The ElectricImage Handbook

The ElectricImage Handbook

Edited by
John Sledd

CHARLES RIVER MEDIA, INC.
Rockland, Massachusetts

Executive Editor: Jenifer L. Niles
Production: Publishers' Design and Production Services, Inc.
Cover Design: Sherry Stinson
Cover Image: John Sledd
Printer: InterCity Press, Rockland, MA

CHARLES RIVER MEDIA, Inc.
P.O. Box 417, 403 VFW Drive
Rockland, MA 02370
781-871-4184
781-871-4376(FAX)
chrivmedia@aol.com
http://www.charlesriver.com

This book is printed on acid-free paper

The ElectricImage Handbook
by John Sledd
   ISBN 1-886801-73-8
   Printed in the United States of America

99 00 7 6 5 4 3 2 1 First Printing

CHARLES RIVER MEDIA titles are available for site license or bulk purchase by
institutions, user groups, corporations, etc. For additional information, please contact
the Special Sales Department at 781-871-4184.

DEDICATION

Another book dedicated to my wonderful wife, Janel, who never ceases to amaze me with her patience. And to my family, whose support and tolerance of my lack of visitation during the writing of this book, is very much appreciated.

Contents

Foreword

It's been a long-time coming, but a book on ElectricImage is finally here. As ElectricImage users, many of you have probably felt a bit like the black sheep of the 3D world, with the herd being mostly composed of users of LightWave 3D, 3D Studio Max, and others, but you probably felt like a black sheep with an ace up your sleeve.

ElectricImage, as a product, has always been great. It sports a fast and beautiful renderer, great animation tools, a superb tolerance for tons and tons of polygons, and all of this is wrapped up in a wonderful interface. And of course, it's always been available for the Mac. But you already knew these things, otherwise, you wouldn't be using it.

The introductions of EIAS versions 2.8 and 2.9 mark wonderful advances for ElectricImage and its users. The interface has gotten even better, rendering has gotten even faster and great new plugins are popping up everywhere. With the addition of the new modeler, EI users now have an extremely powerful and integrated system that simply cannot be matched.

I thoroughly love using it for my work and am looking forward to its future growth.

Enjoy the book.
John Sledd

Acknowledgments

First and foremost, I would like to thank the great people of Electric Image, Inc. for pouring your lives into this magnificent tool (and for getting me updates while I was writing, and calling to answer questions, even on the weekends). Its speed and ease-of-use provide its users with more creative freedom and, most importantly, more time for things other than work. I think I speak for us all when I say "Thank you!"

I'd like to thank the wonderful people who contributed artwork and writings for this book. Putting this book together was a monumental task and I couldn't have done it without you. So, to all you contributors, "Thank You!"

I'd also like to thank the publisher for not killing me every time I said, "Um. It's going to be a little bit later than I thought." The time was well spent.

I also want to thank the production team that took all of these rough text files and folders upon folders of images and turned them into a real-life book. You guys are amazing and I completely appreciate the hell you went through.

Finally, I want to thank the readers out there. Afterall, if it weren't for you, this book would have never made it past the conceptual stage. Your support is what makes things like this possible.

About the Editor

John W. Sledd is a freelance illustrator and animator who prefers lots of trees over lots of people and therefore lives deep within the mountains of Front Royal, Virginia. His illustrations have appeared on magazine and book covers, advertisements, packaging, collectible card games, web sites and more. His animations wind up mostly in games such as Harry the Handsome Executive, Mars Rising and Slithereens, by Ambrosia Software (www.ambrosiasw.com), but occasionally find themselves in other venues as well.

You can reach John at john@sledd.com or see more of his work at www.sledd.com.

1

Welcome

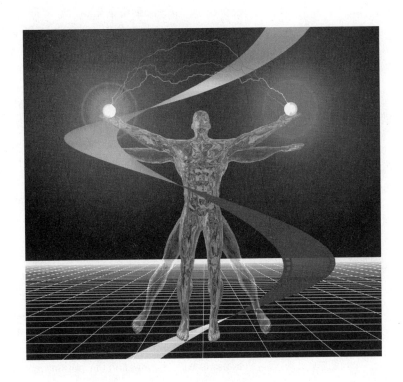

Welcome to *The ElectricImage Handbook,* the essential guide to harnessing the power of the ElectricImage Animation System. To help you get a grasp on this complex yet powerful application, several ElectricImage gurus have graciously poured the content of their brains all over the following pages. Please don't let their sacrifices be in vain.

The objective of this book is to do more than simply teach you how to accomplish specific tasks in ElectricImage. It is my hope that, by the end of it, you will have gained more of an overall feel for the application, which will open you up to other ways of meeting your own challenges. I call this the *Zen* of an application. It's more than knowing which button to push, what number to enter, or where to look for a certain tool. It's an understanding of how the application works, how it's laid out, and a feel for how you might go about accomplishing a certain task or effect—even if it's never been brought to your attention before. This book is about being able to freely explore your creativity. Become one with the app, Grasshopper, and the mouse will beat a path to your door, or something like that.

This book is also designed to fuel your creative engine and to inspire you to further delve into the possibilities of the world of 3D with EI. Since the world of 3D really *is* a world of it's own, and is often a world that you create from scratch, working in 3D should be more adventure than task. Hopefully that's how you view it. If you don't, the amount of work you have to put in to get good at it might not seem worthwhile. If you do have a passion for creating, this is a good place to be.

So—Read the book. Learn EI. Make Mama proud.

What This Book Is All About!

Creating good 3D art can be one of the most intimidating tasks a person can face. Even 3D professionals struggle every day to stay on the cutting edge and to produce animations and illustrations that astound their viewers. If you look at the 3D art of ten years ago and compare it to the 3D of today, there's practically no contest between the two. As computers become faster and cheaper, software becomes more powerful, and digital artwork becomes more accepted, artists are able to experiment with more techniques, challenge more status quos and generally produce better work on tighter schedules. Unfortunately, the schedules seem to get tighter and tighter, but that's just part of the business.

Good 3D requires skills in sculpture, painting, photography, lighting, and organization. A lot goes on in your typical 3D project, and if you can't keep up with the pace of the project, you won't complete the project.

If you plan on animating your 3D project, you must add directorial and motion theory skills to your list of credentials. In adding the element of time to your projects, you suddenly rocket from a three-dimensional project to a four-dimensional one. You become a god-like being creating your own universe from the ground up. Sounds like the plot to a good sci-fi thriller, doesn't it.

This book is here to make it all easier. From illustration to animation. From special effects to the best techniques for realism. You'll find a little bit of everything within these pages.

The ElectricImage Handbook distinguishes itself from other general 3D books because it is the first book to focus primarily on ElectricImage software. It also draws from the real-world experience of several EI artists and animators to help you blow past much of the learning curve and get right to the good part: Creating worlds and seeing them come to life. There are few things more satisfying, in my opinion.

What Software And Hardware Do I Need?

This much is pretty simple. Support for other platforms is on the way but the current version of ElectricImage runs only on the Apple Macintosh platform...so you'll need a Mac (a PowerMac to be more specific).

This book was written using EI 2.8 and 2.9, so it would be best if you have either of those. Version 2.9 is preferred, of course, and should be shipping by the time this book hits the shelves. If you plan on using the files on the CD-ROM, you'll absolutely have to have 2.9 as the files are not backward compatible and all final versions on the CD-ROM were saved out of 2.9.

Many of the techniques in the book apply to older versions as well, but the interface changes that happened between 2.7.5 and 2.8 would require you to do a little bit of rethinking to make things work out right if you're using an older version. Versions 2.8 and 2.9 also include many new features that the older versions didn't have, and this book covers several of them, so if you're still using an older version, you just don't know what you're missing. Might I suggest that you call your local EI dealer and order the newest version immediately. Like I said, 2.9 should already be shipping by the time you read this.

Of course, you don't really have to have any of those to just *read* the book. You just need to know how to read. It would make things more enjoyable, however, if you actually had the proper hardware and software.

How Much Experience Do I Need?

While *The ElectricImage Handbook* was written to be used by beginners as well as intermediates and experts, I must insist that you have at least a basic understanding of how EI works. It would be best if you have already gone through the tutorials that came with your copy of EI and have at least skimmed through the user guide. They put a lot of work into the new documentation so use it and love it.

Although you may be able to follow along and work through these tutorials without having ever touched the manual, I can promise that you'll get a lot more out of the book if you do have a foundation to build upon. Most importantly, however, is that you have a very strong desire to master the art. This book can't turn you into a 3D pro any more than getting that new shiny, powerful piece of hardware can. Both can help a great deal but without the desire, the tools and information are nothing.

How Should I Use This Book?

If you are even somewhat familiar with EI or 3D in general, you should be able to sit down at your computer with EI loaded and go through this book from beginning to end, but this is not really a necessity. Feel free to skip to whatever chapter for help on a technique you need today. Got a problem mapping an object? Head to Chapter 6. Got a problem with a model you are trying to import? Jump to Chapters 3. It's as easy as that. If you're just in an exploratory mood, go straight through, or just close your eyes, flip though the book, and pick a spot at random.

If you are pretty new to EI or 3D in general, I would strongly suggest that you at least read Chapter 2 first and then go wherever you want to from there. Even if you are a pro, you might glean some useful info from Chapter 2. It's full of great general 3D information and just some typical good artistic information as well.

BEGINNER

Definitely start out with the next chapter, *The World in 3D*. It will give you an excellent overview of how to approach the process of 3D creation from an ElectricImage perspective. You really should go through the tutorials provided with EI first to make all of this stuff come together in your head. Being given the answers before you have the questions is practically worthless. Once you get your basic footing, you can keep this book close to your manuals and jump back and forth as the need arises. The book is logically laid out to take you through the different aspects of scene creation as they usually come up in a production environment.

INTERMEDIATE

Intermediate users will also get a lot out of Chapter 2. Although you may know much of it already, it never hurts to brush up on the knowledge. You might even find out something you didn't plan on. Like Mr. Cosby used to say, "And if you're not careful, you may learn something before it's done."

At the very least, you might find out a new way to use the tools that EI gives you. From there you can just browse through the tips and techniques to find the areas that most interest you. You might even find yourself checking out Chapter 16 and how the big guys do it.

ADVANCED

Current EI pros might be a little more difficult to please, but there is a difference between difficult and impossible. No matter how much of a pro you are, you are still holding an excellent reference source for your 3D needs. Sometimes, as you get older, you forget things. Don't worry, it's not your fault. It comes from sitting in front of a computer screen 33 hours a day. But never fear, if the CRT burns a hole in your brain, just pick up the book and fill it back in again.

Seriously though, you'll find tons of new ideas throughout the book. You might want to check your method of operation against Chapter 2 or head over to Chapter 16 to see how your peers handle their jobs.

Overview of the ElectricImage Handbook

The following chapters in the ElectricImage Handbook can be broken down into three parts that are intended to follow the typical 3D scene setup sequence. It's up to you which order you read them in. I promise that the book will not blow up if you get something out of order.

PART ONE: CHAPTER TWO

This first part is only one chapter long, but it's a biggie. Not only is it large in the amount of content, but it's also very important. Without the knowledge in this chapter, you'd be lucky to make it through a big 3D project at all, much less have it look very good. This chapter not only covers the fundamentals of working 3D but also covers general good artistic concerns. You'll also find a big dose of general ElectricImage fundamentals as well.

Even if you have a big headstart in 3D, please try to resist the temptation to ignore this chapter. I don't care if you read it now or later, but do read it. You may find that some things can be accomplished much easier with just a little bit of planning.

PART TWO: CHAPTERS 3–12

This is the bulk of the book. This is where you'll find the tips and techniques that really help you suck the marrow from EI. Marrow-sucking is much easier in 2.9 now that it has bones. (I know it was bad but I couldn't help myself.)

The basic difference between tips and techniques is that tips are more advice-oriented and usually aren't that long. Techniques, on the other hand, are often actual tutorials on how to create specific effects or achieve that perfect result.

The subjects of these chapters are arranged in what should be a logical order based on the creation of a typical 3D scene. We start out with the modeling or importing of models then move on to materials and shading, lighting, camera tips and techniques, animation, rendering, post-production, special effects, and finally to using ElectricImage for the internet.

PART THREE: CHAPTER 13

This last part is only one chapter in length, too, but basically this is a summary of everything you learned in Parts One and Two. This chapter traces a project of one of the most talented ElectricImage users out there, from beginning to finish. The more you know about how others do things, the more equipped you are to be able to decide the best method for you.

Get to Work

Now here's the really important part. Regardless of whether you read this book front to back, back to front, upside down, in a tree, or under a truck, you won't get much out of it at all unless you do something with the knowledge. Experience, experimentation and stick-with-it-ness are the three most important factors in your 3D growth. You have to just get in there and do it.

I was just recently directed to the web site of a person who wanted to learn another popular 3D application. He decided that, in order to really learn the app, he just had to submerse himself. What he wound up creating over the span of ten months was a virtual coffeeshop with a level of detail that went all the way down to the muffin crumbs on the counter. This final scene wound up containing over 7 million polygons (yes, you heard right). I can't vouch for the sanity of this particular individual, but I guarantee he knows his app by now.

As the above example suggests, another key element is to just have fun. If you do this 3D stuff for a living, take some time off every now and then to do something just for fun. Create that spaceship scene or cartoon short just for yourself and have a good time with it.

OK. Enough with the babble. Let's get on with the book.

2 The World in 3D

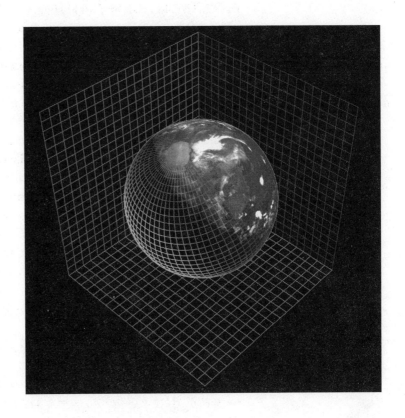

The best place to begin studying the world of 3D is right where you are sitting. The universe around you is the best example of 3D there is. As a matter of fact, the world around us is why art was created in the first place. People wanted to be able to accurately recreate what they saw and what they dreamed. Over the years, new techniques and technologies have brought us closer and closer to being able to realize this desire. 3D technology is the most recent addition to the artistic arsenal and it not only lets you recreate aspects of the world around you, but also allows you to build complete worlds of your own. ElectricImage, with its amazing polygon-handling capabilities and rich renderer, frees your own world-building imagination to create and explore.

While I did mention earlier that the 3D creation process can be intimidating, I didn't say it was impossible. It's gets much easier as you familiarize yourself with your tools and the techniques that make those tools shine. The best place to start with both of these is to find the most efficient working method that will get you from concept to finished product. The more efficient you are, the quicker you'll work, the clearer you'll think and the fewer roadblocks you'll run into. The key to this efficiency is to plan ahead. This chapter will introduce you to a system and many of the considerations of each step in the system. By the end of it, you should be able to completely analyze any 3D project and take the path of least resistance and greatest reward.

I've sectioned this chapter into five different parts. I've attempted to hold true to a common sequence of events for creating a full-blown 3D project, but some of the events can be switched around and some can occur simultaneously.

- **The Modeling Thought Process**
  In order to model well, you need to learn how to approach the building of the model in a fashion that best fits how your chosen modeling application functions. The modeling thought process also entails building the models for the most effective use in your 3D app, namely EI. There are ways to make your life easier and correct modeling is one of them.

- **The Shading Thought Process**
  Some may argue that lighting should come next in the order of things, but I disagree—well, sort of. I prefer to get the object looking right, then light it and make adjustments to either the shading or lighting, if the need arises. Some might even save this part for last, and you're welcome to do so, but this is my favorite part of 3D so I'm going to get to it up front.

  Shading is where you determine the surface appearance of your models. This involves setting Geometry, Diffuse, Specular, Ambient, Reflectivity, Transparency, Luminance/Glow, and Transmission characteristics of your Materials. You can also the use of Texture Maps and Procedural Shaders, which can be applied to any of the above characteristics.

- **The Lighting Thought Process**
  Lighting is the basic mood-setter of your 3D scene. Lighting can make the same model look foreboding or friendly, happy or sad, cold or hot. ElectricImage has some amazing lighting controls and options, and we'll discuss them a bit here.

- **The Composition Thought Process**
  Often, the main difference between a good 3D piece and a really dull one is in the composition of the scene. This is most often the area overlooked by blossoming 3D artists without formal artistic training. You must know how to compose your scene. Very simple scenes can be brought to life by good composition and very complex scenes can be killed by a poor implementation.

- **The Animation Thought Process**
  If you're like many 3D mavens out there, you're not happy with just building the perfect 3D scene. When you've got all of the pieces together, you want to fling them around the 3D world. Blow them up. Crash them into things and generally just cause a lot of mayhem. Well, that's what EI excels at, but you need to know some basics first. Here's where you'll get them.

The Modeling Thought Process

This is where it all starts. Before you can create that perfect animation or illustration, you need to have some models to move around and arrange. Your models will either be of things that already exist in our world, or they can be objects derived directly from your imagination. Whatever the source, they need to be believable. Many objects may seem overwhelming at first, but if you really study them, you'll find out that they aren't so complex after all.

One thing that can be said, with conviction, about 3D modeling is that you'll never look at the world the same again. Chairs, people, cars, planes, and other such objects are no longer what they appear. You begin to mentally convert everything into splines, NURBS, and polygons and think, *now how would I build that?* It's a sickness, to be sure, but it's much better than the flu.

MAKE THINGS SIMPLE

The first thing to understand when trying to get a grasp on modeling is that virtually every object can be broken down into several little objects, which can often be broken down into several other little objects. If you go straight to the bottom of this chain, you are no longer building one big complex model, but several simple little models that, in turn, you can assemble to create the larger finished model.

This still leaves you with a need to model these smaller objects but even they can be broken down into simpler shapes. Let's use the wine glass in Figure 2.1 as an example. The glass itself may look a tad on the complicated side, but when you view the actual shapes that it took to create the finished model, you'll see that one of them is simply a common circle. All objects, or at least parts of those objects, are based on some 2D primitive that we are very familiar with such as squares, rectangles, circles, ellipses, triangles, and so on, the main difference being *how* that 2D shape is modified in the third dimension.

In the case of the wineglass, two shapes, based roughly on rectangles and an ellipse (the curves of the base of the glass), are revolved around a simple circle. By taking a couple of 2D shapes and revolving them around another 2D shape we give the shapes a 3D existence.

To break this idea down even further, let's take the concept of 2D primitives a step further to make 3D primitives. A square extruded along a straight line

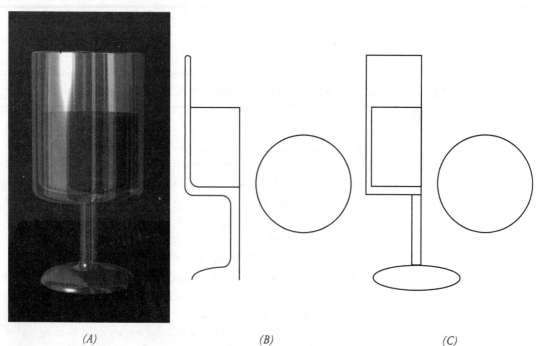

(A)   *(B)*   *(C)*

FIGURE *This glass can be broken down into very basic shapes. (A) Wineglass. (B) Wineglass profile. (C) Wineglass*
2.1 *primitives.*

becomes a cube. A circle extruded along a straight line becomes a cylinder. Of course, as with many things in 3D, there is often more than one solution to any given problem. You can also make a cylinder by rotating a rectangle around a circle. The wineglass illustration is a good example of this. The basic wineglass cross section is made of rectangular shapes, but once revolved, not a single straight edge remains.

And since many 3D objects are based on 2D primitives, it also stands to reason that they would also based on 3D primitives. The little guy in Figure 2.2 is a good example of this theory. He is made up of nothing but 3D primitives. A glance at the guy's hierarchy in his **Project Window** gives that away. Now granted, this isn't an accurate representation of a human, but hopefully you can see the connection. Look at your own arm—it's not much more than a couple of deformed cylinders. Same with your leg. Your head is based on a spherical shape and your chest is based on a more cubical object.

Once you start to break things down like this, modeling becomes a much less daunting task. You'll begin to look at the world in a whole new light. As with any form of visual art, correct execution starts with a proper interpretation. It's much more difficult to draw a hand if you don't look at it properly. You need to see it as a composition of lines and shading, because that is what will go onto the paper. The same holds true for 3D. You need to see the objects at their most basic level. If you're new to 3D, this type of observation can get in the way, because once you start, it's difficult to think of anything else for a while. I remember when I was first getting interested in 3D. I was a graphic designer but my job entailed a little illustration. I would sit in important meetings thinking "hmmmm, I wonder how I would model that chair" or "where would I start if I needed to make that overhead projector?" Needless to say, I didn't get much out of these meetings, but the daydreaming eventually did pay off. Luckily this obsession gets replaced with other obsessions along the way, but you'll never be able to look at a flower or watch a movie without dissecting it. Say goodbye to your innocence.

ORIENT YOURSELF

Now that you've figured out how to look at things before you start modeling them, you need to figure out how to navigate around the virtual 3D space that you have to work in so that you can build the model properly and then position and animate your finished objects. If you were a traditional model-maker working with clay or any other tactile building material, you'd be working in the physical world. Getting around to the back of the object would be as simple as rotating it around on its base or walking around the table. It's not quite

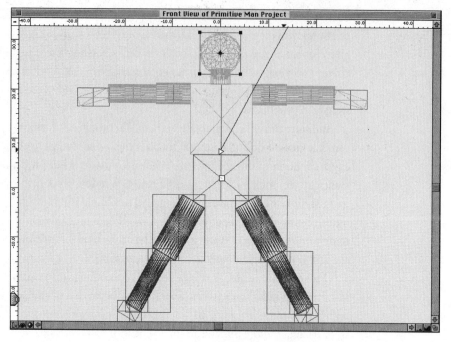

(A)

(B)

(C)

FIGURE *Even a human form can be broken down into its primitive basics.*
2.2

that simple in your 3D app since the world of your application exists only in your computer. Until we get truly immersive, virtual-reality interfaces, you must learn to navigate your digital 3D world using your 2D computer screen. This is no easy task, but it's not impossible either.

In the real world, we refer to the three dimensions as width, height, and length; in the computer world, these dimensions are represented as a three-dimensional graph with X, Y, and Z axes. Getting a grasp of these axes is the second key to mastering the modeling process. Figure 2.3 is an example of how ElectricImage (as well as most other 3D apps) sees its world. All action takes place at some point, which can be charted as a coordinate of X, Y, and Z. You navigate these axes by moving along them linearly or by rotating around them. For example, a point that lies at X=0, Y=0, and Z=0 would be exactly in the middle of your scene. A point that lies at (10, 5, 0) would be 10 units to the right and 5 units high. You can then move this point forward or backward by entering a number for the Z axis position. If you wanted to move the point forward, you'd enter a negative number (which may seem backwards, but that's

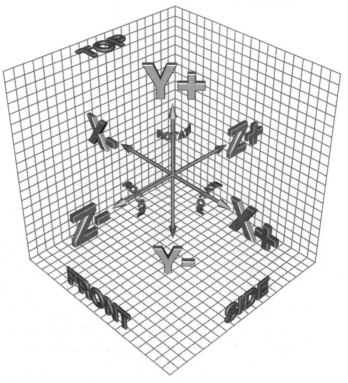

FIGURE   *This 3D graph shows how EI views the world.*
2.3

how it is). If you wanted to move the point backward in space, you'd add a positive number. The same holds true for the other axes. A negative X value moves the point to the left and a negative Y value moves the point down.

If you want to rotate an object, this is achieved by spinning the object around each of the axes. Unlike placement, however, an object's rotation is based on an axis system that uses the object as its own universe where the center of the axis system is the rotation point of your object. So if you imagine that Figure 2.3 is an object, its center of rotation would be where the three axes intersect. You could then rotate the object forward and backward by rotating it around its X axis, rotate it left and right by rotating it around the Y axis, or spin the object like a propeller by rotating it on the Z axis. Figure 2.4 shows a rotation conversion chart. EI will let you enter negative and positive numbers, depending on the direction that you want to rotate your object. So a rotation value of 90° would be a 1/4 rotation counterclockwise, whereas a rotation of

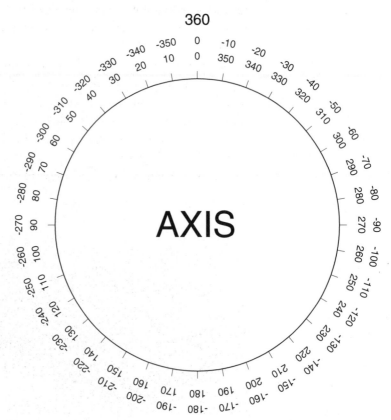

FIGURE *ElectricImage determines the direction of rotation using positive and negative*
2.4 *values.*

–270° would be a 3/4 rotation clockwise. Your object would wind up at the same point, but the negative or positive number tells it in which direction to rotate to get to that point.

Once you understand how to navigate around using this coordinate system and how objects behave in it, you'll have the "thinking in 3D" concept pretty much beaten. Understanding this will not only allow you to understand what EI wants from you as input, but you'll also be able to understand more about the relationships of objects in the world around you and how that information will translate in the world of 3D.

PLAN AHEAD

Understanding the concepts presented up to this point make it easier for you to plan your models ahead of time. You must first decide what you want to build and then plan on how to go about breaking the project apart into subparts to make assembly of the final model a breeze. The end result will be a model that is solidly and simply built, not to mention easily animatable. Adhering to this method will make for much less chaos in your brain and in your modeling environment.

Sketching out your modeling ideas before you start is always a great idea. Once you get the 2D shapes down on paper, it's much easier to convert your thoughts into 3D. I usually do a quick and dirty sketch on paper, then another sketch in Adobe Illustrator to fine tune the curves and overall shapes. I then take parts of the art created in Illustrator and use them as construction elements when building the model.

The car in Figure 2.5 may seem like a ridiculously complex modeling task

FIGURE *A complex model of a car.*
2.5

FIGURE *The wheel is one component of the finished car model.*
2.6

but by breaking the finished model into its separate objects, it becomes much less intimidating. Take the wheel in Figure 2.6 as an example. This object is pretty complex as it is, but if you notice, it's made up of several different objects that aren't very complex at all. Combining these separate objects into your finished piece makes the rest of the car look less daunting. When you're done modeling one component of a model, like this tire, it is wise to link the individual base objects to an object you determine as your master object in the group. For example, Figure 2.7 shows the hierarchy of the tire in Figure 2.6. Notice how the smaller groups in this submodel are all linked to the largest

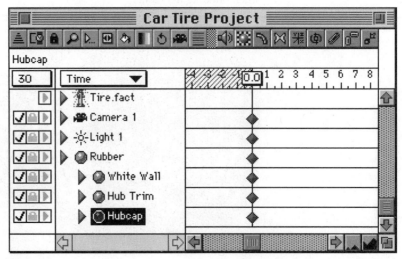

FIGURE *The wheel's hierarchy shows a good method of organization.*
2.7

group, the tire (called *rubber* in this instance), in the collection. This makes the manipulation of the finished wheel object much easier. It's always preferable to link all pieces of a model that move together, the reason being that when the time comes to animate this wheel rolling, you only need to animate the rubber part and the linked objects will follow. This is much easier than having to set up rotation values for each of the separate groups.

BE EFFICIENT

Never model more than you need. Although ElectricImage handles very high polygon counts and numerous groups with ease, there's no sense wasting the modeling time creating objects that won't be seen in the final render. Figure 2.8 shows all of the objects that are really necessary to create a convincing wheel for our car. We all know that a real tire/wheel combo is much more complex in real life, but unless you're creating a technical illustration or animation, there's no reason to add details that will never be seen because they will only chew up your available resources. You should always take your end goal into account when building your models. If your car model is simply going to drive past the camera, this is all you need. However, if the tire needs to fly off the car, then you'd want more of an undercarriage and perhaps more detail on the inside of the tire. If this is not the case, get away with as little as possible.

Another good habit to form is to turn off models or parts of your scene/models that you aren't currently working with. If you don't want to turn

FIGURE *If you aren't going to see it in the final render, don't bother modeling it.*
2.8

them off because you want them to render, but don't want to deal with them while working on the scene, simply assign those objects a preview mode that requires less time to update. The ability to use different preview levels for each group is another great new feature of EI 2.9—a wonderful timesaver when working on those huge scenes.

NAME GROUPS PROPERLY

Always name your groups as you create them and give them names that make sense. This will make your modeling chores much easier and will aid any other person who might find the need to edit your work. That person may just be you, if you are required to put a project on hold for a while (which happens all too often). You might come back to a model that you understood at the time but then find yourself trying to relearn what *object 1, object 2, object 3, . . . object 27* are, when, if you'd named them properly in the first place, you'd be much better off.

LEARN HOW TO MOVE

EI gives you basically two ways to move an object in 3D space, which you will do very often when modeling and/or setting up your scene. The first, and more fun of the two, is by dragging the object around using the four view windows. These four views consist of three **World View Windows** and a **Camera View Window**. The three World View Windows are like virtual viewports into your scene and have no camera attached to them. These are typically what you will use to move objects around in your scene, because you can move your scene around within the window to quickly get to any area that you wish to edit without having to worry about destroying the composition of your shot. The fourth window, your Camera View Window, shows you how your selected camera views your scene. This gives you your compositional info and allows you to make final tweaks that might be more difficult through your World View Windows. You typically do not want to move your scene around in your Camera View Window because doing so actually moves your camera. If you have a perfectly composed scene, you don't want to go flinging your camera around. Figure 2.9 shows the window structure of ElectricImage, while Figure 2.10 shows the window setup for the ElectricImage Modeler. They are very similar and work in a similar fashion. The only real difference being that where the Camera View Window is in Modeler, you actually have an additional World View Window that acts as your Camera View Window. You can move it around to your heart's content without worrying about destroying your composition. Destroying your composition in Modeler isn't really a consideration

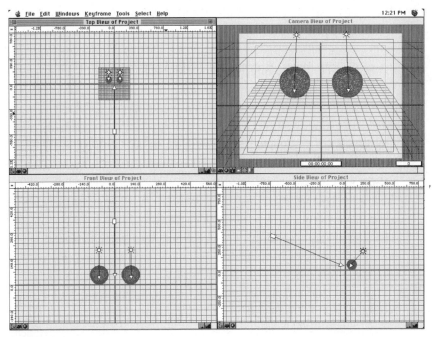

FIGURE   *ElectricImage's window setup.*
2.9

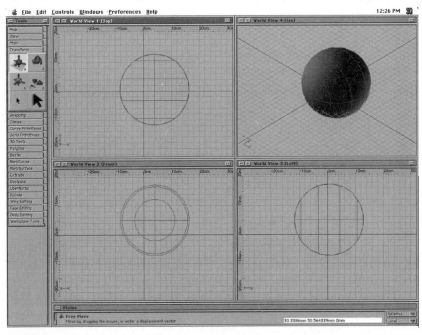

FIGURE   *The window setup of the ElectricImage modeler.*
2.10

unless you are planning on rendering your completed scene in Modeler, but it's worth mentioning in case that is your goal.

The second way to move your groups around in EI is by positioning them numerically. The **Group Info Window**, as shown in Figure 2.11, allows you to position and rotate your groups by entering coordinates and values. This is often reserved for final tweaking or when you know exactly what you want. When you get into numeric positioning and rotation, your knowledge of the X, Y, Z coordinate system will become very useful.

SUMMARY

Well, with all of that said, I suppose the main idea here is that modeling can be tough, but if you plan well, learn how to move around in your 3D world, think the project through, and break it down into bite-size chunks—rather than trying to swallow it whole—the job becomes much easier. The same holds true for every other aspect of 3D. Break it down and work from the ground up.

The next time you look at a great animation or still and think "Wow. I wish I could do that." Chances are, you can. I guarantee that the creator of that wonderful piece approached it in the same step-by-step fashion outlined here. It just takes a commitment of time and the ability to see the project from the proper angle. Chapters 3 and 4 will give you some great tips and techniques to help you through your modeling adventures.

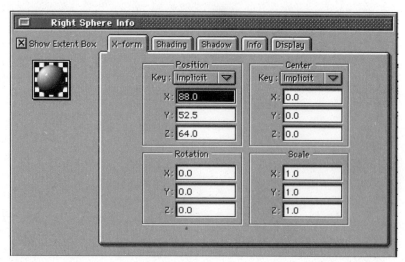

FIGURE *The Group Info Window allows you to position and rotate your groups by the*
2.11 *numbers.*

The Shading Thought Process

The process of assigning the surface qualities to your models and groups is called *shading*. This is my favorite part of working in 3D. No matter how well built or how detailed your models are, they will still look flat, plastic, and dull if you don't assign the right shading properties to them. Many of you probably built kit models as a kid (some of you may still), and I'm sure, if you were like me, you realized—at the end of your hard construction labor and glue-fume induced euphoria—that your model looked nothing like the one on the packaging, that your model came in. That's because they don't bother to tell you that what you see on the box top is not the model you just put together, but simply a good paintjob that this model is holding up. Most likely, nowhere on the box did it say "You need to learn how to paint to make these things look good." Even if it did, it was probably in teeny, barely legible print. Well, 3D is no different, except that you certainly don't even get the teeny disclaimer, so allow this next statement to serve as one. *If you don't know how to paint, your models will not look like the ones on the box top.* The good news is that painting your 3D objects is much easier and far less messy than painting those kit models.

I'll spend the next couple of thousand words or so explaining the basics of shading your model. Hang tight because there are several different layers to making a well shaded model but, like everything else, it's easily broken down into smaller bits of info that are easier to digest.

MATERIALS DEFINED

Materials control the surface characteristics of your groups in EI to determine the most fundamental look of your models. Figure 2.12 shows the interface to these material components, the **Group Material Info Window** (or Material Editor as many like to call it). As you can see, there are several tabs that give you access to the channels of your material: Geometry, Diffuse, Specular, Ambient, Reflectivity, Transparency, Luminance/Glow, and Transmission. You'll want to consult your user guide for specifics on these channels, as it gives just as good of an explanation as I can give here. No use in reinventing the wheel any more than necessary.

Using the Material Editor's channels, you can determine the color of your object, tell it to be shiny like metal, or dull like clay. You can tell it to be transparent or opaque, reflective or nonreflective and many other options in between and beyond. Figure 2.13 gives you a good idea of what each channel does. A basic checker texture map has been applied to each sphere in the specified channel to show you the extremes of the settings available for each. It should be noted here that a light was placed behind the Transmission sphere to properly show the

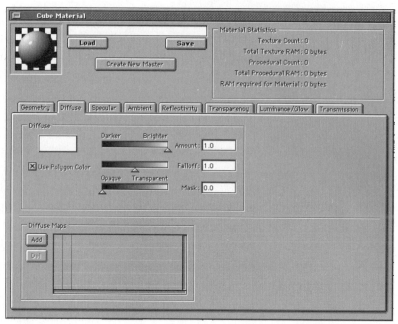

FIGURE **2.12** *The Group Material Info Window gives you access to all of the controls for determining the surface characteristics of your groups.*

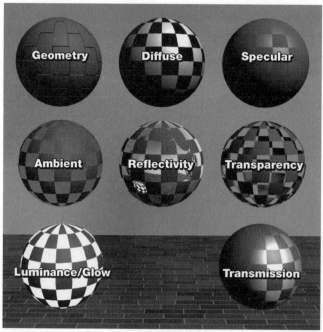

FIGURE **2.13** *This is an illustration of how the various material channels affect the surface of your groups.*

effect of the Transmission channel. Transmission allows light coming from behind your group to be seen through the other side. It should also be noted that
Bump was the only option used for the Geometry channel but is not the only
option available. We'll cover more of those in later chapters.

TEXTURE MAPS DEFINED

Texture Maps are bitmap files that you can place in the map lists in your various material channels that allow you to alter the surface of your groups above
and beyond what you can achieve using materials alone. A texture map can be
used for something as simple as giving a wall a wallpaper texture or for something as obscure as simply dirtying up the surface of your model. Using texture
maps is most analogous to actually painting your model. The big difference is
that you paint a big slab of texture and then project it onto your group when
you're done (unless you happen to be using a 3D paint program that actually
does allow you to paint directly on your model, after a fashion, that is).

Texture maps are most often used when you really need a particular realistic
look, and, used in conjunction with clever material settings, they can create
very believable results. In addition to using texture maps as a basic solution for
creating color surface for you model, such as the wallpaper mentioned above,
texture maps also make it possible to alter your material settings so you can
have an object with, for example, differing levels of reflectivity across its surface.
Figure 2.13 is also a very good example of this.

When using texture maps, you must take several things into consideration,
the first being the size of your maps, both dimension and resolution. Let's address resolution first. The resolution of a texture map is what gives it detail. Texture maps are essentially a grid of pixels, each of which carries one color. It's like
building a picture with colored blocks. If you have lots of blocks to use to make
your picture, you'll be able to add more detail. If you have only a few blocks to
work with, your picture's detail must suffer. Figure 2.14 is a good example of
this. The image on the left has a higher resolution and therefore carries more detail. The image on the right is made up of fewer pixels, or blocks, and therefore
carries much less detail. Same image, different resolutions. This must be taken
into consideration when using texture maps, as EI uses the resolution of your
texture maps to make its final renderings. The more information EI has to work
with, the more detailed your renderings of texture maps will be.

The question that most often arises is "What resolution should my texture
maps be?" An easy answer is "Make your texture maps the same, or higher, resolution as your final rendering." This answer unfortunately doesn't address the
problem extremely well. The reason being that, in 3D, your maps may have to

FIGURE *Resolution determines how much detail a texture map can display. Higher resolutions yield greater detail*
2.14 *whereas lower resolutions sacrifice detail. © 1996 John W. Sledd*

be stretched in order to fit the object you are mapping. They also are seldomly shot head-on in your final render. And most importantly, different objects will be closer to the camera than others and therefore may require a higher resolution to look good. If you're animating, the same object may be far from the camera one instant and then very close to the camera the next. This must be compensated for.

Figure 2.15 shows a texture map of a grid that we'll apply to a plane. Figure 2.16 shows this plane rendered and everything looks just fine. However, if you

01	02	03	04	05	06
07	08	09	10	11	12
13	14	15	16	17	18
19	20	21	22	23	24
25	26	27	28	29	30
31	32	33	34	35	36

FIGURE *A simple texture map of a grid.*
2.15

01	02	03	04	05	06
07	08	09	10	11	12
13	14	15	16	17	18
19	20	21	22	23	24
25	26	27	28	29	30
31	32	33	34	35	36

FIGURE *The map used is a fine resolution for this render.*
2.16

zoom in on one of the grid cells, as in Figure 2.17, you'll see that the texture map begins to break apart. This is because the resolution of the texture map was fine for a distant shot of the plane, but when you zoomed in on it, suddenly the resolution for the area being rendered was not sufficient to produce a smooth image because EI now has much less information to use to build the final render. The jagginess or blurriness that results is called *pixelation*. So the guideline is to decide how close your texture maps will be in the final render and size them accordingly.

FIGURE *When the object is closer to the camera, the resolution of the texture map is not*
2.17 *high enough to yield a good render and pixelates.*

It is often difficult to numerically gauge the proper resolution, especially when objects are flying around in your animation, but some trial and error will give you a good feel over time, and you'll begin to size your texture maps properly from the beginning. A good rule to follow is to create your original maps at resolutions much higher than you think you will need and then resize copies of the maps to use for actual rendering. This is also a good practice because, if you're doing an animation, you never know when the client will ask for a higher resolution image for print work. If you're doing a print piece that is 8.5 × 11, the client may come back and ask for a poster. If you create the original texture at the minimum resolution you think you'll need, you'd have to recreate the maps for the higher-resolution work.

Although low resolution maps are a very bad thing, maps that have too high of a resolution are also bad because they require much more memory and processor time to render. No sense making a render take any longer than it has to. So even though you create your original map at a very high resolution, only use copies of the map with the appropriate resolution for the job at hand.

An alternative here is to create maps that you can tile. Tiling takes one map and duplicates it many times across your image. In Figure 2.18, I've tiled the

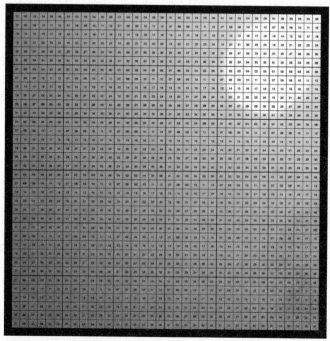

FIGURE   *Tiling your texture map essentially turns one map into many, thus giving EI*
2.18   *more information at rendering time.*

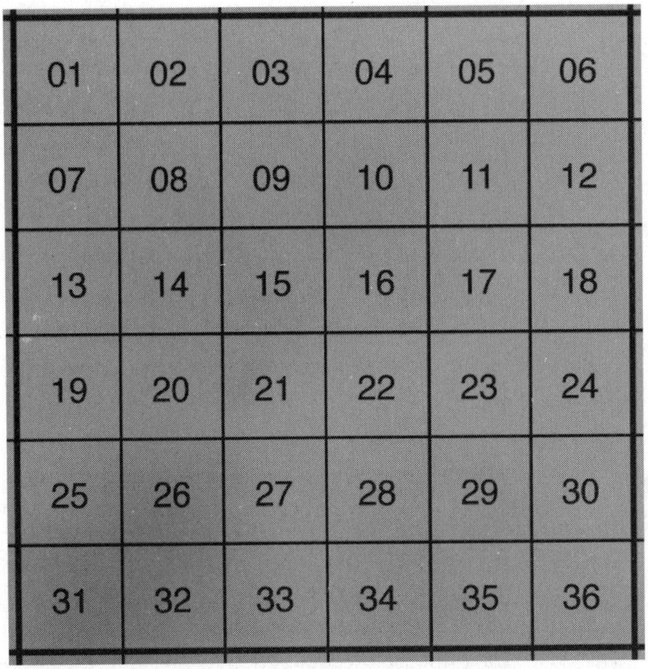

01	02	03	04	05	06
07	08	09	10	11	12
13	14	15	16	17	18
19	20	21	22	23	24
25	26	27	28	29	30
31	32	33	34	35	36

FIGURE   *A close-up render shows that we now have plenty of detail to produce a nice,*
2.19   *sharp render.*

grid image so that we have one full grid image where one cell of the grid used to be. As you can see, we now have more than enough info for the far away shot, but for the closeup shot, the resolution yields a much nicer image (see Figure 2.19).

Once you get the idea for your resolution, you also must determine the proper dimensions for your texture map. The above grid image is fine when applied to a perfectly square wall, but when we apply it to a more rectangular wall, it doesn't take a genius to see that this could cause problems with texture map distortion (see Figure 2.20). This can also be compensated for by either tiling the texture map as in Figure 2.21 or by using a larger, better proportioned texture map as in Figure 2.22. Tiling is often good enough, but it can also yield unnatural patterns in your images that will scream *computer generated,* so tiling should always be used with caution.

Calculating the proper resolution for your maps gets a little more complex when you start using maps that wrap around your model, because then you are only rendering one part of the map at any given time and therefore have to adjust your resolutions accordingly. This can be seen when applying a map to the

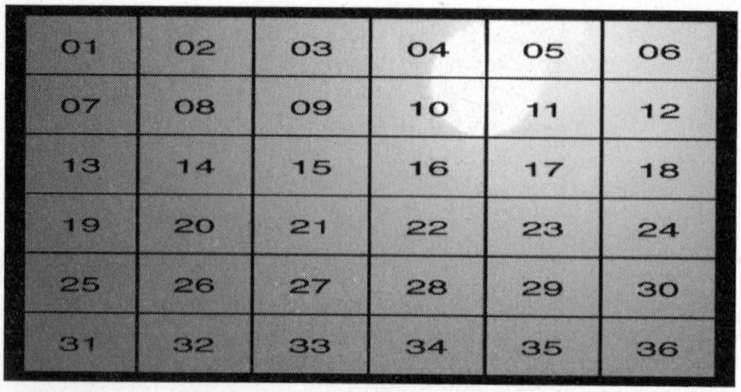

FIGURE 2.20 *Applying a map that has different dimensions than your group will result in stretching and distortion.*

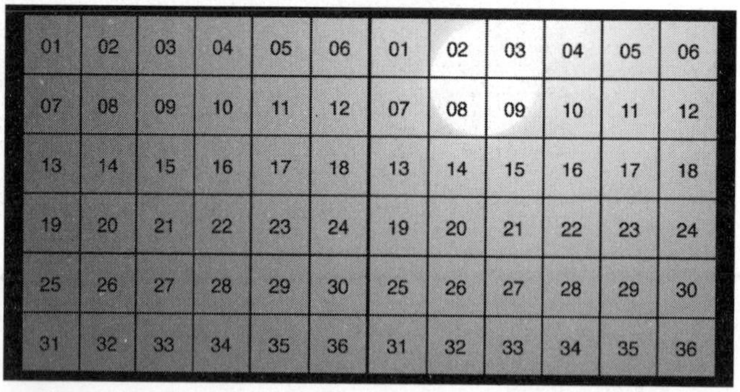

FIGURE 2.21 *Tiling the map can fix this but isn't always what you want.*

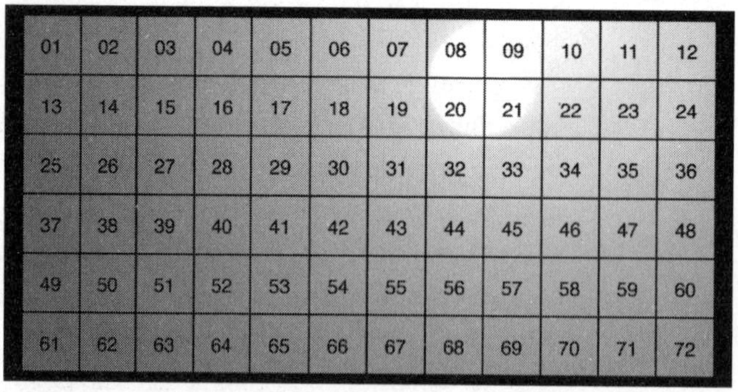

FIGURE 2.22 *Creating the map at the proper size in the beginning can save you a lot of heartache.*

FIGURE *When wrapping your texture map around a group, you must compensate for the*
2.23 *amount of texture that will actually be visible to the camera at any given time.*

sphere in Figure 2.23. This can also be compensated for by tiling the texture map, or by using a larger texture map but you just have to keep in mind how much of the overall map will be seen by the camera at any given time. If your final frame is 640 × 480 pixels and the group you are texturing occupies one quarter of that frame at its closest position to the camera, then the visible portion of your texture map must be at least 320 × 240 pixels to look good in the final render.

Using the larger texture map certainly helps in this case, but, as shown in Figure 2.24, you might still run into some distortions due to the curvature of your model and the stretching that the map must endure as a result. Additional editing of your texture map, as shown in Figure 2.25, can pre-distort your image so that it maps more precisely to your model. The grid in Figure 2.26 holds more of the map's original internal scaling due to the pre-distortion applied to the map.

Map Projections

In closing this section on Texture Maps, I want to say a little about Map Projections. Understanding how mapping modes work is very important to being

FIGURE **2.24** *The curvature of your model and the spherical mapping needed for such a model can result in its own form of texture map distortion.*

01	02	03	04	05	06	07	08	09	10	11	12
13	14	15	16	17	18	19	20	21	22	23	24
25	26	27	28	29	30	31	32	33	34	35	36
37	38	39	40	41	42	43	44	45	46	47	48
49	50	51	52	53	54	55	56	57	58	59	60
61	62	63	64	65	66	67	68	69	70	71	72

FIGURE **2.25** *Pre-distorting the map can correct these problems before they start.*

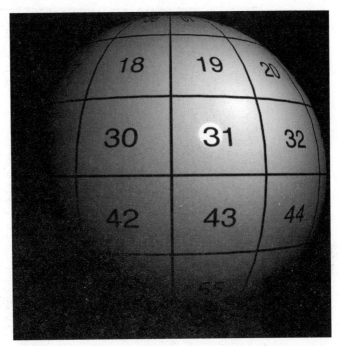

FIGURE   *The pre-distorted map maintains the internal scaling of the map much better*
2.26   *when rendered.*

able to use them correctly. We addressed Flat and Spherical mapping indirectly in the above examples, but let's go over them in more detail and also cover the other two, Cylindrical and Cubic.

What Map Projections do is use a primitive shape, such as a plane, cylinder, sphere, or cube, and then project the map onto your object using that primitive as a sort of slide projector.

Flat Mapping is like projecting a map from a flat surface or plane onto your image. Think of it as a slide projector and your texture is the slide. You could easily project your slide onto a wall for viewing, but you would not want to project it onto a rounded object or an object with multiple sides (unless you use several maps all being projected to separate sides), because you're only projecting your map from one direction. This is very good for walls and other flat objects as shown in Figure 2.27.

Cylindrical Mapping projects the map from a cylinder shape that encompasses your group. It wraps around and projects the map towards an imaginary line (or infinitely thin cylinder) that runs along the Y axis of the map. Figure 2.28 illustrates how this works.

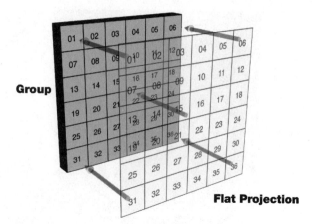

FIGURE **2.27** *Flat Mapping projects the map in a linear fashion onto your group.*

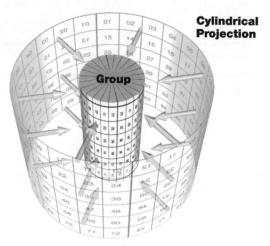

FIGURE **2.28** *Cylindrical Mapping projects your map from a giant cylinder that surrounds your object.*

Spherical Mapping works in much the same fashion as Cylindrical Mapping, but instead of projecting the map from a cylindrical shape towards an imaginary line, it uses a sphere as the projection shape and projects the image towards a point (or infinitely small sphere). Figure 2.29 shows you what's going on here.

Cubic Mapping, as shown in Figure 2.30, projects the map from all six sides onto your group. I have exploded the representation of the cube projection here to give you a better idea of what's going on.

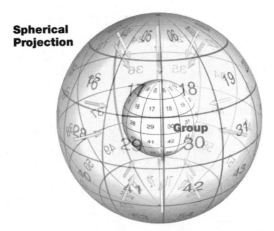

Spherical Projection

FIGURE *Spherical Mapping projects your map from a sphere towards an infinite point in*
2.29 *the middle.*

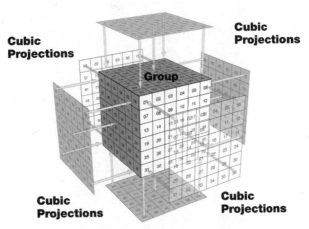

Cubic Projections

Cubic Projections

Group

Cubic Projections

Cubic Projections

FIGURE *Cubic Mapping projects your map from the six sides of a cube primitive.*
2.30

Most of the time, you will want to choose a mapping method that best approximates the shape of the group you are trying to map. As I mentioned in the modeling portion of this chapter, all objects are based roughly on 3D primitives. For example, a wall would use Flat Mapping, a column or tree trunk would be well-suited to Cylindrical Mapping, a head would make very good use of Spherical Mapping, and a cardboard box might look great with Cubic Mapping. This is generally a good rule to follow but always be open to other alternatives. I've mapped a box-like object by creating a map for two of the box's sides and then used Cylindrical Mapping to wrap the resulting texture around the rest of the box. Worked like a charm. There is almost always more than one solution to any given problem.

Taking these considerations to heart will have you texture mapping like a pro in no time.

SHADERS DEFINED

Shaders, also known as *Procedurals* or *Procedural Shaders,* are similar to texture maps in how they are applied and what they can do, but they are different in two main respects. For starters, Shaders are like your own custom texture creation programs right in EI (see Figure 2.31). Each shader gives you several pa-

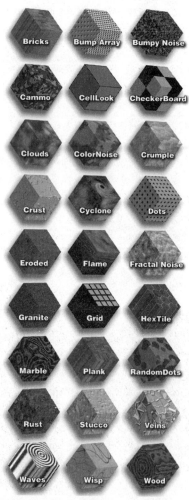

FIGURE 2.31   *EI's procedural shaders are like having your own little texture creation engines right inside EI.*

rameters you can adjust to fine tune your resulting texture, which then gets applied to your model at rendering time. Shaders are also, unlike texture maps, resolution independent. Since the shader is recalculated for each frame, they always render at the optimum resolution so you don't have to worry about using a map that is too big or too small. This makes them very useful for large objects like floors or landscapes that extend far into your scene. See Figure 2.32 for an example of this resolution independence. The image on the left is a distant shot of a cube with the Bricks procedural shader applied to it. The image on the left is a close-up shot of the same cube. Notice how there is no pixelation in the close-up image at all. Not only is there no pixelation, but the detail in the surface of the brick is very good.

EI's Shaders also render very fast, which is a great bonus.

Procedural shaders can affect one or several channels of your material. Most only affect the channel in which they are placed, but some affect others as well. The Bricks shader, for example, affects the bump, diffuse, and specular channels. The BumpyNoise shader will affect the base channel that it is applied to, plus the bump channel. And the Cammo shader will affect only the base channel where it is applied. Consult your user guide for which shader affects which channel(s).

Don't make the mistake of assuming that procedural shaders are only good for creating effects similar to their name. The Flame shader, for instance, makes great clouds. The Cloud shader is great for dirtying up your groups and the Crumple shader creates great ocean waves.

You can also mix and match texture maps with procedurals to get the best of both worlds by using texture maps where you need more control and shaders

FIGURE   *Procedural shaders are resolution independent so they render equally as well at*
2.32   *a distance or up close.*

where you can get by with less control but don't want the problems associated with resolution.

Since most procedural shaders are also animatable, they provide an excellent alternative to using movies when the surface of your group needs to be animated.

Your EI user guide has great explanations of the procedurals and how to go about editing them. It's fun to play with your shader settings, but consult your manual while you're experimenting just so you have some idea of what's going on.

SUMMARY

Experiment with EI's shading tools. Get a feel for what they do and how they do it, then study the various objects around you and work on creating materials that match them in your renderings. With a combination of the Material Info Window settings, Texture Maps, and Shaders, you have a virtually unlimited palette of options to choose from. It takes a little practice but the surfaces of your models are just as important as any other aspect of your scene so it's well worth the time investment.

The Lighting Thought Process

In many cases, lighting is one of the most underutilized aspects of creating a 3D scene. It can't be stressed enough how important successful lighting is. Figures 2.33 and 2.34 illustrate the difference interesting lighting can make in your image. In this case, shadows were disabled for Figure 2.34.

As an exercise, turn off all the lights in your room, including your computer monitor. It's probably pretty dark. Depending on where you are, it could be completely black. Now turn on just one light. Study the pattern of how the illumination of that light washes across your room. What does it illuminate? What does it bounce off? What does it almost reach? Notice the consistency of shadow direction from this one light source. This is the dramatic effect lighting can have on your 3D scene. Imagine, then, the ability to control light precisely and you've got the basis of the Lighting Thought Process.

ElectricImage provides six different types of illumination for your 3D environment. Figure 2.35 shows the **Light Info Window** (available when you double-click any light) and the location of your light options: Camera, Parallel, Radial, Ambient, Spot, and Tube lights. ElectricImage allows unlimited light sources, determined only by the amount of RAM you have.

FIGURE
2.33
An example of how proper lighting enhances the scene. © 1998 John B. Crane

FIGURE
2.34
An example of the difference flat, uninteresting use of lights can affect the scene. © 1998 John B. Crane

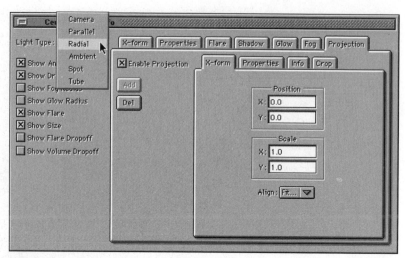

FIGURE *The Light Info Window.*
2.35

TYPES OF LIGHTING

Two basic lighting concepts will be presented here: Environment Lighting (sometimes called natural lighting) and Effects Lighting. Most "successful" images you see employ some combination of the two.

Environment Lighting

Environment lighting can be described as the overall illumination of your 3D scene or environment. It is important for setting the overall mood and establishes a baseline for the viewers' emotions. Soft, cool light brings a sense of calm. Harsh, glaring light tends to raise anxiety levels. Different combinations of the two can have different effects when mixed and used properly.

Lighting should not be considered as an afterthought. How you will light the scene should be ever present in your mind from the very beginning. Having a sense of the "feeling" of your environment from the outset will help focus your lighting strategy.

Effects Lighting

Effects lighting employs a different philosophy. By keying in on certain objects or portions of your scene, you're able to direct the viewer's eye as you desire. Figure 2.36 shows spot lights aimed at a model in an otherwise dark scene. This directs one's eye towards that object. This is the most obvious and straight forward use of effects lighting but there are other more subtle approaches using

FIGURE   *Using volumetric spot lights to accentuate this billboard scene, you can almost*
2.36   *imagine a moth flitting through the beams of light.* © *1998 John B. Crane*

light color, color in shadows, and placement of your effects lights that become
more sophisticated.

SETTING THE MOOD

As stated already, lighting is directly responsible for the overall mood of your
scene. This is accomplished through two primary elements: Color (or temperature of light) and Shadow.

Color

A light's temperature will have an impact on the mood of the scene. While you
may choose to leave a light color at its default white setting, dramatic differences may be seen when experimenting with a scene's overall light color. ElectricImage has the ability to assign any color to any of its lights. Working color
into your lighting scheme is something many people overlook. A winter day,
for example, would simply not appear a winter day with yellowish, warm tones
in the lighting. Cooler blues and grays would more successfully convey the feeling of the cold and snow. The same colors, used indoors, can make a room
seem sterile, clinical, and uninviting.

Conversely, a warm and cozy indoor setting should be lit much differently. Generic colorless lights may get you partially there, but working the color and temperature of light in the room to warm, friendly tones will greatly enhance the effect. The same warm lights used in an outdoor setting would elicit a sense of a hot, sunny atmosphere.

Shadows

Shadows are also a very important element of your lighting scheme. The lack of shadows altogether will produce a generic, sterile image that just won't look "right" to most viewers. Figure 2.37 and Figure 2.38 show the same image rendered with and without shadows. Keep in mind that each shadow casting light adds rendering time so it's important to use shadows judiciously.

ElectricImage allows a variety of controls over the shadow elements of your scene to customize each shadow for optimum efficiency and the desired look. These controls live beneath the **Shadows** tab in the **Light Info Window**. Enabling shadows on a per-light, as-needed basis is very important in establishing an efficient and effectively shadowed scene.

ElectricImage also has the ability to cast colored shadows. While the default is a predictable black, dramatic effects can be accomplished by using color in

FIGURE *In this image shadows are disabled. Yet, the volumetric capabilities are still*
2.37 *operable allowing separate control over the two elements. © 1998 John B. Crane*

FIGURE   *The same scene with shadows enabled. © 1998 John B. Crane*
2.38

shadows to work subtle interest into your scene. This is one of my favorite ways of juicing up an otherwise unremarkable project. You'll be amazed at what properly used shadows can add to your scene. Try, for example, having a orange light cast a bluish shadow or a red light cast a greenish shadow.

DISTANCE AND SCALE

Distance and scale are very important when considering the lighting of your scene. Scale is determined by many different factors (and will be addressed more in the Scene Composition section), and lighting is one of them. As a light recedes into the distance, it will get smaller and dimmer. Emissions become less pronounced and shadows less defined. ElectricImage offers direct visual feedback over the size of lights using the check boxes shown to the left in Figure 2.39. If you were lighting a space station, for example, placing extremely small lights around the perimeter would aid in suggesting a sense of size to the station. In this case you may disable the light's ability to actually emit light (the **Glow** and the **Properties** tabs are separate for a reason) to keep from "flooding" what would otherwise probably be a rather dark scene. Moving lights through the course of an animation can also produce interesting effects with size enabled. Using scale and distance is extremely important in creating the notion of time and space as shown in Figure 2.40.

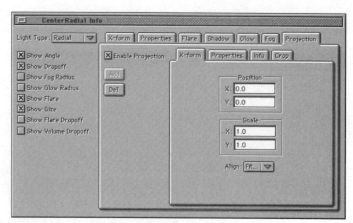

FIGURE 2.39 *Screen grab of Light Info Window.*

FIGURE 2.40 *The number and size of lights are often very important in determining the size of objects. The space-like lighting (a distant light with sharp shadows) helps quite a bit as well. © 1998 John W. Sledd*

MANIPULATING THE MOOD

The addition of the time element in your animation allows nearly infinite variations on your lighting theme. The mood of a project may change during the course of an animation to coincide with various events. If, for example, the same winter's day mentioned above experienced an explosion, the overall balance of light would shift. There may be a warm light activated at the instant of the blast, then ramped down as the blast dissipates into the environment. While in your inviting, cozy room, a door may suddenly swing open and let in a wave of cool air and light. These are both examples of how you may adjust or manipulate the mood of your project. Remember that you have control over all of these aspects of your scene and should use them.

Moving through an environment could also naturally result in different effects. This is all vital in establishing the notion of time and space in your project. Much of this is manipulation of subtle nuances that many viewers may not actually pick up on, but they would view the results quite differently if these nuances weren't present.

Study the lighting of some of your favorite photographs and movies with a discerning eye. Notice the falloff of the light, depth of shadows, and temperature of the scene. Lighting is an art in itself, and there are few hard and fast rules. Experiment and make the lights in your scene work for you. ElectricImage provides all the tools you'll need.

SPECIAL EFFECTS LIGHTING

Special effects have long been a popular realm for the 3D animator. Much of these effects are accomplished through creative use of lighting. These techniques go beyond the use of either environmental or effect lighting and deserve their own mention.

Visible Lights

Visible lights (otherwise called *volumetric* lights) are a great feature of ElectricImage. In short, volumetric lighting means that a light's emission actually has volume in your 3D scene.

Visible lights occur in the real world when light illuminates particles of dust or moisture in the atmosphere. Each ElectricImage light type (except the Camera, Parallel, and Ambient lights) has the ability to "glow." This is accomplished in the Light Info Window under the **Glow** tab. What this means, essentially, is that rather than just emitting light, your light has visible volume assigned to it as well. ElectricImage also allows a light to be able to glow without emitting light, which is handy for adding lighting effects to your scene without affecting the overall illumination.

Visible lights are a fast and powerful way of working real-world effects into your scene. A flashlight sweeping through a smoky or dusty room would produce a visible cone of light. If you're building a space station and wish to add that extra look of scale and realism, sprinkle a few very small glowing lights around your model. The smaller and dimmer the lights, the larger the station will appear. Countless uses exist. Volumetric lights add subtle detail that provide atmosphere, as well. A foggy or rainy night would cause a light to have a visible halo or glow around it. In general, the denser the fog, the brighter the glow.

Volumetric lights in ElectricImage also render in your alpha channel. Figure 2.41 shows a rendering using volumetric lighting. Figure 2.42 shows this rendering's alpha channel as it appears in Photoshop. This is good news for those who wish to do post-work on their images in other applications such as Photoshop or After Effects.

Lightning

Lightning could be considered another visible light or special effect. Figure 2.43 shows a render using a plug-in from Northern Lights called Zeus™ for lightning effects.

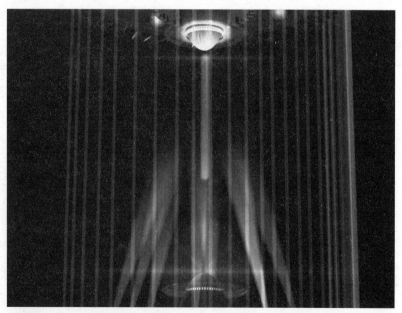

FIGURE *A volumetric lighting sample showing radial, spot, and tube lights.*
2.41

FIGURE
2.42
The same image's alpha channel as it appears in Adobe Photoshop.

FIGURE
2.43
*Using Zeus™, a lightning generation plug in along with a light flare. © 1998
John B. Crane*

Lens Flares and Light Flares

Flashes from explosions, stars in the sky, or just the camera pointed at an intensely bright light are all occasions to use lens or light flares. Lens flares have been a part of ElectricImage for a while now. Version 2.8 added **LightFlares**, another option beneath the **Flares** tab of the Light Info Window. Light Flares offer a more flexible option to the classic lens flare. Although most real-world photographers try to avoid lens flares in their images, they add a sense of realism to your renderings. Just don't overdo it.

Science Fiction Lighting

Because space is dark, with usually only one dominant light source (the sun or other star), light needs to be handled in a special way when floating around out there. Exaggerating pools of light to illuminate islands of activity becomes necessary, but needs to be handled very delicately. Science fiction scenes wouldn't be science fiction scenes without creative use of lighting. Spaceships shooting laser or pulse weapons in outer space, stars glowing, planets reflecting light, and glowing beacons on freighters all require special lighting techniques.

Scale and sharpness of your shadows becomes another consideration in outer space scenes. If a freighter flies over the surface of the moon and casts a huge shadow on the surface, the appearance of scale and distance is completely lost. If it casts a barely discernible, small, fuzzy shadow on the surface, it conveys the idea that it's a greater distance away. You can go back to Figure 2.40 for an example of this.

Using Gels (Projections) and Gobos

There are times you may wish to add shadow detail to your scene that is cast by off-screen objects. Figure 2.44 shows a still life without a gel, and Figure 2.45 shows the same scene with a gel used to mimic light though a window or grid.

In real life, this is accomplished through real-world effects such as sunlight through a window or shadows of leaves of on a forest floor. In 3D, gels are used for such effects. The **Projection** tab in the Light Info Window is where maps are assigned to use as gels. Gels can affect the color of your light as well. This is often unnecessary in 3D because the light's color is determined by a separate parameter, but ElectricImage provides this choice in the event you want to create the effect of a stained glass window or when one light just needs to cast different colors.

Gobos could be thought of as puppets in front of a spotlight. A gobo is either 2D or 3D element in your scene that passes in front of a light source and acts as a *flag*, blocking light from hitting certain elements. Gobos are easily ma-

FIGURE
2.44
A still-life without a gel. © 1998 John B. Crane

FIGURE
2.45
Adding a gel to simulate light coming through a window adds an off-screen life to your piece. © 1998 John B. Crane

nipulated and animated in your project file because they are geometry rather than a map. While adding geometry adds a little to rendering time, gobos can earn their time hit by adding dramatic lighting effects to your project. Figure 2.46 shows a scene rendered with a shadow-casting gobo along with a shot of how the scene is constructed.

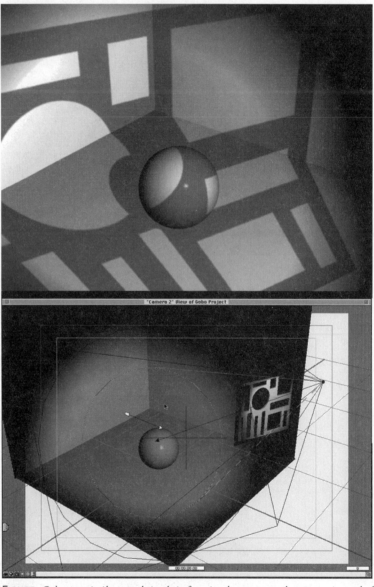

FIGURE   *Gobos are similar to gels in their function but are actual geometry instead of a*
2.46   *map placed in front of the light.*

DRAMATIC LIGHTING

Dramatic lighting could be considered lighting that brings a sense of drama or urgency to the image. Contrast and drama may be suggested by creative use of dramatic lighting. Consider a stage performance, for example, and the critical role lighting plays in real-world theater. Strategically placed and illuminated spotlights key in on certain cast members as they perform. So it is in your animation projects. While there will be many times that your project will not call on dramatic lighting (if it were used all the time it wouldn't be dramatic), selective use brings a sense of isolation and importance to an object in space. We'll cover this more in the Composition Thought Process section.

Ambient Light

Ambient light can best be described as the overall brightness or color of your scene. Ambient light essentially defines how deep or what color the shadow areas are and is often very important in the final image. If your scene is too dark and too contrasty, try adding an ambient light instead of tweaking your existing lights. If it then becomes too washed out, lower your ambient settings until you are happy. ElectricImage provides you with two ways of adding Ambient light effects to your scene and the two should not be confused. Confusing, maybe, but not confused.

Figure 2.47 shows the ambient light control in the **World** object present in every ElectricImage project. This ambient setting defaults to Off. Enabling it requires selecting the check box shown. The world Ambience setting works in conjunction with the **Ambient** tab in your Material Info Window and is responsible for adding an overall color wash to your scene.

Adding an actual Ambient light is another story and is discussed a bit in the Lighting Tips and Techniques chapter. It allows you to lighten your areas of shadow and contrast and can also add a color wash to your objects as well. The actual Ambient light provides more control over the effect than the ambient setting in the World Info Window but each has its place.

SUMMARY

By paying attention to real-world scenarios, you'll begin to build a better appreciation for the role good lighting plays in your 3D projects. ElectricImage offers tremendous amount of control over lighting. Having so many options can quickly get overwhelming and confusing, but with a little practice and study, you'll become an expert. You'll be able to encourage viewers to see what you, as the creator, desires, by directing them through on a deliberate path, or calling attention to a key element or event as it happens. You'll be able to drive

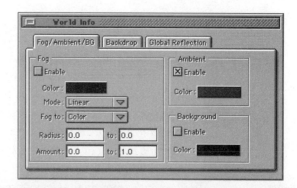

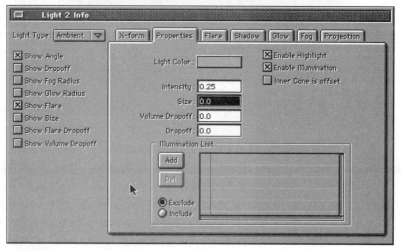

FIGURE   *The World Ambient and Ambient Light windows.*
2.47

events and objects back in space, accentuate prominence and importance on a
sliding scale, and completely control the atmosphere of your projects.

—John B. Crane

**The Composition
Thought Process**

Composition is often what makes the difference between a professional photograph and a snapshot. The same holds true for 3D. The biggest problem with
composition is that it's typically the most difficult skill to really explain, and
even more difficult to master, because there really aren't any hard and fast rules
you can apply. There are some general things to watch out for and details to pay
attention to, but each scene is completely different and can require you to re-

think your technique each and every time. The bar gets raised a little higher when you start animating because you have to then take the motion of your objects into consideration.

In a nutshell, the goal of composition is to add mood and form to your scene by establishing a hierarchy of importance to each of your objects. Sometimes you want more attention to be placed on an object or series of objects and sometimes you want the viewer to look at a scene in a particular order. And often, you want it all.

In this section, we'll cover the main things you need to consider when setting up your scene. From here on, however, it'll be up to you to put all of these together. The key goals for composition are *object placement,* used to make a scene look more natural, *creating emphasis* to bring certain elements to the viewers attention, viewing angle and lens settings to put sizes into perspective and just generally make the scene more interesting, and scene dialogue, which helps the image or animation tell the story.

So let's get on with it.

OBJECT PLACEMENT

This is the most fundamental area of your composition. The basic idea here is to add a natural feel to your scene and give it a pleasing construction at the same time. Since the frame in which you are working creates limitations on your viewing area (as opposed to how you see the world through your own eyes), you have to learn to make the best use of that given area. A general rule to follow is to divide your frames into sections (see Figure 2.48). This is a tried-and-true technique used in all forms of design. These are only a few of the examples showing how you can split up your composition. You can combine any of these or even create your own but they give you a good starting point.

Creating this grid helps you to visualize your scene as an artist or designer visualizes ideas on an empty canvas or sheet of paper. It will help you determine the most appealing and useful placement of your objects. Typically, you'll want to avoid using the first box in that figure because, for most situations, you'll want to avoid centrally located objects because they immediately limit your composition options and create a confrontational feeling between the viewer and the subject. Although there are times when you want to create a sense of confrontation, this is usually not the way to go. Centrally placed objects create an unnatural feeling for the piece because they allow for no flow of action, unless the object is going away or coming towards the viewer, hence the confrontation. Even in a still image, you typically want to create some sense of motion. Even if the object in the image is supposed to be stationary, you typi-

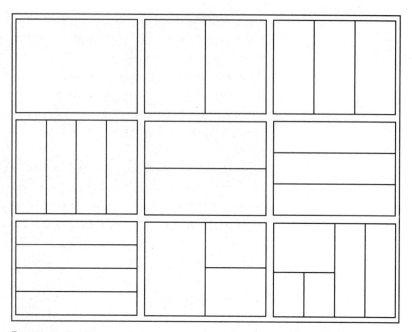

FIGURE *By dividing your frame up into sections, you can get a better feel for how you*
2.48 *should design your scene.*

cally want to give the impression that there is something going on in the scene
other than what you see in front of you. Think of this as a car stopped at an in-
tersection without its turn signal on. You don't know whether it's parked or getting ready to turn left or right. You, as a driver approaching this stationary car,
don't know what to expect. The same holds true for the viewer of your scene.
Figure 2.49 shows an example of this. The top image leaves little room for
adding extra elements unless you want them to encircle the soldier in a very unnatural fashion. It also gives the impression that the soldier is thinking, "Snap
the picture already, so I can get back to work." The bottom image, however,
leaves plenty of room to play with, plus it gives the scene much a more natural
personality and gives the viewer an idea that something is getting ready to happen. Figure 2.50 is a sample of the exception of when a more centrally placed
main image does work. For this image, I was going for a more confrontational
feel. I still mixed things up by making the main image not quite in the center
of the piece and by choosing an interesting viewing angle. There is also a good
bit of motion here. You know, as a viewer, that if you don't get out of this guy's
way, you're likely to get knocked down.

FIGURE *Placing an object in a centrally located position leaves you little room for play*
2.49 *and forces the viewer to deal with the object head on. While this is sometimes*
what you want, it's often not the best solution. The bottom image opens the
scene up for extra action and adds flexibility for the placement of additional
objects.

Since you're working with a third dimension here, you have forward and backward placement to consider. The images in Figure 2.51 show how you can still use a relatively straightforward composition as far as the X and Y axes are concerned but how, by moving things around in the Z dimension, you can spruce things up a bit. The top image is pretty dry but the bottom one is a good example of how tweaking things along the Z axis and moving the camera around a tad can help add a bit more excitement to a scene. If you like, you can randomize the scene a little further to spruce up the action. The image in Figure 2.52 does not pull one object out from the rest but it does give a good bit of life to the scene.

FIGURE **2.50** *This is an example of when a centrally located main object does work and is necessary to convey the proper message. © 1998 John W. Sledd*

EMPHASIS

Throughout your 3D endeavors, you will often want to create emphasis on a specific object in your scene. This can be done a number of ways. Object placement is one of them, as was shown above. The object that is closest to the camera can make a big difference.

There are other ways to create emphasis, however. You can do it through lighting, your color scheme, camera focus, or a combination of all of the above.

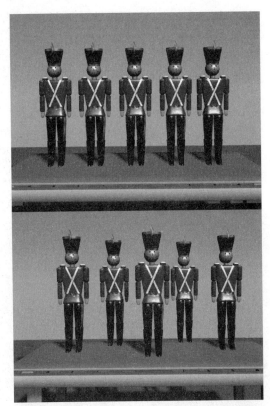

FIGURE *Here we have two basically centrally located scenes. The first one is pretty dry*
2.51 *and gives no indication of action, but the second one gives a much better sense*
of depth. The only difference between the two images is a slight tweak of the
camera angle and a repositioning of some of the elements in the scene along the
Z axis.

FIGURE *Randomizing the position and rotation of your objects can give a scene a more*
2.52 *chaotic, and therefore, lifelike quality.*

Figure 2.53 shows how selective positioning and lighting can pull one object out from the rest. You can combine positioning and lighting with a little bit of tension to add to a scene as well. Figure 2.54 not only does a good job of telling the viewer where to look but also gives an indication of what's about to happen. Watch that first step!

You can leave your lighting alone and use color to augment your composition. Figure 2.55 shows a relatively basic scene. The camera angle helps give interest to the scene, but the color of the one soldier tells the viewer immediately where to look first.

FIGURE
2.53 *Just as with the spotlight in a theatrical production, you can bring all of the attention to an object without working very hard at all.*

FIGURE
2.54 *Adding a little bit of tension to a scene can tell the viewer where to go as well. Of course, if you spotlight it, too, the viewer really has no choice.*

FIGURE
2.55 *If you want to leave the lighting and position alone, a simple color change can add a dramatic effect to a scene.*

VIEWING ANGLE AND LENS SETTINGS

The angle from which you render your scene and the lens settings (field of view) you choose are, in my opinion, the quickest way to liven up a shot. Varying levels of importance can be established and interesting lines can be created by shooting your scene from odd angles or by using extreme lens settings. The image in Figure 2.56 uses a wide-angle lens setting to bring the foreground character into unquestionable importance. The off-center shot also lets the viewer know that there are other objects in the scene that could be ready to challenge the hierarchy of importance at any instant.

The foreground character can also be emphasized by using a depth-of-field effect. This keeps the foreground object in crystal clear focus while blurring out the background objects. Using depth-of-field, however, your foreground object doesn't have to be the most important object of your scene. You can adjust the depth of field to pull the viewer to other objects in your scene. Figure 2.57 shows two options available using depth-of-field. In the top image, the camera is focusing on the foreground object. In the bottom image, the depth of field has been adjusted to focus on the second object in the scene, thus giving it more importance. Depth-of-field can be animated as well, so you can focus on your foreground object and then move the focus to a secondary object to place the emphasis there.

FIGURE *A nice wide-angle lens can dramatically increase an object's importance.*
2.56

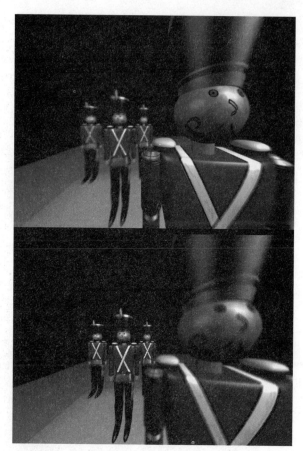

FIGURE *Depth-of-field can be use to place importance on objects, regardless of how they*
2.57 *are placed in the scene.*

Viewing angle can also determine the size of your objects. Figure 2.58 shows two shots of the same object. The bottom shot shows a toy soldier on a table that you could smash with the palm of your hand, whereas the bottom shot, taken from below the object, turns your toy into a giant. Who would be smashed here?

In an animation, the viewing angle can be adjusted to make the best use of your frame space and to get more action into the scene while keeping the object of your desire more prominent throughout the overall motion.

Figure 2.59 shows an animation of a spaceship. In order to get an appropriate amount of motion into this frame, the scene had to be shot from very far away and, as a result, you can barely make out the details of the ship. This looks

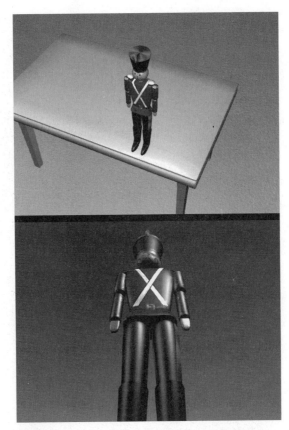

FIGURE **2.58** *Camera angle can make the difference between a rendering a toy and rendering a statue.*

FIGURE **2.59** *This animation was shot from a relatively head-on view. As you can see, we're too far away to tell much about the object that we should be paying close attention to.*

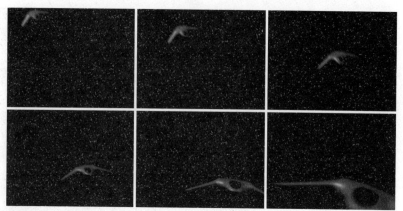

FIGURE **2.60** *By adjusting the camera position and viewing angle, we can see more of the ship and add quite a bit of impact to the scene as well.*

more like one of those UFO camcorder shots. Of course, you should keep this technique in mind because you never know when you're going to have to create a trumped-up close encounter. Another instance of an exception to the rules.

By adjusting the camera angle and position, as in Figure 2.60, you can get more of the motion into the scene and give more frame real estate to the object as well. This is a much more exciting shot.

SCENE COORDINATION AND DIALOGUE

Each object in your scene must work with, not against, each other object and element (such as lighting or motion) in the scene. You do this via a combination of all of the above elements. Even if your objects are all wonderful and your lighting is right on, your final render will suffer if the objects don't work properly together. The images in Figures 2.61 and 2.62 illustrate this very well. The two images are identical with the exception of object placement and camera angle, yet the image in Figure 2.62 is a much better example of composition. Why? Because the image in Figure 2.61 leaves little to the imagination. There is nowhere for the story to go. It was just like someone walked up to the table and took a snapshot with an old Kodak Brownie. The image in Figure 2.62, however, conveys much more mood and leaves you wondering about the story behind the image.

SUMMARY

By using a combination of the above techniques, your images and animations will add to the story behind them instead of relying on it for their existence.

FIGURE   *All of the elements of a scene can be fine, but if the composition is wrong, the*
2.61   *scene winds up dull.* © 1998 John W. Sledd

Like the concept of making all of the objects in your scene work together, your story and images should work together as well. You never want one to totally break apart without the other. Composition is the key ingredient to making this cooperation happen.

The above guidelines are a great place to start, but, as I mentioned earlier, they all have exceptions and, in most instances, you'll have to pull new tricks out of your own hat with regularity. Experimentation is the key, but thinking about your options ahead of time will cut a good bit of travel time from your journey.

FIGURE 2.62 *A little object placement and a creative camera angle can add a great bit of mood to a scene. © 1998 John W. Sledd*

The Animation Thought Process

Question: What's the difference between a 3D illustration and a 3D animation?

Answer: Time.

One of the greatest things about working in 3D is this additional element of time that allows you to move into that fourth dimension. It used to be that animation was the realm of the mega-buck outfits who could either afford large staffs or the high-priced equipment needed to do it "on the computer." No longer. ElectricImage brings top-notch digital animation to the desktop user. Using ElectricImage to animate, you become the writer, director, choreographer, artist, model and prop builder, lighting engineer, sound technician, and producer, all at the same time and all in the same place. But surely it can't be that easy or everyone would be doing "Toy Story" on the Mac at home. The truth is, while desktop computer animation has been made possible and much simpler over the past few years, it's still an art unto itself, warranting volumes and volumes of techniques, information, advice, and time. To the avid computer graphics junkie, it's a never-ending affair. Planning an animation becomes the first step in any successful project.

PLAN AHEAD

Everyone has a slightly different style of working, but if you plan on getting into the animation realm of 3D, you'd better accept this fact right from the start: Animation takes planning. While you can fly by the seat of your pants through many an illustration project, relying on good old Photoshop to cover any of the blemishes, animation is a whole different animal. From the very beginning stages to the final rendered frame, everything you consider in animation adds up to a cost of time. The big-time hit is usually the actual rendering process, but many of the steps along the way can be equally as time consuming.

A few defined steps will get you started. In order, they are the basic idea or story script, a storyboard of the proposed animation, then an animation script, and finally into EI itself. In a perfect world, you'd want follow all of these steps, but many leave out various segments in an effort to hasten the process and cut down on time. If you decide to skip a step, be sure that you are actually cutting down your time rather than simply adding to it by trying to cut corners that you shouldn't be cutting. There's that saying, "There's never time to do it right but there's always time to do it over." Truer words have never been spoken. If you were the kind of kid who liked to put the decals on your model cars before the paint was dry, you're going to have to learn a little bit of patience here. Rest assured, though, that it is possible to maintain a level of spontaneity and creativity without getting completely bogged down in the "procedure." After all, this is still supposed to be fun, right?

THE STORY SCRIPT

The story script is the idea itself. Even if it's in your head and you know it like the back of your hand, write it out on a sheet of paper. Like all of those motivational guys who tell you to repeat your goals to yourself every morning in front of the mirror (does anyone actually do this?), writing out the animation script allows you to begin to formulate a plan of attack. If others will be getting involved, it also helps them see your vision of the project in black and white, and—perish the thought—maybe even offer some suggestions to improve it. If you're in the position of trying to get a concept approved by a paying client, unless that client can read your mind, you're going to have to write it down.

What you're after is a logical stream of events that flows nicely together. A story. This story will more than likely have a beginning, a middle, and an end, no matter how short an animation spot it is. Whether you're selling something for a client, or realizing your personal animation vision, if the story falls apart, nothing else matters. We've all been to movies that have whiz-bang special effects but the story line, writing, and plot are a step up from "see Dick and Jane run." Let's face it: Creativity is important. Writing down that creativity is vital.

If this is your first attempt as an animator, you have an incredibly valuable resource right in your own home. It's called your television. Most things on TV follow some sort of formula. Spend time observing commercials, movies, and yes, even sitcoms. Follow the camera angles, lighting, camera cuts, pans, and how long a shot stays on an actor's face. Watch how lighting may affect what you're feeling or seeing on the screen. Notice the music playing in the background. All of these things potentially contribute to the success of an animation project. Many of them are incorporated every day in the shows we watch on television, so take advantage of this and study. Rent some movies noted for cinematography such as "Citizen Kane," or movies that pertain to your field of interest such as "Alien" or "Blade Runner." All have something to offer. Study how your favorite directors handled tricky lighting situations. It all applies— even if you're only doing a 10-second bit on how to sell soap.

After you've done your homework and hopefully expanded the vision of your project, it's time to get it down on paper. In so doing, do your best to jot down notes to yourself—like the scale of an object relative to the camera, or how fast something moves by the camera, or what you envision the lighting conditions might be like. Remember, you're an artist, not just a technician. All of your notes, however subtle they may seem to you, could be vital in communicating your message.

THE STORYBOARD

Once you have the story penned, it's time to begin to visualize it with drawings. Storyboards are often used for this step. They can be either pre-made or homemade—it makes no difference. There are pads for sale at graphic art stores and there is even a simple storyboard template in EPS format on the CD that came with this book. Look in the Chapter 2 folder.

The storyboard is where your animation starts to assume a life of its own— where you begin to realize the story visually. The first step is to break it down into the major scenes or acts. Once the major acts are delineated, start breaking down these segments into finer detail. How well you can draw has very little to do with this initially. The important thing is that the images convey your message. Be as detailed and precise as you can, but remember, these are fast, rough passes designed to get a point across, be easily and quickly adjusted, and not necessarily win awards. Figure 2.63 shows the beginning of a simple storyboard created completely in Adobe Illustrator. The drawing clearly isn't great, but the message is clear—somebody's in trouble.

If you have a difficult time drawing an element or concept, note it at the bottom of the frame and keep moving. Don't get hung up on trying to draw fog, for example. The idea is to begin to visualize your animation on paper before sitting down to the computer. If you take this step, once you sit down at the computer, your time is more efficiently spent carrying out a plan.

That having been said, if you're an impatient, fly-by-the-seat-of-your-pants worker who wants to see action and results, by all means do as you see fit. If you know you simply want a camera flying by a still model, elaborate storyboarding is probably unnecessary (unless the client requests it). But at least have a vision in your mind as to what you hope to accomplish with this animation. You'll be glad later.

1. Mumble Mumble Mumble

2. FREEEEEEEZE!!!!!

3. EEEEEEEK!!!!!!

4. You Boys are in a LOT of trouble!!!!

FIGURE   *Storyboards can be very simple but are infinitely useful.* © *1998 John W. Sledd*
2.63

THE ANIMATION SCRIPT

An animation script basically looks like a pencil drawing of the ElectricImage's timeline in the project window (see Figure 2.64). There is an EPS file on the CD-ROM accompanying this book with an animation script template that you can use. Time is noted across the top, and your cast of characters and events may be written in along the side.

This animation script acts as a rough draft for when you sit down to work in ElectricImage. You can quickly sketch out how you think the animation should be set up before beginning to work in EI. Once you move the project into ElectricImage, you can fine tune all you want, but this script provides an basic sketch to work from.

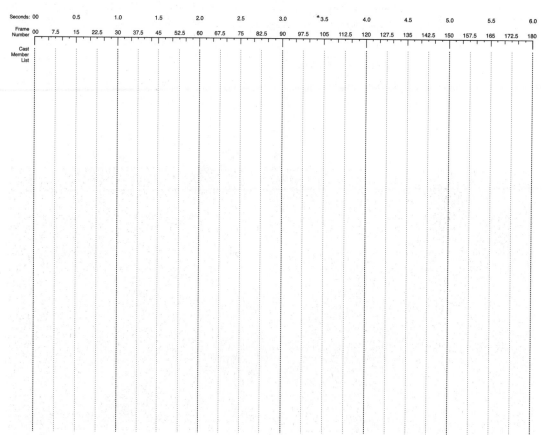

FIGURE *A basic animation script as provided on the CD ROM that came with this book.*

2.64

KEY EVENTS

Key events are, simply put, events in time that have been set by you, the artist. Key events are needed to tell the computer where the action begins and ends and at what points along the way other action occurs. They are the cornerstone of computer animation.

In traditional cell animation, the lead artist, or the "keyman," would draw the key frames, generally thought of as the most important action. Once these key frames were completed, "tweeners" would handle the laborious job of filling in the frames between key events. This was called "tweening" and is important in computer animation because the computer becomes, among other things, your tweener—essentially a staff of artists working for you.

Using a few keyframes, simple or complex movement can be established. Figure 2.65 shows a simple camera rotation. While other keyframes were established to move lights, the main motion in this 15-second video was created using four keyframes controlling the rotation of the camera. Figure 2.66 shows the timeline of the project.

INVERSE KINEMATICS

Animating a camera fly-by or simple movement of an object is a relatively straightforward process. Things get much more complicated when you begin

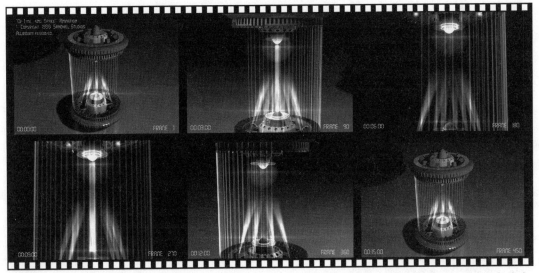

FIGURE *Keyframed segments of a simple camera rotation around a model. Although addition keyframes were set for light*
2.65 *motion, the basic camera rotation is established in four keyframes.* © 1998 John B. Crane

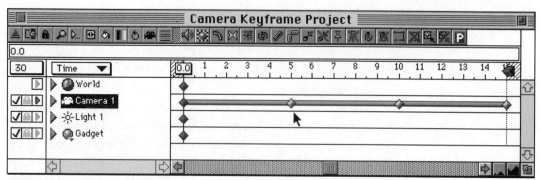

FIGURE **2.66** *The timeline of the project shows the setup of the keyframes for the camera.*

to animate complicated machinery or a character walking. The use of inverse kinematics (IK) is invaluable in these instances.

Inverse kinematics serves as smart links between model parts allowing the movement of one object to affect the movement of another in the IK chain. The aspect of "inverse" means that the motion dictated by one object moves up the chain, affecting objects above in the hierarchy. Figure 2.67 shows a graphic representation of a human arm linked with inverse kinematics. If you IK link the arm as shown, click on the wrist and extend it. As long as the constraints and links are set in a realistic fashion, the new position of the wrist will affect the forearm and upper arm as well. IK offers tremendous time savings over what would otherwise be a nearly impossible task; trying to determine the re-

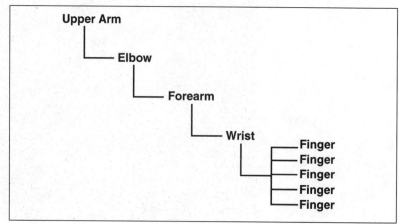

FIGURE **2.67** *A graphic representation of an IK hierarchy. Essentially, the inverse aspects of this hierarchy means motion moves up the chain.*

sult one move has on another. Without IK, there would be a lot more guess-work involved.

HIERARCHY

In order for the IK chain to work correctly, it's important the your hierarchy is established correctly in the **Project Window**. Establishing complex or simple hierarchies in ElectricImage easily done. Figure 2.68 shows an example something you'd greatly benefit from if time was spent constructing a good hierarchy. A term you'll hear used a lot is "parent-child" relationship. This refers to the notion that a "child" object is that which is located beneath the Parent object in the hierarchical chain. Pulling on the toe of the foot will extent all the hydraulic hoses (shown here using CableCraft™) and sliders, telescoping out the legs in accordance with a step this contraption would take.

LINKS

Links are the means by which members of the hierarchy actually attach to the others. These links define how each parent-child relationship moves relative to itself. Figure 2.69 shows an example of the **Link Info Window** in ElectricImage. In this image, a chrome hydraulic rod will be sliding into the sleeve con-

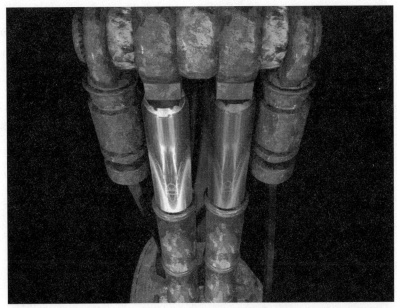

FIGURE   *These hydraulic legs are one of many examples of complex machinery directly*
2.68   *benefiting from Inverse Kinematics. © 1998 John B. Crane*

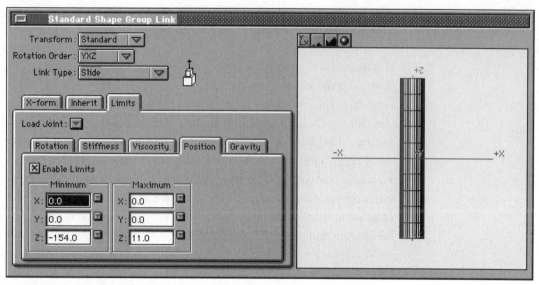

FIGURE *The Link Info window with a Slide Link assigned.*
2.69

taining it. Thus, designating a slider link is appropriate because it most closely resembles the real-world movement constraints.

There are eleven types of links available under the link pull down menu. They are, in order of appearance, Custom, Free, Ball Planar, Cylinder Planar, Planar, Socket, Cylinder, Universal, Slider, Pin, and Lock. In this case, the Slider link allows you to determine the axes on which the object will slide and also establish limits as to how far it will slide, avoiding the possibility it'll shoot out of the end of its sleeve.

Establishing a complex IK hierarchy takes practice. Each area is covered in adequate detail in the ElectricImage user manual. Take your time and study the examples.

BASIC ANIMATION TECHNIQUES

OK. So we know we have the right tools within ElectricImage to create a great animation. But what about actually using these powerful tools to animate something? Where does one begin? Animators, since early on, have operated on a few basic principles that hold true in today's high-tech applications. There are some fundamental concepts that you will greatly benefit from, if understood correctly. They have little to do with the technical jargon and more to do with how motion is portrayed, in any medium. Your endeavors to better understand animation theory would be greatly aided by picking up some good books by the masters. *Disney Animation: The Illusion of Life* by Frank Thomas and Ollie Johnston (two of the original Disney animators) would get you heading in the right direction.

Anticipation

Anticipation plays on the notion that before a major movement, there is usually a minor, sometimes almost imperceptible, movement that precedes it. If you watch a character jump off the floor, for example, you'll notice that preceding the actual jump there is a bending of the knees and legs that facilitates that jump. If the character simply springs up into the air, it would look unnatural. This is anticipation. It can also work on otherwise inanimate objects such as a cartoon gun. In cartoons, if you watch a gun being shot, it tends to swell up around the base before emitting the bullet. Anticipation is used to introduce the motion of the bullet being emitted from the gun. As the gun emits the bullet, it will use other animation techniques to further convince you that it actually shot the bullet.

Exaggeration

Exaggeration helps reveal things otherwise hard to see or that simply require emphasis to create a certain effect. It can also be used as a means to characterize an action. Take that same gun shooting the bullet. We used anticipation to ready the viewer for the bullet being ejected. We could now use exaggeration to swell that barrel up to drive the point home this is a big, nasty bullet that barely fits in this gun. As the bullet is ejected, it could be exaggerated lengthwise to indicate that it's traveling at tremendous speed. The barrel of the gun would also recoil from its original swelling, collapsing slightly on itself in an exaggerated manner. Figure 2.70 shows the use of exaggeration.

Overlapping Action

Natural motion isn't as predictable as the computer can make it seem. Good motion is often not completely sequential. That is, one movement doesn't necessarily start and stop before another begins. Overlapping action is the concept that every motion will have its own individual start and stop points, thereby overlapping in time. If you watch the human figure walking, notice what the shoulders do in relation to the swinging of the arms and in relation to the sway of the hips and the strike of the foot. As the arms move forward in natural motion, the shoulders are posturing themselves in relation to what the feet, hips, and spine are doing, and preparing for the next arm swing as the next footstep falls. A subtle, well-orchestrated set of overlapping actions remains the Holy Grail of any character animator's efforts.

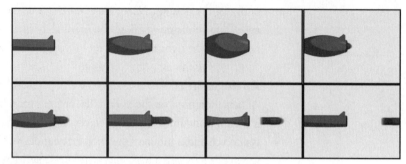

FIGURE **2.70** *Various frames of a cartoon gun shooting a bullet is a good example of Exaggeration and Anticipation.*

The good thing about animation on the computer is that you do not need to concentrate on all of these motions at once. Focusing on getting the leg movement correct, for example, then moving to the hips, then the swagger of the spine and the sway of the shoulders allow the animator to tackle a complex project in bite-sized tasks. By establishing keyframes that determine the timing of the individual motions first, you may then shuffle these independent motions around on the time line to fine tune the overlap of the action.

Squash and Stretch

This is one of the most often used effects in animation, especially in cartoons. Characters being stretched unnaturally as various calamitous events occur, such as getting stepped on, pulled in different directions, or shot out of a cannon. Squashing and stretching also happens in real life. The most often used example is a ball bouncing. As the ball hits the ground, it will compress or squash slightly on impact. This is because the ball isn't made of strictly rigid material but a rather soft, pliable material such as rubber. As the ball leaves the ground after its impact, it will conversely stretch, elongating towards the direction it's heading. Often, squashing and stretching are combined with other methods such as exaggeration, especially in the cartoon style of animation. Subtle amounts may also be very effective in more realistic events.

Follow-Through

Follow-through follows the principle law of physics that every action has an equal and opposite reaction, and that these actions and reactions don't always start and stop abruptly. Think of a character throwing something. As its arm extends forward in an arcing motion to throw the object, upon release of the thrown object, the arm continues through its arc as its velocity decreases.

Another example takes us back to the example of a bullet shooting out of a gun. If you're ever shot a gun, you know about the recoil. The energy expended upon the explosion sending the bullet out the barrel also has an effect in the opposite direction, kicking the gun back. This is also a form of follow-through, and omitting follow-through can cause unnatural looking motion.

The important facet of follow-through is gravity and velocity. Imagine a ball (maybe the ball thrown by the character mentioned above) bouncing on the ground. As the motion of the ball carries it down toward the ground, its momentum picks up because of gravity. Therefore, it's going faster at the bottom of its motion cycle as it nears the ground. As the ball strikes the ground and shoots upward, it will slow towards the top of the bounce, also due to gravity, and then proceed back down. ElectricImage has velocity graphs for such an event. Velocity graphs are an extremely important aspect of working with natural motion. There is good documentation in the ElectricImage manuals and tutorials on your ElectricImage CD. Study them, do the projects, and understand the principles. These lessons will pay off dramatically when you tackle your first complex animation.

BASIC CAMERA MOVEMENTS

If you've ever watched a movie and wondered who was behind the camera, the cinematographer probably didn't do a very good job. Camera motion is an extremely important aspect to animation. If done correctly, camera motion becomes integrated into the scene, virtually unnoticeable except for special circumstances.

One of my favorite aspects of ElectricImage is how easily the camera is manipulated. You simply click on it and move it. No fancy icons to decipher, just click and move like in the real world, but with no cables to trip over. Just the same, there are some fundamental concepts you'll do well to understand. They are Orbit, Pan, Dolly, Track, and Zoom. Figure 2.71 shows where these controls are tucked in ElectricImage's Camera View window. One of the telltale signs of the beginning animator is too much or too radical camera movement. As you get more experience, you'll learn how to be subtle with the camera motion and avoid potentially causing your viewers motion sickness.

Zoom

Zooming is the most basic concept. If you've ever used a telephoto lens on a camera, zooming is accomplished by changing the focal length to pull away from your subject or to zoom in on it. In ElectricImage, you simply move the camera closer to the object it's pointing at. Zooming in quickly can add drama

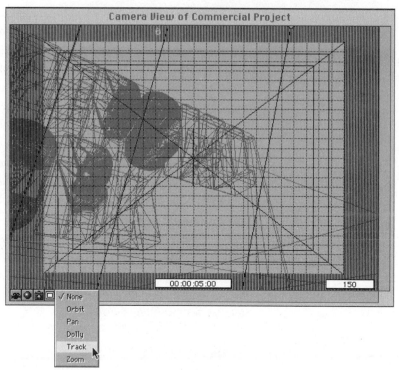

FIGURE *Here's where to find your camera control options.*

2.71

to a scene, but it can also cause a sense of urgency. Start with slow, deliberate zooming. To add a little more interest, try rolling the camera slightly from one side to the other during your zoom. These subtle tricks can add interest to your animation with very little effort.

Model Fly-By

The fly-by is a classic camera maneuver used a lot in scenes where you're following a moving object. Parking your camera at a point in space then passing the model by it can produce some simple, dramatic results. ElectricImage provides easily editable motion paths and using these motion paths as a reference makes it easy to establish your camera near the path of the object's intended course of travel. If you set the camera to follow or *Look-At* your model, it will naturally rotate as the model passes by.

Dramatic effects can be created by setting a spaceship off in the distance, out of sight in the opening shot, then flying the ship past the camera. As the camera rotates with the passing ship, the tail section becomes visible and you are left with a real sense of the ship closing in on your location and then passing.

One of my favorite examples of this is in the opening shot of the original "Star Wars" when a ship passes directly over the camera. This was a miniature model, but the successful notion of immense size and power was pulled off by the position of the camera, the lighting, and the speed at which this ship passed.

Figure 2.72 shows some examples of fly-bys. In Figure 2.72A, the camera's position is halfway between the ship's beginning and ending positions. With this setup, the ship begins small, grows large as it nears the camera, then fades small again as it recedes into the distance. This is predictable, smooth motion. Figure 2.72B shows the camera positioned towards the beginning of the action.

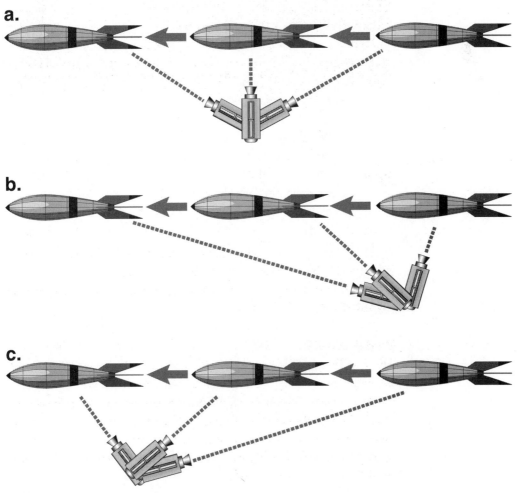

FIGURE   *The basic fly-by.*
2.72

This camera angle would show the ship pass in the first frames, then slowly recede into the distance during a majority of the animation. The advantage to this is that the ship starts off large and in the forefront, immediately grabbing the viewer's attention. This setup has the additional advantage of directing the viewer in the direction where the camera ends, opening the door to a nice segue, if desired. Figure 2.72C shows the camera positioned at the end of the ship's path. This introduces the ship to the viewer in a gradual fashion and is another interesting way of presenting a model into your animation.

Some variations on all of these techniques can produce great animation sequences with minimal effort. As a ship nears the apex of its turn, it could bank slightly to follow the inertia through the turn. Although there is no gravity in space to make this a problem for the ship, it's looks much more interesting and keeps you from sloshing your ship's passengers around.

Try playing with focal lengths in this process, too. ElectricImage allows you to change the Field of View of the camera over the course of an animation. This may be used to accomplish slight exaggeration as the ship draws nearer or recedes, producing the effect of greater speed.

Camera Dollying

Dollying is sometimes used instead of a model fly-by. Dollying makes it possible to follow along with the action. In ElectricImage, it's a simple matter of dragging the camera from one point to another. There are essentially three different types of dolly movement. Figure 2.73A shows the first kind, where the camera moves along parallel with the object. This produces an even, stable, predictable closeup of the model good for showing extreme detail or action within the model. Figure 2.73B shows another kind of dollying where the camera is moving faster than the model, eventually passing it. This shot is good for showing closeups of the front of the model, or playing with the notion that something is moving faster or slower in the scene. By the camera moving faster you're implying that the model is moving slower than the viewer. Figure 2.73C shows the last dollying action where the camera lags behind the model because it's moving slower. This conveys the sense of greater speed of the model and also allows a better view of the back portion of the model.

SUMMARY

Animation is where all of the other aspects of 3D design we talked about come together. Adding the element of time increases the options for details in your work exponentially. It can get a little overwhelming, but you can start small and work your way up.

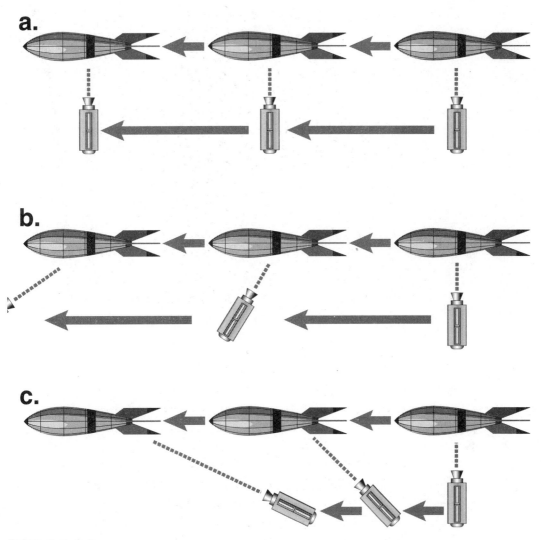

Without a clear idea of your animations goals, however, you run the risk of confusing viewer and losing your message. You're better off with a well-crafted still image than a poorly executed animation. Take heart, though, there are plenty of opportunities for you to practice this time-honored art. With ElectricImage at your side you're well on your way to mastering computer animation.

—*John B. Crane*

CHAPTER

3

Modeling and Importing Tips

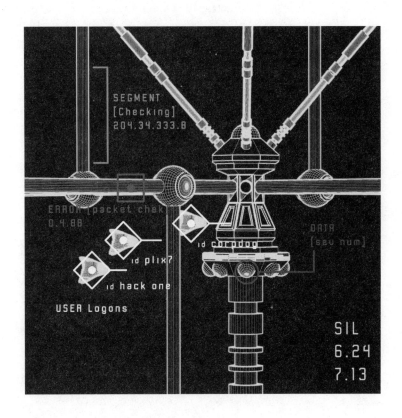

T here are many little bits of good information to keep in mind when creating models for your projects. We'll cover several of them here, which will hopefully make your life a little easier.

Model in Layers

Creating multiple layers in your modeling projects gives you many advantages when working with large scenes. For example, one of the most obvious ways to speed up screen redraw is to turn off objects that you're currently not working with. If you are using layers, you can turn off all of the objects in the layer simultaneously simply by turning off the visibility of the layer. You can also simplify your layer window by clicking on the little arrow next to the layer folder. This closes the folder and frees up more space (see Figure 3.1).

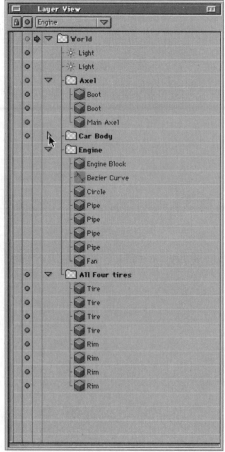

FIGURE *Modeling in Layers can help you be much more organized and can help with*
3.1 *keeping the perceived complexity of a model to a minimum.*

Layers also come in handy when creating objects. Since the ElectricImage Modeler leaves behind your construction objects and creates new objects in the active layer, you can create your construction objects in one layer and then make another layer active right before you create the final object. This will leave the construction objects in their original layer but will place the newly created objects in the currently active layer. This helps keep things organized.

Memorize Keyboard Shortcuts

There are several keyboard shortcuts in Modeler that will help streamline your workflow. For example, **Command-P** selects your **Pick tool**, **Command-R** selects your **Rotate tool**, and **Command-M** selects your **Move tool**. By holding down the **D-key** while using any of these tools, you can create duplicates of the object you are moving.

You can also adjust your views by holding down various combinations of keys. Holding down the **Spacebar** allows you to interactively pan around in your window. **Spacebar-Command** lets you zoom in and out on your scene. **Spacebar-Command-Shift** allows you to orbit your scene. If you find you're running out of fingers here, simply holding down the **o-key** while dragging will let you orbit as well.

Holding down **Option** will give you the zoom tool. Clicking or dragging a marquee will zoom you in on your scene. If you want to zoom out, you simply press **Shift** at the same time and click.

There are many other keyboard shortcuts and learning them will save you a good bit of time and a number of mouse-clicks.

Don't Make More Objects Than Necessary

A good general guideline is, if you aren't going to see it, don't model it. There's no point in modeling the guts of a rocketship if all you are ever going to see in your illustration or animation is the outside of it. This sounds like common sense but many modelers, including myself, get caught up in the details sometimes, which can be fine for a funtime project, but can needlessly cost you time when a deadline is looming. Remember, this is just animation, the rocket will fly whether it's got guts or not. Not only will this extra detail cost you during modeling but it'll cost you during rendering time as well. The next tip addresses this.

Don't Overmodel (Too Many Polygons = Too Much Time)

EI is a wonderful application when it comes to handling large quantities of polygons, but this doesn't mean you should just go hog-wild with your polygon counts. The more polys you're rendering, the longer your screen takes to redraw and the harder your CPU has to work to render the scene. Extra polygons don't just come from extra objects but also result from using too many polygons for the model in question. This is more of a concern when working with polygonal modelers than it is when working with the EI modeler, but the same still holds true when it comes time to export.

When you're working with a polygonal modeler, you need to take into consideration where the object will be in your scene and model it accordingly. If it's only going to appear at a good distance from the camera in your scene, you can skimp on the details because they will never be seen anyway, so why waste the resources. If the object is going to be the focus of your scene, and/or will come very close to the camera, then you would want to use as much detail as possible to avoid the faceted edges that are all so common and ugly in 3D art.

Since the EI Modeler is resolution independent, you really don't even have to think about the amount of polygonal detail when you're modeling, which is a great advantage. You do still need to consider this at the time of export, though. You can find these options under the **Tessellation** tab in the **Document Preferences** (see Figure 3.2). You may find that the default settings work

FIGURE *The Tessellation settings in the EI Modeler control the resolution of your*
3.2 *exported models.*

just great for whatever you're doing, but sometimes you may find the need to up the resolution. You may also find times when you can decrease the resolution to save yourself some time or to try to compensate for other high-poly models in your scene. The point is: Don't just max everything out because you can and because you just want to make sure everything looks great. There is a point of diminishing returns. Every poly you save will buy you extra time during rendering.

Select Objects in the Layer Window

Sometimes you'll find it difficult to select an object in the **World View Windows** because it may be obstructed by other objects, but each object is clearly visible in your **Layer Window** and ripe for the picking (yep, slight pun intended). This can save you a great deal of frustration.

Save Often

Even the best of machines and most solid apps crash. And even if they don't crash all on their own, the power company isn't perfect either and no machine can run very long without juice.

The best insurance you can buy for your hard work is to save often. The last thing you want to happen, after spending several hours on a job, is to have it just disappear right in front of your eyes. So save, save, save, and then save again.

In addition to saving often, you might want to also save versions of your file at various stages of development. Clients have a bad habit of coming back and approving work that they detested the first time they saw it. This usually happens after you've gone through twenty or so versions in an attempt to make them happy. If you were smart enough to save these earlier versions, you'll be no less frustrated, but at least you'll be less likely to commit murder.

Build Your Scene in Simple Wireframe Mode

Working in **Simple Wireframe** preview (draw level) will not only speed up your redraws, but you'll also be able to pay closer attention to the topology of your model. This will help you spot problem areas or potential problem areas early on. The programmers at EI made it easy for you to jump between **Draw Levels**, so switching to Smooth Shade from time to time to check your progress is easy.

Use Real-World Cross Sections

The most precise way to build real-world objects is to create your model based on the actual shapes derived from the real-world object you're trying to mimic. There are a few ways to do this.

If you are modeling something relatively small, like a small rock or a model car, perhaps, you could take pieces of wire and wrap these pieces of wire around the object's profile at key areas. You can then scan these pieces of wire and import them into the modeler for tracing with your 2D drawing tools. The resulting paths can be used to build your final shape.

If you are building a much larger object and have access to the blueprints of the object, you can scan the actual blueprints, import the resulting images into Modeler, and work from there. I have a friend who recently purchased blueprints of the original Star Trek Enterprise and used them to build his 3D version. It apparently worked great.

Model kits are also very helpful reference. They not only offer separate little pieces to use as reference but some even offer great blueprint-like drawings.

Force Correct Your Normals

When pulling models into ElectricImage Animation System (EIAS) from other modeling applications, even those that export the FACT format, you may often run into problems with the shading (see Figure 3.3). The sphere on the left was added as a FACT (**File>Add>Model>FACT**), but some reversed normals cause the obvious shading anomalies. By importing the model instead of adding, you can do a little trick that will usually get the normals all facing in the right direction. To import a model, choose **File>Add>Model>Other**. You

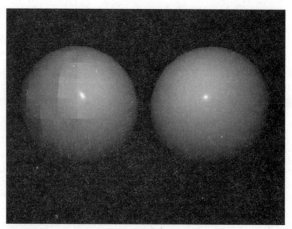

FIGURE *When importing some models, you may run into shading problems such as this.*
3.3

should get the dialogue box shown in Figure 3.4. Find the option at the lower right of the window called **Assume Correct Normals**. Holding down the option key and clicking this checkbox will change the option to **Force Correct Normals** as shown in Figure 3.5. EI will then flip all normals so they face outward.

Modify Your Axes

You will often find that an imported model has a different orientation than you would expect. The model might be facing backward, upward, or turned completely upside down. The sphinx model in Figure 3.6 faced in the proper direction in the modeling package where it was created, but when imported into EI, it wound up facing backward instead of forward. This is because the modeling application used to create the model interpreted the X, Y, and Z axes dif-

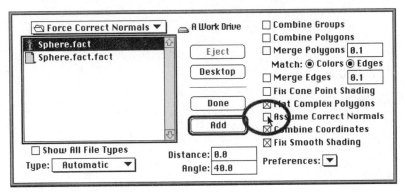

FIGURE **3.4**   *The dialogue box for Adding a model with the Assume Correct Normals checkbox circled.*

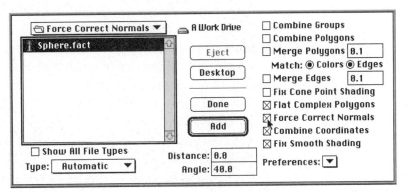

FIGURE **3.5**   *Option-clicking the Assume Correct Normals checkbox will turn it into Force Correct Normals.*

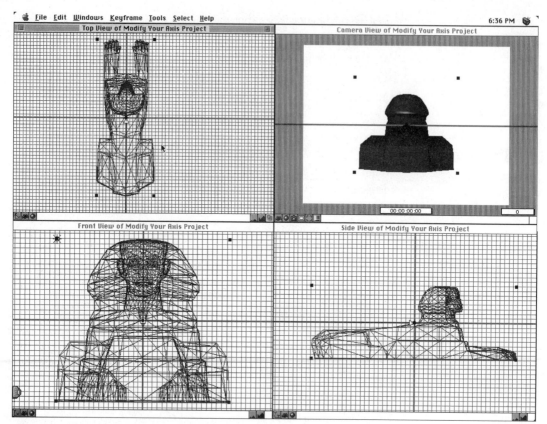

FIGURE 3.6 *This model faced forward in the application in which it was modeled but faces backwards when imported into 7EI.*

ferently than ElectricImage. Many modelers have options for correcting this, but that won't help you if you're just given a model and told to make it work.

You might think this is easy enough to fix, and you would be right, but it might not be the way you're thinking. You really don't want to just rotate the model so that its orientation is correct. While this does work, it can cause problems when it comes time to animate and, at the very least, it'll force you to make calculations that you shouldn't have to make. It's best to just zero out the rotation and start from scratch.

You do this by selecting the object and choosing **Modify Axes** from the **Tools** menu. You'll get the palette shown in Figure 3.7. This particular Sphinx model is not too badly disoriented. It's just facing the wrong direction along the Z Axis. To fix the problem, we simply click on the **Reverse Z** button.

So what do you do if you have a model composed of several groups? That's

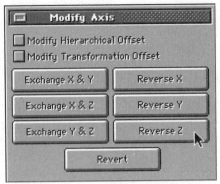

FIGURE   *Clicking on the Reverse Z button in the Modify Axis palette will fix the*
3.7   *problem.*

easy to fix, too. You just select all of the objects in the model, bring up the
Modify Axes window, check **Modify Hierarchical Offset**, and then click
whichever buttons are necessary to reorient your model. You'll notice that
when you do this, the groups all rotate in relation to the parent object. If you
want the objects to rotate around their collective center, you'll want to check
Modify Transformation Offset as well, before realigning the axis (see Figure
3.8).

When importing a DXF, you have the option of making at least one adjust-
ment in the **Importing** dialogue box regarding axis alignment. Figure 3.9
shows how you get to the DXF options and the Exchange Y and Z coordinates.
Basically, this does the same thing as the Exchange Y and Z button in the **Modify Axes Window** so you can do it here or there. It makes no difference.

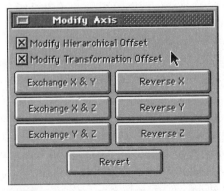

FIGURE   *Check the Modify Transformation Offset to make all of your groups maintain*
3.8   *their positional relationships.*

FIGURE
3.9
When importing a DXF, you can also choose to exchange the X and Y coordinates upon import.

Name Groups Descriptively

I've mentioned this already but I'm going to say it again. You should always name your groups as descriptively as possible. I know it takes a little extra time than leaving your objects with default names such as *Line, ÜberNURBS,* and *Revolved Object* but more appropriate names such as *Cable, Melted Blob,* and *Insulator* would certainly be more descriptive and will buy you more time than they cost in the long run. So name your objects descriptively—you'll be glad you did.

Tear off Some Palettes and Maybe Buy Another Monitor

The EI Modeler allows you to tear off palettes to make getting to their tools easier. My favorite palettes to keep floating around are the **Pick Filter** and the **Snapping** palettes. Both of these tools are very important when working with the EI Modeler and, if you're like me, you'll find yourself getting irritated rather quickly if you have to go looking for them every time you want to change a setting. Keeping these two palettes floating around will save some time.

Also, if you're only running one monitor on your system, I'd strongly suggest that you run out and buy another. My main monitor is a 17-incher, which is just on the edge of being big enough. To gain more screen real estate, I currently use a 12-incher left over from my first Mac LC as my second monitor. One of these days I'll spring for a 14- or 15-incher, but for now the 12 does the job.

Having a second monitor gives you a great place to put all kinds of windows and tear-off palettes while keeping your main monitor free for the geometry. This second monitor is also an excellent place for your **Project Window** when working in EIAS.

Round Your Edges

Very few objects in life have perfectly sharp edges, and you should take this into consideration when building your models. A little bit of edge rounding can add a good bit of substance to a model because it adds a lot of little edges to catch and reflect light. In Figure 3.10, the object on the left doesn't have any rounding on the edges and appears a bit on the flat, computer-generated side, whereas the object on the right has a nice, soft, and more realistic look.

This won't always be necessary but, on the whole, rounding your edges slightly can add good bit of realism to your scene.

What Is a Granger Unit?

By now you've probably noticed that the EIAS measurement system isn't based on any real-world measurement system like the Metric System. Instead, it's

FIGURE   *Rounding your edges can give an object a much more visually appealing quality.*
3.10

based on a unit of measurement which has no real-world equal. It's completely a virtual measurement. These units have been lovingly dubbed *Granger Units*.

Some are bothered by this lack of precision and others look at it as a way of simplifying your life. Since these units are virtual units, you can use them to reference any unit of measurement you like. You can make them millimeters, inches, feet, meters, or miles. The biggest problem, however, is when it comes time to import a model. Depending on how your modeler exports, or how you have it set up to export, you can get very different results.

Basically EI uses the base unit that your modeler exports and converts it in a 1:1 relationship. So if your modeler exports inches and your model is 1 foot tall, then it'll come into EI as 12 units tall. If your modeler is set to export feet and you have a space station that is 5 miles long, it'll come into EI at 26,400 units.

Some modelers have a fixed export and some give you the option to change its export unit. However, if you keep this conversion in mind, it'll only take a few tries to figure out how it works. To find out what your modeler's preferred unit of export is, create a sphere at whatever size you like (just be easy on yourself and make it a round number, like 4 feet or 24 inches or whatever), then export it as a DXF or FACT or whatever you prefer to use and then import it into EI. Check the size in the **Info Tab** of the **Group Info Window** and you should have your answer.

Export Standard Shapes as FACTs

If you're using the **Standard Shape** plug-in, it's a good idea, once you get the Standard Shape the way you want it, to export it as a FACT and then reimport it using the Force Correct Normals trick mentioned earlier. Standard Shapes are known to cause problems that can be avoided by doing this little export/import trick. When you import the newly created FACT, it will be placed in the exact same position as the original.

4 Modeling Techniques

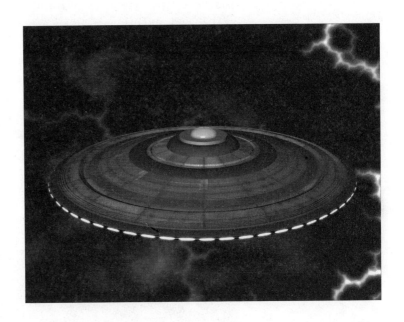

The tutorials in this chapter all concern creating models within EIAS using plug-ins and the new ElectricImage Modeler. Read it, learn it, love it.

Most of the plug-ins have been around for quite a while and are pretty well known, but EI's new modeler requires most people to learn a whole new modeling paradigm. However, its power makes it extremely worthwhile.

I want to take a moment here to extend overwhelming gratitude to Chris Weyers for putting together most of the tutorials you will read in this chapter. He's worked hand-in-hand with those brilliant engineers at EI to learn the application and to provide you with several comprehensive tutorials using EIM.

Since these tutorials were written using beta versions of the modeler, you might want to check the web site (www.charlesriver.com) for updates to anything that may change between now and when the modeler ships. If tools or their usage change, we'll update them there.

So buckle up and let's build some stuff.

Complex Modeling with Zaxwerks' Vector Lathe

This technique illustrates the modeling of a multi-group flying saucer using only Adobe Illustrator™, ElectricImage™, and ZaxWerks Vector Lathe™ (see Figure 4.1). What we're going to do here is create a single object model and then break it apart while maintaining each separate object's orientation and relationship to each other.

FIGURE   *This multi-group model was created in ZaxWerks Vector Lathe with one*
4.1   *Illustrator profile.*

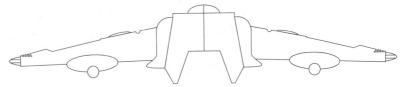

FIGURE *The original Illustrator cross-section sketch.*
4.2

My sketch phase is usually done in a 2D isometric view in Illustrator with a simple thumbnail sketch to use as reference for my composition. This way, I can make my sketches using the basic shapes I'll need to build the model and then import these exact same shapes to build the model in whatever modeler I'm using. In this case, it's Vector Lathe.

STEP ONE

Create the file you wish to use as your Lathe profile. Figure 4.2 shows the cross-section sketch of my flying saucer. You really only want half of this profile but I mirrored mine to get a good idea of the actual size ratios. Notice the separate yet overlapping shapes. This is the key to the whole technique. Figure 4.3 shows what actually winds up being imported into Vector Lathe. Note that I reset the Illustrator file's origin to the midpoint of the saucer. I did this by showing the rulers and then clicking and dragging the lower right-hand corner, where the rulers meet, up to the middle of the saucer (see Figure 4.4). This step is very important because Vector Lathe uses this origin as the Lathe Axis and also for placement of the **Center of Rotation** and **Local Origin** for the created model.

STEP TWO

Create a new project in EI **(File>New)**. Name it SAUCER.PROJECT. When prompted to import a model, click **Done**. Now choose **File>Add>Socket>- Vector Lathe™**. This opens the Vector Lathe interface. Another way to add a Vector Lathe object is to simply click on its icon in the **Object** Palette, as shown in Figure 4.5. When the Vector Lathe interface pops up, load the profile you

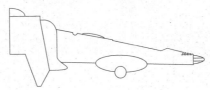

FIGURE *Vector Lathe only needs half of the original profile.*
4.3

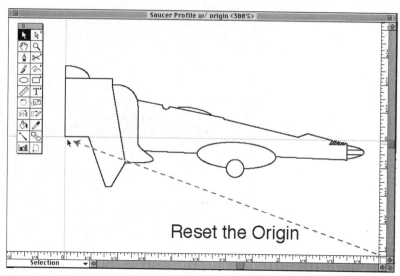

FIGURE *Resetting the origin in your drawing program tells Vector Lathe where to place*
4.4   *the Lathe Axis and the Center of Rotation and Local Origin of you model.*

created (or the SAUCER PROFILE file on the CD) by clicking on the **Load File** button at the bottom left of the Vector Lathe interface. You should wind up with something that looks like Figure 4.6. The default settings should be pretty good for this tutorial, so click on **OK**.

STEP THREE

Here's where the real fun begins. Now we have what appears to be a pretty nifty flying saucer. Problem is, we need to shade areas of it differently. You would probably want to add a different material to the dome on the top and a different material to the main body, and so on. Here's where those separate shapes come in. If you refer back to Figure 4.3, you'll see that there are ten separate

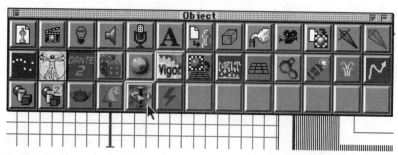

FIGURE *The Vector Lathe Object Palette icon.*
4.5

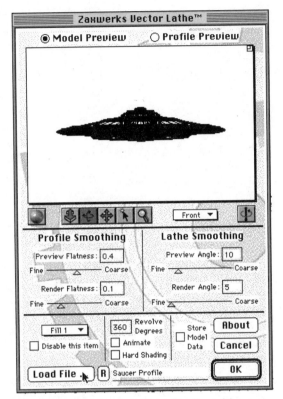

FIGURE *The preview of your initial Lathe model.*
4.6

shapes that comprise the full profile. Each of these separate shapes will become a separate object for shading purposes. Select the **Vector Lathe Group** and duplicate it eight times by choosing **Duplicate** from the **Edit** menu eight times. Yes, only eight, because two of the shapes in this profile will actually be shaded the same so we don't need separate objects for each of them. They are the shapes that are closest to the outside shape of the saucer. You should now have nine (the original plus the eight duplicates) identical duplicates of the flying saucer (see Figure 4.7).

STEP FOUR

In the **Project Window**, double-click the first **Vector Lathe Group** in the list to open its **Group Info Window** and click on the **Plugin** button on the left (see Figure 4.8). This will open up the Vector Lathe interface again. You can also go directly to Vector Lathe (or any other plug-in, for that matter) by holding down the **Control** and **Option** keys while double-clicking on the group.

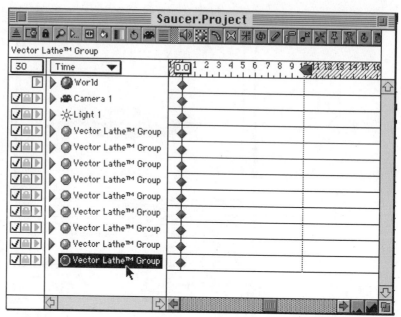

FIGURE **4.7** *Now we have nine exact duplicates of our original Vector Lathe flying saucer.*

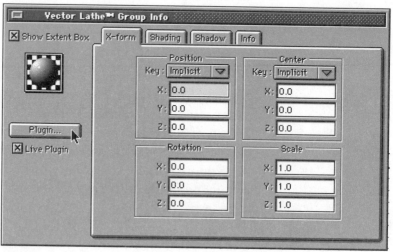

FIGURE **4.8** *The Plugin access button.*

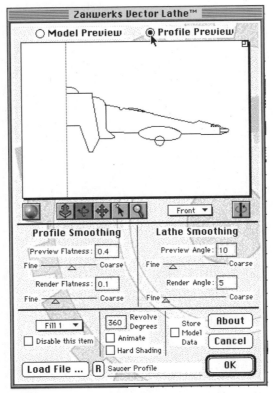

FIGURE *Zoom in on your profile.*
4.9

When the Vector Lathe interface opens, click on the **Profile Preview** radio button at the top of the page. Then select the magnifying glass tool and zoom in on the profile so that it fits nice and snug in the preview window (see Figure 4.9).

Now, using the **Object List** pulldown menu, browse through your shapes. When a shape is selected in the pull-down, it will turn *green* in the preview window. This is how you'll know which shapes to keep and which to throw away (see Figure 4.10). If you used the SAUCER PROFILE file on the CD, all of the objects will be named *Fill 1, Fill 2*, and so on. Vector Lathe recognizes both filled *and* stroked objects. If your file included stroked objects, with no fill, they would be listed as a *Stroke 1, Stroke 2*, and so on. The only difference this makes depends on how your revolving the object. If your **Revolve Angle** is less than 360 degrees, the *Fill* and *Stroke* designations determine whether the model will have endcaps or not. *Filled* objects will have endcaps and therefore will appear solid, and *Stroked* objects will have no endcaps and therefore will appear hollow.

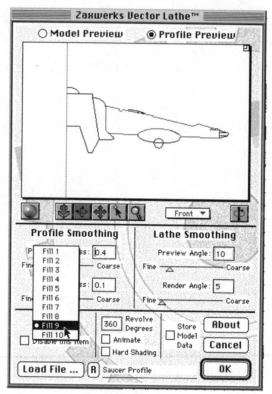

FIGURE *The selected shape turns green.*
4.10

STEP FIVE

Here we'll start building the separate sections. Let's work from the top down in building this saucer model. Find and select the object that forms the top sphere. It should be *Fill 6*. With *Fill 6* selected in the Object List pulldown, you'll see that the top dome turns green. From here you'll want to turn off all of the other objects. You'll see that there is a checkbox right under the Object List pulldown menu that says **Disable this item**. You could go through and select each and every item and click on that check box, but there is a quicker way. With *Fill 6* selected, **Option-Click** on the **Disable this item** checkbox. By Option-Clicking, you turn off all of the objects in the Vector Lathe model (see Figure 4.11). Then you can simply click on the box again (no option key this time) to reenable *Fill 6* (see Figure 4.12). Click **OK**.

This will generate a specific model for just the top dome. In the Project

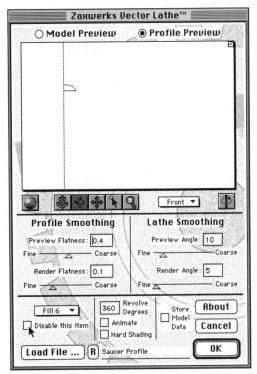

FIGURE   *Option-Click the Disable this item checkbox*
4.11   *to turn off all of the shapes.*

FIGURE   *Re-click the Disable this item checkbox to turn*
4.12   *the selected object back on.*

Window, select the Vector Lathe Group you just performed the above task on (if you were following instructions, it should have been the first one in line) and hit **Enter**. This will highlight the name of the Vector Lathe Group in the edit box at the top of the Project Window. Name the new Vector Lathe Group **Top Dome** and hit Enter again (see Figure 4.13).

STEP SIX

Now **Ctrl/Optn-Double-Click** on the next Vector Lathe Group in the Project Window. When the Vector Lathe window opens, Click on the **Profile Preview** radio button at the top then select *Fill 5*. Option-Click the Disable this item checkbox to turn off all of the shapes again and then re-click it (with no Option key) to reenable *Fill 5* as in Figure 4.14. Click **OK** and name the group **Core** in the Project Window. Repeat this step the rest of the way down the saucer, but don't forget the two shapes that will be combined as one. Figures 4.15 to 4.21

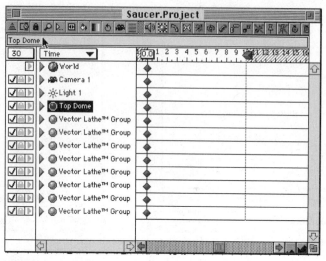

FIGURE *Rename the Vector Lathe Group.*
4.13

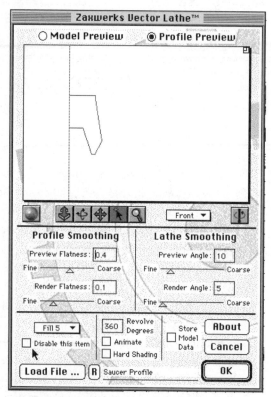

FIGURE *Reenable the Fill 5 (or Core) shape.*
4.14

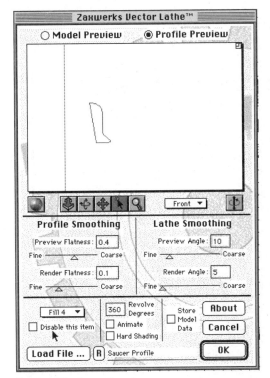

FIGURE *The Outer Core shape.*
4.15

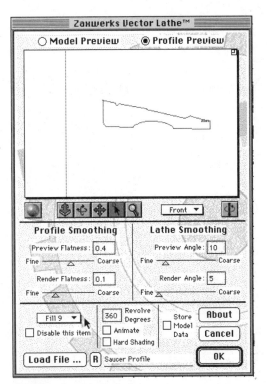

FIGURE *The Main Body shape.*
4.16

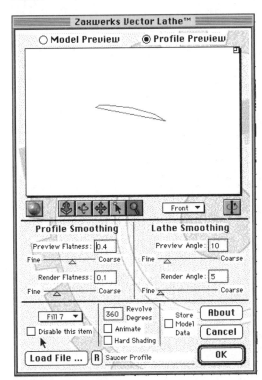

FIGURE *The Top Ring shape.*
4.17

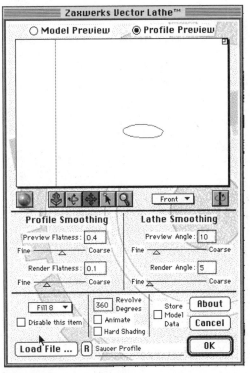

FIGURE *The Bottom Ring shape.*
4.18

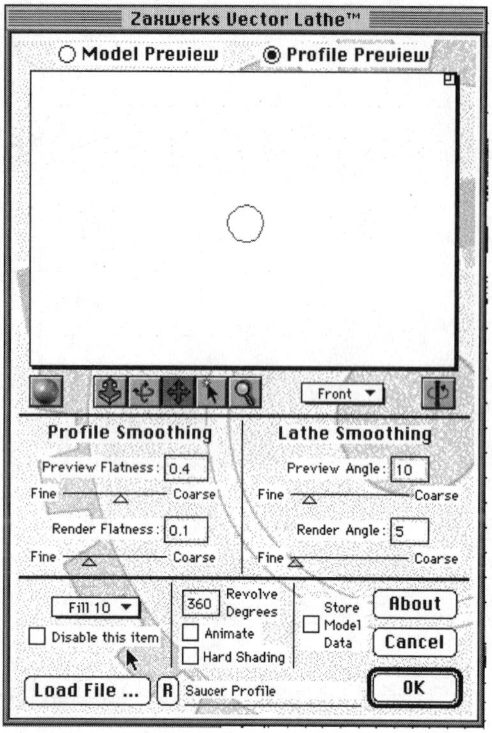

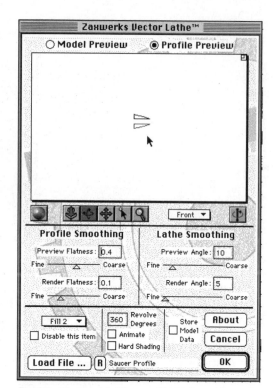

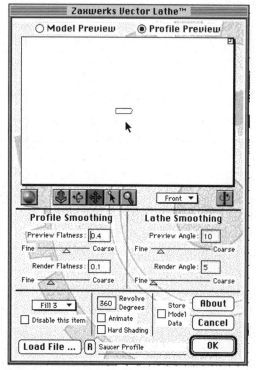

FIGURE **4.19** *The Bottom Thruster shape.*

FIGURE **4.20** *The Outside Thruster Shield shape (this is the two-shapes-in-one shape I was talking about earlier).*

FIGURE **4.21** *The Outside Thruster shape.*

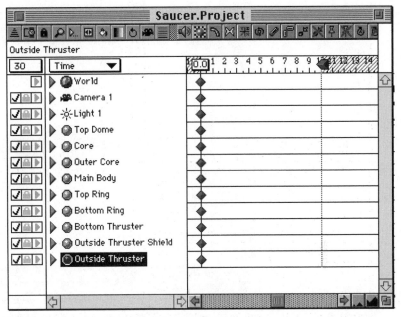

FIGURE   *The Project Window with the nine different models.*
4.22

show the shapes you should wind up with to make the individual saucer groups. Figure 4.22 shows the names I gave my different groups.

STEP SEVEN

When you're done, link the groups as you wish and you've got a perfectly aligned flying saucer ready to shade and animate (see Figure 4.23).

This technique has many uses, and I'll leave you with one of the more useful ones. Suppose you want to create a rough sketch or animation for a client. You can make up the sketch or animation using the single object models and, upon their approval, go through the above steps to create the finished piece while maintaining all motion and/or orientation information from the sketch.

Modeling with Mr. Nitro

Say you've got this nice little stylized tree set up for a visualization project (see Figure 4.24). The client says it's OK but she don't really care for the spherical leaf objects that much and would prefer that you make them look more like leaves. You could do this in a modeling program or you could, in just a few clicks, get Mr. Nitro to do it for you . . . and it would be animatable, too.

Most of the time we use Mr. Nitro to blow things up. And that's exactly

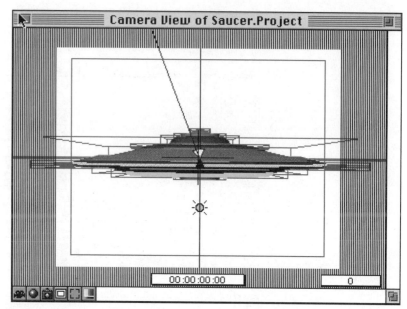

FIGURE *The finished model: Ready to be shaded and animated.*
4.23

FIGURE *A cute little stylized tree.*
4.24

what we're going to do to this poor little tree, but we're not going to blow it to smithereens, we're just going to shake it up a bit.

If you'd like to follow along with this tutorial, you can open the NITROTREE PROJECT on your CD-ROM.

STEP ONE

The first thing you want to do here is send the object you want to blow up to the center of your world. This makes working with Mr. Nitro a bit easier because you don't have to do a bunch of coordinate calculations. After everything is set up however, you can place your tree anywhere you see fit.

So with our tree leaves at the center of our world, add a Mr. Nitro socket by choosing **File>Add>Socket>Mr. Nitro** and enter the settings shown in Figure 4.25. I'll go over these settings a little so you know what's going on.

Ground Zero is the center of the explosion. We want this to be 0,0,0 because that's where our tree is. You could just place your tree anywhere by taking its center information and typing those coordinates in this box, but it's always a good idea to work with Mr. Nitro with these zeroed-out settings. For this particular tutorial, Mr. Nitro could be just about anywhere, but I don't want you to get into any bad habits.

The **Gravity Direction** and force can also be left at 0,0,0 here because we really don't need any gravity to pull our leaves down. You could experiment with this to shape your tree, but for now, let's leave it alone.

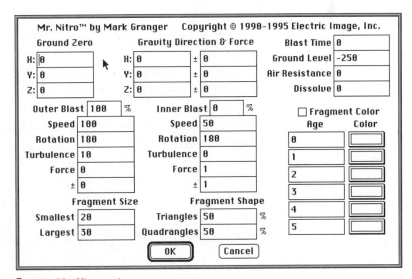

FIGURE *Mr. Nitro settings.*
4.25

Blast Time is when the shockwave from Mr. Nitro starts on its path of destruction. If you want your tree to be exploded on Frame 0, you could set this to a negative number so the blast started before the actual rendering starts. We're going to leave this one at 0, too, because we can preview our tree at different points in time simply by dragging the time thumb around.

Ground Level is the location at which the particles of your explosion stop falling. If you left this at 0, our tree would be flat in the middle. Since that's probably not want you'd want (unless you were making a Joshua Tree), we need to make this a value that is below the Y minimum of our tree's leaf dome. I put in a value of –250 here and it worked fine.

Air Resistance is the setting for the amount of environmental force your fragments will encounter when the shockwave comes barreling through. Again, for this tutorial, we can leave it at 0.

Dissolve fades your fragments out after your explosion. Since we want to keep our leaves around, leave this one at 0 as well.

Now, moving back over to the left and down, you'll find the **Outer Blast** and **Inner Blast** settings. This is a nifty feature for doing explosions, because you can essentially set two different shockwaves. The first will come through and blow away the specified amount of your model and then the Inner Blast will come though and finish off the rest. Great for realism but not necessary here. Leave the Outer blast set to 100%.

Moving down in the Outer Blast column, the first thing you come to is **Speed**. Speed determines how fast the shockwave passes through your scene. For this tutorial, let's leave it alone because it's just fine and dandy the way it is.

Rotation is the next one down and is also fine the way it is. It determines how much your fragments rotate as the shockwave passes through them.

Next in line is **Turbulence**. Turbulence is like a noise function that twirls your fragments around. Since we want our tree to be nice and random, let's bump that way up to 10.

Finally we come to **Force**. I say "finally" not because it's the last in line but because it's really the key to this technique. Force is how much the blast moves your fragments from their original positions. Since we want our tree's leaves to stay put, knock that down to 0 and knock it's ± field down to zero as well (although if you want some of your leaves to blow off your tree, you could leave it set to 1).

The next item on our list is **Fragment Size**. This determines the size of your fragments. What you set this to is totally up to you, but I found the default settings to be a little too small for this project. I upped them to 20 for the smallest and 30 for the largest.

Moving on over to the right, you have your **Fragment Shape**. Mr. Nitro gives you two options for your fragment shape: Triangles and Quadrangles. Since we'd probably want a good mixture of the two to keep things random, I left them at 50.

The only think we haven't covered is **Fragment Color**. This is the particle color settings. You can determine the color of your fragments at various stages of their lifecycle. For this tutorial, leave it alone.

That's the rundown of the Mr. Nitro settings and how they fit in with our grand scheme here.

So now just click OK to exit the Mr. Nitro interface.

STEP TWO

Now this is the easy part. Once you've got your Nitro settings all squared away, you can link your Leaves object to it. If your time thumb is on 0 still, you won't see anything happen at all. To preview our effect, drag the time thumb to 5.0 seconds or so and viola, instant tree leaves.

In the project file on the CD, I've already added a Leaves texture map. You can jump into the **Material Info Window** of the **Leaves** object, click on the Diffuse tab and turn the map on by clicking in the space directly to the right of its name.

If you render your frame now, you should get something similar to Figure 4.26. If you'd like, you can render an animation here to see what Mr. Nitro is doing. If you don't feel like it, you can just look at the movie on the CD-ROM called MR. NITRO TREE MOVIE FAST.

The first few seconds of this movie illustrate how Mr. Nitro's shockwave passes through your tree. The last few frames of the animation show a neat little tree with its leaves blowing in the wind.

If you were using this for an actual job, you probably wouldn't want to show Mr. Nitro ripping through the tree. This is where setting the **Blast Time** to a negative number comes in handy. If you jump back into the Mr. Nitro plug-in and bump this Blast Time back to about –5.0, the blast will start before the rendering does and your tree will be in full blowing fury by the time the first frame is rendered. You can also move your tree around anywhere you like, at this point, by dragging the Mr. Nitro object around. The settings will all stay relative.

STEP THREE

If you don't want the leaves to be animated, or simply don't want to deal with the overhead of rendering Mr. Nitro for every frame (although Mr. Nitro has gotten mighty speedy lately), you can "freeze" the leaves as a static model.

FIGURE *Our "Nitroed" leaves.*
4.26

What you'd want to do here is select the Mr. Nitro group in the Project Window, tap the Enter key to highlight its name, and rename it *Real Leaves* or something along those lines.

Then, move the time thumb to the area of your animation where you like your tree the best. Then, with the Mr. Nitro group still selected, choose **File>Export>Model>Fact**. You'll be presented with the dialogue box shown in Figure 4.27. Choose the **Selected Only** option (otherwise you'd be adding the original leaves object as well as the Mr. Nitro exploded leaves), click OK, and then name your model something like *Leaves Model.fact* and just click **Save**.

You can now add the leaves model, link it to your trunk (or your trunk to it), and you have an instant static tree.

○ Selected with Children   (preserves Hierarchy)
● Selected only   (no Hierarchy)

             OK

            Cancel

FIGURE *Fact export options.*
4.27

You might want to keep your original leaves around if you've textured them because when you re-add the newly created static model, it will not have any of the material settings of the original. If you kept the original around, you can just copy and past the materials into the newly added model.

And that's that.

Modeling a Stylized Chess Set with the EI Modeler: Introduction

Before we begin to model our stylized chess set in the ElectricImage Modeler, we need to cover some basic information. First and foremost I *highly* recommend reading the section of your modeler manual that deals with object topologies. Understanding how EIM creates its topological descriptions is key to getting the most out of the program. You need to keep in mind that EIM is not a polygonal modeler. It describes surfaces in a continuous fashion. There are significant advantages to this method. First and foremost, your surfaces will have a very high degree of fidelity when imported into EIAS. Another advantage is the ability to combine any type of object at any time. For instance, it's no problem to use the boolean subtract tool to subtract a solid 3D object from a 2D curve. One final advantage to keep in mind is that models you create in EIM are resolution independent. If you need to scale them up by a factor of 100, you can do it without loss of surface fidelity.

There is a price to pay for all of this flexibility, mainly a learning curve. Once you've created a body (the generic term for an object in EIM), you can't alter it by pushing, pulling, and deleting polygons. There aren't any polygons. You can edit some surfaces by CV with the NURBS surface editing tools, as you will see in one of the exercises. By and large, though, it pays to try to build up objects by creating a simple shape and then using the boolean and knife tools to add to that object. Because of the resolution-independent topology, you can preform hundreds of boolean and knife operations on an object with absolutely no loss.

If you do want to create organic shapes by pushing and pulling a mesh, you can't beat the UberNurbs tools for the task.

Here are a few things to keep in mind as you do the exercises:

- The x, y, and z keys will constrain translation and rotation to the X, Y, and Z axs respectively.
- The x, y, and z keys will constrain the movement of an UberNurbs cage segment to the X, Y, and Z axes respectively. If you hold down the "r" key plus the x, y, or z key, this will allow you to rotate an UberNurbs cage segment.

- You don't have to click on an object to move it. This means you can select it in one window, and as long as it's selected, click anywhere in any other window and move it.
- The views in the Modeler are based on object position, NOT your position. This means that when you select a **Left Side** view you will actually be looking at the **Right Side** of the object.
- Modeling affects the active layer only. If you create objects and they aren't showing up in the **Layer Window** where you expect them, look to the active layer to find them.
- Pay close attention to the status window, it will walk you through the steps you need to take to use a specific tool.

DESIGN

Modeling is one of the hardest subjects to teach. Different software packages have completely different toolsets and capabilities, as well as modeling metaphors. In an attempt to rise above all of this confusion, I've developed a simple design philosophy that can be applied to any modeling task using any package. It's based on the evaluation of symmetry in an object.

Modeling packages, in general, are very good at creating perfectly symmetrical objects. By evaluating an object I want to model, based on symmetry, I can find the best combination of tools to first create the rough symmetry of the object and then modify, it into a more believable shape.

For instance, everyone has modeled a wine glass (or bottle, or Roman column, etc.) at some point. You define a profile and revolve it around a center to get a perfectly symmetrical object. If you look at the world around you, almost all objects have some degree of symmetry to them. I look at objects I want to model and imagine what they would look like if I sliced them into small pieces on the X, Y, and Z axs. This gives me a better idea of how I could create pieces and profiles in my modeling software that I can put together to form the object.

Even a complex object like a tree has a degree of symmetry. If you were to cut it into slices on the X axis you would get a series of roughly circular slices. If you cut the tree into slices on the Y axis you would get a series of asymmetrical profiles for the trunk and branches. However, if you extrude one of the circular cross-sections taken from the X axis slices along the profiles created by the Y axis slices you would get a rough shape of a tree. By breaking singular objects down into simple component shapes that can be used for modeling you can simplify even the most complex object.

PUTTING IT ON PAPER

One of the most difficult things to do is to fire up your modeling software and just start "modeling something." You may have broken an object down based on symmetry in your mind's eye, but you will always reach a point where the modeling process will bog down. You can spend hours working on what seemed like a simple model when you started.

To avoid this, it's a good idea to sketch your ideas out in a front and side view before you begin modeling. Even if you never use the drawings, you will at least give yourself an idea of how things should fit together.

For the chess pieces, I began by doing rough sketches to get the basic shapes locked in. Once that was done, I translated the sketches onto 4 × 4 grid-square-to-the-inch graph paper in front and side view. This helps in two ways.

First, it allowed me to determine my project's scale. The EIM project was set up to have four minor grid squares to every major grid square, just like the graph paper.

The second thing using graph paper does is allow me to easily project an object's frontal features into a side view. To do the sketches on graph paper I use a pencil, compass, and ruler. I create the volume of the character, like the King, by adding circles. I run a line down the symmetry point and projection lines from front to side views with the ruler, and I simply freehand sketch the rest of the detail in. The resulting sketches aren't 100% accurate (nor do they need to be), but by keeping them aligned I can use the same image in the front and side views. This is a great habit to get into, and it will save tons of time. If you don't feel you have the time or the ability to draw what you want to model, then put your flatbed scanner to use. Scan in front and side views of the model and drag them into the same document. Use the grid snapping feature in Photoshop to create a simple grid and line the pictures up relative to one another.

In the modeling exercises, you will need to add an image to the **Front** and **Left Side** views for each individual exercise. This is done by holding down the **Control** key and clicking in the view. From the popup menu select the **Place Image** command. Once you have the image in the view you will need to position the front drawing so that the Y axis runs down its middle. Then position the side drawing so the Y axis runs down its middle. You can only add one image per view, so when you move on to another part of the exercise, your images will be replaced by the new ones you add. The beginning of each exercise will tell you how large to scale each image once it's been added, you'll just need to remember to center it.

FILLED WIRES AND SOLID OBJECTS

We will be making use of the primitive circle and rectangle tools quite a bit in this tutorial. Sometimes we will need to create a circle or rectangle that refers to a filled circular wire. Other times we will need to create a circular wire or a rectangular wire that is a circle or a rectangle without a face. You can create filled and unfilled wires by changing the option of the circle and rectangle tools. If you double-click on the tool and uncheck both of the creation options, you will be creating a wire body. If both options are checked, you will be creating a filled sheet body. Pay close attention to the terminology in these instances.

Most of the surface generation tools have options to "cap" the resulting body. If a body is capped, it's a solid body. If it's uncapped, it's a surface body. Unless otherwise noted, all surfaces should be created as solids.

PROJECT ORGANIZATION

A "blank" project has already been created with the proper grid scale and all the layers you will need to complete the tutorial. You will notice that each object's layer has a sub-layer inside of it called "Construction Objects." This folder is there to hold all of the items you use to create the final model. All of the wires and faces you use to construct the model should be saved in case you need them. By putting all of the construction objects in one folder, you can easily export only the finished model to EIAS. You can accomplish this by turning on visibility for all layers, and then turning off visibility for the construction object layers. Select the **Visible Only** option from the export preferences (**Edit > System Preferences**).

Also keep in mind that most of the surface tools don't destroy the profiles used to create them. It's sometimes possible to click on an object and the wire used to generate it when using the boolean tools. This means you could accidentally subtract or add a wire to the body you're working on. For this reason, it's best to move a construction object into the construction object's folder immediately after it's been used and turn off its visibility.

PREPARATION

Before you start on the tutorials, open up the design scan images in projector and take a look at them. Evaluate their symmetry and consider how you might model them in other programs you've used. This will help you more fully develop a modeling strategy that suits you.

OK. So with all of that taken care of, let's get to work.

Modeling the Castle

Traditionally the Castle (or Rook) is represented as a castle tower. We're going to add wheels to this structure to keep with a "mobility" theme for all of our characters and, by the end of this tutorial, you should wind up with something similar to Figure 4.28 (minus the shading, of course, we'll leave that up to you.)

STEP ONE

Open CHESS BEGINNING PROJECT and make the "Castle" layer the active layer. Import the "castle.image" into the front view and center the front profile of the drawing along the Y axis. There's no need to add another image to the left view. Scale the image to be 6 major grid units high.

It's pretty easy to evaluate the symmetry of this object. It has a symmetrical profile that's been turned around a circular axis. This makes the **Revolve** tool the ideal choice for creating the base object.

Turn on grid snapping and select the **Polyline** tool. In the FRONT view, start by clicking on the top of the castle where the drawing meets the center, Y-axis line. Continue clicking to trace out the basic shape of the Castle. Don't attempt to trace the contours that are cut into the top of the castle, just create a straight line for the top, as shown in Figure 4.29. Double-click when you set the last knot in the polyline to put the line into edit mode. Use grid snapping

FIGURE   *The Castle we're going to build.*
4.28

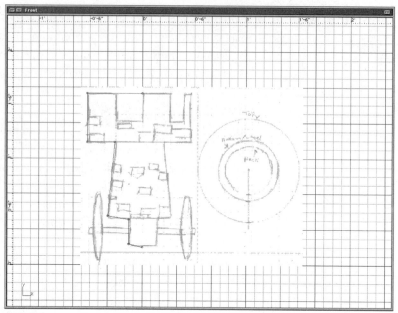

FIGURE *Our Castle outline.*
4.29

to make sure that the beginning and end knots are snapped to the center, then turn grid snapping off to reshape the middle part of the polyline.

TIP

This is one of the best uses for grid snapping. Many of modeler's tools require that the beginning and end points be snapped into alignment. By drawing a rough line or curve with grid snapping on you can get the beginning and end knots (or cvs) in place. Then, turn off grid snapping when in edit mode and work on the middle knots of your curves.

Now that we have our revolve profile, we need to create an axis to revolve around. In the ElectricImage Modeler, any line can act as a revolve axis. We want to revolve around the Y axis, so we need to turn on grid snapping and draw a vertical line down the center of the front view as shown in Figure 4.30.

At this point, the first and last knots of the Castle's profile are intersecting the revolve axis (see Figure 4.31). This can cause the **Revolve** tool to create two identical edges that are occupying the same coordinates. To avoid this problem, it's a good idea to move the revolve profile away from the revolve axis just slightly. To do this, select the profile with the move tool and hold down the "x" key and drag the Castle profile so the knots don't intersect the revolve axis (see Figure 4.32).

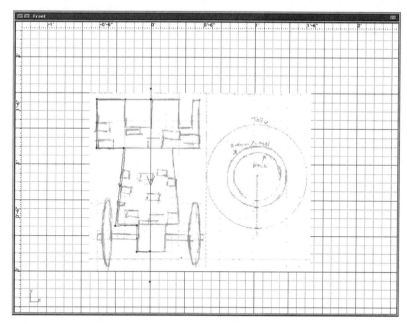

FIGURE *Creating our revolve axis.*
4.30

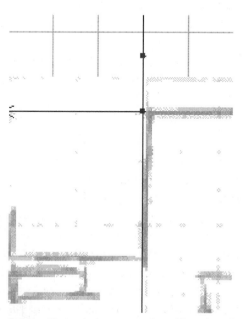

FIGURE *Notice the how our castle profile and revolve axis intersect.*
4.31

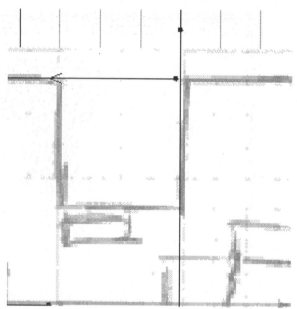

FIGURE *Drag the knots so they no-longer intersect.*
4.32

Now double-click on the **Revolve** tool (in the 3D Tools palette). Make sure the **Solid** box is checked, the **Angle of Revolution** is set to 360, and **Number of Steps** is set to 0. Select the Castle's profile and then click on the center revolve axis line. You will get a revolved, solid Castle shape (see Figure 4.33).

*Setting the **Number of Steps** parameter to zero will produce a revolve with an infinitely smooth surface. Entering any other numeric value will produce a specific number of steps to the revolve. We'll be exploring this more when we build the Bishop.*

STEP TWO

We've got the basic shape down, but we need to create the details that form the top of the castle. We can accomplish this task easily by using the **Boolean Subtraction** tool to cut the details into the basic shape.

Double-click on the **Circle Tool** (Curve Primitives Palette). Make sure it's set to create a filled circle. In the top view, begin by clicking in the center of world space where the X and Z axs meet. You can turn on grid snapping to aid in this if you like. Drag out a circle that comes within 1.5 grid spaces of the outer edge of the Castle's top circumference, as shown in Figure 4.34. Use the

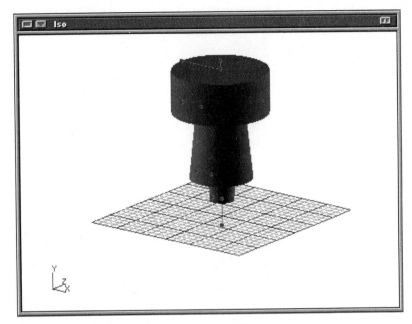

FIGURE *The revolved castle shape.*
4.33

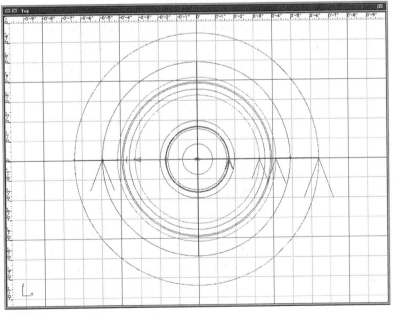

FIGURE *Creating a circle for our boolean operation.*
4.34

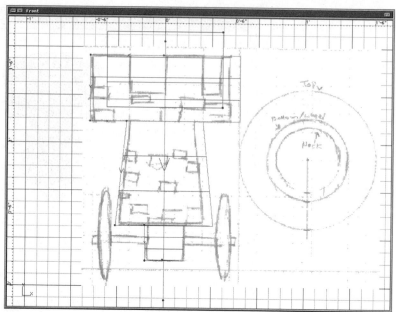

FIGURE *Extruding the circle.*
4.35

Translate tool to move this filled circle up on the Y axis so that it is about 2 grid spaces above the top of the Castle.

Select the **Extrude Tool** (3D Tools Palette) and extrude the circle down into the Castle until it's within 1.5 grid spaces of the point where the crown reaches the neck, as shown in Figure 4.35. Next select the **Boolean Subtract Tool** (Boolean Palette). Select the Castle shape first, and the extruded circle second, then double-click. This will carve the center out of the Castle, as shown in Figure 4.36.

Next we need to carve out the top to create the spire sections of the crown. This will also be accomplished with **Boolean Subtraction**.

In the Front View frame the top of the Castle. Select the **Rectangle Tool** (Curve Primitives Palette) and draw a filled rectangle in the front view that has the approximate size and shape of the hole you would like to cut into the crown (see Figure 4.37). Switch to Top View and use the **Extrude Tool** to extrude the rectangle so that it goes all the way through the crown, as shown in Figure 4.38.

Double-click the **Linear Copy Tool** (Copies Palette) and set the options up to those indicated in Figure 4.39. Now, select the extruded block, double click

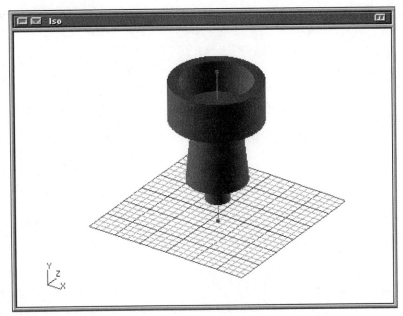

FIGURE *Carving out the center.*
4.36

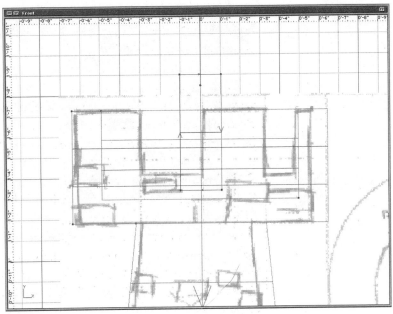

FIGURE *Creating the rectangle for our spire cutter.*
4.37

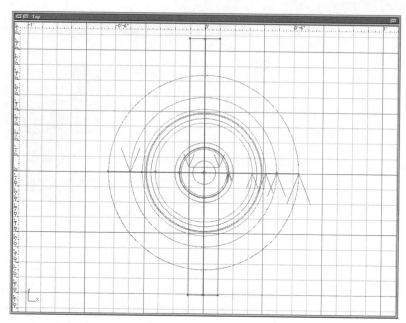

FIGURE *Extruding our spire cutter.*
4.38

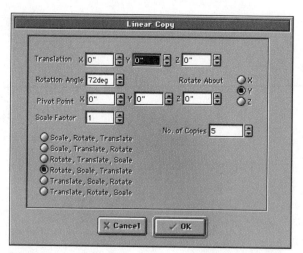

FIGURE *Linear Copy Tool Settings.*
4.39

on the **Linear Copy Tool**, and hit the **OK** button. The block will be copied and rotated into a radial array of blocks.

The Linear Copy Tool will retain the values that were last entered in its options dialogue. For this reason you must first double-click on the tool, enter your settings, and then select the object you wish to duplicate.

NOTE

Now select the Boolean Subtract Tool. Click first on the Castle Solid, and then on each of the rectangular blocks, then double-click. The blocks will be subtracted cleanly from the Castle's crown, giving you the spires, as shown in Figure 4.40.

STEP THREE

To create the axle frame the bottom of the Castle in Front View, add a horizontal line that runs through the center of the drawing. We will extrude a circle along this path in a moment to create the axle, but first we need to create the wheel shape to revolve.

Frame the left wheel in the Front View. Select the **Ellipse Tool** (Curve Primitives Palette). Use the axle line you just created as the center point to start the ellipse from, click and drag until the circumference of the ellipse represents

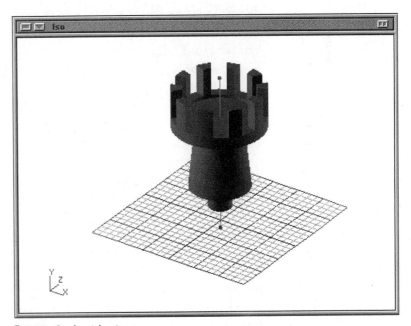

FIGURE *Castle with spires.*
4.40

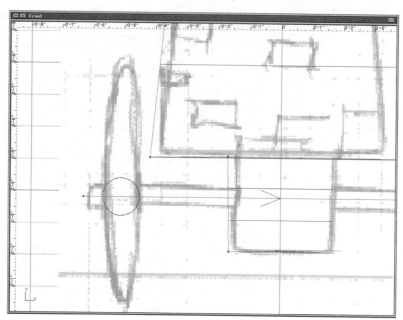

FIGURE *Specify the circumference of the wheel.*
4.41

the width you want the center of the wheel to be, as shown in Figure 4.41. Now let up on the mouse and drag upwards to establish the height of the wheel's ellipse (see Figure 4.42).

Turn off the visibility for the newly created ellipse and create a circle in the middle of the axle line that represents the thickness you would like the axle to be. Select the **Sweep Tool** (3D Tools Palette). Click on the circular face to select it as the sweep profile and the axle line to select it as the wire to sweep along. Your axle is now generated.

Turn visibility back on for the ellipse. Select the **Straight Knife Tool** (Knife Palette) and click on the ellipse to select it as the surface for cutting. Drag out a horizontal line across the ellipse that's aligned with the top part of the axis. Delete the lower half of the cut, as shown in Figure 4.43. Revolve this shape around the line you used to create the axle profile to get the wheel. The wheel will have a hole in the middle that lines up perfectly with the axle.

TIP

It's often a good modeling technique to bounce back and forth between creation stages for various objects that are related. This way you can see the relationship forming between objects as you build them, rather than attempting to create those relationships after the fact.

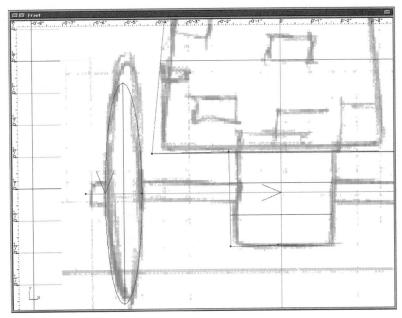

FIGURE *Specify the height of the wheel.*
4.42

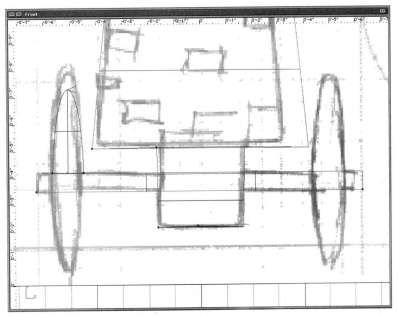

FIGURE *Creating the revolve profile for the wheel.*
4.43

Select the **Symmetry Tool** (Transform Palette). Click once on the left wheel to select it as the object to be mirrored, then double-click. Click once on the center line you used to revolve the Castle's profile around. A duplicate of the left wheel will be copied to the other side of this line. This is a mirror copy of the wheel, rotated 180 degrees. We'll get a better look at the **Symmetry Tool's** effects when we model the Pawn in the next exercise.

This finished the basic Castle. Take a look at the model. You've done a significant amount of Boolean subtraction work on it, but its edges are all crisp and defined. Maybe a little too defined? Too perfect? Well then, we should fix that.

STEP FOUR

We can give this Castle a little more organic feel by using the **Rounding Tool** (3D Tools Palette) on the edges.

The rounding process will take all selected edges and create a bevel of the size you determine on them. It's important to keep in mind that rounding is actually creating new faces, so your model will become more complex as you apply rounding to various edges. For this reason it's important to make rounding the last part of your modeling process.

Another important consideration for rounding is that it has to evaluate all edges associated with the edge(s) that you picked for rounding. To take our castle as an example. The rectangular holes we cut into the crown have edges that travel in x, y, and z and are joined at a common point. If you select an edge that runs in Y, but it is connected to one that runs in X, they will both be evaluated for the rounding operation. If a face (and the resulting co-edges) can't be generated for the point where these edges meet, the operation will fail. For a more thorough description of rounding make sure and read that section of your ElectricImage Modeler manual.

We're going to begin by rounding the entirety of the Castle. This is accomplished by leaving the pick filter set to **Body** level. Double-click on the **Rounding Tool** and set the **Constant Radius/Offset** to .1 inch, as shown in Figure 4.44. Frame the Castle in the ISO window in such a way that you can see one of the edges that makes up the crown. Click with the Rounding Tool on one of the edges. Because you are in **Body** pick mode, all edges that make up the object will be selected. The little blue circles represent the radius of the rounding operation that will take place when you double click, as shown in Figure 4.45.

Double-click and sit back in amazement as the rounding tool goes to work. Watch the status window and you will see each edge called out as it is rounded and blended. This relatively simple-looking object has several hundred edges

FIGURE *The Rounding Tool settings.*
4.44

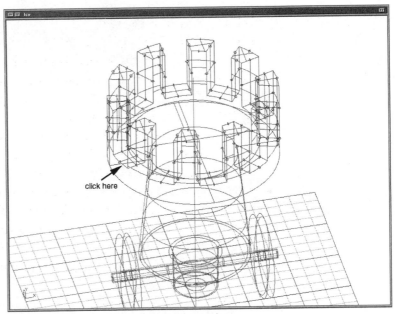

click here

FIGURE *Little circles indicate the rounding preview.*
4.45

that are all being blended at once. When the operation is done, you will have a Castle that looks a lot less edgy (see Figure 4.46).

To finish the Castle we're going to round the point where the axle and wheel come together. To do this we need to be in a different topological selection mode. Select the **Edge** pick filter. Frame the left wheel in the ISO view so that you can clearly see the outer edge of the hole through the center.

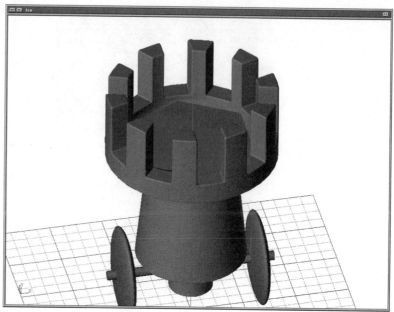

FIGURE *The rounded castle.*
4.46

TIP

When rounding individual edges, it's almost always easier to work in the iso view to select them.

Click on the outer edge with the **Rounding Tool**. (If you accidentally select an edge you don't want, hold down the **Shift** key and click on it again to deselect it.) The edge will be highlighted and a rounding icon will appear. Double-click to round this edge, as shown in Figure 4.47. Turn the axle's visibility on and round its outer edge as well. When you're done, you will have a clear visual cue that shows the viewer that the axle does truly go through a hole in the wheel (see Figure 4.48).

Now we're really done with the Castle. From this point on, we won't be covering rounding operations, except for special cases. It will be up to you to round edges of the remaining characters in a way that suits your tastes.

—*Chris Weyers*

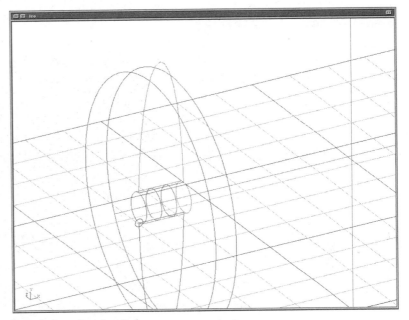

FIGURE *Rounding the wheel.*
4.47

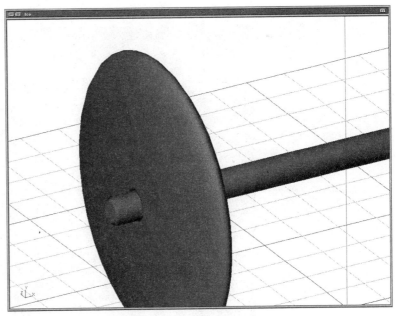

FIGURE *Both the wheel and the axle should be rounded.*
4.48

Modeling the King

STEP ONE

Here we're going to model our King as shown in Figure 4.49. Open the CHESS BEGINNING PROJECT file again and make the "King" layer the active layer. Add the KING.IMAGE to the front view and the left view and scale it up to be 9 major grid units high. Turn off visibility for all other layers if they aren't already.

Examine the images in the Front and Left views. The King appears roughly symmetrical, with the exception of his baggy trousers, which are symmetrical from the front, but asymmetrical in the back. As with the Castle, we will create symmetrical base objects first and then use the Boolean tools to alter their symmetry.

Frame the bottom part of the King in the Front View and create 3 circular wires. The first wire should represent the circumference of the King's waist. The second will represent the largest "flared" portion of his trouser leg. The third will represent the tapering inward that happens at the bottom of the trousers, as shown in Figure 4.50. Rotate each circular wire 90° on the X axis and translate them into positions that roughly match the width of the trousers in the drawing (see Figure 4.51).

FIGURE *The final King.*
4.49

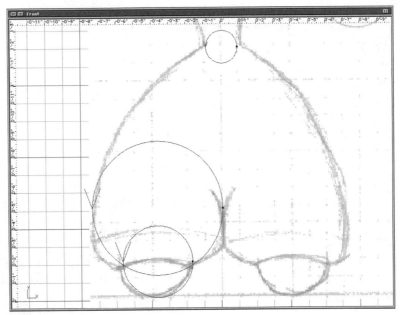

FIGURE   *Creating the cross-sections for the trousers.*
4.50

This is a great shortcut for generating skinning profiles for an object. Simply use a front of side view, begin creating your shapes to the width of that view, then rotate them to orient them for the sweep. This way you don't need to draw top views in your drawings.

Double-click on the **Skin Tool** (3D Tools Palette) and make sure all options *except* **Use Spine** are checked. Also set the skin type to **Smooth**. In the front view select the bottom circle, the middle circle, then the top circle and double-click. Now you have a billowy pant leg, as shown in Figure 4.52. This "billowing" was accomplished by leaving the Smooth option on in the skin dialogue box. This option will attempt to create a smooth blend between the ribs you pick. By creating a small circle and a large circle and keeping them far apart we gave the skin surface plenty of room to "round off." This works much the way f-curves do in the animation system. Creating two wildly different values (size in this case) creates a more pleasing blend the farther apart these values are. You can use this to your advantage when modeling. Ribs that are closer together will produce a more pronounced blend. Ribs that are farther apart will produce a less pronounced (smooth) blend.

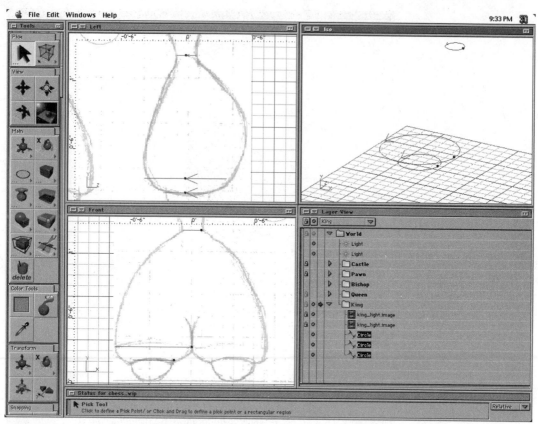

Select the Sphere tool and create a sphere for the wheel at the bottom of the leg. We'll use this sphere to Boolean a hole in the bottom for the wheel. Because Boolean objects are not preserved, we first need to make a copy of the sphere. We want this sphere to stay exactly in place, however. To do this, we will use the **Linear Copy Tool** with its settings set to the defaults, as shown in Figure 4.53. This will create a duplicate of the sphere in exactly the same position as the original turn off the visibility for this copy. Now select the **Boolean Subtract Tool,** click on the pant leg solid, and then on one of the spheres. Double-click to subtract the sphere from the pant leg and turn visibility back on for the sphere copy. You now have a completed left pant leg/wheel section (see Figure 4.54). We can use the **Symmetry Tool** to copy this section to the right side.

Turn grid snapping on and use the **Line Tool** in the Front View to create a vertical line that runs down the center of the King on the Y axis. Select the Symmetry Tool and select the pant leg solid and the sphere/wheel. Double-

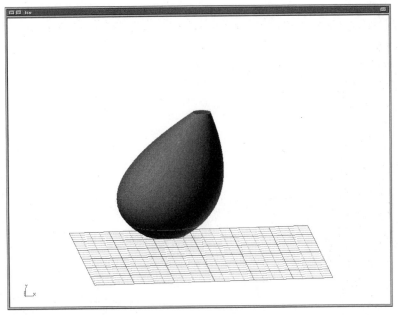

FIGURE   *Our skinned billowy pant leg.*
4.52

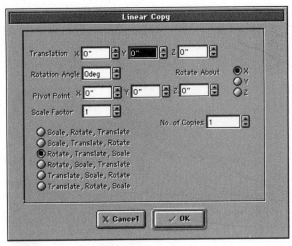

FIGURE   *The Linear Copy Tool settings.*
4.53

click, then click once on the vertical line. An exact duplicate will be reflected across the Y axis to complete the pants/wheels of the king, as shown in Figure 4.55. Use the **Boolean Union Tool** to join the right and left pant leg halves together into one object.

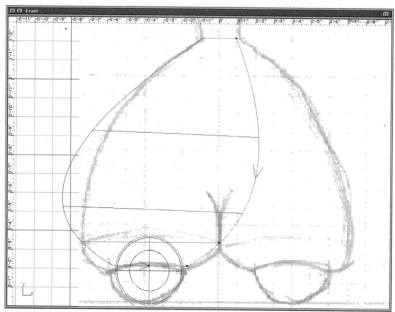

FIGURE *The completed left pant leg/wheel.*
4.54

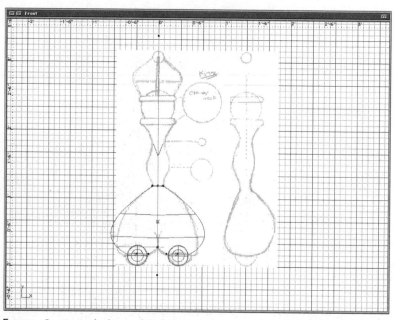

FIGURE *Creating a duplicate of the leg.*
4.55

STEP TWO

Now at first glance you might expect that the midsection of the King is a perfect candidate for the **Revolve Tool**. We have two things to consider, however. First, we want the base of the mid-body to line up exactly with the top of the pants. Second, we're going to be using the NURBS surface editing tools to adjust the topology of the midsection, so we don't want to have the seam that a revolved surface would create. We will use skinning to solve both of these problems.

Turn off the visibility for the pant legs, spheres, and the bottom two circular wires you used to create them. Make three duplicates of the top pant leg circle and translate them into positions that are even with the bulges in the mid-body.

*Hold down the "d" key while dragging to make a duplicate. Scale the circular wires accordingly to create four cross-sections, as shown in Figure 4.56. When the cross-sections are placed, select the **Skin Tool** and skin them together (make sure capping is turned on). This will create a mid-body that has a continuous surface. It will also be perfectly symmetrical. If you frame the mid-section in the Left View, you will see that the King sketch has a bit of a potbelly. To create this potbelly we're going to use the NURBS Surface Editing tools to pull out the mesh.*

TIP

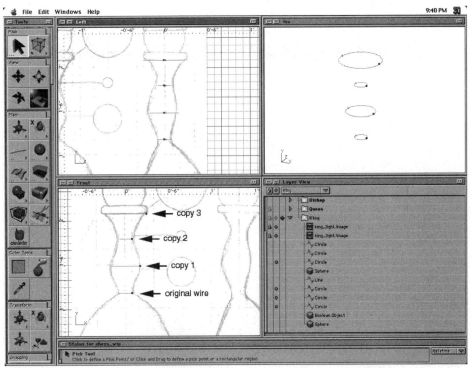

FIGURE *Creating duplicates using the "d key drag."*
4.56

Select the **NURBS Surface Edit Tool** (NURBS Surface Palette). Click on the midsection. This will turn the skin solid into an editable NURBS surface with blue control hulls and red CVs where the isoparms were (see Figure 4.57). This NURBS cage is too complex for our needs, so to save some time we'll reduce the degree of the surface. Click once on the **Reduce Degree Tool**. This will immediately reduce the number of NURBS CVs and control hulls used to represent the surface (see Figure 4.58). With the **NURBS Surface Edit Tool** active, drag a marquee around the center of the control cage, as shown in Figure 4.59. With the center of the control cage selected hold down the "z" key and drag forward, as shown in Figure 4.60. When you double-click to restitch the face to the solid body, the king will have a potbelly, as shown in Figure 4.61.

Technically, when you are editing with the NURBS Surface Tool, you are temporarily pulling a face out from the body that contains it. This means that there are limits to how much you can manipulate the NURBS surface. If you alter the surface too drastically, the surface won't be able to be stitched back onto the body that contained it. In these instances, the NURBS Surface Tool will revert to the original, unaltered, body so you can try again.

NOTE

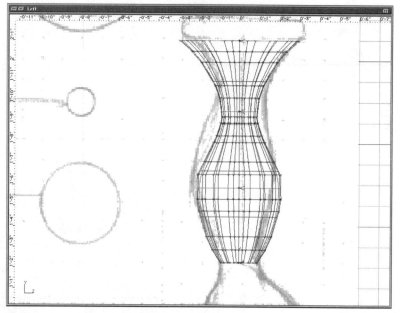

FIGURE *Turning the surface into a NURBS surface.*

4.57

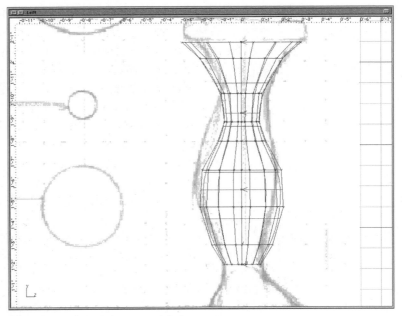

FIGURE   *Reduce the degree to simplify the geometry.*
4.58

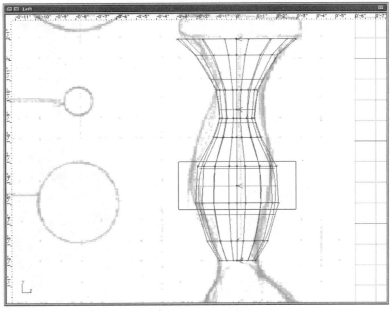

FIGURE   *Selecting the CVs to manipulate.*
4.59

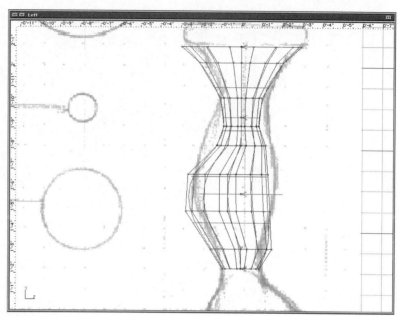

FIGURE *Pull the CVs out to form the belly.*
4.60

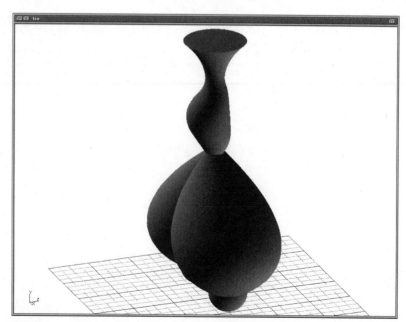

FIGURE *The potbelly in all its shining glory.*
4.61

A helpful analogy might be to envision a picture frame. Imagine that you could unhook the canvas from the frame and alter its shape. To get the canvas back into the frame, the outer edges of the canvas must line up with the frame edges that they came from. You could alter the interior of the canvas, but any modifications to the outer edges would mean the canvas would no longer be able to fit back into the frame. In the case of NURBS surfaces, this would mean the stitch would fail. This is why we skinned the King's midsection. If we had revolved the midsection, we would have created a vertical edge where the revolve attached itself. If we had unhooked the face with the NURBS Surface Tool and pulled it out, the edge of the face would no longer match the edge of the body that it came from, thus it would not have been able to be stitched. If it helps, envision this edge as a "zipper" on the back of the King's midsection. If we had pulled the revolved faces forward, the "fabric" would no longer match up to the "zipper," which stays in place during the editing process. For a more thorough explanation of these issues see your manual.

STEP THREE

Frame the upper part of the King in Top View and create two circular wires, one for the neck collar and one for the bottom of the crown. Then create two circular wires for cross-sections to sweep around these wires, as shown in Figure 4.62.

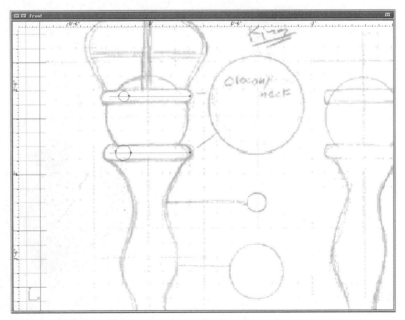

FIGURE *Create two circular wires to sweep for the collar and crown base.*
4.62

Select the circular cross-section, then the circular wire that represents the circumference of each body and use the **Sweep Cross-Section Along Path Tool** to form the objects. After you've created both shapes, add the sphere for the head (see Figure 4.63). The head doesn't have to seat perfectly on the collar at first, we can adjust it later if needed, after we create the crown.

The rails of the crown can be created by sweeping an oval (or square or circular if you like) along a **Bezier curve**. Select the Bezier Tool (Bezier Palette) and begin creating a curve by clicking in the middle of the left edge of the crown's base and move up to the sphere that will top the crown. Add an oval for a sweep profile, as shown in Figure 4.64, and use the Sweep Cross-Section **Along Path Tool** to create the first rail. Use the **Linear Copy Tool** to create the remaining three rails by selecting the rail you just created, then double-click on the Linear Copy Tool. Enter 90° for the angle of revolution, 3 for the number of copies, and select the Y axis for the revolution, as shown in Figure 4.65. Click OK and the copies will be made, as shown in Figure 4.66. Since you pre-picked the rail, it wasn't necessary to reopen the linear copy dialogue box.

To create the circular joining detail in the middle of the crown, simply sweep a rectangular wire around a circle as you did with the neck and crown base (see Figure 4.67). Add a sphere to the top of the crown to complete the

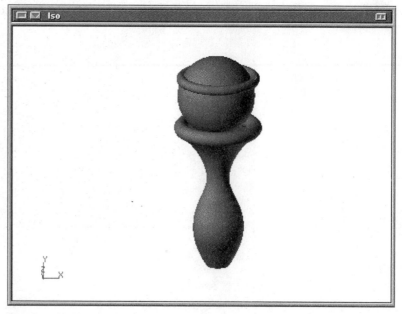

FIGURE *Add the sphere for the head.*
4.63

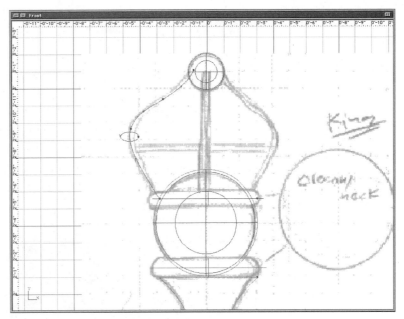

FIGURE *Creating the construction geometry for the crown.*
4.64

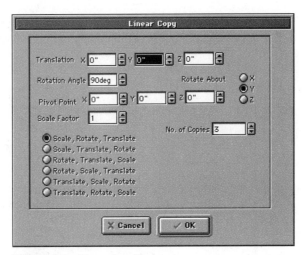

FIGURE *More Linear Copy Tool settings.*
4.65

FIGURE *The created copies of the crown rails.*
4.66

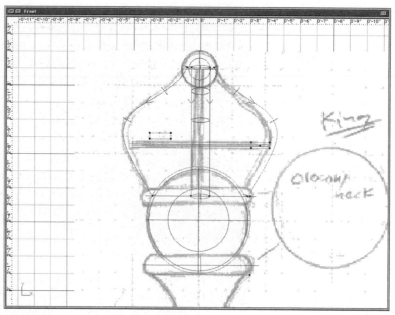

FIGURE *The last touch of crowning detail.*
4.67

King. If needed, select the crown and the head and move them down on the Y-axis until they meet the neck collar. And you're done.

—*Chris Weyers*

Modeling the Bishop

STEP ONE

Figure 4.68 shows the Bishop model we're going to be creating in this tutorial. Open the CHESS BEGINNING PROJECT and make the Bishop Layer the active layer. Add the BISHOP.IMAGE file to the front view and the left view and scale it up to 7 major grid units.

By now it should be fairly easy for you to evaluate the methods we will use to create the Bishop. The midsection is ideally created with the **Revolve Tool**. The base can be created by Boolean subtracting several spheres, and the top television monitor can be created by skinning. We're going to introduce a new tool to create the rails at the top and bottom of the Bishop, the **Bi-rail extrude**.

In the Front View, frame the midsection of the Bishop. Use the **Bezier Tool** to create a curve that conforms to the drawing, as shown in Figure 4.69. By now you should be an old pro at creating a revolve axis and revolving shapes. We're going to throw a twist into the process, however. The Bishop's midsec-

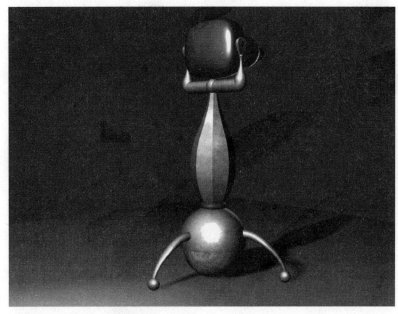

FIGURE *This is the Bishop we'll be creating.*
4.68

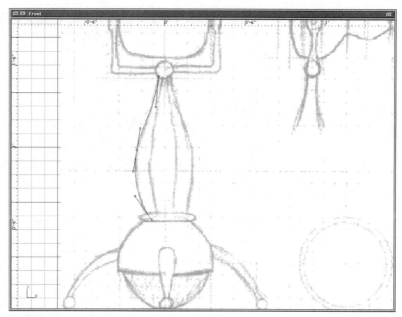

FIGURE *Create the initial Bezier curve.*
4.69

tion is designed to be segmented, not smooth. We can easily accomplish this by double-clicking on the **Revolve Tool** to open its options dialogue. Change the number in the **Number of Steps** box to 8, as shown in Figure 4.70. Close the options dialogue and revolve the midsection profile around the revolve axis. You will get a midsection created out of eight sections.

We need to create a small collar at the bottom of the midsection that will join it to the spherical base. Ideally, we want this collar to tightly conform to the shape of the midsection. We can accomplish this by extracting a wire from the base of the midsection.

FIGURE *The Revolve Tool settings for the faceted body.*
4.70

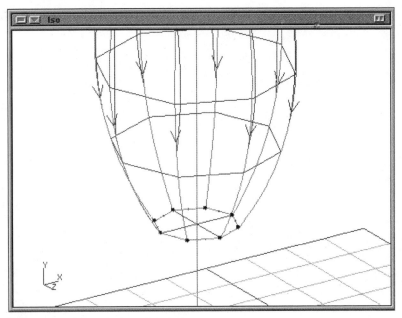

FIGURE *Zoom in on the base of the body.*
4.71

Select the **Convert Loop to Wire Tool** (Wire Editing Palette). In the iso window, frame the base of the Bishop so that you can see the bottom edge clearly, as shown in Figure 4.71. Click once on the bottom edge of the midsection. This will extract an octagonal wire from the base of the midsection. You will have to turn visibility off for the midsection in order to see this wire as it is in the exact place the wire on the solid body is.

The only problem with this octagonal wire is that we want our collar to be round. We can easily round off this wire with the **Convert Polyline to NURBS** Tool (Wire Editing Palette). Select the Convert Polyline to NURBS Tool and click on the Octagonal wire. It will be copied and converted to a NURBS curve that is circular, as shown in Figure 4.72. It may not be perfectly circular, but it's close enough. It is also as exact a circular match for our midsection base as we can get. Hide the octagonal wire.

In the Front View create a circular cross section and sweep it around the NURBS curve, as shown in Figure 4.73. This will create the circular collar at the base.

To create the base of the Bishop, start with by adding a large sphere that is the size of the largest part of the base (see Figure 4.74). Select the **Scale Tool** and hold down the "d" key. Click on the sphere and drag to create a copy that is scaled smaller than the original, as shown in Figure 4.75. Use the **Linear**

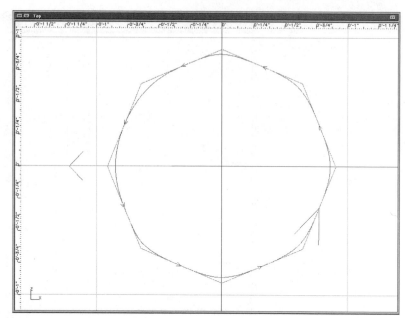

FIGURE **4.72** *Round off the octagonal shape with the Convert Polyline to NURBS Tool.*

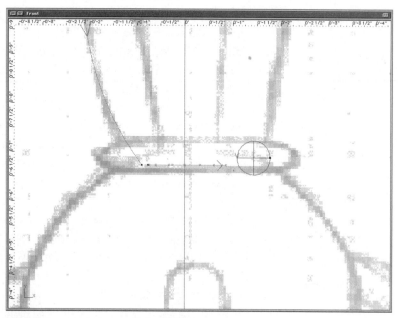

FIGURE **4.73** *Sweep a circle around the NURBS curve.*

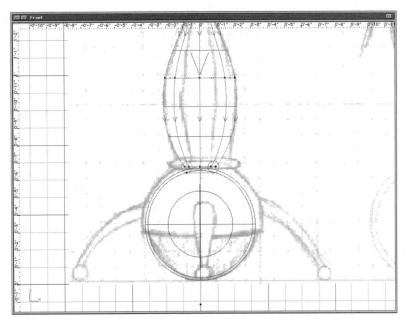

FIGURE   *Add a large sphere for the start of the base.*
4.74

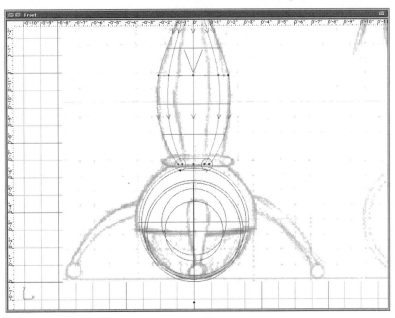

FIGURE   *Create a smaller copy of the larger sphere.*
4.75

Copy Tool to create a copy in place of this scaled down sphere and use the **Boolean Subtract Tool** to subtract the small sphere from the large one. Use the **Straight Knife Tool** to cut the bottom of the booleaned base shape off just below the center line, as shown in Figure 4.76.

To create the small legs for the base, we'll use a bi-rail extrusion. This tool is similar to the sweep tool in that it will extrude a shape along a path, but it will scale the shape based on two profiles.

Frame the left side of the base. Use the **Bezier Create Tool** to create two curves that match the curve of the top and bottom of the leg. Make sure that these curves begin and end far enough into the base shape and the sphere shape that will be at the end.

You can create the first bezier, then duplicate and edit it to create the second.

TIP

Then add a circular wire in the middle of the two bezier curves. To create a bi-rail extrude, the ends of the rails and the shape profile must be intersecting. To do this, size your circle as close as you can to the space between the two wires, then turn on Edge Snapping. Use the **Bezier Edit Tool** to put the curves in edit mode, then snap the end points to the edges of the circular wire, as shown in Figure 4.77.

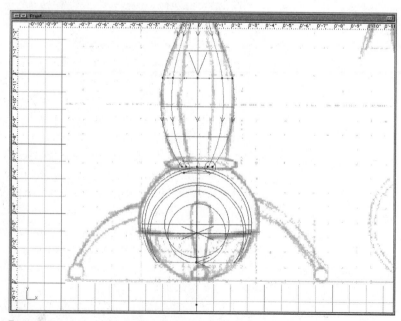

FIGURE *Cut the resulting booleaned object in half.*
4.76

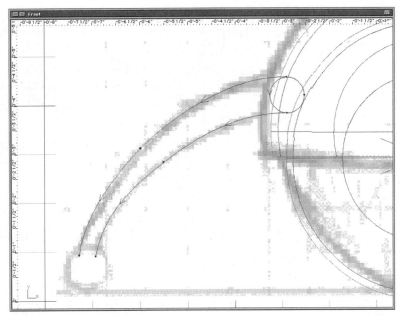

FIGURE *Snap the edges of the beziers to the circle.*
4.77

> **NOTE**
>
> *The shape profile can exist anywhere on the curves, it doesn't have to be on the ends.*

Now select the **Bi-Rail Tool** (3D Tools Palette), click first on the top rail, then on the bottom rail, and finally on the circular shape profile. The circle will be extruded along, and scaled between, the two rails. Add a sphere to the bottom of this rail and Boolean union the rail and the sphere into one object.

The Bishop's rails are designed to be in a tripod-shaped support structure, so we need to move the rail we just created to the front of the body before we use the **Linear Copy Tool** to create two duplicates. Frame the base and the rail in Top View and in Front View. Turn on visibility for the center revolve axis line, if it isn't already on. Select the **Rotate About Center Tool** by clicking and holding on the **Rotate Tool** and selecting the last tool in the palette that pops up. This tool allows you to rotate an object around the axis of an object you choose. Select the rail, then double click and choose the revolve axis line. Enter 90 in the rotation field that pops up in the **Status Window**. This will rotate the rail to the front of the Bishop.

Now select the Linear Copy Tool, then click on the rail. Double-click on the Linear Copy Tool and set the **Rotation Angle** to 120°. Click the **about Y-axis** radio button, and enter 2 for the number of copies, as shown in Figure 4.78.

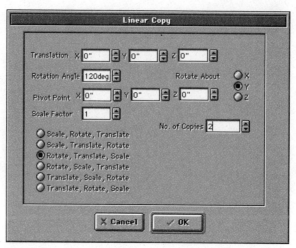

FIGURE *The Linear Copy Tool settings.*
4.78

When you click **OK**, two copies will be made and rotated into place on either side of the body (see Figure 4.79). Use the **Boolean Union Tool** to join the three rails to the hollowed out base. (Be careful not to join the wheel sphere.)

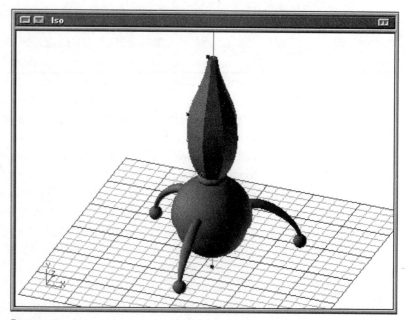

FIGURE *Two leg copies made.*
4.79

STEP TWO

To create the bracket that holds the Bishop's head monitor in place, we will be using the Bi-Rail Tool as well, but this time we're going to shape the rails a bit more.

In the Front View, use the **Bezier Curve Tool** to create a wire that runs down the center of the left bracket. Make sure the wire starts far enough into where the sphere on the top will be. Also be sure to insert an extra knot just below the point where the bracket turns circular. This will help us reshape the curve in the side view (see Figure 4.80). Switch to the Left View and put the Bezier Curve in edit mode. Reshape the curve to conform to the fluted shape at the top of the bracket, as shown in Figure 4.81.

In the Left View, select the bezier wire and move it forward on the X axis to put it in front of the revolve axis, then use the **Symmetry Tool** to duplicate the wire to the other side. Add a circular profile to the point where the fluted shape is the narrowest and add a rectangle about 1 grid space above, as shown in Figure 4.82.

Rotate the circular and rectangular wires so that they intersect the rails. This will set you up to do the bi-rail (see Figure 4.83).

Select the Bi-Rail Tool, click on the two rails, then select the circular wire, and finally the rectangular wire. Double-click to generate the bi-rail. The circle

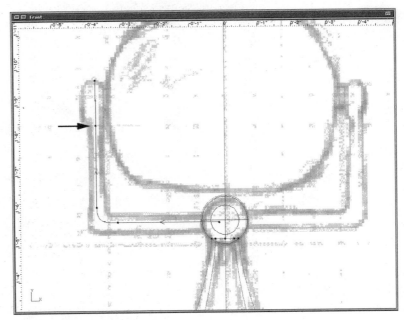

FIGURE *Insert an extra knot.*
4.80

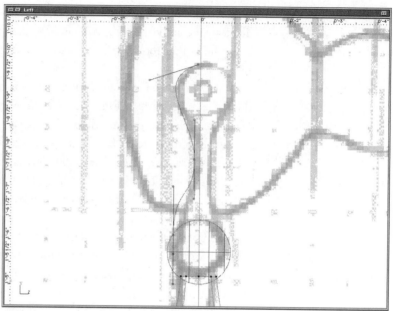

FIGURE *Reshape the bezier curve to fit the fluted shape.*
4.81

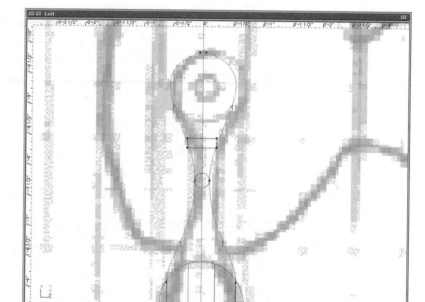

FIGURE *Mirror the curves and add two profiles.*
4.82

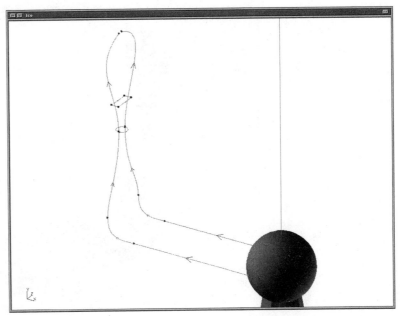

FIGURE *Rotate the profiles perpendicular to the direction of curves.*
4.83

will be swept downward to the base of the neck, and the rectangle will be swept upward to create a squared off end to the bracket. Both of these shapes will conform to the width defined by the rails, as shown in Figure 4.84.

You can use as many profile shapes as you like in a bi-rail extrude. The bi-rail tool does not blend smoothly between disparate shapes like a circle and a square. We used this to our advantage in this case to create a bulge at the top of the bracket. If you would like a smoother transition between circular and square profiles, you would need to create intermediate wires that slowly transition from circular to square and place them along the rails at the points where you would like the blend to occur.

Using the Convert Polyline to NURBS Tool will turn a rectangle into a smooth, ovoid wire. By weighting this wire, you could easily create a transition from rectangular shape to circular.

TIP

Before we mirror this half of the bracket to the right side we need to put a hinge pin on the top. Frame the top of the bracket in the Left View and create a circular wire in the center of the flat part. Use the **Extrude Tool** to extrude this wire on the X axis to a point where it would intersect the TV screen. (Make sure capping is turned on in the extrude options.) Turn off the visibility for the

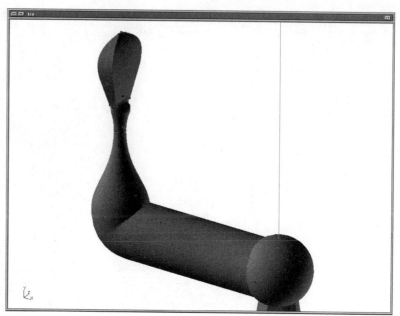

FIGURE *The bi-railed extrusion.*
4.84

extrude and select the **Wire Knife** (Knives Palette). Click once on the bracket and once on the circular wire you used to create the pin. This will cause the circular wire to cut a hole through the top of the bracket. Delete the circular slug that is created and use the **Rounding Tool** to round off the edge of the pin and the edge of the hole in the bracket, just like you did for the Castle's wheels (see Figure 4.85). By using the same wire to both create the pin and cut the hole, we have a perfect fit. Keep this technique in mind as we'll be using it to cut holes in the Pawn's legs in the next exercise.

Select the bracket and the pin and use the **Symmetry Tool** to copy it to the right side. Add a sphere on top of the neck and boolean the sphere and the two brackets together.

Step Three

To create the monitor, we're going to skin together several profiles of differing shapes, similar to how we did the midsection of the King's body.

Frame the monitor in Front View and use the **Bezier Tool** to create a curve in the shape of half of the monitor, as shown in Figure 4.86. When you're done, turn on grid snapping and make sure the beginning and ending knots are snapped to the center axis. Use the Symmetry Tool to mirror a copy of this

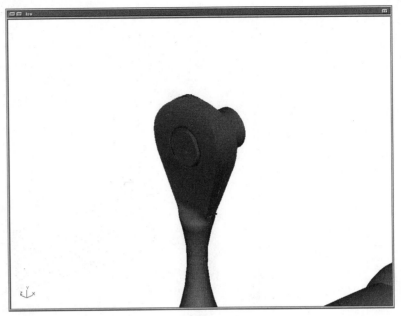

FIGURE *The rounded hole and pin.*
4.85

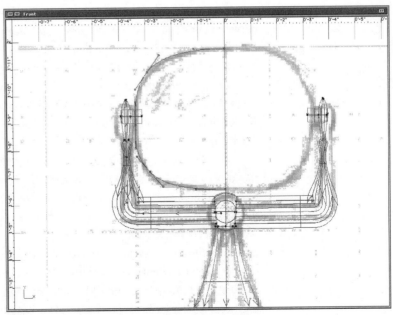

FIGURE *Use the Bezier Tool to create half of the monitor.*
4.86

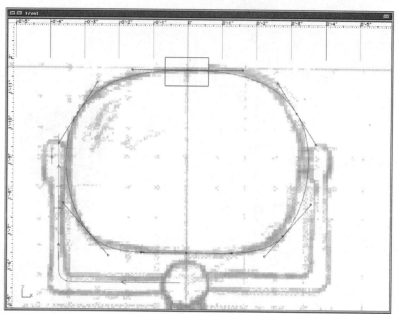

FIGURE *Join the two bezier curves.*
4.87

curve across the center axis. Select the **Bezier Edit Tool** and click on *both* curves to put them in edit mode. Select the **Bezier Join Tool** (Bezier Palette) and drag a marquee around the point where the beginning knots of the two curves overlap, as shown in Figure 4.87. Do the same thing for the point at the bottom where the end knots overlap. This will produce a single closed bezier curve. At the points where the two knots (top and bottom) overlapped, use the **Bezier Edit Tool** to move them apart, and delete one of them. Reshape the curve if needed (see Figure 4.88).

Switch to Left View and duplicate/translate (that is, use the move tool with the "d" key depressed) a copy of the curve to the very front of the monitor. Duplicate another copy of this curve in the opposite direction to the point where the back of the monitor begins to taper off. Scale the copy that is at the front of the monitor down to .1 inches. In the Front View, create a circular wire that represents the circumference of the rear of the TV screen. Translate/duplicate two copies of this circular wire and scale them to the appropriate circumference to create the bulge at the rear of the monitor. (Just like we did for the King's mid-section.) This will leave us with 6 wires to skin (see Figure 4.89).

Select the **Skin Tool** and pick the wires starting with the front, small bezier curve and ending with the back circle. Double-click to create the skin. Your

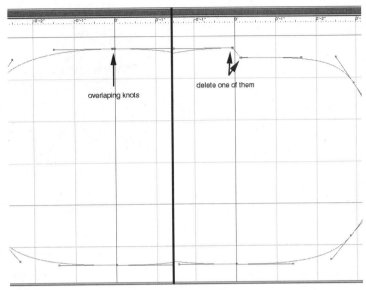

FIGURE   *After joining the beziers, remove the additional point.*
4.88

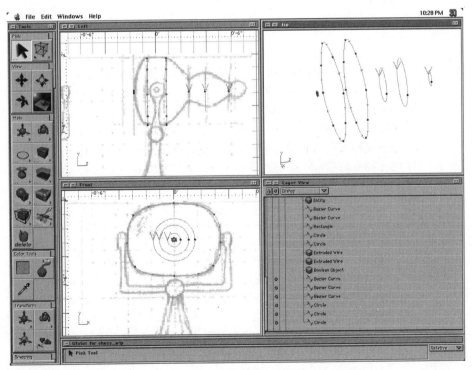

FIGURE   *Six skinable wires.*
4.89

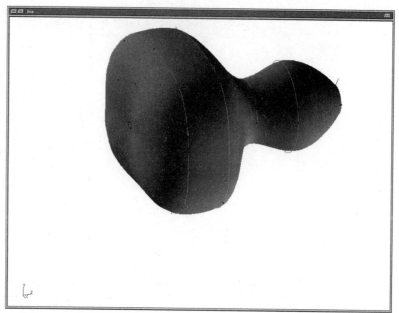

FIGURE **4.90** *The front of your skinned object may have an unsightly bulge . . .*

skin body may have an unsightly bulge in the front, as shown in Figure 4.90. If so, this situation can easily be remedied by undoing the Skin operation, adding a fourth copy of the bezier between the small wire in the front and the large wire, as shown in Figure 4.91, and then redoing your skin.

Add a sphere to the back of the TV monitor and you're finished with the Bishop.

—Chris Weyers

Modeling the Pawn

STEP ONE

Open the same Chess project and make the Pawn layer active. We're going to make the Pawn in Figure 4.92 so get ready. Import the PAWN.IMAGE file into the front and the left view windows and scale the image up to be 5 major grid units high.

A quick evaluation of the image points to the head/helmet as being the most complex object to model. The legs can be created from simple extrusions, as can the eyes. The foot can be created by skinning. But the helmet doesn't have an immediately identifiable symmetry. It does, however, have one area that ex-

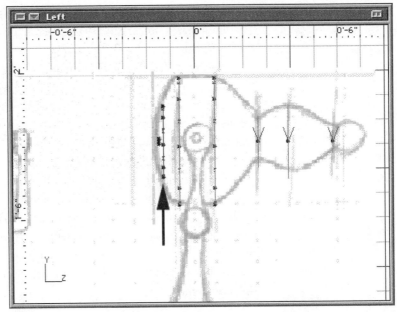

FIGURE   ... *correct it by adding another cross-section and redoing the skin.*
4.91

FIGURE   *Our target Pawn model.*
4.92

hibits some symmetry. Look at the edge of the helmet in Front and Left view. They both share a similar curve shape. We can use this as the starting point for the Pawn's helmet.

In the Front View, frame the helmet of the Pawn. Select the **Create New NURBS Curve from CVs** tool (NURBS Curve Palette). Create a control hull that roughly mimics the shape of half the helmet. If you haven't used NURBS before, the secret to using a control hull to create a curve is to think of it as a polyline. You just draw straight lines that are parallel to the curves you want to create. Because NURBS curves are continuous, each CV you place will effect a portion of the curve between itself and the next CV. As you continue to add edges to the control hull, you will be rounding off the curve between.

When you've drawn the curve, select the **NURBS Edit Tool** and adjust the weight of the curve at the tip of the helmet, as shown in Figure 4.93. You do this by holding down the "w" key and dragging on one of the CVs (not the Knots). This will add more influence to that area of the curve and tighten up the curve at that point.

Don't add so much weight to the CV that it causes the two knots in that area to overlap. This will destroy the curve's continuity and create geometry that won't boolean properly.

NOTE

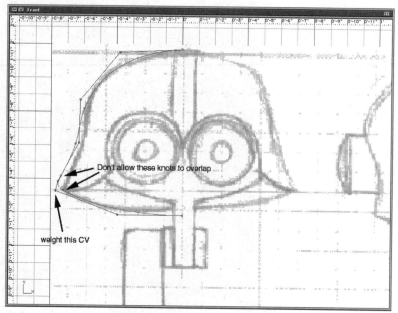

FIGURE *Adjusting the weight of the helmet.*
4.93

Turn on grid snapping and make sure the beginning and end points are snapped to the center Y axis. Select the **Line Tool** and create a Y axis revolve line. Use the revolve tool to revolve the NURBS curve. You can immediately see that there is a difference between this revolve and others that you've created with beziers. It may be difficult to see all the detail in the shape. This is because we have created a single continuous face to describe this body's surface. If we had used a bezier curve, we would have been creating one face for each segment in the bezier. This would have left us with three or four separate faces, which makes things easier to see. By using a NURBS curve, which is a single continuous edge, we have only one face. This will be a benefit when we start to cut and boolean this helmet shape, as we won't need to cut through multiple faces. It simplifies the topology. It does however make it harder to see. We can remedy this situation by adjusting the Spline Tessellation settings.

Choose **Edit>System Preferences**. Select the **Tessellation Tab** and look to the lower right area called **Spline Tessellation**. There you will see an area where you can change the **Number of Splines** in the **U** and **V** directions (see Figure 4.94). Change the Number in **U** and **V** to 4 and click **OK**. You won't be able to see your changes until you choose the **REGEN Tool** (Body Editing Palette) and click on the helmet shape. Now you should be seeing twice as many isoparms in the U and V direction.

Now we need to hollow out the center of our helmet. To do this select the

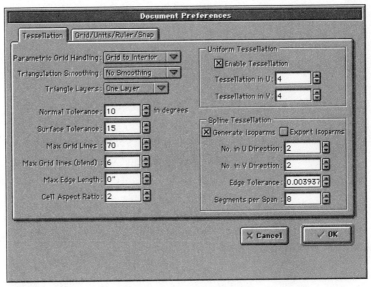

FIGURE *Setting the tessellation to get a better preview.*
4.94

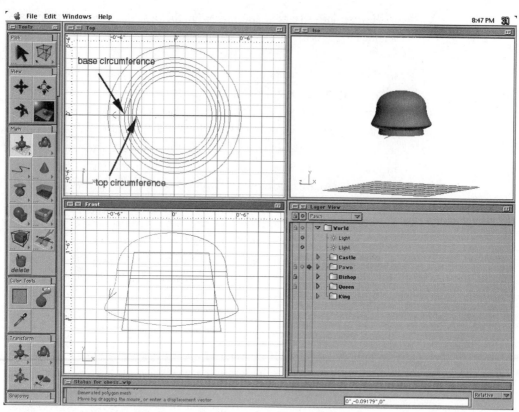

Cone Tool (Solid Primitives Palette). In the Top view, begin by clicking in the center of the helmet where the X and Z grid lines meet. Drag out the base circumference of the cone to be just within the inner circumference of the helmet. In the front view, drag the height of the cone up to about 7 grid spaces. Back in the top view, create the top circumference to be about 2 grid spaces smaller than the base. What you should end up with is a shape like an inverted cork (see Figure 4.95). Translate the cone up on Y until it intersects the helmet. Use the **Boolean Subtract Tool** to cut the cork shape out of the helmet.

In the Left View, frame the helmet and select the **Bezier Tool**. Create a curve that roughly matches the curve that the eye tubes come out of in the drawing, as shown in Figure 4.96. Select the **Wire Knife Tool** (Knives Palette) and click first on the helmet and then on the bezier wire you just created. The wire will cut its shape through the helmet, leaving two pieces. Delete the front (smaller) piece. You should be able to see the basic form of the helmet taking shape now (see Figure 4.97).

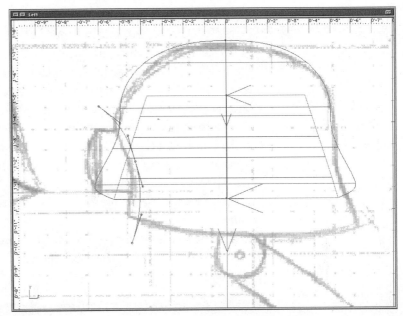

FIGURE   *Creating a curve to cut away the front portion of the helmet.*
4.96

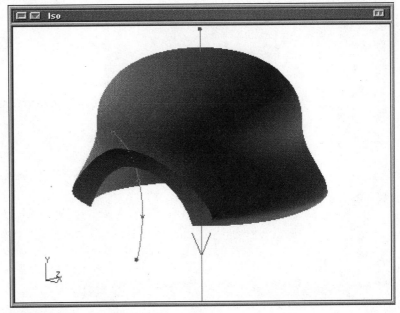

FIGURE   *The basic form of the helmet.*
4.97

Switch to the Front View and create a filled circle that is the circumference of the eyes. Extrude this filled circle back into the helmet at least halfway. Use the symmetry tool to duplicate it to the opposite side, as shown in Figure 4.98. Now select the left cylinder and use the **Linear Copy Tool** to duplicate it in place, then turn off the visibility for the duplicate. Use the Boolean Subtract Tool to subtract both of the cylinder shapes from the helmet, as shown in Figure 4.99.

Now turn on the visibility for the copy you made of the cylinder. Select the **Circular Knife Tool** (Knives Palette). Click in the center of the cylinder and drag out a circumference that comes within one-fourth grid space of the radius of the cylinder. Delete the center slug that is left in the cylinder and you will have the left eye tube (see Figure 4.100). Now we need to create a lens for this eye tube.

In the Left View, select the eye tube with the **Scale Tool** and hold down the "d" key as you drag. Scale the copy up to the point where the inner face of the

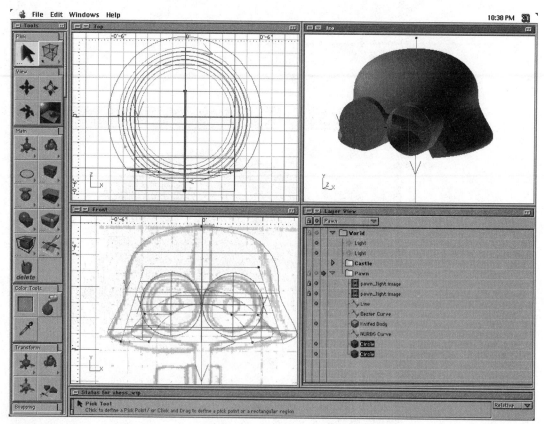

FIGURE *Creating the eye hole cutters.*
4.98

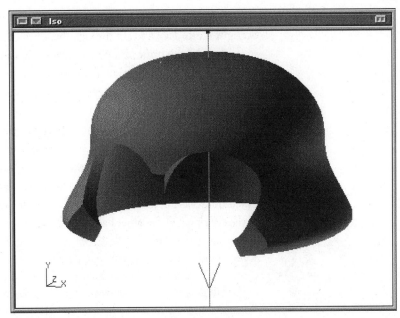

FIGURE   *Booleaned-out eye holes.*
4.99

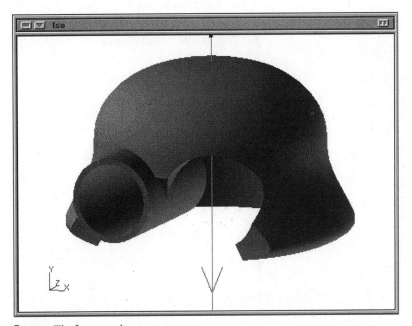

FIGURE   *The first eye tube.*
4.100

copy is touching the outer face of the original. When you're done, select the **Straight Knife Tool** and cut through the scaled tube on the Y axis about 2 grid spaces behind the front of the tube. Delete the back larger half of the cut, as shown in Figure 4.101. This will leave you with a lens ring.

We'll create the lens for the eye in the same way we've been creating wheels for other characters. Start in the Front View by creating a sphere that fills the eye ring. Make sure the edges of the sphere intersect about halfway into the eye ring. Select the sphere and **Scale/Duplicate it**. Make the duplicate about 10% smaller than the original and use the Boolean Subtract Tool to subtract the smaller sphere from the larger. Select the Linear Knife Tool and cut the hollowed-out sphere in half on the Y axis. Move one-half of the sphere to the front of the eye ring and the other back into the tube, as shown in Figure 4.102.

When you animate this model, apply a reflective surface to the back half of the sphere to give depth to the character's eyes. As a final touch to the eyes, add a sphere in the middle of the tube to represent the pupil. Select the entire left eye assembly and Symmetry-duplicate it to the right side.

TIP

To create the part of the head that fits inside the helmet, use the Bezier tool to create a curve that represents the left half of the head shape and revolve it around the center Y axis, as shown in Figure 4.103. To create the neck, switch

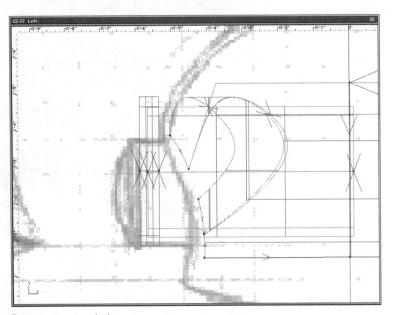

FIGURE *Creating the lens ring.*
4.101

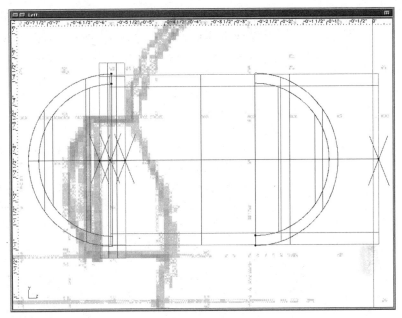

FIGURE *Creating the eye.*
4.102

FIGURE *The head is a simple revolve.*
4.103

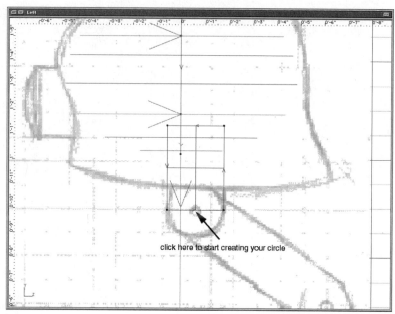

click here to start creating your circle

FIGURE *Creating the rectangular part the neck shape.*
4.104

to Left View and create a filled rectangle that starts inside the head and extends to the middle of the pivot point for the neck, as shown in Figure 4.104. Create a filled circle starting in the bottom center of the rectangle. Use the **Linear Copy Tool** to make a copy of this face and turn off its visibility. Boolean union the circle to the rectangle for the neck, as shown in Figure 4.105, and extrude this face to the proper depth.

STEP TWO

Begin the upper leg by turning on the visibility for the duplicate circle. Create a second duplicate and translate it into position at the lower end of the leg (see Figure 4.106.) Now turn on **Edge Snapping** and select the **Line Tool**. Begin drawing a connecting line between the two circles by clicking on the top edge of the upper circle and then on the top edge of the lower circle. Because you have edge snapping on, you will easily be able to connect the line between the two circles and keep it tangential. Do the same thing for the bottom, as shown in Figure 4.107.

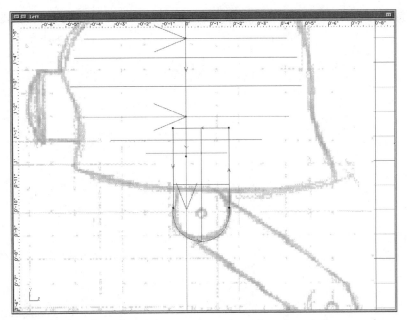

FIGURE *Boolean the circle and the rectangle together to form the neck shape.*
4.105

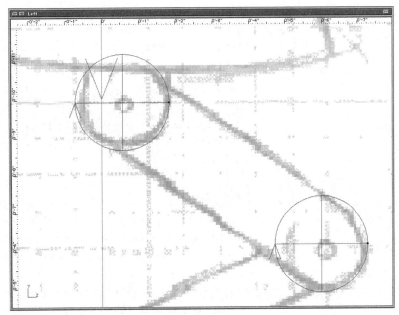

FIGURE *The two circle shapes for the rounded ends of the leg.*
4.106

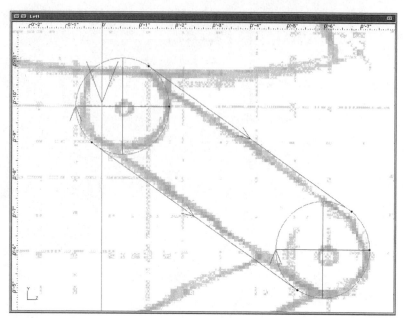

FIGURE *Connecting the circles with lines.*
4.107

Edge snapping is an excellent tool for modeling objects that have been designed at an angle. Just start by creating a part of the object you can use for snapping and connect it with lines.

TIP

Select the **Skin Tool** and skin the two lines you just created together to form a face. Select the **Boolean Union Tool** and join the rectangular face to the two leg circles. Extrude this face to get the upper leg (see Figure 4.108).

The wire lines you used in the skinning operation are still visible and it would be very easy to accidentally include them in the Boolean operation so turn their visibility off. Keep in mind that 2D (wires and edges) objects and 3D objects can be booleaned in EIM, so you'll want to keep a close eye on where the wires you use to create objects are at all times.

NOTE

The lower leg is created exactly the same way as the upper leg—just start with a slightly smaller circle. Create a duplicate of this circle to use at the beginning point for the ankle. The ankle joint is created exactly the same way as the neck, just turn on edge snapping to draw your rectangle so that it matches the edges of the circles.

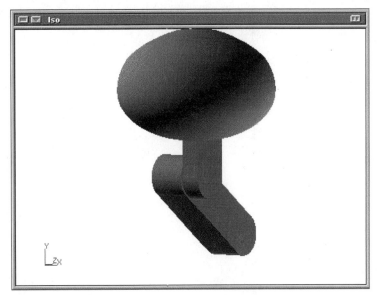

FIGURE *The upper leg extrusion.*
4.108

To create the foot, we'll use a skin. Remember that we can work the profile spacing to create a "puffy" shape like the foot. Start in Top View by creating a closed bezier curve in the shape of the foot, as shown in Figure 4.109. Duplicate this curve and scale it up to be about 15% bigger than the original. In the Left View, rotate it so that the rear part of the curve is down toward the heel and the front part of the curve is sticking out of the top of where the toe would be. Duplicate the original curve again, and this time, scale it down by about 70%. Translate this small duplicate up to the top part of the foot and rotate it so that it's at the same angle as the top line of the foot in the illustration. Position this curve so that it is within the ankle, as shown in Figure 4.110. Use the **Convert to Single Spline Tool** to turn the bezier curves into NURBS curves. This will allow us to create a continuous surface that will have a smoother shape. Select the **Skin Tool** and click on the original bottom curve, then on the middle larger curve, and finally on the small curve. Double-click to create the skin. You should have a nice puffy looking foot (see Figure 4.111). The placement of the larger curve is what allowed the skin to puff out on its way to the smaller curve.

Now before we Symmetry-duplicate the left leg to the right side, we want to put some hinge pins in it and round off the sharp edges. You should remember how to create the hinge pins from the Bishop exercise. In the Left View, create three filled circles that are positioned where the hinge pins need to go, as shown in Figure 4.112. In the Front View, translate these circular wires into po-

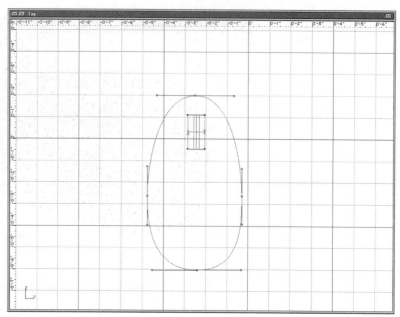

FIGURE *The first shape for the foot.*
4.109

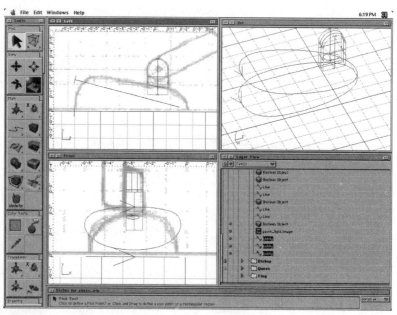

FIGURE *The three foot cross-sections.*
4.110

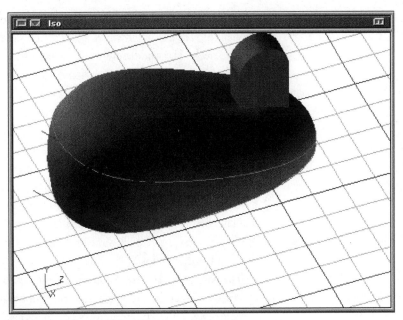

FIGURE *Our final puffy foot.*
4.111

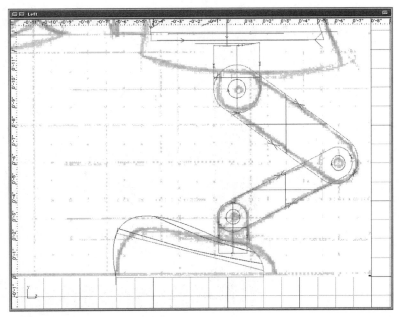

FIGURE *Creating the circles for the hinge pins.*
4.112

sition and extrude them into the legs. Make sure you extrude each pin far enough into the leg that it will be a part of. This means the top pin must intersect the neck. The middle pin must intersect the Upper Leg, and the bottom pin must intersect the ankle (see Figure 4.113). Select the three pins with the **Linear Duplicate Tool** and copy them in place. Hide the copies. Use the **Boolean Subtract Tool** to subtract the top pin from the Upper Leg. Subtract the middle pin and the bottom pin from the middle leg, as in Figure 4.114.

Turn the visibility on for the 3 pin duplicates you created. **Boolean Union** the top pin to the neck. Boolean Union the middle pin to the Upper Leg and the bottom pin to the ankle, as shown in Figure 4.115. The middle leg will have two holes in it to receive both the middle and the lower pin.

Now, before we symmetry the left leg assembly to the right, we want to round its edges first. You'll want to do most of your selecting in **Edge** pick mode in the iso window.

The pawn's legs represent a special case for rounding as they contain linear and convex edges. If you switch your pick mode to Edge and select all of the Left Side edges and attempt to round them with a .1" radius, as shown in Figure 4.116, you will most likely get the error message shown in Figure 4.117.

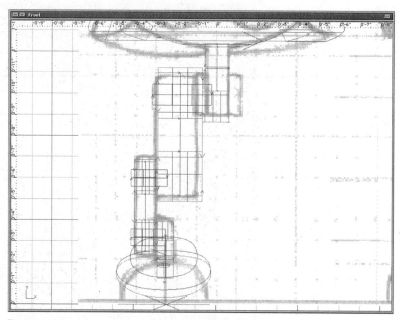

FIGURE *The pins must intersect the appropriate leg parts.*
4.113

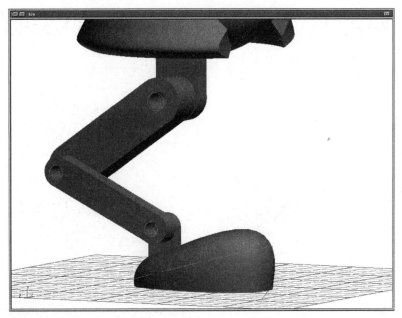

FIGURE *Subtract the pins.*
4.114

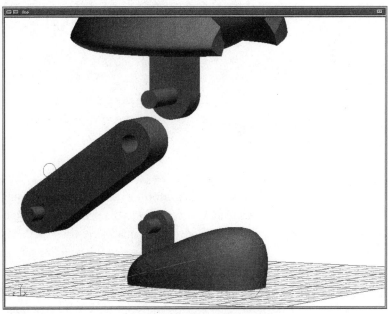

FIGURE *Boolean the pins to the leg parts so they will interlock.*
4.115

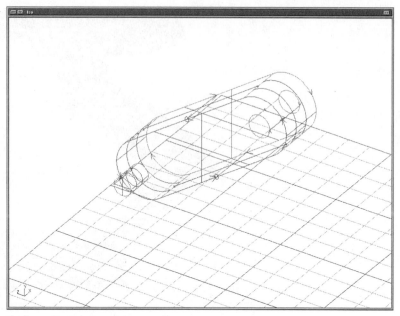

FIGURE *All edges selected for rounding.*
4.116

FIGURE *The error message that will probably result.*
4.117

Most rounding errors can be attributed to a couple of things. The first is that you simply haven't chosen the right edges to round together. The second is that you have edges with a small space between them. You may not be able to see that space, but it can prevent the rounding mechanism from bridging the gap between the edges.

In the case of the upper leg, we're dealing with a series of edges that have a little too much space between them. To get around this problem, we can round the flat (straight) edges first. Pick all of the straight edges on the upper leg and round them with a .1' radius, as shown in Figure 4.118. Once the straight

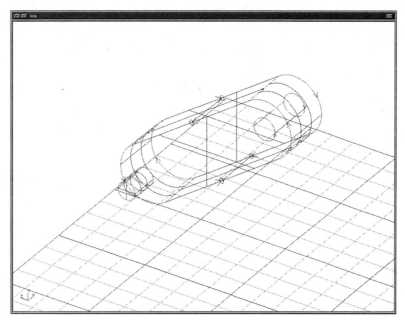

FIGURE   *Round the straight edges first.*
4.118

edges are rounded, select the convex edges and attempt to round them. You may get another error message at this point. What's happening here is you're attempting to fit a .1″ radius into an area that already has a .01″ round. There isn't a way for you to push the new face out of the way so, to solve this problem, just drop your rounding radius for the convex curves down a tiny bit to .09″. This will allow the convex edges to blend into the existing round edge coming from the straight sections (see Figure 4.119). The lesson here is to always evaluate complete topology in all three dimensions and attempt to round the straight edges first if you can, then the convex edges. Don't forget to round the hinge pin and the outer edges of the hole in the upper leg.

To round the lower leg, work the same way you did on the Upper Leg. Round the straight edges first at .1″ and then round the convex edges at .09″.

One thing you may be noticing, if you've been switching to and from shaded mode throughout this process, is that your rounded edges aren't really that round. They may appear jaggy or octagonal. You can control these artifacts by changing the maximum grid lines that will be displayed in blends. This is done in the **Document Preferences > Tessellation Tab**. By selecting the **Max grid lines (blend)** option and raising the number, you will be telling the modeler to draw more lines for the blends, which will make them smoother when

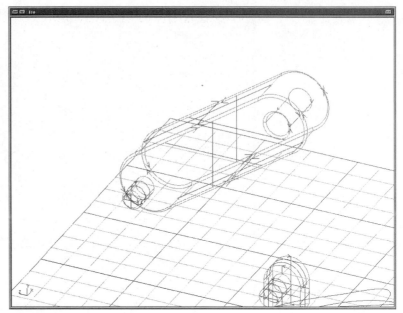

FIGURE *Round the convex edges next.*
4.119

you shade them (see Figure 4.120). Note that this setting doesn't have anything to do with how the edges will look when exported to a FACT file, it's only for display while in modeler.

We also need to round off the edges of the ankle. Rounding the upper part is just like the work you did on the legs. First round the straight edges, and then round the convex edges. Once you've done that you can select all of the edges that join the ankle to the foot, as shown in Figure 4.121. Notice that everywhere you created a round, there are now extra edges.

Once the rounding is done, symmetry duplicate the left leg over to the right leg position.

STEP THREE

Rounding the outer edges of the helmet is also going to require some special care. A very complex set of edges bounds the inner and outer faces of the helmet where you created the boolean. In this case we need to round the convex edges first, because they're bordered by a single straight edge that is part of yet another convex edge. To begin rounding the helmet, choose the edges that are facing outward. The easiest way to start selecting these edges is to switch to Right or Left View and select the first one. Then select the second one in the iso

Document Preferences

Tessellation | Grid/Units/Ruler/Snap

Parametric Grid Handling: Grid to Interior ▽

Triangulation Smoothing: No Smoothing ▽

Triangle Layers: One Layer ▽

Normal Tolerance: 10 ⊟ in degrees

Surface Tolerance: 15 ⊟

Max Grid Lines: 70 ⊟

Max Grid lines (blend): 6 ⊟ ◀━━

Max Edge Length: 0" ⊟

Cell Aspect Ratio: 2 ⊟

Uniform Tessellation

[X] Enable Tessellation

Tessellation in U: 4 ⊟

Tessellation in V: 4 ⊟

Spline Tessellation

[X] Generate Isoparms [ ] Export Isoparms

No. in U Direction: 2 ⊟

No. in V Direction: 2 ⊟

Edge Tolerance: 0.003937 ⊟

Segments per Span: 8 ⊟

[X Cancel]   [✓ OK]

FIGURE *Setting the Max Grid Lines (blend) option to make your rounds smoother.*
4.120

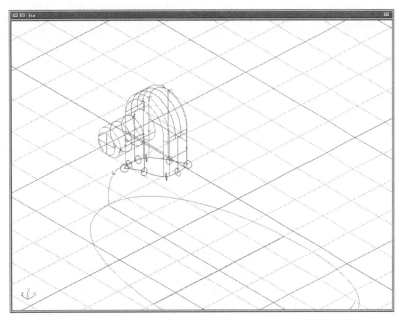

FIGURE *Finally you can select the edges that join the ankle to the foot.*
4.121

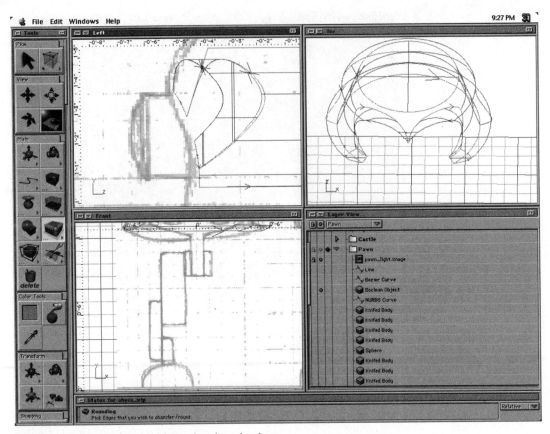

FIGURE *Switching views will help you select the right edges.*
4.122

view once the first has given you a clue to the position (see Figure 4.122). Once you have these large convex edges rounded, choose the straight edge that connects them to the rim of the helmet, as shown in Figure 4.123. Once this edge is rounded, choose the remaining edge in the loop and round it, as shown in Figure 4.124.

An easy way to evaluate a topology for rounding is to select the **Loop Pick Filter** *and click on edges. This will display the other edges that make up the loop and give you clues as to how the faces have been created. You can then switch to edge pick mode and be able to pick edges in the proper sequence to avoid errors.*

You may want to round off the edges of the eye rings that hold the lenses before you complete the model of the Pawn. After that, though, you're done.

—*Chris Weyers*

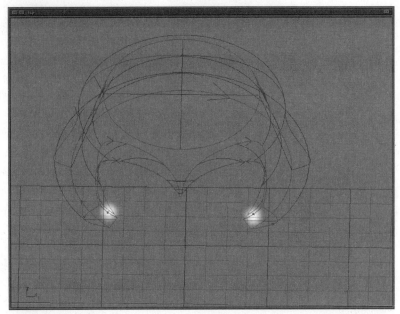

FIGURE
4.123
Once the large convex edges are rounded, select the edges that connect them to the rim of the helmet.

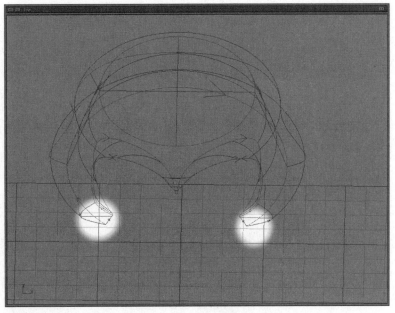

FIGURE
4.124
Finally, select the remaining edge and round.

Modeling the Queen

In evaluating the Queen object (see Figure 4.125), symmetry may be a little harder to find. There is an obvious Left to Right symmetry when viewed from the front. The side view, however, reveals a surface that curves in a non-symmetrical way. The neck and leg stems build off of the body and are roughly symmetrical. By now you may be able to guess we'll be using the skin tool to make those structures.

The body could be made in several ways. The Profile skin tool could be used to create a 3D skeleton of wires that form the shape. The Net surfaces tool could be used to create multiple segments of the shape that you could stitch together. The easiest (and most fun) way to build the body structure is with ÜberNurbs. If you haven't yet experimented with ÜberNurbs, it's suggested that you do so just to get a feel for the tool. Just create a simple block and click on it with the **ÜberNurbs Edit Cage Tool** and pull on the edges and vertexes. You can see that the ÜberNurbs cage controls the Nurbs surface it's attached to, almost like magnets from the cage are acting on the surface below. This is the primary metaphor for ÜberNurbs. You adjust a cage by adding CVs, edges, and loops to shape the actual NURBS surface.

FIGURE *The goal of our Queen exercise.*
4.125

STEP ONE

Start by opening the Chess project and placing the QUEEN.IMAGE file in the Front and the Left Views. Scale the image up to be 8 major grid spaces high. Center the Front image and the Left side image along the Y axis.

One of the first things you have to consider when working with ÜberNurbs is what kind of base shape to start with. Most of the time, a simple block is the easiest way to start. It creates a simple, symmetrical cage, with minimal edges. What you need to do is figure out how big to make the block. Because Über-Nurbs works primarily by adding edges and pulling them out into world space, it's usually a good idea to add a block that represents only the "core" of your character. This way you don't have to push edges and CVs inward or begin the process by deleting edges or CVs. For our Queen, we start with a block that represents her entire frontal surface area and only the "core" of her side surface area (see Figure 4.126). Now the block does extend outside of the image in the

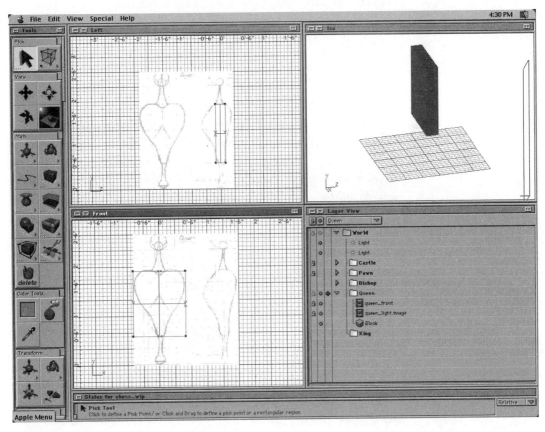

FIGURE   *Our initial shape is a simple cube.*
4.126

front view and will have to be pulled back inward. In this case, however, it will be easy, as that part of the object is symmetrical.

Select the **ÜberNurb Edit Cage Tool** (ÜberNurbs Palette) and click on the block.

For the ÜberNurbs part of this exercise, you can collapse all of the palettes but Über-Nurbs, Pick, and Snapping. Your block becomes surrounded by a ÜberNurbs cage and the surface looks like a lozenge. One of the most important things to realize about modeling with ÜberNurbs is that the cage forms your surface, so the shape of the cage is where you need to focus your concentration. For this reason I recommend turning off visibility for the surface, especially in the early stages.

Press the **TAB** key to turn off the visibility for the surface.

*Pressing **Shift + tab** will turn off the display of the CVs. A good setup for Über-Nurbs is to keep your iso window in shaded mode, and use the TAB key to turn vis-ibility off and on as you shape the cage to evaluate the surface. This makes the process of modeling more fluid, and it's easy to see what effect changes have by simply tak-ing a quick look at the iso window in shaded mode.*

The first thing we want to do is add some ribs that will divide up our block into areas that can be shaped to fit the Queen's body. To do this, select the **Add Rib Tool** (ÜberNurbs Palette) and drag horizontal lines across the cage in front view to divide the cage up into four sets of loops, as shown in Figure 4.127. You will be able to see in the iso view that the ribs form complete, symmetric loops all the way through the cage. If you press the TAB key to display the surface, you will see that it has flattened out significantly. This is an important concept in ÜberNurbs. The farther you pull a face away from its original position, the more the surface will round. To flatten out a surface, you add edges or ribs in the intermediate space. Our ribs are going to act as a series of pivot points for shaping the Queen's body.

As we model the Queen in the Front View, we want the changes we make on the Left side of the cage to translate to the right side. This can be done by creat-ing a line of symmetry. Select the **Symmetry Tool** (ÜberNurbs Palette) and drag a vertical line through the center of the ÜberNurbs cage, as shown in Figure 4.128. Now any changes you make to the left side will translate to the right.

Symmetry only works on identical, original loops. If you add an edge or loop to one side of the symmetry line, it will not be reflected to the other side of the cage.

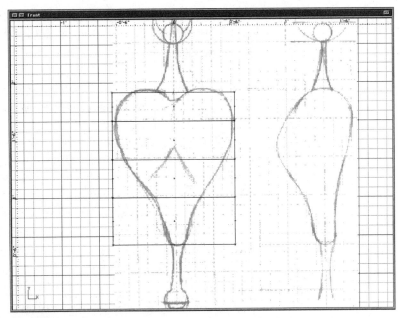

FIGURE   *Add four additional ribs.*
4.127

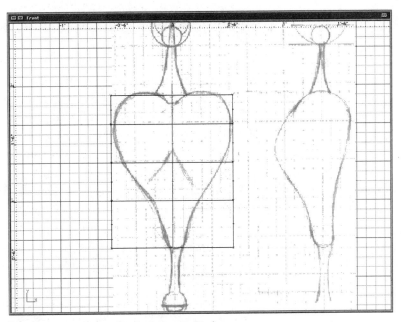

FIGURE   *Creating a line for the Symmetry Tool.*
4.128

Select the **ÜberNurbs Edit Cage Tool** and select the top left CV on the cage. Hold down the "x" key on the keyboard and slide the CV over to meet the Queen's shoulder.

TIP

The x, y, and z keys will constrain ÜberNurbs movement to those axes. You should see the right side of the cage update as you move the CVs on the left.

Continue moving the outer CVs on the left side of the cage to roughly trace the shape of the Queen's body, as shown in Figure 4.129. Now switch to the Left Side view and begin dragging the outer edge cvs out to meet the outline of the Queens body, as shown in Figure 4.130. Once you're done shaping the side view of the cage, turn on visibility for the surface and shade it. Orbit around in iso view and you will see that the shape of the surface has been made to resemble that of the Queen's body in only a few simple steps. It's generally very quick to get an ÜberNurbs cage into the basic shape of a body. Now we need to go in and add the details.

One of the defining features of the Queen's body are the "dents" in the chest and shoulder area. To create these, we need to add edges to break up the frontal surface of the Queen's chest so we can pull out the details. Before we start this, however, we need to hide the back part of the cage. You may have noticed that

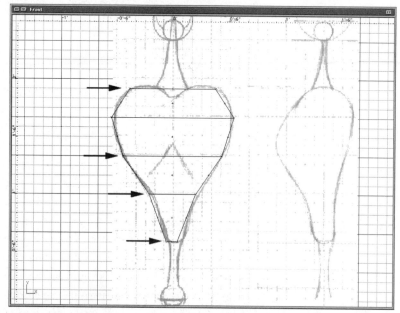

FIGURE *Trace the body from the front with your ÜberNurbs cage.*
4.129

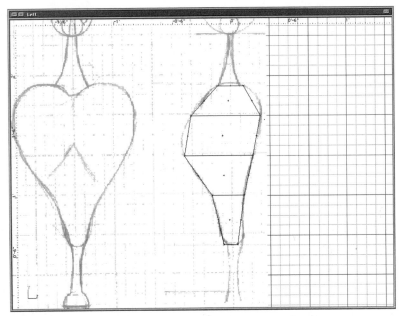

FIGURE *Then trace it from the side.*
4.130

when we selected CVs in front or left view, we select the front and back CVs. In this case it's not desirable, so hiding part of the cage we don't want to affect will be needed.

Select the **Visibility Tool** (ÜberNurbs Palette) and frame the cage in the top view. Drag out a marquee in the top view that covers the back part of the cage, as shown in Figure 4.131. The selected parts of the cage will have their visibility turned off. If you don't get the results you want, you can hold down the Shift key and drag out a marquee over the hidden area to restore the cage. The secret to understanding the Visibility Tool is that it will hide all edges associated with a particular set of CVs. So if you select the CVs on the front edge of the bottom loop on the cage, you will also turn off the edges that run up the front of the cage from those CVs.

Frame the cage in the Front View and select the **Add Edge Tool** (ÜberNurbs Palette). Starting at the top of the cage, add two identical edges that connect the second and third horizontal ribs. Space these edges about 2 grid spaces apart, as shown in Figure 4.132. Add another two edges that connect the second and the first horizontal ribs in the same manner. Now add a third vertical edge in the center of the two sets of edges you just created, as in Figure 4.133. Don't worry if these edges don't line up perfectly—it's not needed.

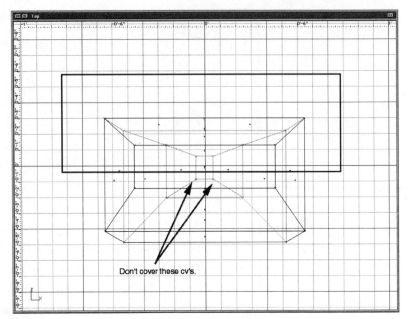

FIGURE *With the Visibility Tool, drag a marquee around the area you wish to hide.*
4.131

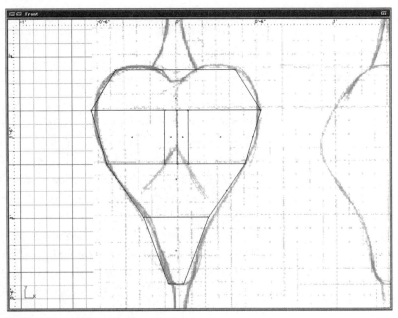

FIGURE *Create a few more ribs.*
4.132

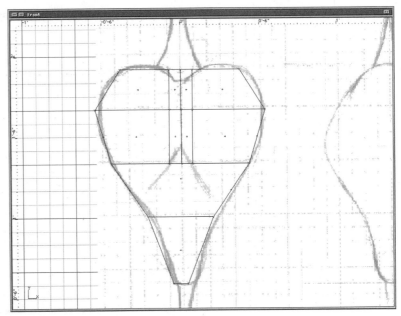

FIGURE *Create a vertical rib to define the dent.*
4.133

In the Front View hold down the Shift key and select both of the center vertical edges we just added. In the Left View hold down the "z" key and drag the edges back into the Queen's body, as shown in Figure 4.134. Press the TAB key to turn visibility back on for the surface and notice what we've done. By pulling back the center edges, we've created a dent in the Queen's chest. This is one of the most common techniques for shaping an ÜberNurbs cage. If you want to pull a shape into an object, you first create a series of edges that border that area to "hold out" the rest of the surface. In our case, the left and right edges hold the remaining volume of the chest out into space. If we had not added these, the chest would have gently sloped inward. (You can see this if you want by using the **Delete Edge Tool** to delete the left and right edges. Just make sure you put them back when you're finished.)

Now we need to shape the top part of the Queen's shoulders. To do this we need to add two more edges between the top and second horizontal ribs.

Turn on **Edge Snapping** (Snapping Palette) and click once on the top horizontal rib on the left side and once on the second horizontal rib on the left side (see Figure 4.135). With edge snapping turned on, the cvs for the edge you're adding will snap to the center distance of the edge you click on, regardless of

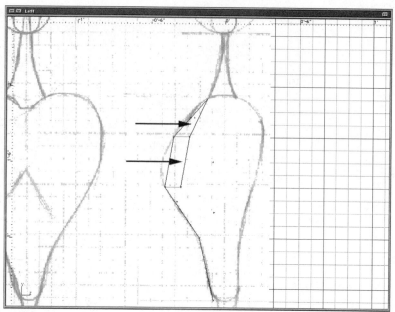

FIGURE
4.134 *Drag the edges back into the body.*

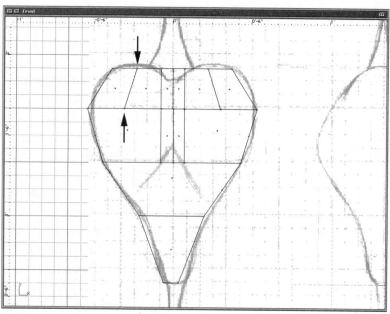

FIGURE
4.135 *Snap the edges.*

where on that edge you initially click. Add a second edge on the right side that connects the top and second ribs.

This is one of the best way to model with ÜberNurbs. Often you need to add an edge to part of the model that you can't get to completely in any of the orthographic views. By rotating the model in the iso view and using edge snapping, you will be assured that the edge is being inserted in the center of an edge or loop. Then you can modify it in an orthographic view.

With both edges in place you can form the top of the Queen's shoulders by dragging all of the cvs on the connecting edges inward, and downward, as shown in Figure 4.136.

Turn the visibility back on for the rest of the cage by selecting the **Visibility Tool** and **SHIFT + Drag** a marquee around the whole model. Shade your iso view and take a look at it. You can see the details you've added to the front part of the shoulders, but it smooths out as it moves back. This is because there is no connection between the front loops where you added this detail and the back loops. To give the shoulders definition on the Z axis you will need to add edges that connect the front and the back. To do this, hide all of the cage except for the top loop. Use the **Add Edge Tool** to connect the CVs on the front edge of the loop to the back edge of the loop, as shown in Figure 4.137. Now unhide

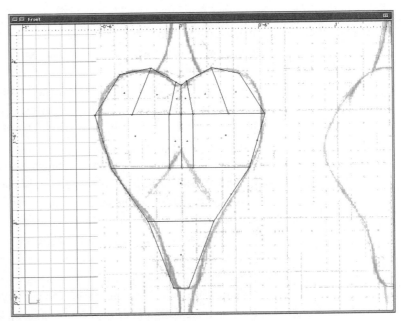

FIGURE *Drag the CVs to form the shoulder area.*
4.136

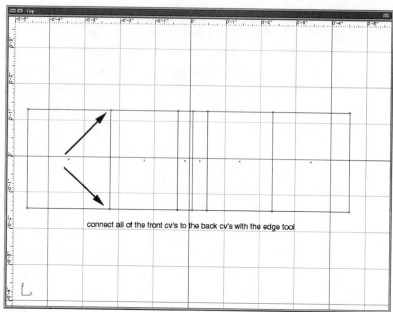

connect all of the front cv's to the back cv's with the edge tool

FIGURE *Add an edge.*
4.137

the cage and reshape the top shoulder area on the Z axis by pulling the center edges down on the Y axis. Add an edge that connects the center of the top rib's back edge to the center of the second ribs back edge (see Figure 4.138). This rib will help keep the surface shape on the back side of the shoulder more even.

The Queen's midsection should now be looking pretty good. However, there is one thing to be aware off. In the iso view, rotate the body around to the front side so you can get a good look at the area between the third and fourth ribs (see Figure 4.139). This area represents a complex loop with multiple CVs (similar in concept to a complex polygon in a polygonal modeler). All of the cvs on the third rib affect the surface between the third rib and the fourth. They can cause a striation in the surface because these cvs represent space between separate edges on the third rib, but they have no counterparts to connect to on the fourth. As you model any object in ÜberNurbs, look for open areas like this that border complex ones and break them up with extra edges. This will give you a smoother surface transition. To break this area up, connect the CVs of the vertical edges on the third rib to the fourth edge, as shown in Figure 4.140.

Hopefully, this has given you a good idea of how ÜberNurbs works. It takes some getting used to, but once you learn to see modeling your object in less de-

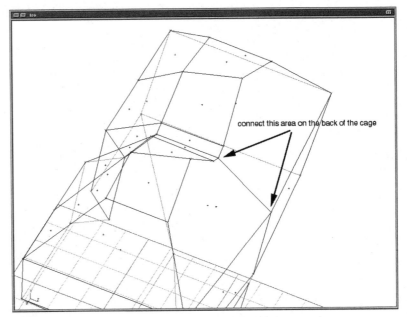

FIGURE *Add another edge.*
4.138

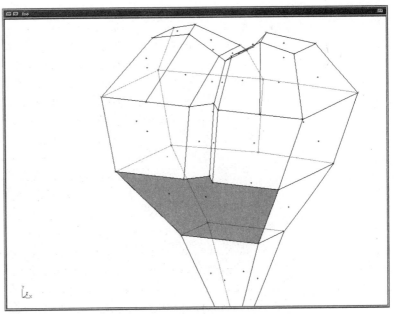

FIGURE *This is a complex loop, which can create problems.*
4.139

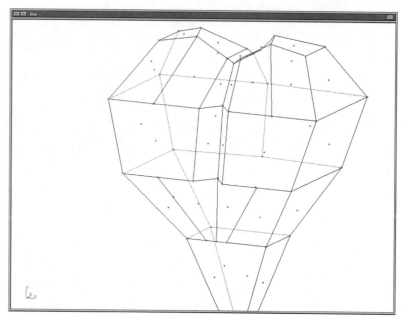

FIGURE *Connect the CVs to break up the complex loop.*
4.140

tail, you will grow to like it. Metaphorically, the process could be compared to carving wood. You can carve a blocky version of what you want to see out of a block of wood, and then sand it down to see a more refined object. ÜberNurbs is similar, only the "virtual sandpaper" works in real time.

STEP TWO

To model the Queen's base, we're going to project a wire onto the ÜberNurbs surface. For this reason we need to convert the ÜberNurbs object completely to an ACIS body. To do this, double-click on the **ÜberNurbs Edit Cage Tool** and check the **Convert Fully to ACIS** option.

TIP

Generally, you want to keep ÜberNurbs Attributes, unless you want to use other modeling tools such as booleans or knives. Then you must convert the ÜberNurbs body to ACIS.

In the Front View, frame the lower half of the Queen's midsection. Create a circular wire that is about 2 to 2.5 grid spaces wide. Rotate the circular wire 90°

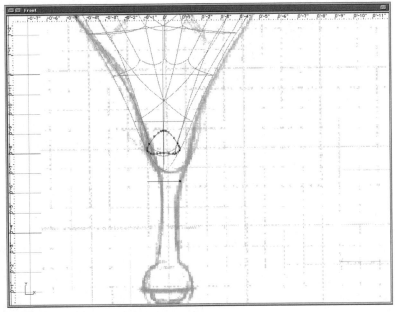

FIGURE *Projecting a wire onto the Queen's body.*
4.141

and move it so that it is 1 grid space below the midsection. Select the **Project Wire Tool** (Wire Editing Palette) and click first on the Queen's midsection and then on the wire. Drag out a vertical line along the Y axis to tell the circular wire what direction to project. When you let up on the mouse, the circle will be wrapped along the bottom of the Queen's midsection (see Figure 4.141). Select the circular wire that was used for the projection and make two duplicates. Place one duplicate at the bottom of the Front View where the wheel will be. Place the second duplicate in between the bottom of the midsection and the bottom circular wire. We're going to use these wires, plus the projected wire, to skin the Queen's base, just like we did for the King's midsection (see Figure 4.142).

Select the **Skin Tool** and click on the bottom circular wire, the middle circular wire, and the projected wire (skipping the original circular wire). This will create a skin surface that exactly matches the base of the Queen's midsection (see Figure 4.143). This surface will not be capped because the projected wire at the top is non-planar.

By now you should be an expert at creating the spherical type of wheel that's at the bottom of the Queen's base (if not, refer back to the King and Bishop exercises).

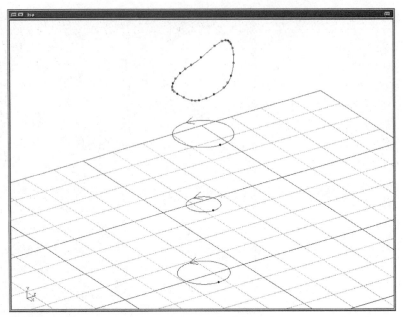

FIGURE *Creating the wires to use for skinning the base object.*
4.142

STEP THREE

The Queen's neck is created the same way we created the base. Begin with a circular wire that is about 3 or 4 grid spaces wide. Project this circle on the Queen's shoulders. Create two more copies of the circular wire that you used to project, scale each by 50%, and translate them in Y to form the ribs for a skinning operation (see Figure 4.144). Select the **Convert to Single Spline Tool** (Wire Editing Palette) and click on the projected wire. This will turn the piecewise projected wire into a single NURBS curve. Because we're making such a large jump in size (50%) between the projected wire and the next skinning rib, a NURBS curve is preferable to keep the surface smooth and controlled.

NOTE

Be careful in your use of the Convert to Single Spline tool. All curves in EIM need to be at least C2 continuous. This means there can be no cusps, sharp bends, or kinks in a NURBS curve. If you use the Convert to Single Spline Tool on a curve with a cusp in it, you'll be creating a curve that is discontinuous, and any geometry you create with this curve will be degenerate. Realisticly, it may not affect the look of your model, but degenerate surfaces will produce error messages as you attempt to use other tools like booleans or knives on them.

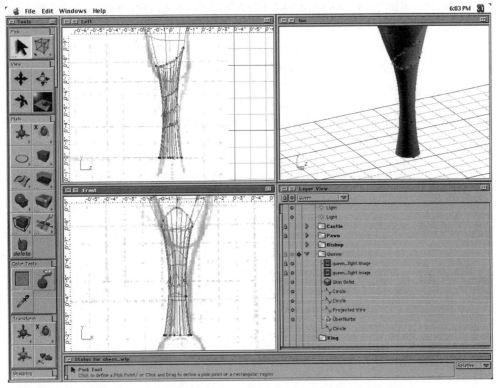

FIGURE   *The resulting skinned object exactly matches the Queens midsection.*
4.143

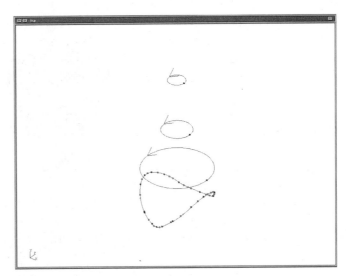

FIGURE   *The neck cross-sections.*
4.144

Select the **Skin Tool** and click first on the projected wire, second on the middle circular wire, and finally on the top circular wire (skipping the original projected wire). This will, again, create a skin surface that joins smoothly to the Queen's shoulders, as shown in Figure 4.145. For the head, simply add a sphere to the top of the Queen's neck.

To create the crown, start by creating a filled circle that represents the outer circumference of the crown. Select the circular knife and click down about one-half of a grid space above the center of the circular face and drag out until the cutting circle is outside of the face, as shown in Figure 4.146. Delete the center part of the cut and extrude the remainder to the desired depth for one set of crown points. Round the edges of the crown points and duplicate/rotate it 90 degrees.

Finally, use the pick tool to select all of the objects that make up the Queen, except for the crown and the spheres that make up the head and the wheel. Select the **Boolean Join Tool** (Booleans Palette) and double-click. This will join all of the objects together into one body. Unlike the **Boolean Union Tool**, you can use the **Boolean Unjoin tool** at any time to unlink all of these objects.

—Chris Weyers

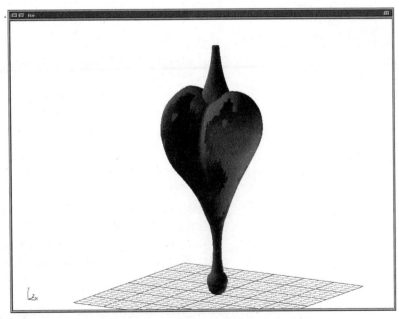

FIGURE *The skinned object joins perfectly with the Queen's shoulders.*
4.145

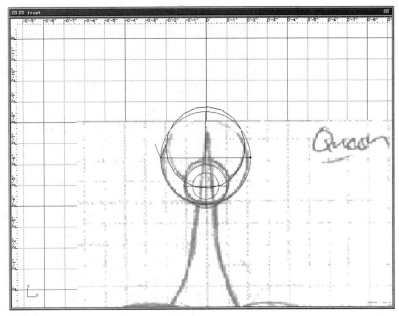

FIGURE *Setting up the crown geometry.*
4.146

Modeling the "ÜberKnight"

Figure 4.147 shows the Knight that we're getting ready to build. Open the Chess project and import the KNIGHT.IMAGE file into the Front and Left Views. Scale the images up to be 6 major grid units high.

In looking at the images, symmetry doesn't jump out at us immediately. The "pot" that the knight's head seems to be planted in is a good candidate for a revolve, and the wheels and support should look suspiciously familiar (they're borrowed from the Castle and the Bishop). The Knight's head, however, presents a problem. It has left-to-right symmetry, but overall it has a complex organic topology that doesn't lend itself well to being created with any of the surface tools we've used up to this point. This makes the Knight a prime candidate for modeling with ÜberNurbs. We've already had some experience with ÜberNurbs with the Queen model. We're going to build on that experience and focus on working with a fairly complex ÜberNurbs cage. Before we get started, let's keep some things in mind about ÜberNurbs.

ÜBERNURBS POINTERS

First, and foremost, ÜberNurbs has no undo feature. If you make a mistake, you have to attempt to fix the mistake or quit without saving and reopen the

FIGURE *The ÜberKnight model complete.*
4.147

last saved version of the file. For this reason you should periodically double-click to generate the ÜberNurbs object and save the project file. I suggest doing this after each major change you make to the cage.

We will be working extensively with the **Add Rib Tool** and the **Add Edge Tool**. They both seem to do similar things, but there is an important difference. When you add a rib to an ÜberNurbs cage, you are subdividing that section of the cage through one axis to create new loops in a symmetrical fashion. This means that you can then use the symmetry tool to have changes to one side of the cage mirrored to the other. You do have to re-drag your symmetry line after adding a rib, but thereafter, you can edit the cage symmetrically.

By contrast, when you add an edge, you're merely subdividing one loop on one side of the cage. This means that edits you make to that edge will not be translated to the other side of the cage. When you begin modeling any Über-Nurbs project, the best course of action is to begin breaking down your cage into component sections with the Add Rib Tool and then begin to add local details with the Add Edge Tool.

It's often the case that you can't select one of the CVs or edges you're after in the orthogonal windows, as they are parallel with the CV or edge that lies on the other side of the cage. For this reason, it's often necessary to select the item you wish to move in the iso window and then move it in one of the orthogonal windows. You don't need to reclick on the object once it's selected. You can click anywhere in any window and just start dragging. It's also important to have a little patience when selecting and dragging parts of the cage. Select the item you want to move and take a look at the window to make sure the CV or edge you clicked on was the only one to highlight. If you just click and drag like a speed demon, you will almost certainly pick the wrong thing at some point and bend your ÜberNurbs cage into a horrible mess.

Get in the habit of scanning all four of your modeling windows, even though you may be working primarily in one view. By keeping a constant eye on the entire object, you will catch CVs and edges that become accidentally selected.

As you work through the tutorial keep these keyboard shortcuts in mind:

- Pressing the x, y, or z key while dragging a cage will constrain the item you're moving to the X, Y, or Z axis respectively.
- Holding down the s key and dragging on an edge or a loop will scale the loop or edge.
- Holding down the r key will put the **Edit Cage Tool** in rotation mode. By holding down the r key with the x, y, or z key will constrain the rotation to the X, Y, or Z axis, respectively. Rotation occurs around the center of the selected edges or loops.

Also keep in mind that it's possible to select CVs on edges in parallel when you are in the orthogonal views. This means, for instance, if you are in the top view looking down on a square cage and you click on the upper left CV, you will also select the bottom left CV and the edge that connects them. This is the easiest way of modeling symmetrically without actually using a symmetry plane—we'll rely on it a great deal in this tutorial. Unless otherwise noted, any time you're guided to select a CV or edge in a view, you should be selecting the parallel CV or edge on the other side of the cage.

As the modeling process continues, it will be necessary to hide parts of the cage that are getting in the way. Hide parts of the cage as you see fit to get the job done. It will also save you some scroll time if you collapse all of the tool pallets you're not going to use. We'll be using the ÜberNurbs palette, the Pick palette, the Transform palette, and the Snapping palette for the majority of the exercise.

Let's do it.

STEP ONE: CREATING THE BASIC HEAD SHAPE

Start by adding a primitive block to the scene that represents the volume of the head in the Left View and about the width of the snout in the Front View, as shown in Figure 4.148.

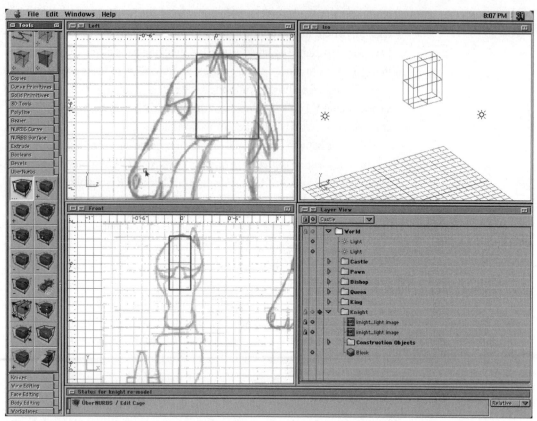

FIGURE   *Add the first block.*
4.148

Select the ÜberNurbs Edit Cage tool and click on the block to turn it into an ÜberNurbs surface. Press the TAB key to hide the surface. We will be doing the majority of the modeling with the surface turned off—just press the TAB key every now and then to see what's happening to the surface as you change the cage.

Leave your iso window set to **Smooth Shade** *mode. This will make it much easier to separate the surface from the cage.*

TIP

Select the **Extrude Loop Tool** and orbit the cage in the iso view until you can clearly see the loop center in the middle of the front face. (Every loop has a loop center that is represented by a CV that is "hanging in space" rather than appearing attached to an edge.) Click on the loop center with the Extrude Loop Tool. This will push a copy of the loop you clicked on out into Z axis space, as shown in Figure 4.149.

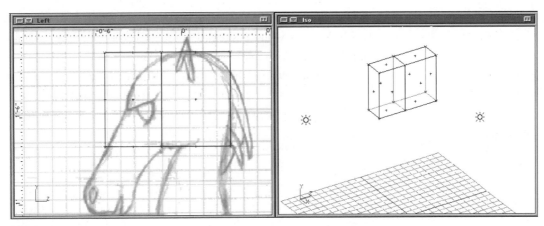

FIGURE *Extruding a loop.*
4.149

With the **Edit Cage Tool**, select the loop center on the front most part of the cage. Hold down the "s" key and drag to scale down the loop to be about the thickness of the snout. With the loop still selected, drag it down to the point just behind where the nose begins to take shape. Hold down the r and the x key to rotate this loop on the X axis until it's parallel with the back of the nose (see Figure 4.150).

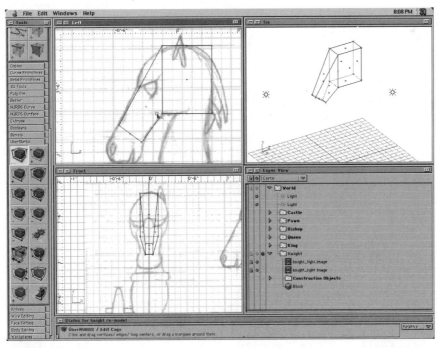

FIGURE *Rotate the loop.*
4.150

In the iso window, rotate around the cage until you can clearly see the loop center of the loop you've just positioned and rotated. Select the Extrude Loop Tool and click on the loop center. This will push another loop out beyond the nose. Select the loop center of this new loop with the Edit Cage Tool and drag it back into a position approximately one-fourth grid space in front of the original loop (behind the Knight's mouth). Scale this loop up just a little until it's approximately the height of the bulge on the nose, as shown in Figure 4.151.

Now orbit around the cage once more so that you can see the loop center of the front loop and use the Extrude Loop Tool to push out one more loop. Drag this loop back to the beginning of the nose, as shown in Figure 4.152. Take a look at your cage. It actually is starting to resemble the shape of a horse's head. The Extrude Loop Tool is an excellent way to add to a simple cage, in a controlled way, to reshape it into something more complex. If you look at the cage in top or front view it looks a bit skinny. We can fix that very quickly.

In the front view, use the **Symmetry Plane Tool** to drag out a line along the Y axis. In the top view, click on the back left corner of the cage. This will select the back left edge of the cage. Hold down the x key and drag the edge to the left. Keep dragging until the width of the back loop is the same as the image of the Knight's head in the front view. In the iso view, select the front three edges

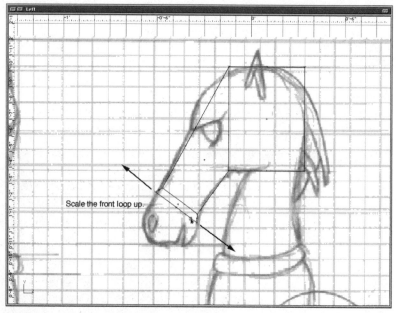

Scale the front loop up.

FIGURE *Scale the group to the height of the nose.*
4.151

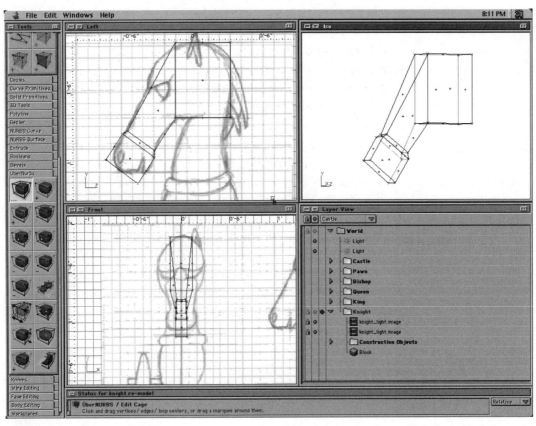

of the nose on the left side. In the front view, hold down the x key and drag them to the left until the nose matches the width of the image in the front view, as shown in Figure 4.153.

STEP TWO: MODELING THE NOSE AND MOUTH

One of the biggest keys to creating a complex organic object with ÜberNurbs is to concentrate on the specific areas of detail one at a time. We're going to start by adding the details that form the mouth/nose area. Use the **Visibility Tool** to hide all of the cage except the front four loops that form the nose.

What we need to do is subdivide these simple loops to form a more complex cage that we can push and pull into the shape of the mouth. The easiest way to accomplish this is to use the **Add Rib Tool** to essentially trace the details in the drawing. We'll start with the mouth and add six ribs.

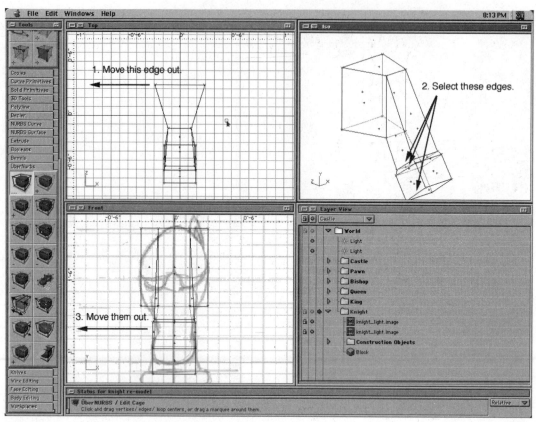

FIGURE *Drag to match the width of the background image.*
4.153

Select the Add Rib Tool and, beginning in the corner of the mouth, drag out a rib that follows the line of the upper lip. Drag out a second rib that traces the line of the bottom lip. Drag out a third rib that is parallel to the one you just created for the bottom lip, that is offset about one-fourth of a grid space. Now add a fourth rib just above the upper lip line that is parallel and about one-fourth grid space above. Add a fifth rib that is parallel and one-fourth of a grid space above the rib you just added. Finally, add a sixth rib that divides the upper portion of the cage just below the nose, as shown in Figure 4.154. We now have the nose divided up into edges we can work with to sculpt it, but we need to open the mouth up. To do this select the **Delete Edge Tool** and click on the two edges at the front of the cage that are connecting the upper and lower lips. This will leave you with an open mouth for the Knight (see Figure 4.155). If you make the surface visible, you will notice that a star pattern is

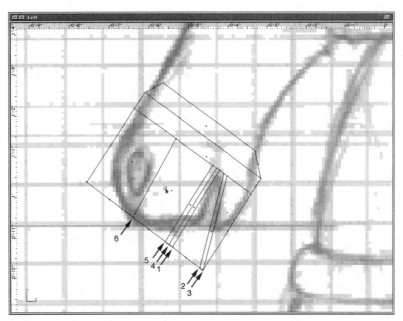

FIGURE *Add a sixth rib.*
4.154

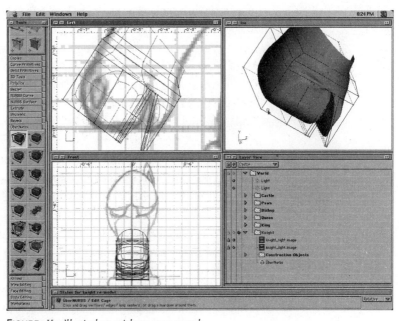

FIGURE *You'll wind up with an open mouth.*
4.155

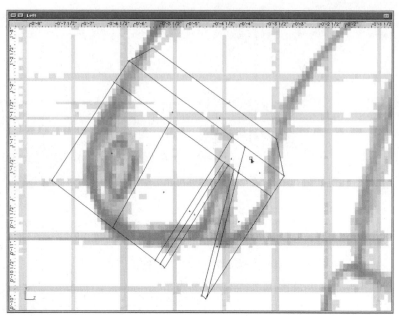

FIGURE *Add edges to get rid of artifacts.*
4.156

showing up just above the corner of the mouth. This happens because we have an edge with 6 CVs opposite of an edge that has only two. We can get rid of these artifacts by using the **Add Edge Tool** to add two edges that join the corner of the mouth to the long edge opposite of it, as shown in Figure 4.156.

Now we're going to use all of the edges we created to form the lips. In the left view, use the **Edit Cage Tool** to select the CVs on the front edge of the third loop up from the upper lip. Pull this edge upward on the Y axis and backward on the Z axis. Once this is done hold down the s key and scale this edge inward about 1 grid space (see Figure 4.157). This will create the "dent" where the lip begins to puff out. Notice also, as you move this edge, that the edges below and above are not affected. The extra edges we added are going to give us more control over the surface as we create the puffed out lip. In the left view, select the front CVs on the second (middle) loop of the upper lip, pull it forward on the Z axis, and scale it larger by a tiny bit, as shown in Figure 4.158. This will give the upper lip a little "puff." If you want more puff in the lip, you can scale the front edge up more. If you just want thicker lips, you can move the front edge up a bit more. You can control the shape and thickness of the upper lip by simply translating and scaling these two edges. This is one of the key concepts to creating facial features of any kind. By creating a series of ribs that subdivide a

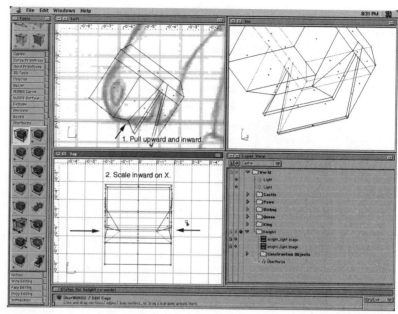

FIGURE *Scale and move the edge.*
4.157

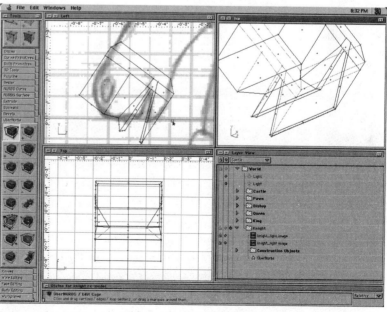

FIGURE *Give the lip some puffiness.*
4.158

shape, you can pull edges around in a controlled fashion. If you want a "puffy" shape like a lip, nose, or eyebrow you have to create two extra ribs (or edges) to hold part of the mesh back while you pull the detail out into space.

The lower lip is created the same way the upper lip was. You notice that we only added 2 ribs to this area earlier. This is because the corner of the cage at the bottom of the lip will form a natural edge that we can manipulate. Start shaping the lower lip in the left view by clicking on the CVs on the front of the second rib (the bottommost edge at the front of the cage). Drag these CVs back until they line up with the point at which the lower lip in the drawing begins to curve back. Scale this edge inward about 2 grid spaces, as shown in Figure 4.159. Now select the front CV of the lower corner of the lip and move it backward until it is aligned with the drawing. Scale this edge outward about half of a grid space, as shown in Figure 4.160. Finally, select the top front edge of the lower lip and drag it backward until it's aligned with the top of the lower lip in

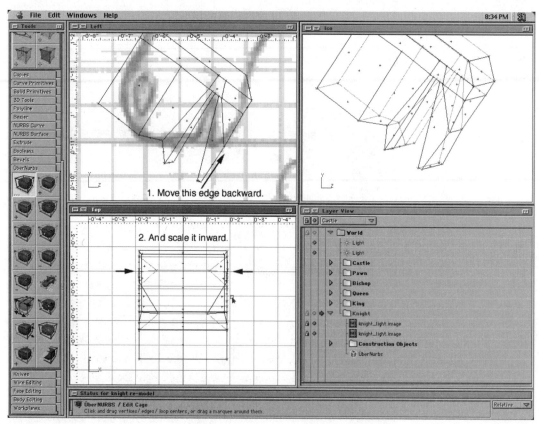

FIGURE *Scale the edge inward.*
4.159

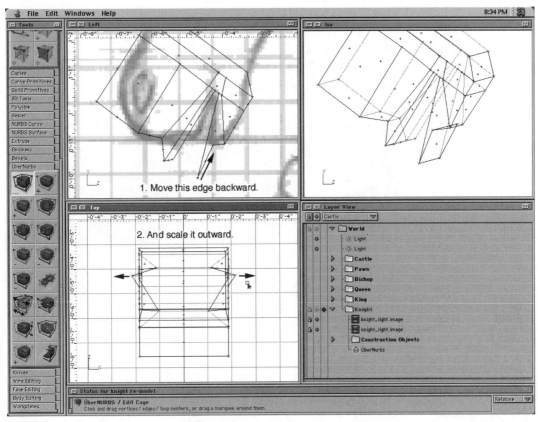

FIGURE *Moving back and scaling the corner of the lip.*
4.160

the drawing, and scale it down by about 1 grid space, as shown in Figure 4.161. Again, by pulling a middle edge outward and scaling it upward between two edges that are farther back and scaled smaller we've created a puffy lip.

To shape the nose, select the top front edge of the cage and move it backward until it meets the curve of the nose in the drawing. Scale this edge down by about 1 grid space to give the nose some taper (see Figure 4.162). We will have to add the nostrils one side at a time, so use the **Visibility Tool** to hide the left side of the model. Select the **Inner Border Tool** and click on the center of the loop that is surrounding the nostril at the top of the cage. This will add a second loop within this loop (a border), as shown in Figure 4.163. Now use the **Inner Border Tool** to add a second loop by clicking on the loop center of the border you just created. This will give you a loop within a loop. In the left view, select the loop center of the innermost loop with the **Edit Cage Tool** and drag

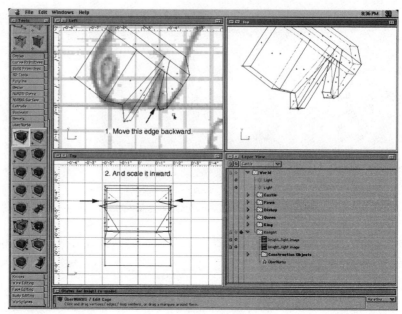

FIGURE *Adjusting the top front edge of the lower lip.*
4.161

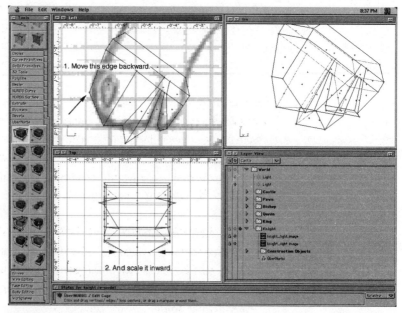

FIGURE *Taper the nose.*
4.162

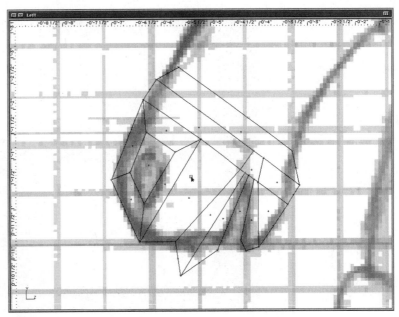

FIGURE *Add a loop to start the nostril.*
4.163

it inward on the X axis in the top view, as shown in Figure 4.164. Do the same thing on the opposite side of the cage. If you make your surface visible and shade it, you will see that we have nostrils and a completed mouth (see Figure 4.165). The first inner border acts as a containment that holds the mesh between it and the edges of the cage in place, while the second inner border is pulled to the inner part of the cage. In modeling the nose and mouth you have gained experience in a key concept to creating a detailed ÜberNurbs model. It's very easy to pull an edge and get a gradual smooth change in the surface. To create pronounced detail, however, you need to add edges around the area you're pulling on. It's often the case that you need to add two containing edges for every edge you pull out into a detail.

STEP THREE: MODELING THE EYES AND FOREHEAD

To model the head and eyes, we will use the same methodology of breaking up the cage with ribs, and then pushing and scaling those ribs to form the details. You may want to hide the nose, but I will keep it visible for reference as we work on the upper part of the cage.

Begin in the left view by using the **Add Rib Tool** to trace out the details around the eyes. First, add a rib that starts just in front of the cheek bone and

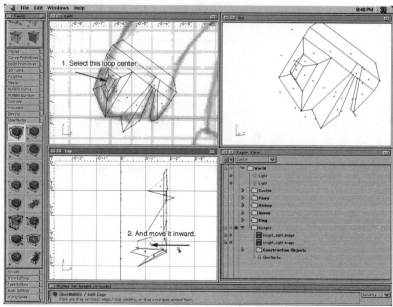

FIGURE *Drag to form the inside of the nostril.*
4.164

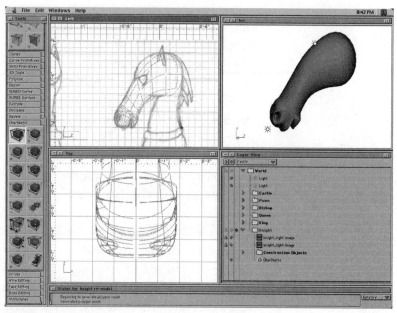

FIGURE *The completed nostril and mouth.*
4.165

extends up to the top of the snout just in front of the eyes. Second, add two ribs that divide the eye area into top and bottom. Finally, add a fourth rib that starts just above the corner of the eye and extends to the curve of the forehead. You won't be able to make these ribs an exact match at this point, you only need to get them close, as shown in Figure 4.166. Add a rib that divides the cage along the Y axis about 1 grid space behind the corner of the eye. If you shade the surface, you will notice that once again we have a star pattern showing up. This is coming from all of the extra CVs that are at the point where the corner of the eye joins the longer edge that runs down the face. To break this up, add a short horizontal rib that breaks up these two long vertical ribs at the corner of the eye, as shown in Figure 4.167. Use the **Edit Cage Tool** in the left view to move the front edges of the ribs you just added into alignment with the curves of the Knight's head in the drawing (see Figure 4.168).

We'll start shaping the features by adding a crease to the forehead. To do this, select the front edge that is at the curve of the forehead and scale it down by 50%, as shown in Figure 4.169. This will round off the front of the head. Now select the front edge of the loop that is between the top edge of the eye loop and the forehead loop you just scaled down. Scale this edge up about 50%, as shown in Figure 4.170. This will give the brow a nice bulge. We need

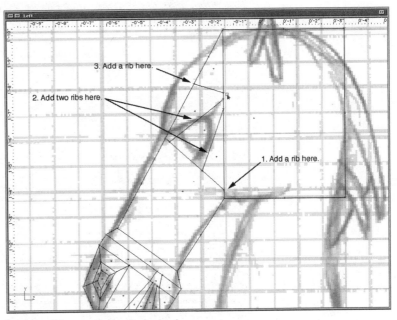

FIGURE *Add some ribs for the forehead.*
4.166

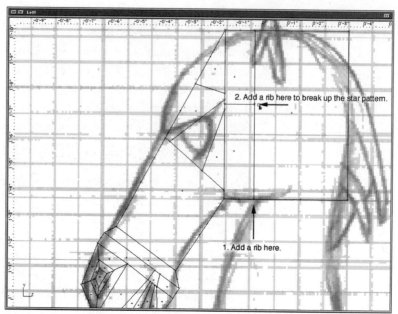

2. Add a rib here to break up the star pattern.

1. Add a rib here.

FIGURE *Add some ribs to get rid of the star pattern artifact.*
4.167

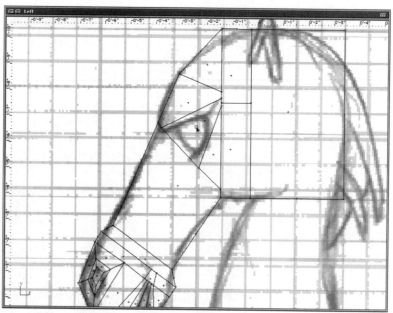

FIGURE *Move the front edges of the ribs to align.*
4.168

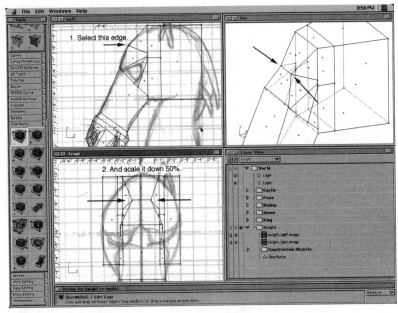

FIGURE *Scale to make the crease in the forehead.*
4.169

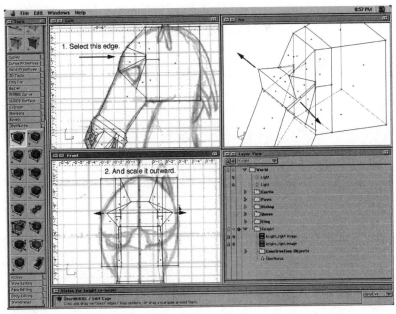

FIGURE *Give the brow a bulge.*
4.170

to add a vertical crease to the center of this forehead/brow mass. To do this, we have to break up the center of the 3 forehead loops with an edge. The easiest way to do this will be to draw these edges in the iso window. To insure that we create the edges exactly down the center of these loops, turn on **Center Edge Snapping** in the **Snapping Tools** palette. Orbit the cage in the iso view until you have a clear view of all three of the edges that make up the front of the forehead/brow area. Select the **Add Edge Tool** and click first on any part of the top edge, then click on any part of the middle edge. With edge to center snapping on this will create an edge in the middle of this loop. Now click on the ending CV of the edge you just added and click again anywhere on the front edge of the bottom loop, as shown in Figure 4.171. This will divide up the brow and give you a way to control the bulge in the center area. To define the crease, select the CV in the middle of the center edge and pull it back about 1 grid space on the Z axis, as shown in Figure 4.172 (the point where the first and second edges you just added meet). Now select the top CV of the first edge you added and move it downward and inward. Select the bottom CV of the second edge you added and pull it upward and inward. This will create a slight pinch in the brow that looks like a bow tie and gives it a more convincing shape (see Figure 4.173). This is the general technique you can use to also create any type of primate-style brow.

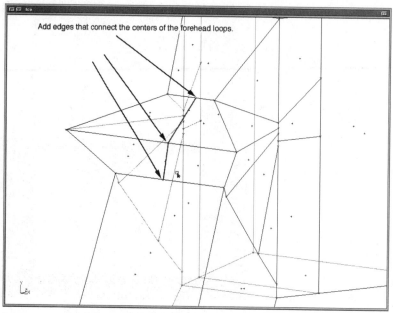

Add edges that connect the centers of the forehead loops.

FIGURE *Add an edge for more control.*
4.171

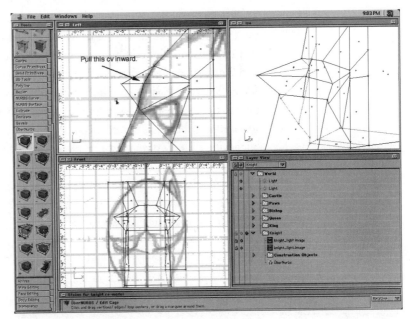

FIGURE *Pull back the CV in the middle of the center edge.*
4.172

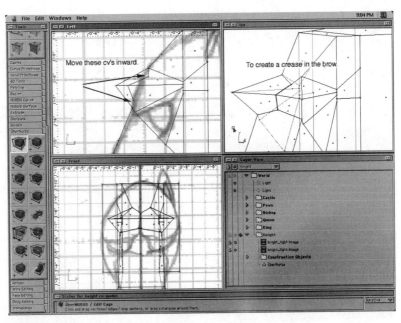

FIGURE *Creating a pinch in the browline.*
4.173

The Knight's eye socket is created in the exact same way we created the nostril. Hide the left side of the model with the **Visibility Tool**. Select the **Inner Border Tool** and click in the center of the loop that defines the eye. Click a second time with the Inner Border Tool on the loop center of the border you just added. With the **Edit Cage Tool**, click on the loop center of the innermost border and in the top view pull the loop inward on the X axis about 1 grid space into the head (see Figure 4.174), You can reshape the contour of the eye by moving the CVs of the first inner loop you added into different positions.

*You can break up an edge by using the **Add CV Tool**. If your eye loop doesn't have enough CVs to reshape it the way you would like, add CVs to the edges of the middle border to break it up into more edges.*

TIP

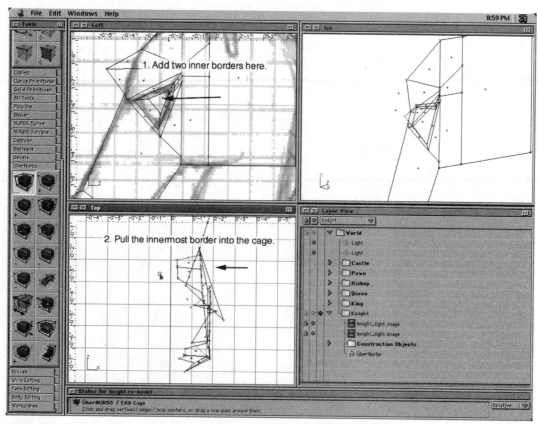

FIGURE *Creating the eyesocket by adjusting the inner border you just created.*
4.174

STEP FOUR: CREATING "ÜBEREYEBALLS"

We're going to create the eyes with ÜberNurbs objects. The advantage to using ÜberNurbs objects versus simple spheres is that you can shape an ÜberNurb object into the exact eye curvature you want.

Start by double-clicking to make the ÜberNurbs surface for the head. Lock the head in the Layer view so you don't accidentally click on it. In the left view, add a simple block that is a little taller and a little wider than the eye socket.

Keep your iso view shaded so you can see the interaction of the eye with the head mesh.

TIP

Rotate the block so it's at the same angle as the eye, as shown in Figure 4.175. Click on the block with the ÜberNurbs **Edit Cage Tool** and reshape it by pulling the back CVs outward to give the eye more bulge in the back. Work

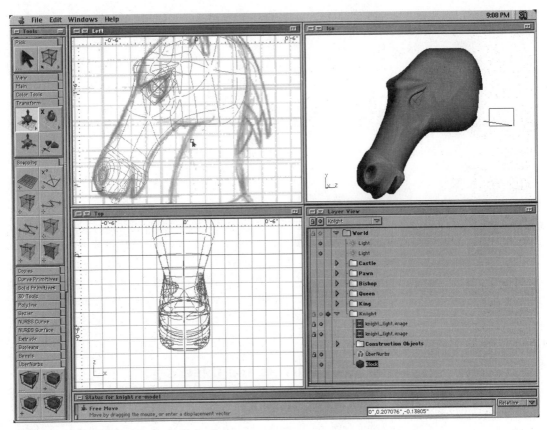

FIGURE *Creating and rotating the block for the eye.*
4.175

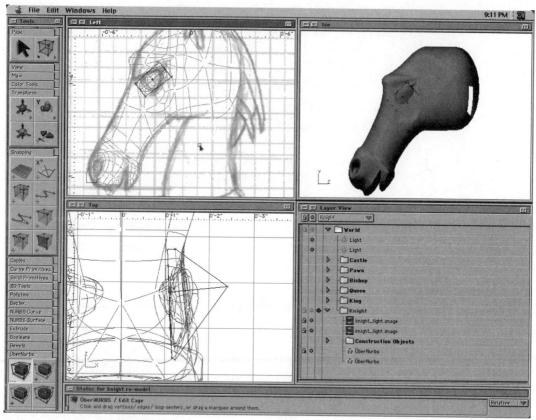

FIGURE *Adjust the eyeball to get a natural protrusion from the socket.*
4.176

with the cage until it fits the eye socket the way you want it to. You don't need to get the back part of the eyeball to match the inner part of the eye socket, you just want a natural looking protrusion out of the eye socket (see Figure 4.176). Once you have the eyeball the way you like it, double-click to create the surface and use the **Symmetry Duplicate Tool** create a copy on the other side of the head. When you're done, hide the eyeballs, unlock the head, and click on it with the ÜberNurbs Edit Cage Tool.

STEP FIVE: PUFFING THE CHEEKS

To create the puffy cheeks of a horse, we need to add a rib that will break up the top part of the cheek. In the left view, add a horizontal rib just below the corner of the eye that joins the two vertical ribs, as shown in Figure 4.177. Select the left CV of the edge you just created and move it backward on the Z axis

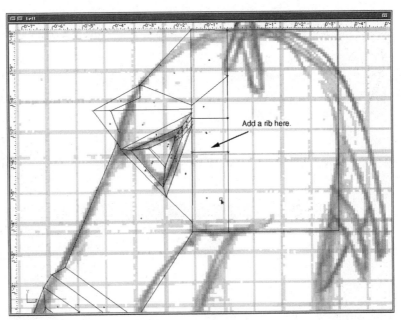

Add a rib here.

FIGURE *Add a rib for the cheek.*
4.177

about half a grid space. Select the right CV of the edge you just created and move it backward on Z as well. This will keep them from overlapping the snout in the scale operation we're about to do. Now select the edge of the rib you just added and scale it up by about 1 grid space. Keep your eye on the top view to see how far out these edges are going. This is what will add the puff to the cheeks (see Figure 4.178). Once you've scaled this edge up, select and move any CVs you need to bring the edges of the cage back into alignment with the drawing. By adding the small horizontal rib we were able to puff out the cheek without affecting the corner of the eye and the brow.

STEP SIX: ADDING AN EAR

To create the ears, we first need to add a rib to the top rear portion of the head to create a contained area for the ear. Select the **Add Rib Tool** and, in the left view, create a rib that connects the second vertical rib in the head with the top of the head. This will create a triangular loop that has 4 CVs around it (see Figure 4.179). Use the **Edit Cage Tool** to drag the 4 CVs that form the triangle into alignment with the shape of the ear in the drawing in the left view (see Figure 4.180). This mainly entails dragging the bottom CVs backward and dragging the top CVs toward each other.

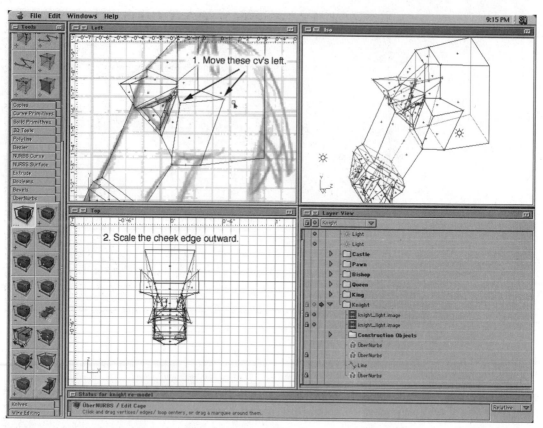

1. Move these cv's left.

2. Scale the cheek edge outward.

FIGURE *Scale the edge of the rib you just created to pull the cheeks out.*
4.178

To create an ear, we first have to create a base and then an earlobe. Select the **Extrude Loop Tool** and orbit around the cage in the iso window until you have a clear view of the loop center for the loop surrounding the ear. Click on this loop center to push out a copy of the loop. Because the original loop sits at an angle, the copy will also be angled outward, as shown in Figure 4.181. Select the loop center on the end of the extruded loop and drag the entire loop inward toward the cage. The goal is to get this loop to be about one-fourth of a grid space away from the original from which it was extruded to act as the base of the ear (see Figure 4.182). Once you have the loop positioned, use the Extrude Loop Tool to extrude a second copy. This is the copy we will use to shape the earlobe. Select the loop center of the new loop and drag it inward on the X axis until it is about 1 grid space from the base loop. Select the top edge of this new loop in the iso window and move it upward on the Y axis in the left view. Scale

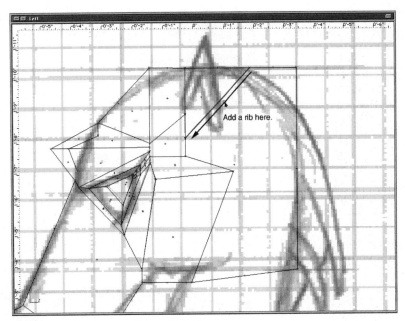

FIGURE   *Starting the ear with an added rib.*
4.179

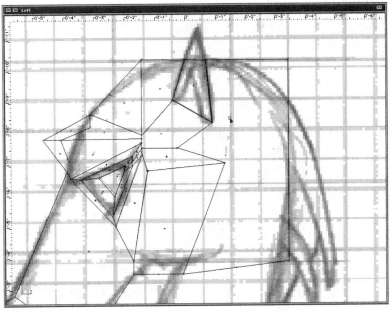

FIGURE   *Use the Edit Cage Tool to align the CVs with the sketch.*
4.180

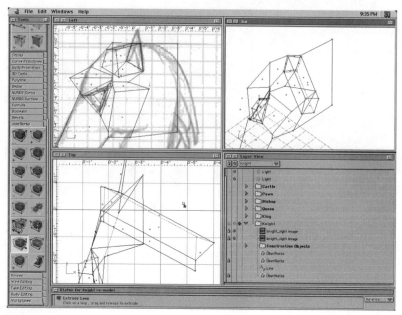

FIGURE *The extruded loop should be angled outward.*
4.181

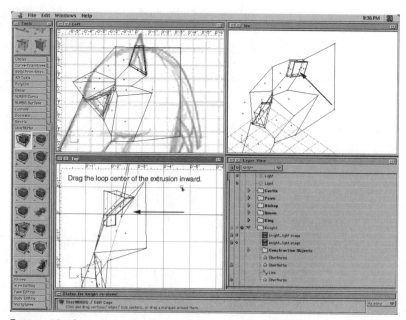

FIGURE *This forms the base of the ear.*
4.182

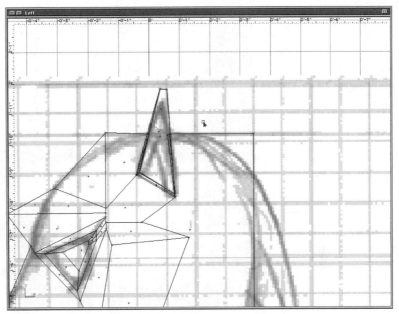

FIGURE *Scale the top loop to give the ear a point.*
4.183

the top edge down to give it a point (like a Mr. Spock ear) (see Figure 4.183). Creating an indentation in the ear is done the same way as for the nostrils and eyes. Select the Inner Border Tool and add an inner border to the pointy ear loop you just formed. Now select the bottom edge of the border you just inserted and drag it inward about one-fourth of a grid space in the top view, as shown in Figure 4.184. You now have one nice ear for the Knight: you will need to add another ear to the opposite side in the same manner. You can see how extruding the first loop and pulling it back created a nice smooth transition into the actual formation of the earlobe (see Figure 4.185).

STEP SEVEN: EXTRUDING THE NECK

To create the neck, orbit around the cage in the iso window until you have the bottom part of the head clearly visible. Use the **Extrude Loop Tool** to push out a loop from the bottom. Pull the bottom of this new loop down below the top of the collar in the drawing in the left view. Add a horizontal rib across the middle of the neck in the left view and select the edges of this new rib and pull them into alignment with the neck in the drawing. Orbit around the cage in the iso view and select the front edge of the middle rib, then **SHIFT + Click** on the back edge of the middle rib. In the front view, scale these ribs down until

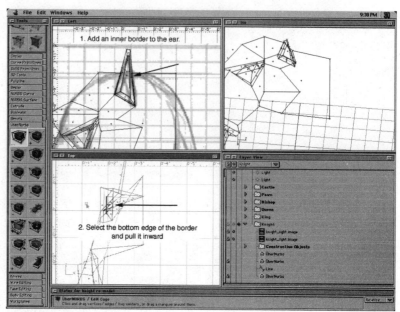

FIGURE *Create the inside of the ear.*
4.184

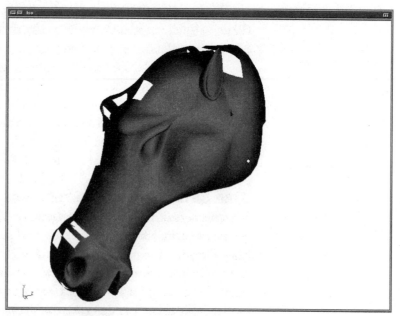

FIGURE *The finished ear.*
4.185

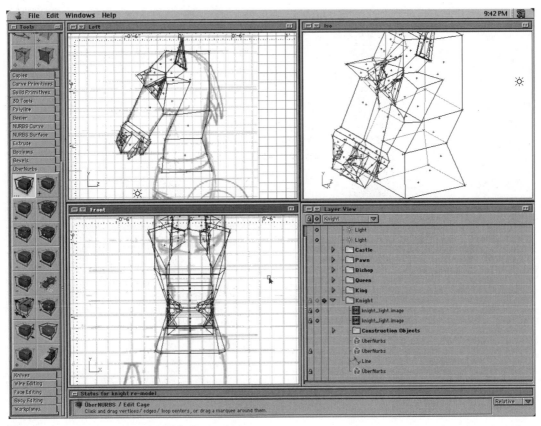

FIGURE *Scale the ribs down to fit the background image.*
4.186

the neck has the approximate thickness of the neck in the drawing, as shown in Figure 4.186.

STEP EIGHT: EXTRUDING THE MANE

The Knight's mane can be created in the same way we created the nose/snout from the simple block earlier. Use the **Visibility Tool** to hide all of the cage except for the rear portion. Switch the front view to back view and use the **Add Edge Tool** to add three edges to the back of the head, as shown in Figure 4.187. Select the **Extrude Loop Tool** and click on the loop center of the top loop. Select the center of this extruded loop and scale it down by at least 50%. Use the Extrude Loop Tool again to extrude a copy of the loop you just scaled. Scale the end of this copy down to a small point. Use the **Edit Cage Tool** in the left view to move the edges of the two extruded loops into the shape of the

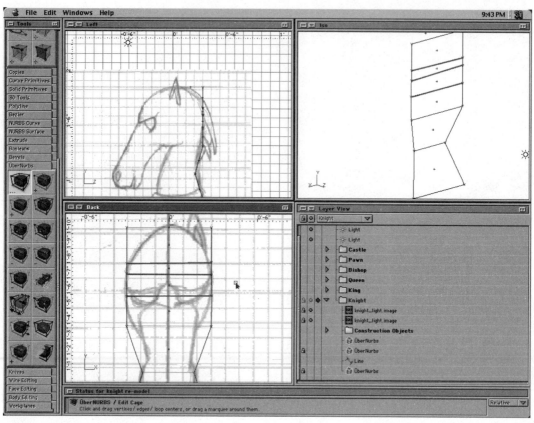

FIGURE *Add three edges to give a foundation to build the mane.*
4.187

mane, as shown in Figure 4.188. Now repeat this process on the third loop down from the top, as shown in Figure 4.189. You will need to hide at least part of the top mane piece to create the bottom one. This will complete the Knight's head and the ÜberNurbs portion of the exercise (see Figure 4.190).

Before you move on, take some time to examine the cage and work out any areas where star patterns might be showing up. When you're done, double-click to create the surface and lock it in the layer window.

STEP NINE: MODELING THE KNIGHT'S BASE

The base of the Knight looks like a clear candidate for the **Revolve Tool**. The only problem is the vents that are in the front surface. This is a case where the Boolean tools will prove very handy.

In the left view, use the **Bezier Create tool** to create a bezier curve that represents half of the pot-shaped base. Revolve this shape around to form a solid

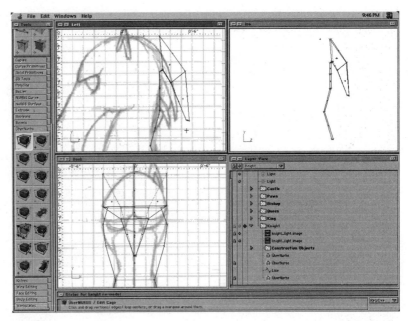

FIGURE   *Use the Edit Cage Tool to shape the mane.*
4.188

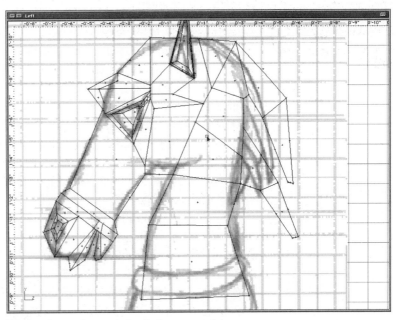

FIGURE   *Repeat the process for the lower part of the mane.*
4.189

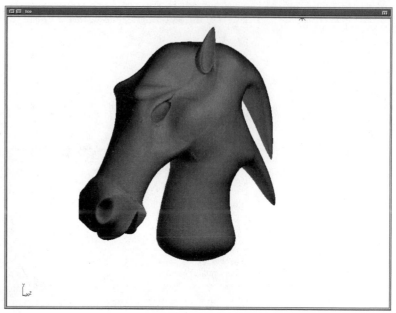

FIGURE *You've completed the head.*
4.190

body and use the **Linear Duplicate Tool** to create a copy that is scaled to .9. Use the move tools to center the scaled down pot copy inside of the original, as shown in Figure 4.191. Create and rotate 2 solid blocks that are about three-fourths as wide as the pot in the Front View and extend back at least two-thirds of the way into the pot in the Side View. Rotate the blocks so they angle downward into the pot, as shown in Figure 4.192. Use the **Boolean Subtract Tool** to subtract the two blocks from the outer (original) pot revolve. This will cut two vents into the surface. Because we have a smaller version of the pot on the inside, we keep the rounded shape on the inside of the vents, as shown in Figure 4.193. If you keep the smaller copy of the pot as a separate object (rather than Boolean unioning it), you can give it a different surface in ElectricImage to make it stand out more.

To create the collar for the pot, we need to extract a wire from the top and extrude a circle along this path. Orbit the pot in iso view until you have a good clear view of the top face. Click on the edge of this face with the **Convert Loop to Wire Tool**. This will extract a circular wire that is an exact copy of the loop that contains the top face of the pot. To see this wire, you will have to hide the pot. Create a circle in the left view that has the same width as the collar in the drawing. Use the **Sweep Tool** to extrude the circle around the extracted wire to create the collar, as shown in Figure 4.194.

FIGURE **4.191** *Make a copy of the base and scale it down.*

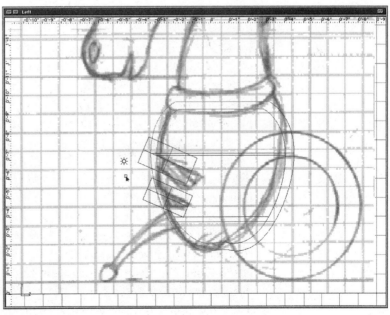

FIGURE **4.192** *Rotate the blocks we'll use for the Boolean operation.*

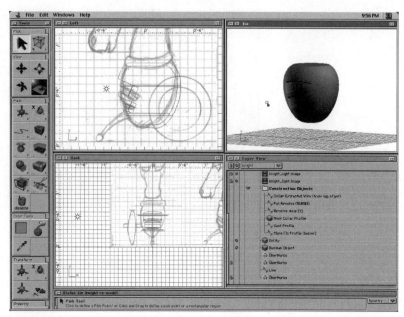

FIGURE 4.193 *The inner copy of the base we created will show through the holes we just booleaned out.*

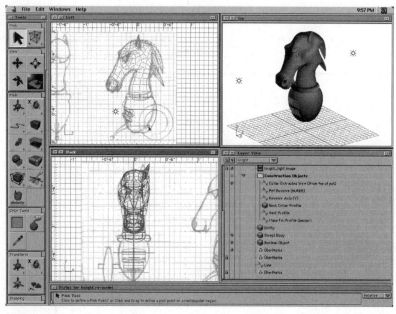

FIGURE 4.194 *Use the sweep tool to create the collar.*

The final pieces of this model should be familiar to you. The wheels are from the Castle and the front leg is from the Bishop. You can easily create copies of these items and scale them to fit the Knight model.

Keep the Knight layer selected as the active layer and turn on the visibility for one of the Bishop's legs. Select the Bishop's leg and use the **Linear Duplicate Tool** to make a copy in place. Because the Knight layer is selected as the active layer, the copy will automatically be created in the Knight folder. Turn off visibility for the Bishop and turn visibility on for the Castle's wheels and axle. Select these items and duplicate them in place. Again, the copies will be moved into the Knight layer. Move the wheels and axle back into place and you're finished with the model (see Figure 4.195).

—Chris Weyers

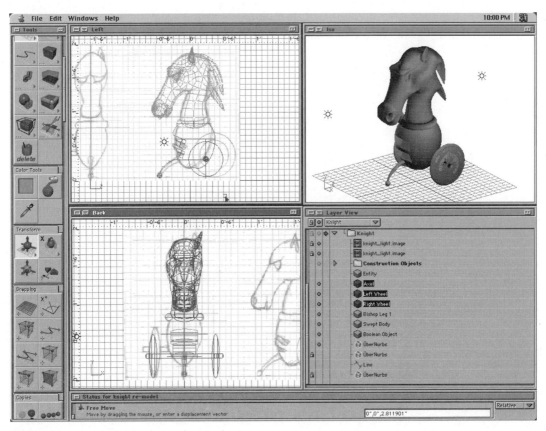

FIGURE *Move the wheels into place and you're done!*
4.195

Exporting Our Finished Models

Because we've modeled each chess piece in a layer, we will be able to export each one as a separate grouped hierarchy. However, we don't want to export all of the construction objects we used. We can set an export option to take care of this. Make all of your models visible and position them in modeler the way you would like them to be when they import into ElectricImage. Turn the Visibility off for all of the construction objects' layers. From the **Edit** menu, choose **System Preferences** and select the **Export** tab. Choose the **Layers as Groups** export option and the **Visible Only** option. This will export each layer as a separate linked group and ignore the construction object layers since they aren't visible.

—Chris Weyers

5 Material, Shader, and Mapping Tips

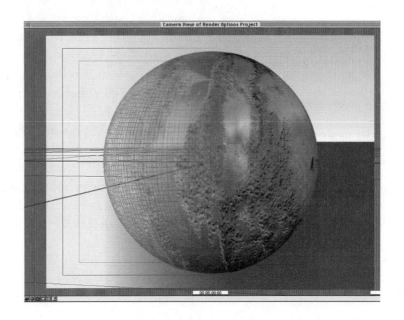

Much of the success of good material creation and group shading comes from just knowing a few good tricks. Nothing major, just little tidbits of info that make you look at things differently, streamline your workflow, and just genuinely make things look better. The following are some neat and tidy tricks that will make your material, texture map, and shading creation go much further.

Study the Real World

Reality is never as it seems—or rather, it's exactly as it seems—but we seldomly have any idea what it really looks like based on memory. What kind of image comes to mind when you think of a rock? Now keeping the rock in mind, tell me if it's dirty or clean. Does it have veins running through it or spots of color? Are there crystallized formations embedded in the rock that glitter as your roll it around? Exactly what kind of rock do you have there? If it's clean, why is it clean? Did it take a bath? If it's clean, maybe it's not a rock at all. Maybe it's just a poor dull little virtual rock.

My point? Well, currently it has very little to do with rocks. My point is that you should look at everything you come in contact with and try to translate every aspect of the surface of that rock into material channel settings, texture maps, and shaders. I realize you're probably growing tired of reading about how you should look at the real world when trying to create your own 3D world, but this is one of those very important points that deserves to be run into the ground.

Forget about rocks for a moment. When you think of the texture to use for a model of a VCR, take a look at your own VCR. You might notice things that you wouldn't have necessarily considered in the creation of your material. If you're like me, you probably have about a quarter of an inch of dust on the top and buttons of your VCR. There are most likely a number of areas that are free of dust due to fingerprints. There might even be scratches on the screen. Most likely, none of these would have been considered when you were putting your materials and maps together to shade your 3D VCR. Of course, you might not want to include all of these things for a product shot (marketing people don't usually want consumers to realize that their products will ever need to be dusted), but if you're creating the studio of a grubby 3D artist, such as myself, you'd most likely want all of this extra stuff.

So next time you're out and about, really take a look at the surfaces of things. Notice how parts of the same surface might be reflective while others are dull. Notice how there may be smudges or scratches. Life is full of imperfections, so unless you're trying to create a pristine environment, a little bit of grunge goes a long way.

Add Complexity

As you may have assumed from the above tip, the key to creating realistic materials is to add lots of detail. You can do this as you paint your texture map, or you can do something as simple as popping a Clouds shader (or other shader) into your Diffuse channel and setting the RGB option to "As Value." This will add some good detail to the surface of your objects without a whole bunch of added work. This technique can even make a regular basic color in the Diffuse channel look much better.

Most materials you create should also have at least some form of Bump, Diffuse (of course), and Specular setting. There are exceptions to this rule but very few objects in the real world are perfectly smooth and most have some sort of specular highlights. Everything has color, too. Even very clear glass will have some color tint to it. All of these may be subtle but they are there.

Learn by Example

One of the best ways to learn what combinations of values and channels make the most realistic materials is to dissect materials created by others. Any time you find a material that you really like, take a run through the channels and see how things are put together and what settings are used (see Figure 5.1). Play around with the material and change the settings a little to experiment with the differences. Only alter a copy of the material though, you don't want to destroy your point of reference. Also, only change one setting at a time—it's easier to keep track of how the changes you make affect the overall look if you're only changing one of them at a time. You will find several materials on the CD-ROM for this book that are free for the taking and you can also find several materials on the web. Gord Lacey's EI Resources site (www.eiresources.com) has a great collection of materials for your perusal.

Disable Rendering Options

Disable rendering options to test render your particular material channels. When you're editing a material such as the one in Figure 5.2, it may be difficult to see the changes made to individual channels. But by turning off rendering options that you're not using, as in Figure 5.3, only the material channel that you're working on shows up, such as the Diffuse in Figure 5.4. This gets a little more complex when previewing channels other than the

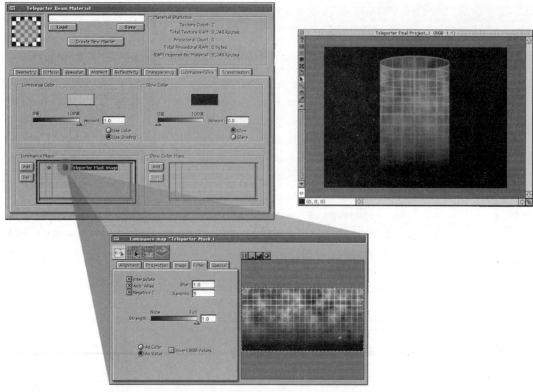

FIGURE *Dissecting the materials of others is a great way to learn.*
5.1

FIGURE *Rendering a complex material may create a little havoc when trying to preview*
5.2 *specific channels.*

FIGURE
5.3
Turning off the render options that you're not using for testing can simplify things quite a bit.

FIGURE *A render of the Diffuse channel only.*
5.4

Diffuse channel because you can't just disable the Diffuse channel or you'll get a big black object in your render. So while keeping the Diffuse render option checked, simply turn off any texture maps you may have in the Diffuse map list. Figure 5.5 is the setup you'd use to get the Specular-only render in Figure 5.6, and the same can be done to preview any other channel like the Bump settings as shown in Figure 5.7.

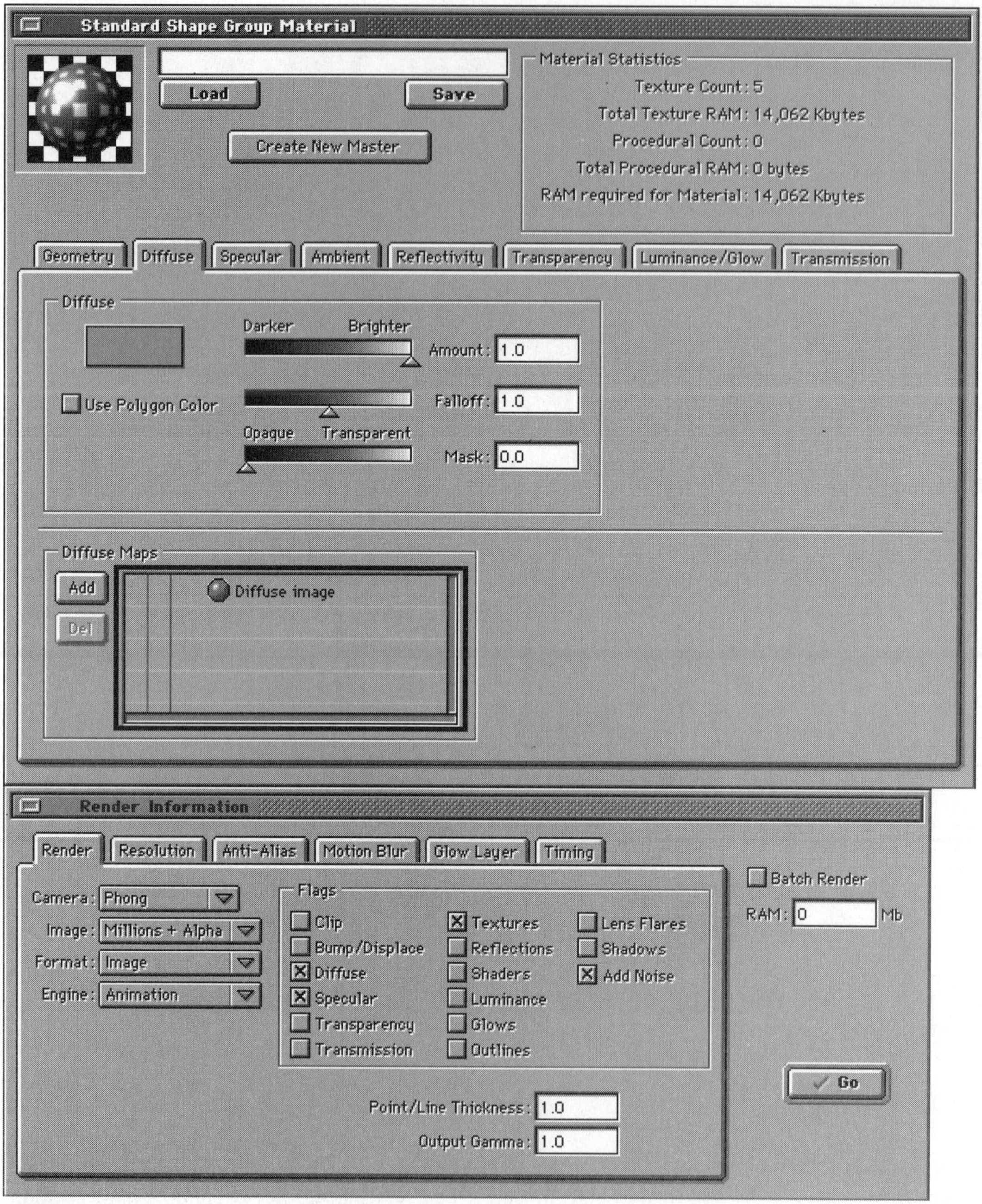

Standard Shape Group Material

Load　　　　Save

Create New Master

Material Statistics
Texture Count : 5
Total Texture RAM : 14,062 Kbytes
Procedural Count : 0
Total Procedural RAM : 0 bytes
RAM required for Material : 14,062 Kbytes

Geometry | Diffuse | Specular | Ambient | Reflectivity | Transparency | Luminance/Glow | Transmission

Diffuse

Darker　　Brighter
Amount : 1.0

☐ Use Polygon Color
Falloff : 1.0

Opaque　Transparent
Mask : 0.0

Diffuse Maps

Add
Del

◯ Diffuse image

Render Information

Render | Resolution | Anti-Alias | Motion Blur | Glow Layer | Timing

Camera : Phong ▼
Image : Millions + Alpha ▼
Format : Image ▼
Engine : Animation ▼

Flags
☐ Clip
☐ Bump/Displace
☒ Diffuse
☒ Specular
☐ Transparency
☐ Transmission

☒ Textures
☐ Reflections
☐ Shaders
☐ Luminance
☐ Glows
☐ Outlines

☐ Lens Flares
☐ Shadows
☒ Add Noise

☐ Batch Render
RAM : 0 Mb

Point/Line Thickness : 1.0
Output Gamma : 1.0

✓ Go

FIGURE *Instead of turning off the Diffuse option, simply disable the map . . .*
5.5

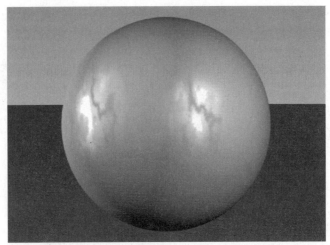

FIGURE   . . . *to get a render of the Specular channel.*
5.6

FIGURE   *Preview your bump map the same way.*
5.7

EI as a Texture Generator

You might not think of EI as a texture generator, but it really is a great one. As I mentioned in Chapter 2, EI's procedural shaders are very powerful for creating certain effects, but they are also a little limited in that you don't have as much control over Shaders as you do your texture maps. By the same token, it's often difficult to find texture maps that are exactly what you are looking for. So

FIGURE *Use EI and its shaders as a texture generator to create raw material for more*
5.8 *complex maps.*

what do you do when you need a floor that is partially Brick and partially Hex-Tile? Simple, you crack EI open, create a plane, map a shader or two to it, and render away. You can create a separate render for each texture that you need and then composite in Photoshop to get the final texture (see Figure 5.8). This turns EI into a quick and easy resource for base materials for texture maps which you can then use for your final project.

Layer Textures to Break up Monotony

One of the problems with 3D is that often there is a lack of randomization in the textures and shaders used, which can make a render look less realistic. You can build this randomization into your texture maps or you can layer shaders or combinations of shaders and texture maps to break things up. Figure 5.9 shows a Clouds shader composited with a BumpArray shader to give a dirty and worn look. In this example, the Clouds shader uses the **RGB as Value** option and a map strength of .26. Figure 5.10 shows a texture map that, when layered on top of a Bricks shader, produces the effect in Figure 5.11.

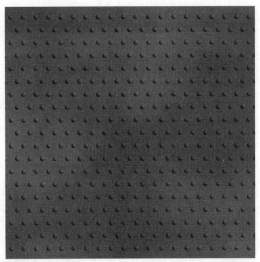

FIGURE *Layering a Clouds shader onto your object creates a nice weathered look.*
5.9

FIGURE *A texture map . . .*
5.10

FIGURE *. . . layered on top of a Bricks shader produces*
5.11 *a nice texture.*

Reflect Something

A common problem that people run into from time to time when first starting out in 3D is they assign a reflective property to an object but don't get the result they are looking for because of no or too few objects around the reflective object to create a believable reflection. In order for a reflective object to look reflective, it must reflect something. Figure 5.12 shows the difference a good

FIGURE *A good reflection can work wonders.*
5.12

reflection can make. The glass on the left has no reflection, whereas the glass on the right has a simple but effective reflection map applied.

As with many other things in EI, there are several ways to accomplish this. Basically, you can assign a reflection map, an auto environment, or mirror reflection. The reflection map takes a map and projects it onto the object at the level of reflectivity you specify. The automatic reflection features (mirror and environment) actually render the scene from the point of view of your object and then map the resulting render onto the object as if it were a normal reflection map.

If you're using a regular reflection map, you must make sure that enough of the reflected map is visible on the area of the rendered object to produce a pleasing effect. If using one of the automatic reflections, you must make sure there is something to reflect. Figure 5.13 is a sphere with a reflection value assigned but no map. There's no reflection at all, much less a convincing one. Figure 5.14 is the same object but with a nice Bryce render applied in the reflection maps list (see Figure 5.15). Figure 5.16 is the same object with the

FIGURE 5.13   *Assigning a Reflectivity level does nothing if you don't give the object something to reflect.*

FIGURE 5.14   *A Bryce reflection map shapes things up nicely.*

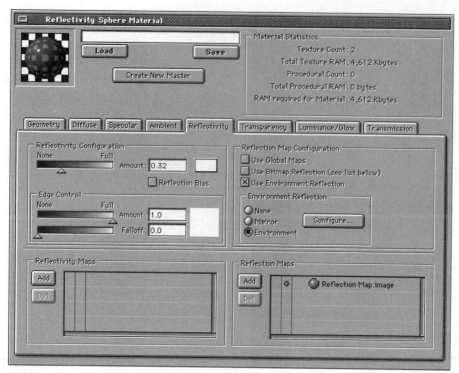

FIGURE
5.15
The map in the Reflection Maps list.

FIGURE
5.16
Environment mapping creates automatic reflections of objects surrounding the reflective object.

FIGURE *Enabling the Environment reflection.*
5.17

automatic **Environment** map feature enabled (see Figure 5.17) and several objects placed around it so that it has something to actually reflect. This image also has the **Backdrop** feature enabled, which gives it a faux sky to render as well. You can also use both options simultaneously to get a layered reflection effect as in Figure 5.18, but be careful with this one because instead of the surrounding objects being reflected first and then the reflection map, both are rendered and composited so you get this partially layered effect instead of a reflection that represents the complete surroundings.

Color in the Reflection Channel

There are very few objects in the world that are completely reflective. Most objects have reflections that overlay the regular color of the object. As an example, you can look at your computer monitor while it is off. It's reflective, but it's a very dark reflection because the monitor color is black. EI makes it easy to use the Diffuse color as the tint of your reflections. To do this, simply check the **Reflection Bias** checkbox in the **Reflectivity Configuration** section of your **Materials Reflectivity** channel. Sometimes, however, you

FIGURE 5.18 *Using Reflection maps along with your Environment map can create more complex effects.*

may want to tint your reflection with a different color. Not a problem, simply uncheck the Reflection Bias checkbox and click on the little color swatch right above it. You can then use the color in this box to tint your reflection. When a mirror-like reflection is what you're looking for, use a very light color and crank the reflectivity level up high.

Copying Maps and Colors

What do you do if you need to place maps of the same size in several different channels of a material yet retain the exact map placement so that the details of each map line up properly in each channel? Well, you could place and position your first map, write down all of the settings, and then reenter those settings for each subsequent map, but that's the long way around. The easy way is to set up your first map then select the map in the maps list, copy it, then paste it into each channel where you need the other maps to go. This is a pretty simple procedure. You select the map, choose **Copy** from the **Edit** menu, then go to the channel where you need to paste the map, click in the map list that you want to place it into and then choose **Paste** from the Edit menu. Repeat this for every other channel where you need to place your different maps. Once you're done,

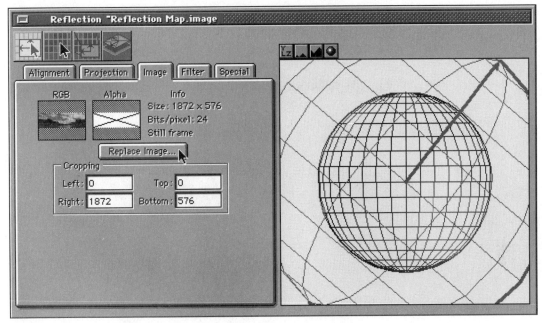

FIGURE *Replacing an image keeps all of your projection settings.*
5.19

go through each channel and double-click on the map you just pasted. When the **Texture Map Info Window** comes up, click on the **Image** tab and then click on the **Replace Image** button (see Figure 5.19). From here, you simply navigate to the map that you want in that channel and open it. All of the settings from the first map will remain but will be applied to the new map instead. A great timesaver.

A similar trick can be done for your various color swatches, only it's much easier. Once you get that perfect color, exit the color picker and then click and hold down on the color swatch. From here you can drag the color swatch into any other channel in your material. To do this, simply drag the swatch over the top of one of the other tabs. The tab will come forward and allow you to drop the color swatch into any existing color swatch in the channel.

Mapping and Deformations

If you're concerned about mapping an object that will be deformed, don't be. For the most part, maps will follow your model even through its various deformations. Figure 5.20 shows a character whose body was mapped using regular old Flat mapping. The textures will follow the group even through complex bone manipulation as shown in Figure 5.21.

FIGURE *Flat mapping was used to texture this character. © 1998 John W. Sledd*
5.20

Try Different Map Projections

As mentioned in Chapter 2, you most often want to use a **Map Type** that most closely represents the object you will be mapping. This doesn't always hold true though. For example, the bottom section of the box in Figure 5.22 might indicate that you need a **Cubic Map Type**; however, I wanted the map to wrap around the edges of the box, so I chose cylindrical mapping. I did this by first creating a map for two adjoining sides of the box (see Figure 5.23). I then mapped the texture to the box using Cylindrical Map Type and then rotated the map around the Y axis so that the beginning of the map started in the proper place (see Figure 5.24). Figure 5.25 shows the final render. It should be noted that you will get some distortion toward the center of each side of the box, but, in most cases, this will be minimal.

FIGURE *Even through bone deformation, the map knows where it's supposed to be. ©*
5.21 *1998 John W. Sledd*

FIGURE *A box in need of mapping.*
5.22

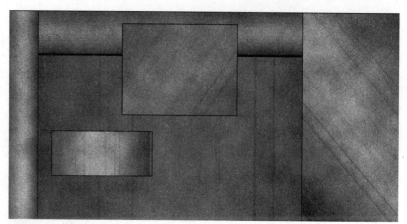

FIGURE
5.23 *A map is created for two adjoining sides of the box.*

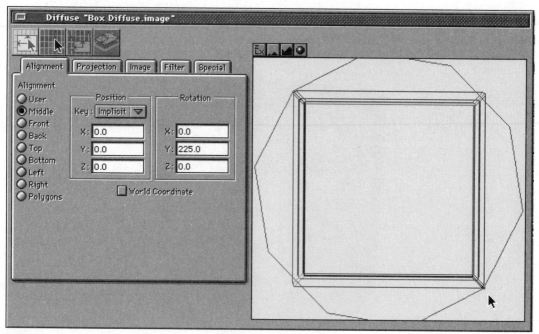

FIGURE
5.24 *The Cylindrical Map Type is chosen and the map is rotated.*

FIGURE *The final mapped box.*
5.25

6

Material, Shader, and Mapping Techniques

I n this chapter, we'll go over some things that will help you stay a little less frustrated and give a good bit of punch to your images. Fortunately, EI 2.9 came with the much requested feature of real-time texture previews. This makes placing your textures much easier than in previous versions, but there is still some good info to be had and there are still some tricks involved, so let's get started.

Mapping Formulas

First and foremost, let's cover some mapping formulas and trickery to make the most out of EI's various projections. Creating maps for cubic or planar objects is pretty straightforward. You simply create a map with the same dimensions as your object. For example, take a look at Figure 6.1. Here we have a regular old planar object we'll call a wall. You may or may not create your own planes to fit easy ratios like this one, which is 2:1, but if you don't, finding out the dimensions couldn't get much easier. Simply open the **Group Info Window** and click on the **Info** tab. The bottom set of numbers gives you your X, Y, and Z size, as shown in Figure 6.2. This particular plane is 400 units wide by 200 units tall, so when you create a texture map for it, use a map with a similar ratio, like 400 pixels by 200 pixels or 6 inches by 3 inches or whatever. Simple enough. If you had a cubic object, you'd get a Z value too, which you could then use to get the measurements for other sides of your group.

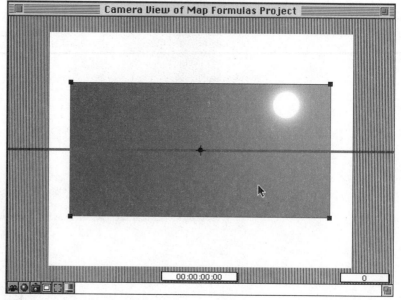

FIGURE *A plain ol' plane.*
6.1

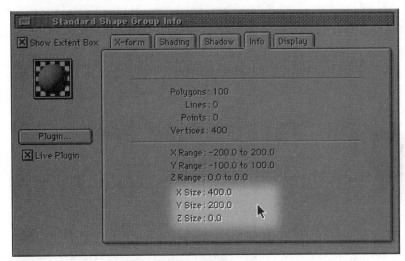

FIGURE *Getting the dimensions of your object.*
6.2

Spherical and cylindrical objects aren't quite as straightforward, but they don't take much more work. Spheres, like the above plane example, use a 2:1 ratio. If you were going to map a globe (and most of us 3D artists have to create a globe at one time or another), you'd want to use a map with a 2:1 ratio. But it doesn't end there. Figure 6.3 shows a sphere mapped with a nice grid

FIGURE *A sphere with a basic grid map applied.*
6.3

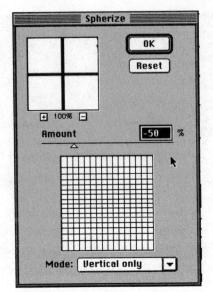

FIGURE *The Spherical Distort filter.*
6.4

map that fits our 2:1 requirement. This might work for most situations, but if you'll notice, the grid is distorted. It's stretched around the middle and scrunched at the top. Fixing it is a piece of cake. Open your sphere's map in Photoshop and under the **Filters>Distort** menu, choose **Spherize**. Set the **Amount** to –50%, the **Mode** to **Horizontal Only**, as shown in Figure 6.4, and apply the filter. What you'll wind up with is a map like the one shown in Figure 6.5. What this trick does in predistort your map so that when it gets stretched

01	02	03	04	05	06	07	08	09	10	11	12
13	14	15	16	17	18	19	20	21	22	23	24
25	26	27	28	29	30	31	32	33	34	35	36
37	38	39	40	41	42	43	44	45	46	47	48
49	50	51	52	53	54	55	56	57	58	59	60
61	62	63	64	65	66	67	68	69	70	71	72

FIGURE *The altered map to be applied to your sphere.*
6.5

FIGURE 6.6 *The sphere with the pre-distorted map.*

out, it's actually being unstretched and you wind up with a much more even projection, as shown in Figure 6.6. I've used this trick when mapping everything from perfect sphere objects, such as globes, to sphere-like objects such as heads.

Mapping cylinders requires that you remember a little bit of high school geometry. The key formula for correctly mapping a cylinder is πd. What this means is that you take the diameter of your cylinder and multiply it by 3.14. (Yes, I know that π isn't exactly 3.14, but it'll get you close enough for this task.) The figure you will get here will give you the width of your texture map, or the height, depending on how your cylinder is oriented. We'll say that our cylinder is oriented along the Y axis, so this formula will give us our texture map's width, which just also happens to be the perimeter of the circle part of our cylinder. Getting your texture map's height is as easy as getting a measurement for a plane. Just click on the Info tab in the cylinder's Group Info Window and look at the appropriate field. In our case, that would be the Y axis.

Oddly enough, we can get our diameter here, too, by taking either the X or Z measurement. So, if we need to map the cylinder whose Group Info Window you can see in Figure 6.7, we'd take the X measurement (400 units), multiply it by π to get a map width of 1256 units, and take a look at the X or Z field to get our map height of 350 units. You can then double, halve, or whatever to get an appropriate map—just make sure your ratio stays the same.

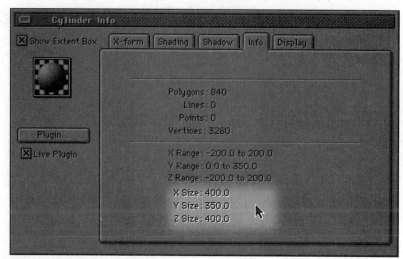

FIGURE *The statistics of a sample cylinder.*
6.7

Now, that you've learned the hard way for all of these, I'll show you an easier way. This tip applies to all of the projections and is something that I use with just about every single project I do. Say we're mapping the same cylinder we just talked about. The first thing you'd want to do is create a placeholder map—any old map will do. Ratio is completely irrelevant, but make it low res so it'll take less time to load. I've included one on the CD-ROM in case you're feeling lazy. Anyway, you'd open your cylinder's **Material Info Window**, go into the channel you want to place the map into, and add your placeholder map as shown in Figure 6.8.

The next step is to open the **Texture Info Window** (you can't get to the Texture Info Window without a map, which is why we made, and are using, our placeholder map). You'll notice that the map is perfectly sized and aligned to your object. Don't worry about your projection mode just yet. This isn't the map we want to use so we'll deal with that later.

Now click on the lower right-hand corner of your Texture Info Window and drag it to make the window as big as you can get it on your screen. It doesn't have to be huge, just a respectable size (see Figure 6.9). Now hold down the **Option** key and click and drag a nice tight marquee around your object to zoom in on it, but make sure it fits within your preview window, as shown in Figure 6.10. Note that I've chosen the Wireframe preview mode as opposed to a preview mode that shows my placeholder map because I often need to see the

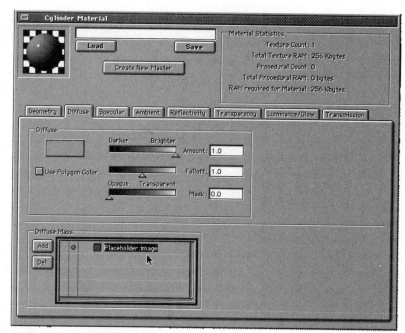

FIGURE *Add a placeholder map.*
6.8

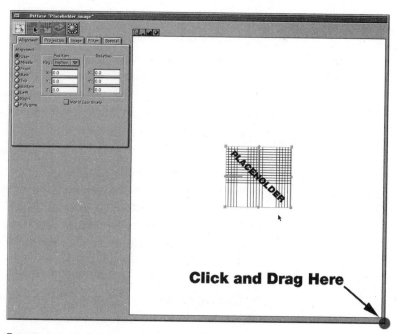

FIGURE *Resizing the texture preview.*
6.9

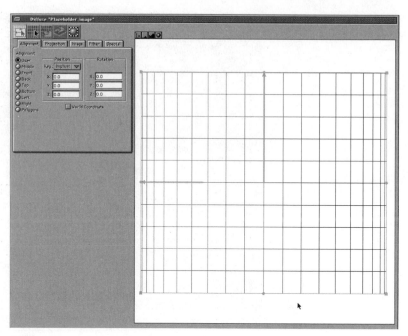

FIGURE *Zooming in on the object.*
6.10

details of my object's geometry for map detail placement. The placeholder map just gets in the way of this.

Finally, take a screen capture of the resulting image. I use a shareware capture utility called Flash-It™ to make my captures because I can crop the image as I capture it, but a regular system screencap works just as well since you can crop the final image in Photoshop. The big drawback of system screen captures is that you get a list of captures called Picture 1, Picture 2, etc. With Flash-It™, however, you can either capture to the clipboard and paste directly into Photoshop or you can make a capture and save it to disk with the appropriate name. So I'd recommend a utility like this but it's not absolutely necessary.

You then take this image into Photoshop. If you haven't done so in the actual capture process, you'll want to crop it based on the guidelines provided by the map's wireframe, as shown in Figure 6.11. Once you've done that, you have a basic template for your object.

If this were a plane or cube, you'd be pretty much done as the proportions will be fine. Since it's a cylinder, the height is fine but you still have to do the math to get the width. The good news is that you can get all the numbers you need for your calculations from Photoshop's **Canvas Size** dialogue box. You

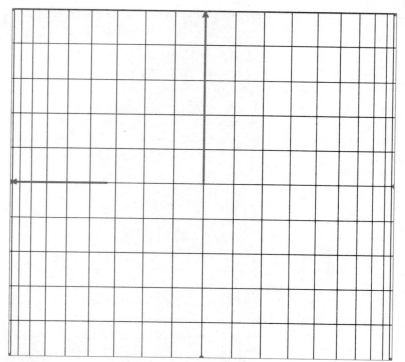

FIGURE   *Cropping the image based on the map's wireframe.*
6.11

can then add area to the map here, in the case of a cylinder or sphere, and work away. If it's a sphere, you'd simply increase the size of your canvas by 200%. You might want to rez the map up at this point using Photoshop's **Image Size** dialogue, since a screen cap probably won't give you the needed resolution, but since you're only using it as a template, it doesn't matter if it gets all funky during the resizing. You'll just throw the template away once your map is done.

Once you're done working on the map, export it as an Image file, go back into the appropriate **Texture Info Window** and click on the **Replace Image** button in the **Image** tab. Set up your placement and you're done. Render away.

Mapping Rotated Objects

A problem with importing objects into EI is that objects come in at the default 0,0,0 orientation regardless of how they were rotated in your modeling application. This isn't typically an issue, but when it comes to precise texture mapping, it can be problematic. Since the object is rotated, but EI thinks it has no

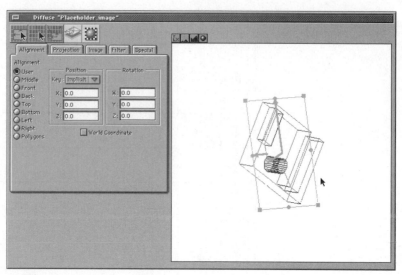

FIGURE 6.12 *The standard map alignment tools don't work very well with objects that were imported with rotational values.*

FIGURE 6.13 *The Select Polygons and Fit To Selected tools.*

rotation at all, the typical alignment controls don't work very well, as you can see in Figure 6.12. The great guys at ElectricImage recently gave us some tools to make it *less* problematic, though. They are called the **Select Polygons** and **Fit To Selected** buttons (see Figure 6.13).

Use the **Select Polygons** tool to select a few polygons on the face that you want to project your map onto. You don't have to select them all, you just need to select enough to give EI an idea of the outer boundaries of the model, as shown in Figure 6.14. Once you have your polys selected, click on the **Fit To Selected** button and your map snaps to *almost* the proper orientation, as shown in Figure 6.15.

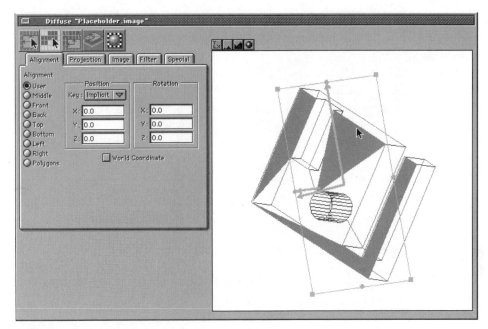

FIGURE *Select a few polygons to give EI the outer boundaries of your to-be-mapped face.*
6.14

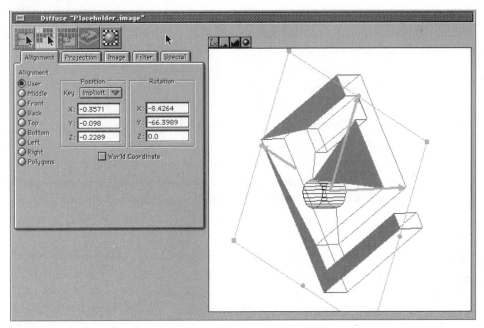

FIGURE *The map snaps to the selected polygons.*
6.15

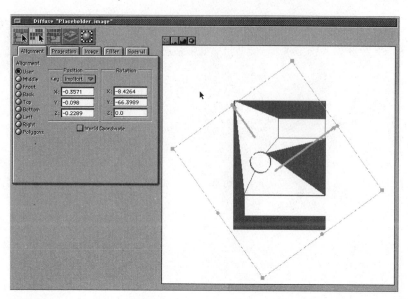

FIGURE *Rotate your view so that you're looking directly at the face you wish to map.*
6.16

As you can see, the map still doesn't know which way to be rotated on the Z axis, but that is easily enough fixed. Choose the **Orbit** view and hold down the command and spacebar keys and drag to orbit around your object. What you want to do is rotate your view until you are looking straight at the side of the object you wish to map. This can be tricky but it's far from impossible. Just use the edges of the object and the wireframe of the texture as your guide and rotate the object until it looks something like Figure 6.16. From here you can use your rotate and drag tools to rotate, position, and scale the map into the proper orientation, as shown in Figure 6.17. You can then take your screengrab for your map template. When you come back and replace the Placeholder map with the final map, EI will remember the orientation of the map and you'll be good to go.

Smoking with PowerParticles

Particles are used for all kinds of things from water to bubbles to smoke. What separates water from bubbles and bubbles from smoke is the material applied to the particle system. Figure 6.18 shows a sample of a PowerParticles emission with almost-default settings. This would be good for many things but not for smoke like we want to make here. Like I said, the difference is in the material, and this is a default material.

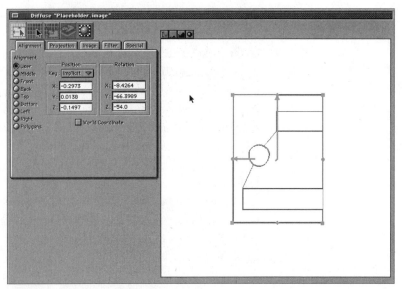

FIGURE *A perfectly aligned map.*
6.17

FIGURE *A sample particle emission.*
6.18

To make smoke, we need to adjust the surface of the particles. We're mainly going to focus on the transparency channel. This will be a very simplified version of what you can do with this technique, so feel free to play around with the settings.

STEP ONE

The first thing we want to do is give the particles a more smoky color. We can do this in either the plug-in interface or via the Material editor. I'm going to do it in the **Diffuse** tab of the Material Info Window to keep things simple. So let's open the particle system's Material Info Window. In case you haven't figured it out yet, there is a file on the CD for you to experiment with.

With our Material Info Window open, let's change the Diffuse color to a nice smoky gray. I don't want to make it too dark because we are rendering against a black background. Oh, and don't forget to uncheck the **Use Polygon Color** box.

The next thing we want to do is zero out the specularity. The reason you'd want to do this is because we're going to be using the transparency channel to cut away portions of the smoke. If we had specular value, we'd still get highlights on completely transparent areas of our geometry.

STEP TWO

Ambient and **Reflectivity** are fine just the way they are, so let's move on to **Transparency.** This is where the real effect comes into play. You'll want to add a **Clouds** shader in the **Transparency Maps** list. Open the Clouds shader and choose **Front Alignment** in the **Texture Info Window's Alignment** tab. Skip on over to the **Filter** tab and click on the **RGB As Value** button as shown in Figure 6.19.

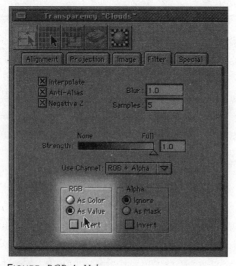

FIGURE *RGB As Value.*
6.19

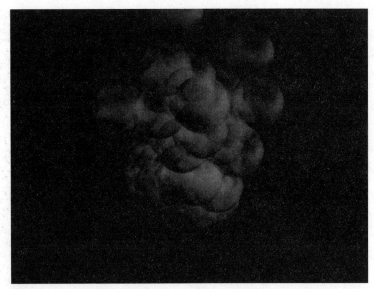

FIGURE *Almost smoke.*
6.20

Now go to the **Special** tab and click on the **Procedural** button. This will open the interface for the Clouds shader. Change the **Density** to **10** and the **Cloud Threshold** to **.5**. Finally, change the blue color to a solid black and close out the shader interface. Then close the Texture Info Window. If you rendered the scene now, you'd get something like Figure 6.20. Almost smoke but not quite. You can still see the spheres plainly, and last time I looked, smoke wasn't in the shape of perfect spheres. That's OK, we can fix this.

Step Three

Hop on over to the **Edge Characteristics** portion of your **Transparency** channel and change the **Amount** to **1.0**, the **FallOff** to **1.5**, and click on the **Transparent** radio button as shown in Figure 6.21.

And that's it. Render the image and you should have some pretty decent-looking smoke (see Figure 6.22).

Building a Chain Link Fence Using Clip Mapping

In this tutorial, we're going to be using pretty much the same technique shown in the above smoke tutorial, but we're going to use **Clip Mapping** instead of Transparency Mapping. The big advantage to using Clip Mapping over Transparency is, unlike Transparency, the holes created by Clip Mapping will let light through so the non-clipped areas will cast shadows.

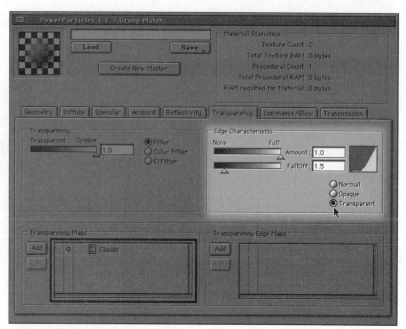

FIGURE *Setting the Edge Density.*
6.21

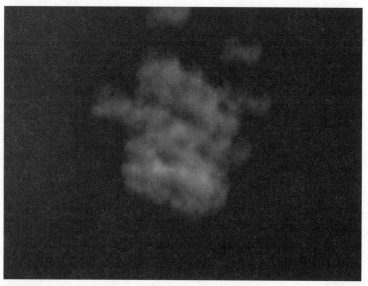

FIGURE *And here's our smoke.*
6.22

FIGURE   *These maps are all we need to "model" a chainlink fence using Clip Mapping.*
6.23

Clip Mapping has many uses, but for this particular tutorial, we're going to create a chainlink fence using the images in Figure 6.23. I created this map using a great program called TextureScape. It was originally made by Specular but then killed off shortly after MetaTools (now MetaCreations) bought the company.

The top map in this sample is the RGB channel of our Chain Link Fence.image file, which we'll be using for our bump map. The bottom map is the alpha channel of the file that we will be using for our clipping map.

FIGURE *Our starting fence.*
6.24

STEP ONE

Figure 6.24 shows our starting fence. Apart from the posts, it doesn't look much like a chainlink fence at all. We can fix that with the maps I just showed you. Let's begin by selecting the Fence object and adding the CHAIN LINK FENCE.IMAGE file into the **Clipping Maps** list of the **Geometry** tab in the Material Info Window, as shown in Figure 6.25. Now open the map's Texture Info Window and you'll see that it's stretched out to fit the fence. We don't want to do this, so let's enter some scaling values in the Texture Info Window's **Projection** tab. Make them **X = .001**, **Y = .001**, and **Z = .001**. Also change the **Tiling** to Repeat on both axes. This image is tilable so it'll work fine (see Figure 6.26).

Once we have this looking right, we can set up the clipping map. In the **Filter** tab choose **Use Channel: Alpha Only**, since we don't want the RGB channel here. We'll save that for the bump channel.

In the **Special** tab, enter a value of **1.0** for the **Clip Factor** and close out the Texture Info Window.

STEP TWO

Now that you have everything set up for the Clipping Map, select it in the Clipping Maps list and choose **Copy** from the **Edit** menu. Click in the **Bump/Displacement Maps** list and select **Paste** from the Edit menu. This makes an exact copy of the map, placement coordinates and all, in the Bump/Displacement Maps list. Now all you have to do is jump over to the **Filter** tab and choose **Use Channel: RGB Only.** And you're all set.

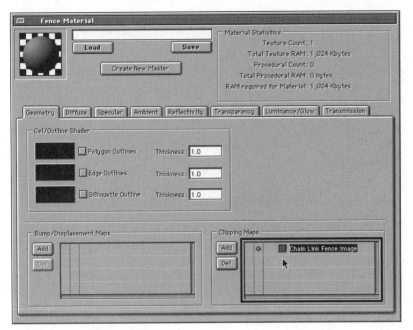

FIGURE *Add the Clipping Map.*
6.25

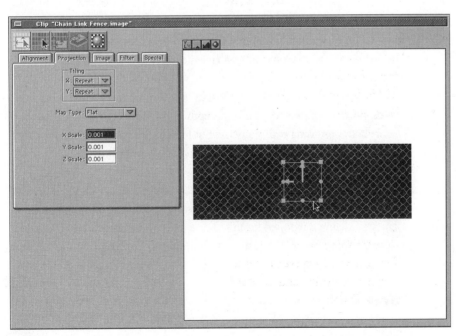

FIGURE *Set the map to repeat on both axes.*
6.26

FIGURE *The final fence.*
6.27

Figure 6.27 shows our nice chain link fence in all it's shadow-casting glory. Feel free to experiment with this quite a bit. The fence could use a good materials workover. You'd be surprised what a nice dirty map or shader can do in the Diffuse channel.

One point of caution: this clip mapping trick only really holds up at a distance, since the geometry has no real depth. If you want a closeup, angled shot, you're better off using real geometry. But for a background fence in your next architectural animation marvel, this technique will work fine.

Sun Project

Here we're going to create a stylized sun with flares licking out into space. No fancy modeling is required for this. There really isn't even much in the way of fancy mapping required. It just needs to be precise mapping, and most of that is done by the computer.

STEP ONE

Start this tutorial by opening the SUN W/ GLOW PROJECT on the CD. I've set most of this up for you so we can get to the nitty gritty a bit sooner, but let me explain what we have here. For starters, if you look at your Project Window, you'll see three objects, two spheres and a plane, and these three objects intersect at the middle. For this effect, the inner and outer spheres will be the actual sun and the plane will become our solar flares. If you rendered this thing as is, you'd just get a big bright glowing square with a sphere in the middle. I've set up all of the other material attributes so we'll only have to worry about the mapping. Be sure to run through the tabs to get acquainted with how the different material channels are set up, but it's pretty straightforward. Also make a note of the fact that I've set a glow set up for you with the plane as our glow object. This will give our flares a nice bright quality.

STEP TWO

Now the first goal here is to turn the flat plane into animated solar flares. So turn off the inner and outer spheres. Open the Plane's Material Info Window and head on over to the **Luminance/Glow** tab. We're going to use a Marble shader for the flares so go ahead and add one to the **Luminance Maps** list. Open the Marble shader's Texture Info Window, click on the **Filter** tab, and click on the **RGB As Value** button. Now click on the **Special** tab and then click on the **Procedural** button. This will get us into the Marble shader's interface.

Change your values to those shown in Figure 6.28 and click OK. Now move your time thumb to the 3.0-second mark and change the settings to those shown in Figure 6.29. This will give us our outward animation of the flares. If you render the scene now, you should get something like Figure 6.30.

Since most suns aren't square, the next thing we want to do is cap off the edges of the flares so they are circular and fade at the end of their lifetime. We do this by using the map shown in Figure 6.31. This is a simple enough con-

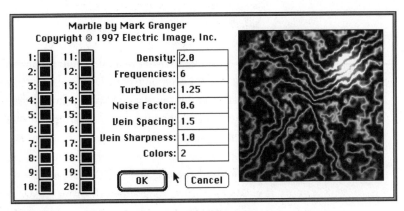

FIGURE *Your marble shader settings at time 0.0.*
6.28

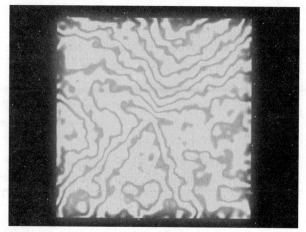

FIGURE *Your marble shader settings at time 3.0.*
6.29

FIGURE *Our initial render.*
6.30

cept. By using this map as a mask for our luminance, the flares are at 100% luminance at the beginning of their life and then fade out toward the edges of the circular map where it fades to black. So add the map called SUN OUTER MASK IMAGE to your **Luminance Maps** list and open its Texture Info Window. From here you'll want to go to the **Filter** tab and click on the **As Value** button. Render your image again and you should see that our marble pattern is now in the shape of a circle. The square is still visible but that's because of the glow applied to it. To get rid of that square glow and to sharpen up our flares, you'll want to copy the maps in our Luminance Maps list and then paste them into the **Glow Maps** list. This couldn't get much easier. Just shift-select the

FIGURE   *This is the map we'll use as a mask to nip off the square edges of our flare plane.*
6.31

maps in the Luminance Map list and select **Copy**, then click in the Glow Maps list and paste. This will copy both maps into the Glow Maps list with all of their current settings (animation included), which is exactly what we want. If you render your image now, you should begin to see the workings of our flares (see Figure 6.32).

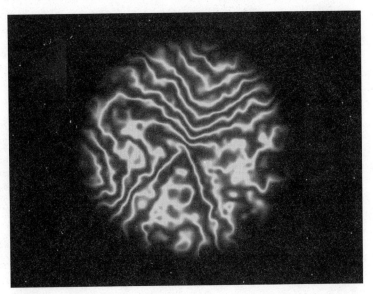

FIGURE   *Our flares begin to emerge.*
6.32

The obvious glitch here is that we now have our flares projected onto a big black plane. To get rid of this black plane, shift-select your map and shader from the Luminosity Maps list again copy and paste them into the Transparency Maps list. This will knock out all of the extra geometry of the plane. If you do another test render, you should see a perfect circle of flares and still be able to see the background between them.

And that's it for our flares. Since we've been copying and pasting our maps, they will be identical in each channel throughout the animation.

Now let's move on to our spheres.

STEP THREE

Turn on both of your sphere objects. The inner sphere is all set up already so you can leave it alone. It's only there to give the sun some depth by filling in the holes we're about to create in the outer sphere. We only need to do one thing to the outer sphere to get it going and that's add a shader in the **Transparency** channel. Make sure your time thumb is on 0.0 and then, once again, copy the Marble shader from the **Luminance** or **Glow Maps** list and paste it into the **Transparency Maps** list. We're not going to use the exact same settings, but they are close, so you'll save yourself a little work by copying and pasting.

Once you have the Marble shader pasted in, open its Texture Info Window, click on the **Special** tab and change the settings to those shown in Figure 6.33. Then move your time thumb to the 3.0-second mark and change the settings to those in Figure 6.34. Like the settings for the Marble shaders on the plane, this simply adds some motion to the shader so you get that swirling gaseous effect. If you render your scene now, you should get something similar to Figure 6.35.

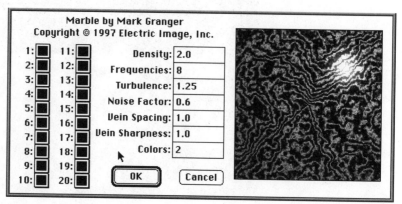

FIGURE *Changing our sphere's Marble settings at time 0.0.*
6.33

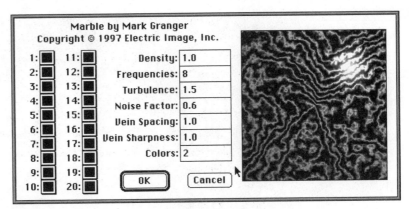

FIGURE   *Changing our sphere's Marble settings at time 3.0*
6.34

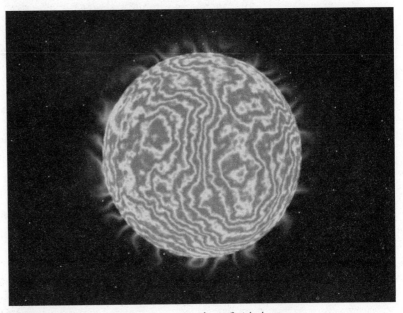

FIGURE   *A render at this point gets you an almost-finished sun.*
6.35

Now I personally didn't care for quite so much swirling gaseous effects and there are several ways to tone this down a bit, but I chose the easy way out and simply turned on the light in the scene. The light washed out the Marble effect on the leading parts of the sphere, allowing only the edges of the effect to peek through as shown in Figure 6.36.

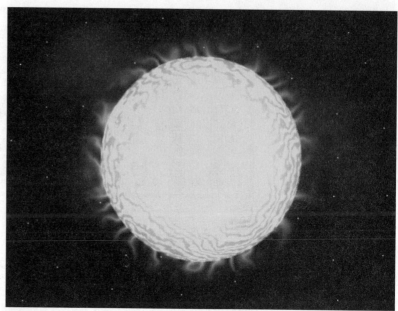

FIGURE *The final sun render.*
6.36

From here you're done, and you have a good start towards a great flaming sun effect. If you wanted to move the camera around the sun, you would want the plane to always be perpendicular to the camera. Otherwise, you would move around to the side of the plane and the illusion would fall apart. To get the plane to follow your camera, simply use the **Look At** tool. Select the plane, click on the Look At tool and then click on the camera. Then, wherever your camera goes, the plane will always be perpendicular to it and your illusion will remain intact.

From Lump to Pear in Eight Easy Shaders (Using AG_shaders from TripleDtools)

The solution to a realistic surface texture has for the most part been solved by high-resolution texture maps that eat up disk space and sometimes stretch, or pixelate, as you get closer to them. Wouldn't it be nice if the image would increase resolution as you got closer to it, and decrease it as you went further away? Since texture maps are a fixed resolution, this is quite difficult to do, but with shaders it is a much easier task.

Photorealistic textures have one concept that drives them all, and that is *layered complexity*. Most shaders are a combination of functions that produce a layering of multiple calculations designed to look real. In effect, you have shaders that make brick, dirty brick, red and yellow brick, old brick, and so on. They are all bricks, but they are modified by other functions as well, so that there is variation in them.

Typically this requires a lot of programming and experimentation to get that one perfect shader. If you are a programmer, the best way to get a desired effect is to create a custom shader, but for everyone else this might seem out of reach. Buck up! The solution is here.

AG_Shaders, by Agrapha Productions and TripleDtools, provide a set of building blocks that are used in the programming of shaders. Using EI's ability to layer shaders, you can build up complexity with multiple instances of these simple building blocks.

RIPENING FRUIT

Let's look at a pear. Normally you would model a pear and texture it with a photo or PhotoShop creation. But look at it closer, and you will see a layered amount of detail that can be broken down to simpler colors and quickly handled with shaders like the one we're getting ready to make. Before we get started though, here are the basic colors you will need:

> Apple Green (APGN) = r65 g73 b0
> Apple Brown (APBRN) = r55 g51 b5.5
> Dark Green (DKGN) = r22 g24 b16
> Brown (BRN) = r47 g25 b9
> Dark Brown (DKBRN) = r21 g12 b9
> Grey/Brown (GBRN) = r49 g45 b40

You will actually get better results if you slightly vary the APGN color between shaders, more green on some, less on others. With that taken care of, let's get started.

First, we need to place the overall colors of the pear. These are darker toward the stem, and faded to an overall green color. Apply **Ag_ramp**, change **x = 0**, the **y = .5**, **y gamma = 3.5**, **Gain = 1.6**, **BegColor** to **APGN**, and **EndColor** to **DKBRN** (see Figure 6.37).

Now the streaks at the stem cap area need placement so apply **AG_fturb**, change the **Iterations = 10**, **Detail = 1.5**, **Scale = 2**, **StretchY = 20**, **Density** to **.6**, as shown in Figure 6.38. The colors here are tricky. You need to remove the alpha value of the **HighColor**, so that it will be transparent and lie over the top of our previous shader. To do this, drag down the **RGBA** slider in the **Color Picker** and reduce the **A Value** to **zero**. This will be called NOALPHA from now on, so **HighColor = NOALPHA** and **LowColor = DKBRN**.

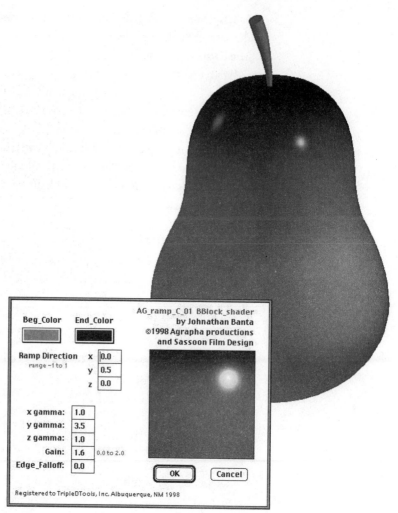

FIGURE *Applying the base colors.*
6.37

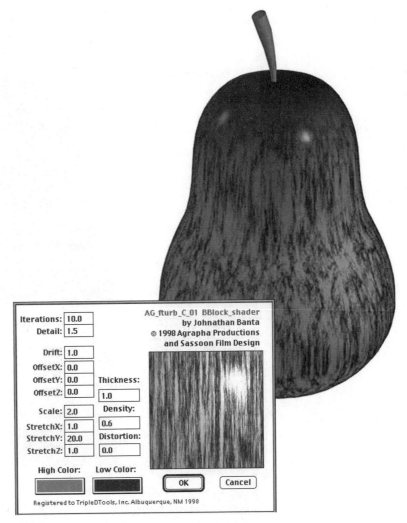

FIGURE *Streaks at the step cap.*
6.38

We need to fade the streaks out as they go lower so apply **AG_ramp**, change **x = 0, y = 1, y gamma = 2, Gain = 1.6, BegColor = APGRN, EndColor = NOALPHA** (see Figure 6.39).

Now we will add some irregular blotches to break up the linear ramp pattern. **Apply AG_fsum**, change **Scale = 20, Density = 1.6, High Color = APBRN, Low Color = NOALPHA** (see Figure 6.40).

Next, we need to create the little flecks of color that appear all over the skin of the pear. To do this, apply **AG_fturb**, change **Iterations = 10, Detail = 1.5,**

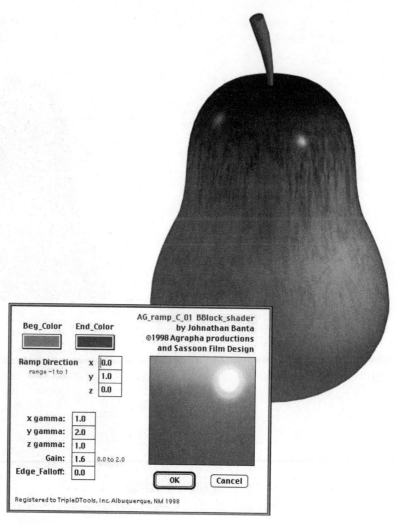

Registered to TripleDTools, Inc. Albuquerque, NM 1998

FIGURE *We need to fade the streaks out as they go lower.*
6.39

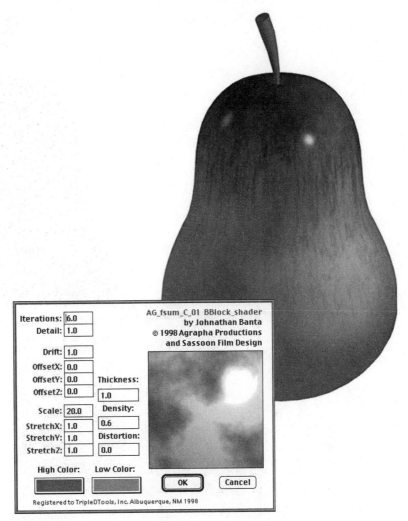

FIGURE *Add some irregular blotches.*
6.40

Scale = .5, Thickness = 2, Density = .4, High Color = DKGN, Low Color = NOALPHA, as shown in Figure 6.41.

The flecks appear a little regular and dark, and so we want to bring them down a bit, and vary their density so as to appear more natural. Apply **AG_fsum,** change **Drift = 10, OffsetX = 5, OffsetY = 1, Density = .5, High Color = APGN,** and **Low Color = APGN** with its alpha set to 40% (see Figure 6.42).

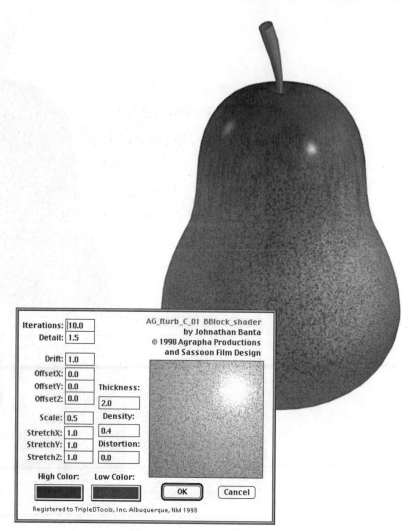

FIGURE *Creating the flecks.*
6.41

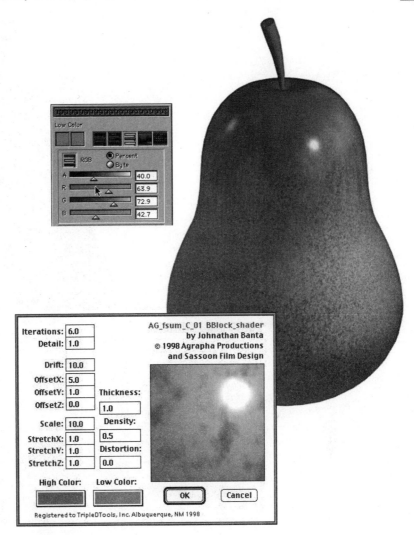

FIGURE *Making the flecks more natural.*
6.42

We need to add a few irregular bruises to the skin so apply **AG_fturbwisp**, change **Scale = 25**, **Thickness = 2**, **Density = .15**, **High Color = BRN**, **Low Color = NOALPHA** (see Figure 6.43).

Now comes the finishing touch for the skin. Currently the pear looks perfectly smooth, and the specular highlight gives it away. This specular highlight will tell our eyes more about this surface and convince us it is real, if done properly.

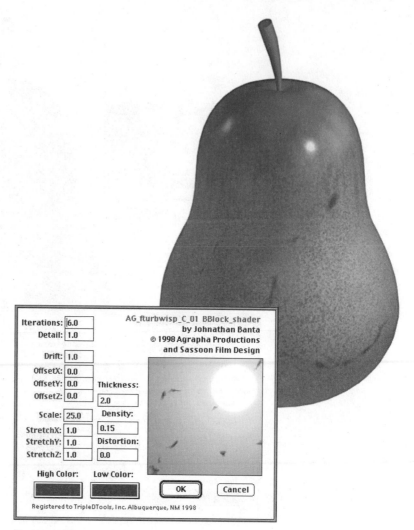

FIGURE *Adding some bruises.*
6.43

Add the standard EI shader **Fractalnoise** to the bump channel. Change **bumpstrength** to = **.4**, as shown in Figure 6.44. For a slight variation in the specular, Apply the **AG_fsum** shader at default values, and change the colors to black and white. Now decrease the **specular value** = **.4**, and increase the **gloss factor** = **.05**.

There. The main body of the pear is done, and can be rendered close up or far away (see Figure 6.45). The stem is merely an extension of these same concepts combined with the crumple shader.

Fractal Noise by Mark Granger
Copyright © 1997 Electric Image, Inc.

Density: 10.0	☐ Sharpen Bumps
Noise Level: 8	Noise Factor: 0.5
Bump Strength: 0.5	Bump Factor: 1.0
Color Factor: 1.0	Sharpness: 4.0
High Color:	Low Color:
OK	Cancel

FIGURE *Breaking up the specular highlights.*
6.44

My final image at 1024 pixels wide took 1 minute 15 seconds to calculate, as opposed to the 26 seconds for the nontextured item. Because we are calculating so many different shaders, rather than one super shader, we are slowed down a bit; however, that is a small price to pay for photorealism.

—*Johnathan Banta*

FIGURE *This is our final pear, both at a distance and close up.*
6.45

7 Lighting Tips and Techniques

Lighting is often one of the most overlooked components in 3D. Light has the power to turn a mediocre scene into a work of art or a magnificent scene into a stanky, lumpy pile of still-warm moist foodcourt refuse. Most likely it'll be somewhere in between, but you get the gist.

Hopefully, after going through this chapter, we'll have you on the way towards that masterpiece and put more distance between you and that noxious pile of rubbish.

Tips: Accentuate Textures and Bump Maps with Low-Angle Lighting

A bump map is an illusion—trick of light—and as such, relies heavily on how you set the lighting up in your scene. In photography, when you want to accentuate the surface of your subject, you tend to lower the light source(s) so they "strafe" the beams of light across your object. This same method works in the ElectricImage world, only better.

The idea is to aim your lighting so that the rays are beaming diagonally at your object's surface rather than directly perpendicular to it. Figure 7.1 shows two bump maps. The only difference between the two is the angle of the light. Notice how the image on the bottom shows a much clearer and more pronounced bump. Not only is the bump more pronounced but the light is much softer and not so overbearing.

The fact is that lights in EI don't render (like they do in the real world), and the clever use of the Exclusion/Inclusion sets for lights give the user a lot of control over the final image. Use some lights to accentuate the bump and others to set the mood of the scene.

—*Rick Greco*

Aiming Your Lights

The proper aiming of lights is a very important part of creating a great animation. EI has some deceptively simple tools for doing just that. For starters, there's the light reference point as shown in Figure 7.2. Hopefully, you have seen this before and are very familiar with it already. If not, try opening a new project and just playing around with lights (and cameras) and their reference points. Also, hit the manual. Reference points are very important for both lights and cameras as they are the first place you will probably go when you want to aim the thing. In addition to their interactive uses, you can also enter numeric values in their info boxes to accurately aim lights.

FIGURE   *Lowering the angle of lighting can really bring your bumps to life.*
7.1

EI also offers this nifty little tool called **Look At**. Basically what Look At does is to tell your light's reference point to track the object you tell it to look at. Figure 7.3 shows a few frames of a traveling sphere being followed by a spotlight. The only work here was to animate the sphere and then tell the spotlight to look at it. Wherever you position that sphere in the animation, EI will automatically update the light's animation to follow it. But it gets even better than

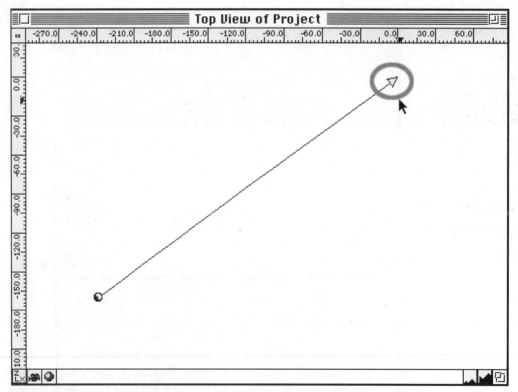

FIGURE *You should know this already but, in case you don't, this is your light's Reference point.*
7.2

FIGURE *By using the Look At feature, the light will automatically follow the sphere without any additional keyframing.*
7.3

that. This Look At feature is animatable as well. Say you want your light to look at a different object at a different point in the animation. You simply go to the point in the timeline where you want the change to occur and tell your light to Look At another object. Figure 7.4 shows this type of thing in action. The light follows Sphere A until it meets with Sphere B and then the light Follows Sphere B back to the left of the screen.

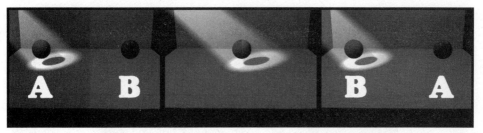

FIGURE
7.4 *The Look At feature can be told during the course of the animation to switch it's attention from one object and place it on another.*

Types of Lights and When to Use Each

In EI you have a choice of six types of lights. These lights are Camera, Parallel, Radial, Ambient, Spot, and Tube lights. Each of these lights has a separate purpose and a separate place in your scenes. Here is a basic rundown of what each light does and where you would use it.

The **Camera** light, an example of which is shown in Figure 7.5, is similar to attaching a radial light to the top of your camera. Everywhere the camera goes, the light is sure to follow. This is especially useful for exploration-type effects where the point of your animation is to take a viewer through an old castle, cavern, tunnel, or some other place that needs discovering.

The **Parallel** light (see Figure 7.6) is best described as an infinitely large wall that emits light. Since the rays of light are coming from a wall, they are parallel to each other as opposed to lights like radials and spots where the light emits

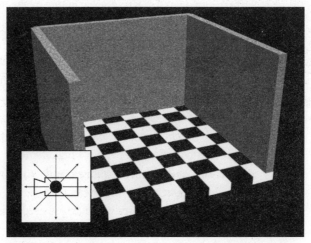

FIGURE *The Camera light is like a Radial light attached to the top of your Camera.*
7.5

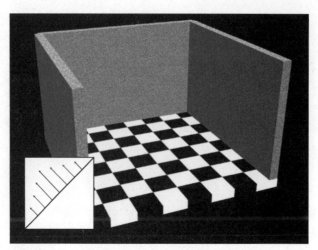

FIGURE 7.6 *The Parallel light is like a giant light-emitting wall.*

from a single point. They are thus emitted at an angle that intersects at the point of origination. Parallel lights creates a lighting effect similar to that of the sun or any really big light source.

Parallel lights are also spaced an infinite distance away from your scene. You can still see the icon for the light, but it behaves as though it was placed an infinite distance away from your scene in the opposite direction of the reference point. Since this is the case, Parallel lights can be placed anywhere in your scene and the light will always travel in the direction of the reference point.

For example, if you have a scene with a sphere in it and you place a Parallel light behind your sphere with the reference point pointing away from the sphere, the front of the sphere will still be illuminated. See Figure 7.7 for an example. Don't go crazy with this though—if you want to cast a shadow, you still need to have the light in front of the sphere with the shadow cone pointing at the sphere.

You might be looking at the samples of the Camera light and the Parallel light and wondering what the big difference is. Well, in this particular sample, it's difficult to discern but there is a big difference. You can set the falloff and such for the Camera light and the light will only go where the camera goes. The Parallel light, however, is everywhere.

The Parallel light is best used when you need a distant and powerful lighting effect. Outdoor scenes, including space scenes, are best lit with a Parallel light. Parallel lights are also good when you want an overall lighting effect similar to Ambient light—which I'm getting to—but with directional shading.

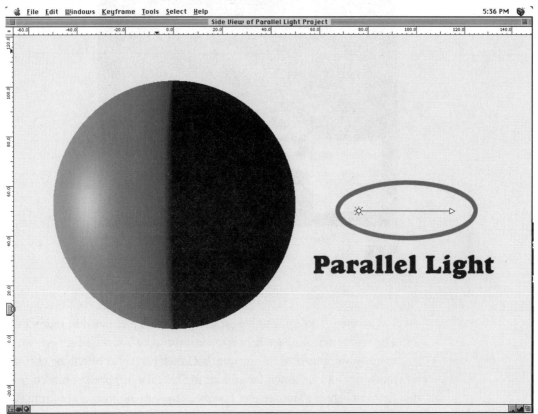

FIGURE *In this example, the light's icon is placed behind the sphere, but since the Parallel light travels along the*
7.7 *reference point from outside your scene, the front of the sphere is still illuminated.*

The **Radial** light is synonymous to a real-world lightbulb. It is a source of light that radiates in a spherical pattern from the center point. You can adjust the falloff and intensity of a radial light to simulate various real-world bulb-based lights. Figure 7.8 illustrates the effect of a Radial light. Radial lights are great for lots of effects, such as when you have something that needs to cast a light in a spherical pattern.

Ambient light is light that is just everywhere. It doesn't come from any specific direction, it just is. Actually, if you had to describe what direction the rays came from, you'd have to say that they come from every direction at all times. I prefer to use Ambient light when I want to make my scenes look like crap. Of course, I've never really had a desire to make my scenes look like crap so I've really never found a use for Ambient light in my work and am very happy that EI defaults to having it set at 0.

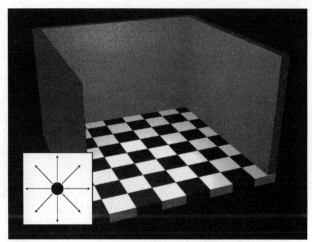

FIGURE *The Radial light casts light in a spherical pattern.*
7.8

However, Ambient light is a great way to add a nice mood to your scene. The key to using Ambient light is to use it sparingly. You probably never want to use Ambient light at full intensity because it just blows everything out and totally destroys the reason for working in 3D in the first place. A nice colored Ambient light at a low intensity, however, can give your scene a wonderful flavor. Personally, I'll still probably never use it but stranger things have happened.

All of the figures in this "Types of Lights" tip section (with the exception of Figure 7.10) have an Ambient light in the scene with an intensity of 0.5 just to show you what the whole box looks like. Since the light comes from everywhere, the objects take on none of the shading they would if the light was coming from a specific direction. This is what makes things ugly. It's also what makes Ambient light useful. If you have a scene that simply has too much contrast in the shaded areas, you can use Ambient light to soften and lighten things up. Outdoor scenes are a good place for Ambient light. Space scenes, however, are not a good place for Ambient light.

To give you an idea of the difference with and without Ambient light, Figure 7.9 shows a scene with nothing but Ambient light at 1.0 and Figure 7.10 shows a scene with a Radial light and no ambient light at all.

The **Spot** light is pretty much what it says it is: a spotlight. Spot lights give you a focused beam of light and are useful for things like flashlights, searchlights, headlights, and any other light where a tight focused control is desired. Figure 7.11 shows the effect of a Spot light.

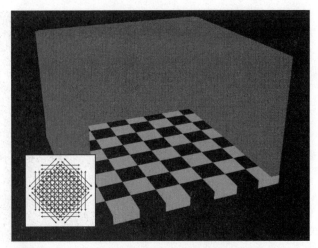

FIGURE **7.9** *This is a scene with nothing but 100% Ambient light. Kinda ugly, if you ask me.*

FIGURE **7.10** *This is a scene with no Ambient light and one bulb light. The lighting here is much more realistic.*

The **Tube** light is basically a stretched out Radial light. In the World View windows, the Tube light looks just like two radial lights tied together. You can make tube lights long or short, straight or angled. Tube lights are good for when you want a long field of uninterrupted light. Fluorescent tubes are a great, and obvious, use for Tube lights, but another use you might not think of is a scene that has a long row of light sources. A corridor, for example. Instead of having every single one of those light sources actually illuminating your

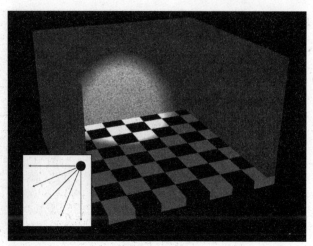

FIGURE **7.11** *The Spot light give you a focused beam of light similar to that of a flashlight.*

scene, you could stretch one long tube light down the corridor to simulate the effect of many lights with one. This won't always fit your needs, but when it does, it could certainly cut down on rendering times. It could also cut down on setup times because, instead of having to alter multiple lights to get the right look, you only have to alter one. Figure 7.12 shows an example of a tube light.

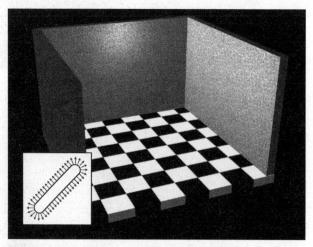

FIGURE **7.12** *A Tube light is essentially a stretched out Radial light.*

The Difference between Fog And Glow

This question comes up very often, and I have the answer for you (I learned it in a Zax class). Basically speaking, Glow lights let lighter areas behind the glow effect to show through whereas Fog lights effect the background, no matter what the luminosity, uniformly. Now this does not mean that Fog lights totally block out background elements (unless you increase the intensity) but if you look at Figure 7.13, you'll see what I mean. The light beam on the left is a Glow light. The light on the right is a Fog light. Look at the mortar between the bricks at the top of the cones of light. Under the Glow light, the mortar is very light but under the Fog light, the mortar is much darker. This is because the Glow light is adding to the lighter areas of the mortar so they show through whereas the Fog light is overlaying the fog effect onto the mortar.

Number of Lights and Rendering Times

The number of lights you have in your scene can dramatically increase rendering time. There are, however, a number of things you can do to minimize this hit if you do need to use tons of lights. And the fact is, sometimes tons of lights are required to get a scene to look the way you want it to look.

The first thing you should decide is whether each light needs to cast shadows. Shadow-casting lights cause a tremendous hit on rendering times because

FIGURE **7.13** *The differences between a Glow light and Fog light can be seen here. Glow lights let the background elements show through whereas Fog lights obscure the background elements.*

a shadow map must be rendered for each shadow-casting light. The best way to determine whether your light needs to cast a shadow is to check and see if there are any objects that will pass between your light and another object, such as the floor or a wall. And even if an object passes between a light and another object, make sure the shadow will be visible if you do render it. No sense in rendering a shadow that will never be seen.

If you do decide that a shadow is in order, the first thing you want to do is change the default shadow buffer size. The shadow buffer defaults to 1280, which creates a great-looking shadow but is also a resource hog. Figure 7.14 shows two spheres. Each has a different light shining on it and casts a shadow. The shadow of the sphere on the left is the result of the default shadow buffer of 1280×1280, while the shadow of the sphere on the right is the result of a shadow buffer of 128×128. As you can see, the 128×128 shadow is much fuzzier around the edges but also took much less time and ram to render. Now granted, you may not like a 128×128 shadow because it simply doesn't have enough info in it to create a good-looking shadow, but a 1028×1028 shadow creates a much larger file (6.5 megs, to be exact) and takes longer to render. A 512×512 buffer would be a pleasant compromise in most instances.

FIGURE *A larger shadow buffer creates a more pleasing shadow but is also a resource hog.*
7.14 *Smaller buffers require less time and RAM but compromise quality. A good in-between shadow is often your best bet.*

View Your Scene through the Perspective of Your Lights

Now, you may be wondering why you would ever want to view your scene through the perspective of one or all of your lights. Several reasons pop into mind right away. One is rather obvious and another is not so obvious, but probably even more useful.

The first, and most obvious, use of this is getting the right aim for your light. You don't just aim your camera by dragging the reference point around, you aim it by looking through the camera view window. The same holds true for lights. If you are looking for just the right position for your light, try viewing the scene through the light by holding down the Option key and clicking in the title bar of the **Camera View Window** (see Figure 7.15). When you do this, you'll get a list of all of the cameras and shadow-casting lights (you cannot view a scene through non-shadow-casting lights, the exceptions being Parallel

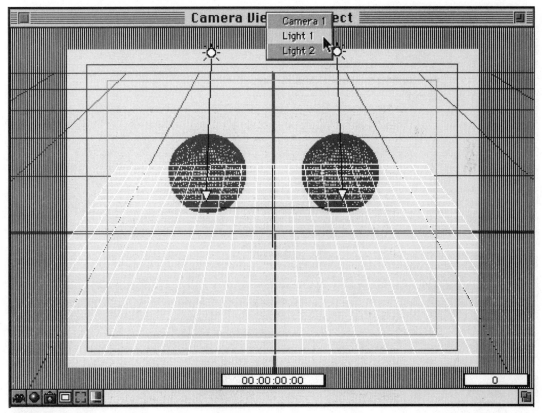

FIGURE *Hold down the Option key and click in the Camera Window's Title bar to choose a light to view your scene*
7.15 *through.*

and Spot lights, which don't care if you have shadows enabled or not) and you can choose any of them to view your scene from. You'll see why the proper naming of cameras and lights is so important the first time you do this in a complex scene.

The second, and not so obvious, use for this feature is getting the best (and most efficient) results from your shadow buffer. You'll find that you can use much smaller shadow buffers if you aim them correctly. Figure 7.16 shows the view from a light placed in a scene and pointed willy nilly at a sphere. The viewable area represents your shadow buffer. You can see how the sphere occupies only a small area of the shadow buffer, so what you want to do is adjust the shadow cone so that you get more sphere and less white space. There are two ways to do this. First, if you are using a Parallel light, you can simply zoom in on the sphere using the typical camera controls. The nature of the Parallel light makes this possible without really affecting the lighting of your scene. If you are

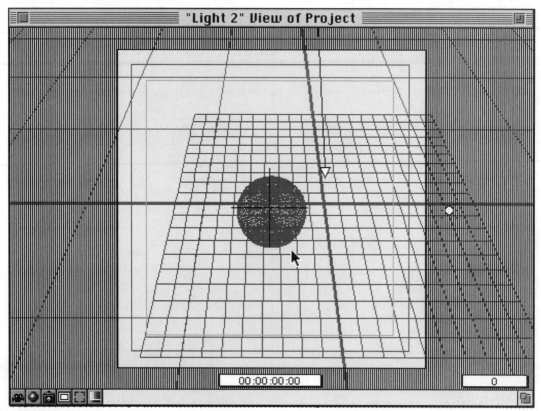

FIGURE *This illustrates a poor use of a shadow buffer.*
7.16

using another type of light, however, you should adjust the **Shadow Cone** setting (in the **Properties** tab) instead. This leaves the light in the same position, so your lighting effect doesn't change, but will still pull the shadow buffer area in around your sphere. For example, the Shadow Cone setting for Figure 7.16 is 45.0 degrees but Figure 7.17 has a Shadow Cone setting of 15.0 degrees. As you can see, we are making much better use of our shadow buffer here.

Randomize Your Lighting

One way to add a good bit of realism to your scenes is it randomize your lighting values. If you have a long hallway with ceiling lights or maybe a city street lined with streetlamps, for example, don't just duplicate a light 50 times and move on. Go back through your lights and adjust the color, intensity, or falloff slightly and intermittently. Typically, you'd want your changes to be slight, perhaps somewhere between 1.1 and .7 instead of 1.0 for intensity, and changes of

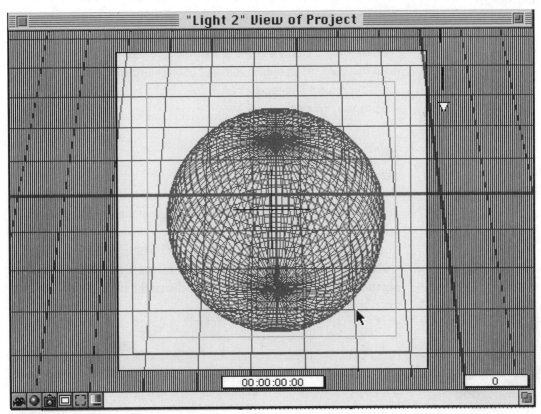

FIGURE *By utilizing more of the shadow buffer area, you can get a much better shadow with a smaller buffer area.*

7.17

similar ratio for the other settings. On the whole you'd want to keep the values all similar but slightly different. The eye will pick up on a bunch of lights with exactly the same settings and something just won't be quite right. In the real world, bulbs can vary slightly due to age, manufacturer, or even the condition of other components of the light's hardware. Your renderings should reflect this kind of real-world details. This doesn't mean each light needs to be different, just go through at random and adjust various parameters to mix things up.

Also, depending on how the people in your scene maintain their premises, you might want to take some of the lights and turn them off completely. When was the last time you drove down a street where all of the lamps worked all of the time?

Many Factors to Consider

Many features of lights in EI allow you to adjust **Factors**. You might be curious as to what this Factor setting does. Basically, this setting determines the degree of falloff between the inside cone and the outside cone of a light or lighting effect. The default setting of 1.0 produces what appears to be a sharp transition between where the light is at 100% and where it fades out. There really isn't a sharp transition, it's an optical illusion, but one you can get rid of by lowering the Factor setting. Dropping a Factor down to 0.5 will eliminate most of the banding your eye thinks it sees.

Sun Angle and Time of Day

This might be one of those things many take for granted but some may not pay that much attention to it. When lighting an outdoor scene or a scene where you can see the outside, pay attention to the angle of the sun if the time of day is important. If it's noon, the light should be very close to directly above your scene. This will cause very short shadows. If it's later or earlier in the day, the sun should be more angled, which creates longer shadows. You might want to pay attention to the season, too, as this can change the angle of the sun to your scenes position.

Use Your Illumination Lists

Selection Sets and Illumination Lists are very powerful features. You may have objects in a scene that have too little or too much light or simply need to be brought out of the background. The problem is, the lighting on all of the other objects looks fine. What do you do?

You set up a selection set for the objects that need the additional lighting. You then create a light and use that selection set as a set in your light's Illumination list with the Include radio button selected. And presto! You are set.

I used this feature in a recent project where I had to give a little extra highlight to a character's hand to separate it from the background. I made a selection set that included only the hand of the character and added a light to the scene. I then added the hand's selection set to the light's illumination list. I also turned off the **Enable Illumination** checkbox in the light's **Properties** tab. This let me add the highlight I needed to the hand group only and also not add any additional illumination that might have washed out the hand group.

Techniques: Three-Light and Four-Light Studio Setups

Two basic lighting schemes are available that work well in virtually any situation. They are the three- and four-light setups. These two setups certainly aren't your only choices when lighting a scene, but they will give you a good place to start, and a working understanding of how light works to augment your scene. Think of lighting as another brush in your 3D artist's toolbox. Let's take a look at several of our light-brush setups.

The three-light setup entails lighting a model using, yep, you guessed it, three lights. The lights are placed in strategic positions around the model to give you the best detail without washing out everything. Figure 7.18 illustrates the basic three-light setup. In this setup the three lights are as follows:

The **Key** or **Primary** light provides the most illumination and should be the most powerful light in the scene. This is also the light that should do the shadow casting. It's best to play around with the settings of the light, starting at about 75%. While most programs have a default light value of 100%, you may find that this is too bright and will add too much contrast between the shadows and the illuminated area. It is best to start out lower and add light if needed.

This light should be located at a 45-degree angle to the front of the model, either to the left or the right of the camera. The light should be a little bit over head-high or over the height of the model. A Spot light with a wide cone (or even a Parallel light) would make a good Key light.

The **Fill** light, as its name suggests, fills in the shadowed areas in your model. It's used to soften the contours and make the transition from light to dark areas. You should start out with about 25% on this light and work up if needed. In contrast to the Key light, if the Fill light is too intense, the model could appear washed out.

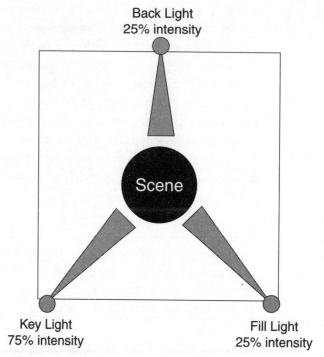

Back Light
25% intensity

Scene

Key Light
75% intensity

Fill Light
25% intensity

FIGURE   *This is a diagram of the basic three-light studio setup.*
7.18

This light should be located on the opposite side of the Key light at a 45-degree angle to the model. Set this light just a tad lower than the Key light. Both Spot and Bulb lights make good Fill lights. A good render-efficiency trick is to disable the shadow-casting properties of your Fill light since its shadows are usually overpowered by your Key light. Being able to add light without worrying about the additional shadow is one of the benefits of your 3D virtual studio.

The **Back** light is placed behind the model to cast a halo or rim of light around the object. A Back light defines the edges of a model from the background. The Back light, like the Fill light, should start out with an intensity of 25% and be increased only if necessary. If the model blends too much into the background, increase the intensity of the Back light. That's what it's there for.

The Back light should be placed directly behind and/or below the model for the best results. Like the Fill light, both Spot and Bulb lights make good Back lights.

The four-light setup in Figure 7.19 is essentially the same as the three-light setup with an additional light and a little different placement. With the four-

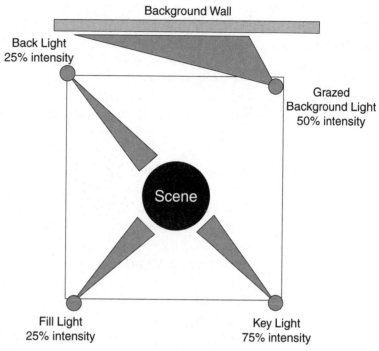

Background Wall

Back Light
25% intensity

Grazed
Background Light
50% intensity

Scene

Fill Light
25% intensity

Key Light
75% intensity

FIGURE   *This is a diagram of the basic four-light studio setup.*
7.19

light setup, the Back light can also be placed directly opposite the Key light. The fourth light is a **Grazed** background light that is used to illuminate a backdrop screen. The Grazed light is placed close to the ground plane and is pointed upward at the background screen at a 45-degree angle. It is best to start the grazed light out at 50% and work up if necessary.

Illusion of Form

The success of a 3D rendering relies heavily on the ability of the artist to maintain the original shape characteristics of the models involved. Understanding the shapes that you are going to model and render in your 3D application will help you to envision the most appropriate lighting setup for those particular models. Analyzing original reference materials such as photographs, sketches, or even real objects makes the process of creating the illusion of form much easier. There are several ways to set up your lighting in 3D. The simplest and the most commonly used is the three-light setup. More complex setups can involve many more lights but this requirement will, of course, vary based on the scene and the final look you are shooting for.

Sample Exercise: Flower Pot

For this particular exercise, we are going to use the three-light setup. As you go though the exercise, pay attention to how the lights are positioned. This is especially important because simply adding three lights in the scene does not necessarily mean you will get a realistic-looking rendering. The intensity, angle, and the distance of the light from model are among the basic elements that will help you create the look you desire. The easiest way to determine the proper lighting for a particular model is to use a secondary model which has similar shapes and contours of the original model. We will be using the free **Standard Shape 2** plug-in from Northern Lights Productions within ElectricImage to create our secondary model to test our lighting setup before we apply them the final model. You can find this plug-in in the Third Party folder on the CD or on the Northern Lights Productions website at www.northern-lightsprod.com. Once we are satisfied with the results of our lighting on the secondary model, we will replace it with the final model.

STEP ONE

Launch ElectricImage and add the Standard Shape 2 plug-in to the scene. Go to **File>Add>Socket>Standard Shape 2** (see Figure 7.20). The Standard

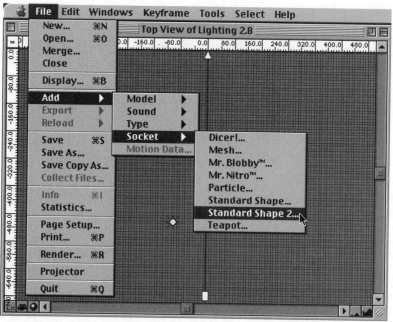

FIGURE **7.20** *Add a sphere from Northern Lights Production's FREE Standard Shape 2 plug-in.*

FIGURE *The Standard Shape 2 Dialogue Box.*
7.21

Shape 2 dialogue box appears (see Figure 7.21). Select **Sphere** and click **OK**. If your **Project Window** is not yet open, go to **Windows>Project Window** (or Command - L). Select the Sphere group then go to **Tools>Linkage**. The **Sphere Link Window** appears. In the **Link Alignment Position**, click on the pull-down menu and choose **Bottom** as shown in Figure 7.22. Close the Sphere Link Window.

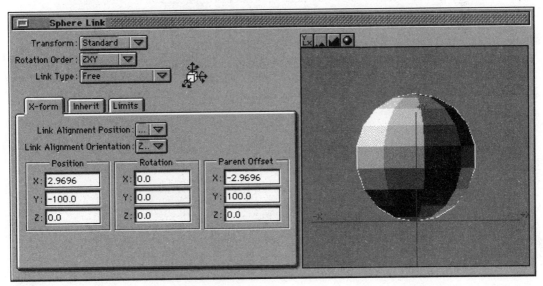

FIGURE *Adjusting the sphere's Link Alignment Position.*
7.22

STEP TWO

Double-click on the Sphere group to open the **Sphere Info Window**. Click on the **X-Form** tab and, in the **Scale** field, type **Y=2.0**. Set the **Position**, **Rotation**, and **Center** numerical settings to **X=0.0**, **Y=0.0**, **Z=0.0** (see Figure 7.23). Close the Sphere Info Window.

STEP THREE

Double-click on the **Camera 1** group. The **Camera 1 Info Window** appears. Click on the X-form tab. Enter the following values: **Camera X=0.0**, **Y=194.5152**, **Z=-850**, **Reference X=0**, **Y=194.5152**, **Z=5.0**. Click on the **FOV** tab and make sure the **Focal Length** is set to **2.0** and the **Field of View** is set to **36.8699** (see Figure 7.24). Close the Camera 1 Info Window.

STEP FOUR

The next step places a copy of the final model of the flower pot in exactly the same position as the sphere. Go to **File>Add>Model>FACT** and choose FLOWERPOT.FACT. Click **OK**. In the Project Window, click on the master group called FLOWER POT. While the group is still selected, press **Command-H** to hide all children. Press the **Option** key and click on the checkbox next to the FLOWER POT group to temporarily hide all of the groups.

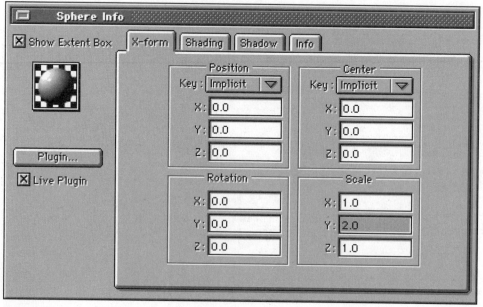

FIGURE *Resizing and positioning the sphere object.*
7.23

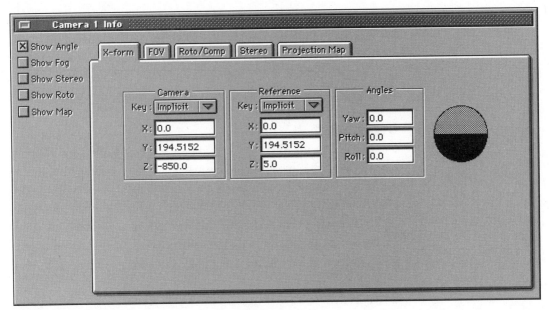

FIGURE *Setting up the Camera.*
7.24

STEP FIVE

We are now ready to add the lights to the project. For this particular exercise, we're going to use a basic three-light setup but with slight variations from the setup described in the three- and four-light setups technique earlier in the chapter. By default, ElectricImage will add one light the first time you launch the application. You need to add two more lights to the project. Go to **File>Add>Type>Light**. Click anywhere in the scene to add the second light. Repeat the process one more time to add the third light.

STEP SIX

It is a good practice to name all groups with a simple name. This is a useful technique to avoid confusion, especially if you are working with a very large project. Click on **Light 1** and hit the **Enter** key. Type in **Fill** at the top of the Project Window and hit **Return**. Repeat the same process for **Light 2** and **Light 3**. Name these light as follows: **Main** and **Side**. It doesn't matter which light gets which name at this point.

STEP SEVEN

We are going to assign a different intensity and position for each light based on the name given. Double-click on the **Fill** light icon. From the **Light Type**, choose **Spot** from the pull-down menu. There are several options that you need to set. Click on the **X-form** tab and, in the **Light** section, enter the following values. **X=2700, Y=4830, Z=-5500**. In the **Reference** section enter **X=-1.8984, Y=154.3649, Z=-5.1201**. Now, if you have put these numbers in correctly, the **Angles** section should read: **Yaw=26.1839, Pitch=-37.365, Roll=0**. Finally, click on the **Properties** tab and change the **Intensity** to **0.5**.

STEP EIGHT

Double-click on the **Side** light icon to open the **Side Light Info Window**. Choose **Spot** from the pull-down menu. Click on the **X-form** tab and enter the following values in the **Light** section: **X=5000, Y=20, Z=3200**. In the **Reference** section, enter **X=-100, Y=200, Z=-20**. If the info is correct, the **Angles** section should read: **Yaw=122.2627, Pitch=1.7094, Roll=0**. Now, click on the **Properties** tab and change the **Intensity** to **0.8**. For the **Outer Cone**, enter **30** and change the **Inner Cone** setting to **15**. Now close the Side Info Window.

STEP NINE

Double click on the **Main** light icon to open the **Main Info Window**. For the **Light Type**, choose **Spot** again. Click on **X-form** tab and enter the following values. **Light: X=-3570, Y=710, Z=-6800**, and **Reference: X=42, Y=25, Z=28**. As above, if you entered these numbers correctly, the **Angles** fields should be as follows: **Yaw=-27.8788, Pitch=-5.0677, Roll=0**. Click on the **Properties** tab. Click on the **Light Color** swatch. Drag the little triangles to the following values. **Hue 30%, Saturation=100%**, and **Value=100%** (see Figure 7.25). In the **Intensity** field, enter **0.8**. For the **Outer Cone**, enter **30**. And for the **Inner Cone**, enter **15**. Close the **Main Light Info Window**. The **Top View** of the scene should look like Figure 7.26.

STEP TEN

We are now ready to test render the scene. To perform the test render within ElectricImage, click and hold on the **Camera** icon located at the lower left-hand corner of the **Camera View Window** and select **Window Size** from the pull down menu as in Figure 7.27. It is important that your system have enough memory to keep EI and Camera open at the same time when doing test renders. If it doesn't, do a regular render instead. Your render should look like Figure 7.28.

STEP ELEVEN

Once you are happy with the lighting effect, it's time to hide the sphere and reveal the flower pot model we brought in earlier. To do this, click on the check

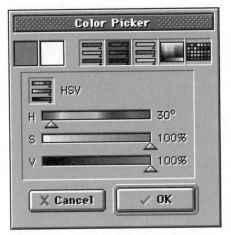

FIGURE *Setting the attributes of the Main light.*
7.25

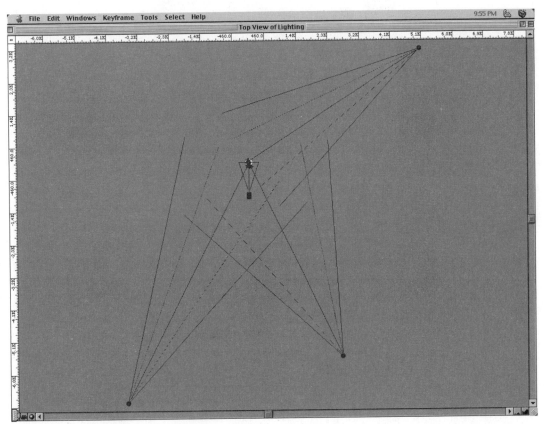

FIGURE *Note the positioning of the three lights.*
7.26

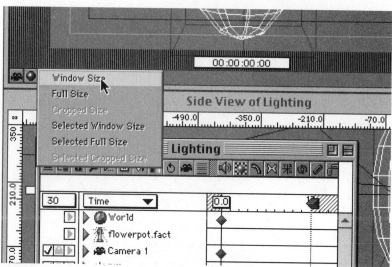

FIGURE
7.27
Doing a Window Size test render.

FIGURE
7.28
This test render shows the results from our lighting setup. Using similar shapes to imitate the original model is a quick way to suggest the appropriate lighting for particular models without having to render the full model each time. This can save you time in the initial stages of your lighting setup.

box icon next to the group named **Sphere** to turn it off. Now, **Option-click** on the empty checkbox icon next to the master group, FLOWER POT. Click and hold on the Camera icon as in Step Ten to perform the test render. Study the final rendered image shown in Figure 7.29. This exercise provides the basic guidelines for understanding how lights can be controlled to create the illusion of form, but feel free to make further adjustments to best suit your personal preference. Experimentation is the key to understanding.

—Sharkawi Che Din

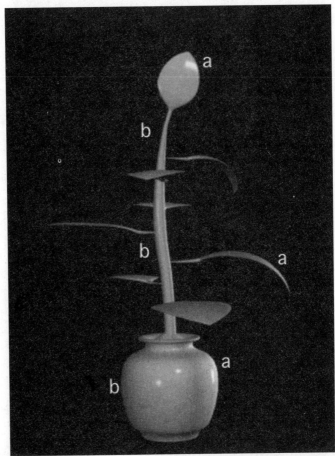

FIGURE   *The final rendered image shows the quality of lighting that creates the illusion*
7.29   *of form. The parts labeled "a" and "b" are lit by both the main and side lights,*
which creates the overall effect of the object's volume.

Monochromatic Palette

Using single-colored lights with different intensities can add dramatic effects to your scenes. In addition, the monochromatic palette will help artists understand how lights can be manipulated in EI to create the effects they desire. Choosing the right color for a particular scene can convey a sense of time and space. For example, if we were to apply sepia-colored lights to a scene that contained old castles, we immediately create a sense of time that reflects the melancholy feeling and mood that might be associated with the genre. Likewise, using deep blue colors would greatly enhance an underwater scene.

The possibilities with monochromatic palette are endless and will offer the ability to create amazing impact to the final composition. With the power of ElectricImage, these effects can be enhanced through the use of built-in volumetric options such as Fog, Glow, Light Ray, Smoker plug-in, Projection map and many more. The following is a quick tutorial to get you started.

TUTORIAL

STEP ONE

Launch ElectricImage. Go to **File>Render**. The **Render Info Window** appears. In the **Render** tab, choose **Still** from the **Engine** pull-down menu. Click on the **Resolution** tab, and in the **Aspect Ratio** section, click on the sub-menu and choose **Custom...** The **Custom Aspect Ratio** dialogue box appears. From the pull-down menu, select **inch**. Enter the following values for the **Horizontal Size** and **Vertical Size**: 8″ and 11″ as in Figure 7.30. Close the Render Info Window.

STEP TWO

Go to **Windows>Object Palette** to display the **Object** palette, as in Figure 7.31. Click on the model icon. The **Add Model to Project** dialogue box appears. Locate the TERRAIN.FACT model in the MASTER MONOC folder

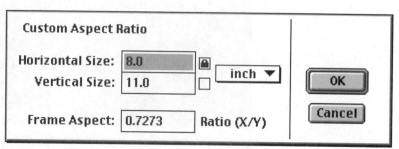

FIGURE *Changing the render Aspect Ratio.*
7.30

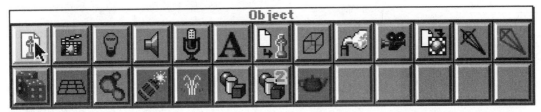

FIGURE *Choose the Add Model Tool from the Object Palette.*
7.31

on your CD. Click **Add**, then **Done**. If your Project Window is not yet open, go to **Windows>Project Window** or press **Command-L**. Select the terrain group by clicking on the **terrain** group icon once in the Project Window. While the group is still selected, go to **Tools>Linkage**. The **terrain Link Window** appears as in Figure 7.32. In the **Link Alignment Position** select **Bottom** from the pull-down menu. Close the window. Double-click on the terrain group in the Project Window and the **terrain Info Window** appears. In the **X-form** tab, make sure all Y values are 0, then close the window and click in the small lock box located next to the terrain group in the Project Window to lock the model.

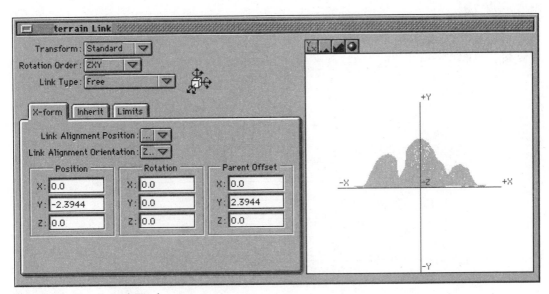

FIGURE *The Terrain Link Window.*
7.32

STEP THREE

Double-click on the **Camera 1** group. The **Camera 1 Info Window** appears. Click on the **Show Angle** checkbox. The Show Angle option helps you to visualize the angle of the camera within the scene. In the **X-form** tab, enter the following values: **Camera: X=58.5316, Y=13.0275,** and **Z=8.6876, Reference: X=3.3738, Y=8.8732, Z=17.9706.** Click on the **FOV** tab in the **Focal Length** section and enter **145.0998** for Focal Length. Type in **70.0** for **Field of View.** Close the Camera 1 Info Window.

STEP FOUR

We are now ready to add the submarine model to the project. Go to **File>Add>Model>FACT.** Select the SUBSMALL.FACT. In the Project Window press the **Option** key, locate the mouse pointer in the middle of the checkbox next to the **Camera 1** group, and click once to lock all groups in the project. Notice that the lock icon appears on every group in the Project Window (see Figure 7.33). All groups in the scene are now locked. When working with a

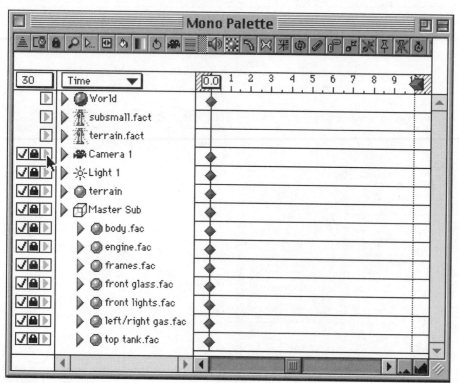

FIGURE *Locking groups prevents accidental movement.*
7.33

complex scene that consists of several elements, such as this one, it is a good idea to lock all prepositioned groups to prevent accidentally moving a group from its already perfect place in the scene. You can always turn off the lock later if you wish to move a group to a different location or when you ready to animate.

STEP FIVE

Click on **Light 1** and rename it **Sub Spot 1**. To rename the light or any other groups in the **Project Windows**, simply select the group you want to rename and hit the Enter key, then type in the name as you wish at the top of the Project Window. Unlock Sub Spot 1 and then double-click on it . The **Sub Spot 1 Info Window** appears. From the **Light Type** pull-down, choose **Spot**. Click on the **X-form** tab and enter the following values: **Light: X=28.136, Y=18.72, Z=21.033**, and **Reference: X=67.9, Y=2.0, Z=-6.8**.

Click on the **Properties** tab and then click on the **Light Color** swatch and select the following values: **Hue 180%, Saturation 100%, Values: 46%**. Click OK (see Figure 7.34). and then set the **Intensity** to **0.7**. In the **Outer Cone**

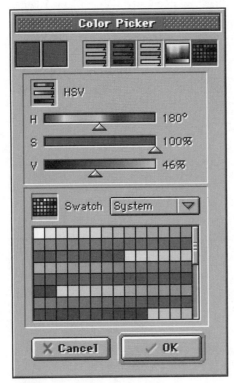

FIGURE *Setting the light's color.*
7.34

field enter **20**, and then type in **10** as the **Inner Cone** value. Click on the **Glow** tab and check the **Enable Glow** check box.

Click on the **Outside Color** swatch and enter the same color settings as you did for the light but change the **Value** slider to **80%**. Click OK. In the **Inner Radius** field, enter **0.0**, and enter **50.0** for the **Outer Radius**. Set the **Intensity** to **0.7** (be sure not to confuse the light intensity from **X-form** tab with the **Intensity** from the **Glow** tab). Close the Sub Spot 1 Info Window.

STEP SIX

Now duplicate Sub Spot 1, rename the new light **Sub Spot 2**, and then double-click Sub Spot 2. The **Sub Spot 2 Info Window** appears. Click on the **X-form** tab and enter the following values: **Light: X=30.39, Y=18.72, Z=22.33, Reference: X=76.4, Y=0.0, Z=4.4**.

Click on the **Properties** tab, then click on the **Light Color** swatch and select the following values: **Hue 180%, Saturation 100%, Value: 70%**. Click OK. Set the **Intensity** to **0.7**. Leave the **Inner** and **Outer Cone** settings the same. You can also leave all of the **Glow** settings the same because they carried over when you duplicated the Sub Spot 1 light. Now check the **Show Glow Radius** box to preview the **Glow** areas that are being covered by the Glow effect as in Figure 7.35. Close the Sub Spot 2 Info Window.

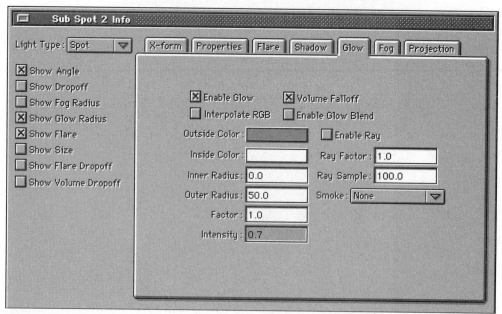

FIGURE *Checking the Glow settings.*
7.35

STEP SEVEN

This is a good time to test render the scene. Click on the small **Camera** icon located in the lower left-hand corner of the **Camera View Window** and choose **Window Size** from the pull-down menu. Your test render should look similar to Figure 7.36.

STEP EIGHT

Notice that the key to success for this particular technique is to apply a white material to all groups. For this exercise the surface material has already been set to **100%** white and no **Specular** values. Feel free to experiment with different settings as you go through this tutorial. Different results can, however, also be achieved with the use of different surface materials as well as the use of different light colors.

STEP NINE

It's now time to add one more light to the final composition. The best way to determine the position of light needed in the scene is to view it from the Top

FIGURE *The test render shows the light's placement.*
7.36

FIGURE
7.37
Adding your final light.

view. Go to **Window>Object Palette** and the **Objects** palette appears. Click on the light bulb icon and drop it into your scene (see Figure 7.37). Rename the light to **Side light**. Double-click on the Side light to open the **Side light Info Window**. Click on the **X-form** tab and enter the following values: **Light: X =32.5**, **Y=30.0 Z=57.0**, **Reference X=0.0, Y=0.0, Z=0.0**. Click on the **Properties** tab and click on the color swatch. Set the slider bar to the following values: **Hue 180%, Saturation 100%**, and **Value 100%** and click OK.

STEP TEN

It's now time to give the final touch to our scene. Double-click on **Camera 1** to open the **Camera 1 Info Window**. Check the **Show Fog** option as in Figure 7.38. Now double-click on the **World** object in the Project Window. En-

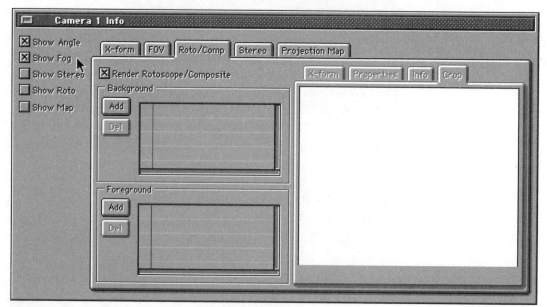

FIGURE
7.38
Setting the Show Fog option in the Camera Info Window.

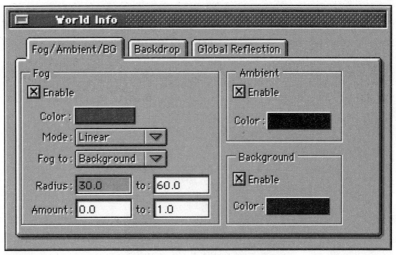

FIGURE *The World Info Window.*
7.39

able the **Fog**, **Ambient**, and **Background** features by clicking the checkbox next to the appropriate names as in Figure 7.39. Make sure Camera 1 is still selected so when you enter the values for fog radius you will be able to see the real-time preview of the coverage area of the fog. In the **Fog to** option choose **Background** from the pull-down menu. Click on the **Color** swatch and set the following values: **Hue 180%, Saturation 100%, Value 45%** and click OK. In the **Ambient** section, click on the **Color** swatch and set the following values: **Hue 180%, Saturation 100%, Value 12%**. In the **Background** section, click on the **Color** swatch and set the following values: **Hue 180%, Saturation 100%, Value 20%**. In the **Fog** section set the **Radius** to **30.0 to 60.0**. Go ahead render your scene. You should wind up with a color version of the image in Figure 7.40.

—*Sharkawi Che Din*

GLOWING SIGN TECHNIQUE

The idea here is to create the effect of backlit letters on a sign using the **Luminance/Glow** channel of the object's material.

SAMPLE PROJECT

I created the 2D outlines or cross-sections for the sign model Adobe Illustrator™ (see Figure 7.41). The reason I have done so is to give me precise control over the map size to be used in the **Luminance** channel. Map dimensions are

FIGURE *First I set up the art for the cross*
7.41 *sections in a third-party drawing*
application.

FIGURE *The final render.*
7.40

critical since the Luminance map must line up exactly with the letters on the sign. You could just eyeball it render after render after render, but why bother when a little planning can save you all this trouble? Notice how this cross-section includes both the type and the back wall of the sign. This will allow me to keep the type aligned properly with the sign and its Luminance map because I can use the Illustrator file as both the beginning geometry for the sign model and as the template for the letters in Photoshop. Remember that you must convert your type into outlines if you are preparing the art for your cross-sections in a third-party drawing program. Most modelers cannot read type imported in this fashion without it first being converted.

STEP ONE

I have already built the model for you in this case, so let's start by opening the GLOWING SIGN PROJECT on the CD. If you rendered the project as is, you'd get Figure 7.42.

FIGURE *The sign with no glow effect.*
7.42

STEP TWO

What you want to do at this point is create your map to be used as your glow mask for the sign. Since I created the sign shapes in Illustrator, all I did was change the sign part of the illustrator file to black and the text part to white. I then copied this file to the clipboard and pasted into a new Photoshop document. From here I simply added a little Gaussian Blur and adjusted my levels a bit to brighten the image a tad. If you wanted a larger glow, you could run a Maximize filter on the text first to create more white space before your blur. Figure 7.43 shows my mask before and after the Gaussian Blur treatment. What this does is create a map that we will use to tell EI the levels of glow we want on the sign and where we want them. From here I save the blurred image as GLOW MAP IMAGE. Since I've done that already for this tutorial, you can proceed onward.

What you want to do at this point is set up the Luminance parameters in the **Glow/Luminance** channel. To do this, **command-double-click** on the **Glow_sign0** object. This will bring up the **Material Window**. Click on the **Luminosity/Glow** tab and then click on the **Luminosity Color** swatch. Choose whatever color you like.

Once you have chosen the color, jump down to the **Amount** slider and

FIGURE *The Glow map before and after the Gaussian Blur.*
7.43

crank it up to **100**. Also make sure that the **Use Color** radio button is selected (see Figure 7.44). If you rendered the scene now, you'd get a nice big glowing sign with some text in front of it. That's not what we want, so here's where the map comes in.

STEP THREE

While you are still in the **Luminance/Glow** channel, go down to the section marked **Luminance Maps** and click on the **Add** button. Navigate to, and open, the file called GLOW MAP IMAGE from the CD. Once it appears in the Luminance Maps window, double-click on it to open the Luminance Map Window. You'll get a window similar to Figure 7.45.

To align the texture map, simply click on the **Front** radio button from the alignment section in the **Alignment** tab. We want a flat projection so we can keep the settings as is in the **Projection** tab. The **Image** tab is also fine so let's skip to the **Filter** tab. In the Filter tab, click on the **As Value** radio button at the bottom of the window. This will tell EI to use a Luminance of 0% where the image area is black and 100% where it is white—and, of course, all of the varying levels in between. This value is directly related to the **Amount** slider in the **Luminosity** channel. For example, since you set this slider to 100%, the pure white in this map will equal 100% of the Luminance color, but if your Amount slider was set to 50%, the white areas of your map would be read as 100% of that 50%. This makes it very easy to control the effect once the map is in place.

Close the Luminance Map Window.

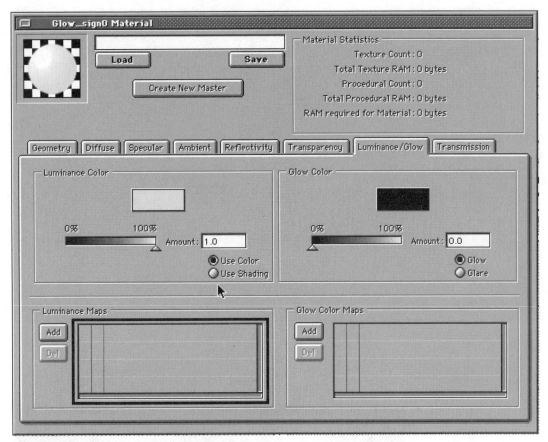

FIGURE *The Luminance settings required for this effect.*
7.44

STEP FOUR

You are done. Now render the image either via a test render or regular render and you'll get something like Figure 7.46.

This technique can also be used to create lights on buildings for city scenes or for spaceships and spacestations to give the impression of many windows. You can also use this technique to simulate radiosity effects. Check out the Radiosity Fake Project and the Inset Ceiling Project in the same folder where you found the Glowing Sign goodies (see Figures 7.47 and 7.48). There is simply no end to the uses for creative mapping in the Luminance/Glow channel.

Glowing Light Source

This is a quick tutorial on the restrained use of a light's Glow attribute. Most times, when we use an effect, we really crank it up to get the most out of it.

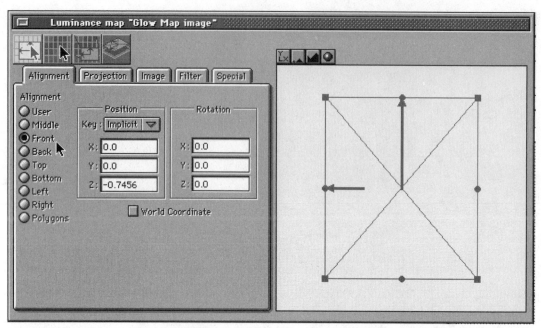

FIGURE **7.45** *The Luminance Map Texture Window.*

FIGURE **7.46** *The rendered wall with glow.*

FIGURE *This effect can be used to create quick Radiosity effects as well.*
7.47

FIGURE *Need inset lighting? Luminance maps are the way to go.*
7.48

The most convincing effects, however, are often the ones we don't really pick up on right away. They can mean the difference between a dead scene and a magical one.

THE CANDLE FLAME

Creating visible light sources that look like real light sources can be a challenge at times. Take the candle flame in Figure 7.49 for example. As it is, it looks okay, but it could certainly use improvement. The first thing that makes this object challenging is the fact that the flame itself is not the light source of the scene because it's only an object with a luminance setting that doesn't actually affect the lighting of the scene. We can fix this, though, by placing a Radial light in the same place as the flame. So what's missing? Life. The flame has no life. Even if you animate this flame dancing around, it still wouldn't be enough.

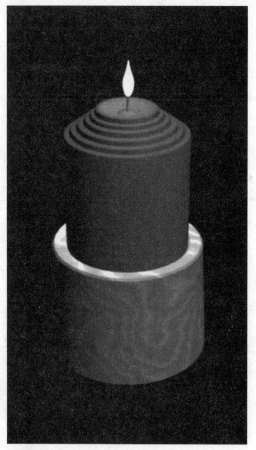

FIGURE *A flame without life is just boring.*
7.49

Hubble   Don Foley

Hubble *is a fantastic example of ElectricImage at work in the world of scientific illustration.*

Rivety Anne John W. Sledd

Rivety Anne *illustrates concepts covered in just about every chapter of this book: clever, yet simple modeling; efficient texture-mapping and procedural shading; good composition; and effective lighting top the list.*

 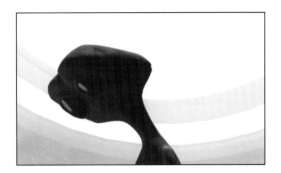

Daycare For Junior

Keith Lango

Daycare for Junior *is not only a fantastic example of character animation, in general, it also shows that there are no boundaries once you set your mind on a goal. It is also testament to good concept, design and execution.*

© 1997 Albert Kiefer and Frans Mensink

Images from the Zeeuws Meisje Project　　　　　**Albert Kiefer and Frans Mensink**

These images show off the realism and complexity that can be achieved with ElectricImage in the hands of talented artists. Notice the depth created by the use of fog, the dramatic use of lighting and the realism in the texturing.

Tiburon is another of Don's masterpiece examples of intricate modeling, creative lighting and delicate use of the Material editor.

Tiburon   **Don Foley**

Landing, is an example of Sharkawi Che Din's signature use of color, shadow and strong texture-mapping.

Landing   **Sharkawi Che Din**

Laser Sail *plays with just about every lighting doodad and trick in the book. Deep space lighting, scale lighting, light flares and glows can all be found on the ship. The planet behind the ship also uses some nifty techniques including various lighting, shading and plug-in enhancements. Notice the atmospheric glow around the planet, courtesy of a glow light, and the ring around the planet courtesy of Northern Lights Productions, Big Dipper (which was also used for the stars).*

Laser Sail John W. Sledd

Network Navigator *showcases a number of special effects techniques using particle systems, material channels and some simple post-production trickery.*

Network Navigator John W. Sledd

Travel   Sharkawi Che Din

Travel *is another of Sharkawi Che Din's excellent lighting and color examples.*

Runner   John W. Sledd

Runner *has it all. Moody lighting, intricate shading,*
bones, post-production techniques, lots of polygons
and, most importantly, 1 guy in a jumpsuit with cool
glasses and a big gun.

Off-Road   John W. Sledd

Off-Road *is a good example of how dirtying up your textures*
can breathe a little more life into your imagery. While not
photorealistic, the dirt and grime gives the image a realistic-
quality that is often missing in 3D work.

You can't just give something life through motion—you have to give it life through spirit. Enter the **Glow** attribute.

STEP ONE

The candle scene is all set up so open CANDLE GLOW PROJECT from the CD. You now have your flame and you have your light (see Figure 7.50.)

All that's left to do is set up your **Glow** attributes. Double-click on the Candle Light in the Project Window. When the **Candle Light Info Window** opens, jump straight on over to the **Glow** tab. You might also want to check the **Show Glow Radius** checkbox at the left of the window. This will give you visual feedback as you adjust your Glow settings.

Now let's check the **Enable Glow** checkbox and proceed with the rest of the settings.

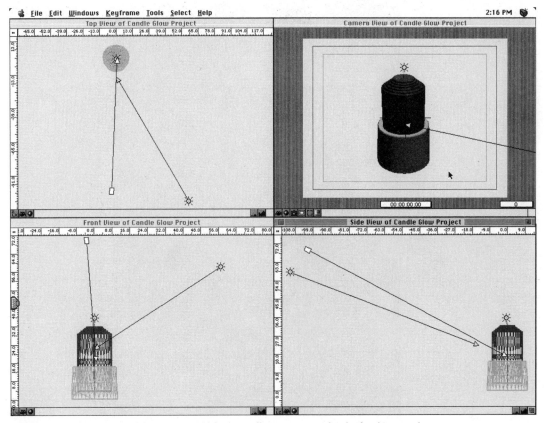

FIGURE *Everything you need for a warm and fuzzy candle scene, except for the finishing touch.*

7.50

From here let's set the Inner and Outer colors of the Glow. I don't care what colors you put in here, just make them rather light . . . but not the bright white that the light defaulted to. I used a cream color for my **Outer Color** and a bright yellow color for my **Inner Color**. When you have picked your colors, jump down and enter **1.0** for the **Inner Radius** and **7.0** for the **Outer Radius**. Render a test image and you should get something similar to Figure 7.51.

STEP TWO

Well, that's rather overwhelming. I guess the only thing to do is use something *other* than the default settings (gasp). I mean, don't get me wrong, it's not that bad (if you happen to like translucent ping pong ball glows that wash out your flame and overwhelm the whole scene) but it could use some finesse.

FIGURE   *This is our first test render. Not bad for a nuclear-powered candle, but we*
7.51   *really just want a regular wick-and-wax model.*

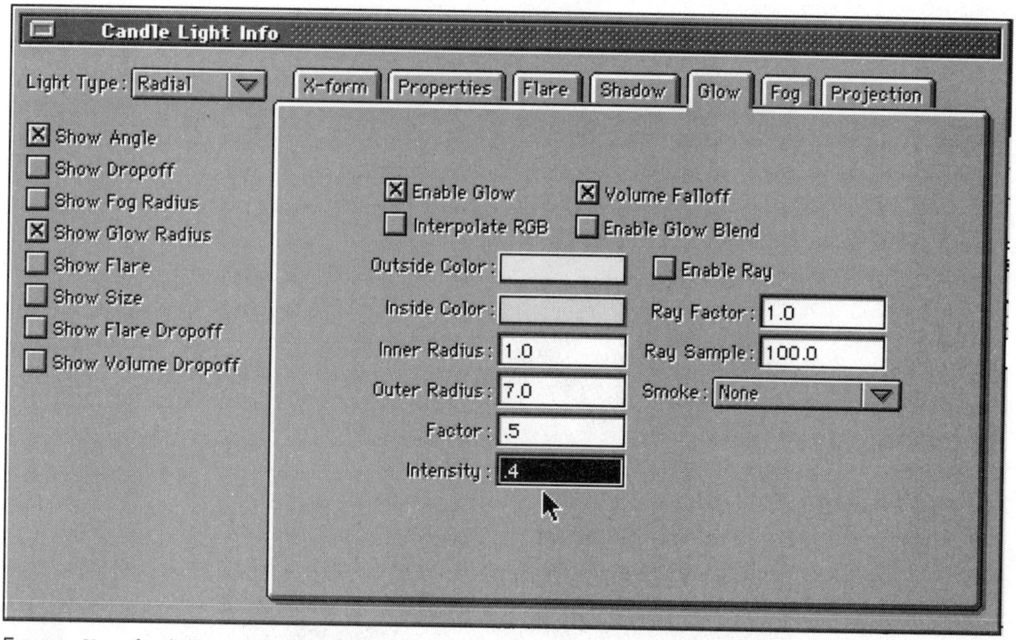

FIGURE
7.52
Your final Glow settings.

Let us go back into the **Glow** tab of the **Candle Light Info Window** and fix this. The first thing you want to do is to change the value in the **Factor** field. A value of **.5** will produce a much better blending of the glow. The next thing you want to do is to knock that transparency down a few notches. Actually, let's take it down more than a few notches. Enter **.4** in the **Intensity** field. Your Glow settings should look like Figure 7.52. Now you should be set to do a test render and get the image in Figure 7.53. This is much better.

Energy Beams

Sometimes you need to have lights do things that the lights in EI just won't do—like illuminate or glow in a certain pattern or look more like a sci-fi energy beam than a light. Sometimes you might even want a light beam to follow a certain path. What do you do in a case like this? Well, you roll your own light.

You can shape visible lights in EI via Projection maps or Gobos, but if you are looking for a parallel light shaft (that is, one that remains a constant width and does not taper), you are out of luck. With this technique, however, parallel light beams for lasers and transporters are but a few more mouseclicks away.

When you are after that specific look, it's nice to be able to unleash the power of the **Material Editor** on your visible light beams.

FIGURE *A softer glow is a better glow.*
7.53

SAMPLE PROJECT: TELEPORTER

This technique is more of a lesson in the Zen of EI than it is a specific project with a specific ending. I've already taken care of the model for our teleportation beam. All you really have to do from here is play around with different settings to get your creative juices flowing.

The file you will need to open is the TELEPORTER PROJECT in your Chapter 7 directory on the CD. Open that file now if you want to follow along. Figure 7.54 is what you would get should you render this scene as is. After we are done, however, we'll have a nice spooky beam coming down to claim our teleportee.

FIGURE   *Teleportee suspended in mid-air.*
7.54

STEP ONE

This first step will be to get acquainted with the scene. I've set most of it up for you, so let me explain what's going on so you'll have some idea why you are doing what and when.

What we have here is a figure being suspended in the air by a beam of energy. We want this beam of energy to be visible and we want to be able to see the figure inside the beam. We'd also like the beam to glow and illuminate the area surrounding it. Since the beam must be a uniform size from top to bottom, this rules out using a visible spotlight. This beam is more of a light source, in and of itself, rather than the visible manifestation of light traveling through particle-filled space, so it would need to illuminate not only the teleportee, but the area around the teleportation station as well. A **Tube** light would work here as long as you only wanted a flat beam of light, but you'd still run into illumination problems. In addition, if you wanted to add a texture to the beam, you'd be out of luck with a Tube light.

To solve the first problem, the shape of the beam, I modeled geometry to serve as the Teleporter Beam. You'll find that object in your Project Window. You can't see it now in the World View because I've turned it off momentarily. We'll get to it in a moment, since it's going to be the actual "work" part of the tutorial.

To solve the illumination problem, I created two **Radial** lights and placed them at the top and the bottom of the Teleporter. Go ahead and turn these lights on in the Project Window. Also turn off the **Light 3** object. This was a parallel light I set up just to illuminate the scene for test-rendering purposes.

A minor problem I ran into was that the Radial lights needed to be positioned inside the ceiling and floor of the teleportation station to keep them from being too close to the teleportee and to keep the light even. This meant that the light had to pass through the ceiling and floor of the station to illuminate the teleportee and the ground. There are two ways that this can be accomplished. The first option, and the one I chose, was to simply turn the shadows off for each of the lights (see Figure 7.55). Nothing really needed to cast a shadow in this scene because of the position of the beam.

The second option would be to turn off the shadow-casting options on each of the objects that block the light sources. This would be a good option if there were objects just outside the station that really needed to cast shadows. You'd simply turn the shadows off on the objects you didn't need shadows from and leave the feature enabled for the objects that you did want shadows from. If you like, when you are done here, you can go back through the tutorial and try that option instead.

Anyway, on with the show. Now that you understand the crucial points of how the scene was set up, let's proceed to Step Two.

STEP TWO

Locate the **Teleporter Beam** object in your Project Window and turn it back on by clicking on the grayed-out checkbox. This will bring in the beam object

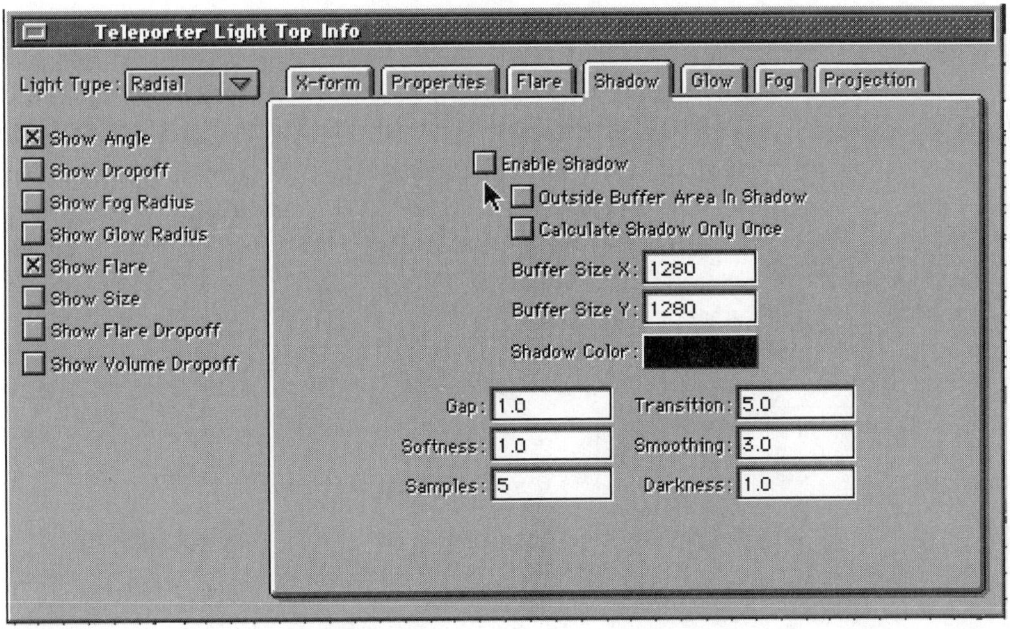

FIGURE *Turning off the light's shadows.*
7.55

that I created (see Figure 7.56). The object, by the way, is simply an uncapped cylindrical object. The endcaps might have interfered with the floor and ceiling of the teleporter and we couldn't have that.

Now command-double-click on the object to open the **Material** editor.

STEP THREE

This entire technique from this point on relies on your material. Let's create a simple initial material to mimic the effects of a visible light. Click on the **Diffuse** tab in the Material editor and then double-click on the color swatch and create a light blue color (I'm a big fan of light blue energy beams for some reason, but phosphorescent greens are just as cool). Now click on that color swatch and drag it over into the **Luminance/Glow** tab. When you get to the Luminance/Glow tab, the tab will come forward and allow you to drop the swatch into the **Luminance** color swatch. This copies the **Color** of the color channel into the Luminosity/Glow channel. Crank the luminance value up to 100%. Now go back to the **Specular** tab, **zero** out the amount, and then set the **Transparency** value to **75%**. You can now render the file and should get an image similar to Figure 7.57.

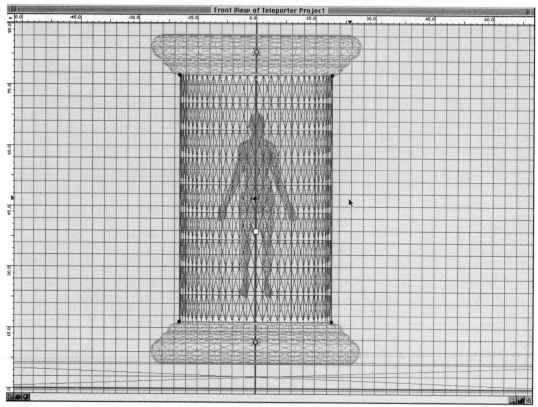

FIGURE *The Transporter Beam object ready to be shaded.*
7.56

STEP FOUR

Well, that's great, but let's do some more experimenting. Let's go back into the material of the beam object and jump back into the **Transparency** channel. Instead of just the simple **Value**, let's drop in a Marble shader. In the **Transparency Maps** section, click on the **Add** button and navigate to your Marble shader. When the shader becomes available, double-click on it to enter the **Texture Info Window**. Click on the **Filter** tab and choose RGB **As Value** from the radio buttons at the bottom of the window as in Figure 7.58.

Now render the file and you should have something similar to Figure 7.59. Cool, huh. Feel free to experiment with different shaders for different effects. The Cloud shader, for example, with its colors set to black and white, creates a nifty gaseous effect as shown in Figure 7.60. The cool thing about using Shaders here is that they are easily animatable to create an energy beam that is, well, full of energy.

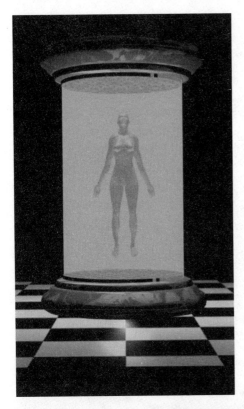

FIGURE *The scene already starts shaping up with the use of a*
7.57 *simple material.*

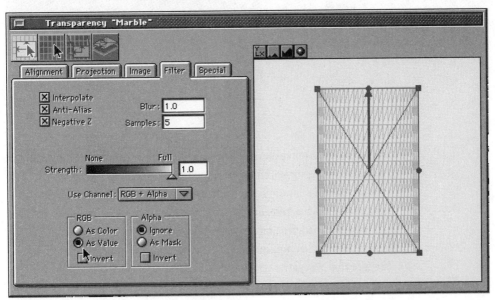

FIGURE *Figure 7.58 Adding a Marble Function.*
7.58

FIGURE
7.59
Here's a nice electrical effect.

FIGURE
7.60
Cool gaseous effects.

By using a map like the one in Figure 7.61 and a little Material editor creativity, complex effects are a breeze (see Figure 7.62).

Lastly, if you plan on using the **Glow** rendering effect—that is, the Glow that creates a volumetric haze around your objects—you would want to place a copy of the shader or map you used in the Transparency channel into the Glow section of the Luminance/Glow tab. Otherwise, the entire object, Transparent or not, will glow.

FIGURE   *Use an image map instead of a shader for more complex results.*
7.61

FIGURE   *Endless*
7.62   *possibilities*
        await you.

Camera Tips and Techniques

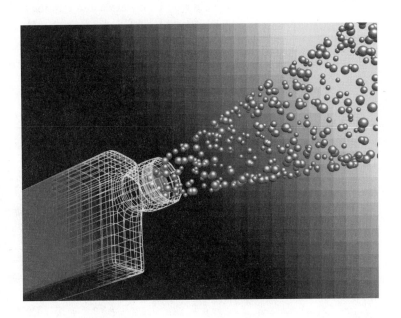

The following is a collection of nifty tips and tricks for EI's virtual camera. You might use some every single day and others might prove themselves useful once every seven years, but at least you'll know where to look for them.

Create Additional Cameras

Sometimes Top, Front, Side, and Camera views aren't enough. Figure 8.1 shows what you get with a typical scene setup of one camera and your three World View Windows. But what if you want to see the bottom or left of the scene as well? Or if you want to view the scene from other angles not provided by the World View Windows, but you don't want to move your current rendering camera (Camera 1 in this case)? Simple. Insert a few extra cameras. In Figure 8.2 you can see that I've added three new cameras to the scene and named them appropriately.

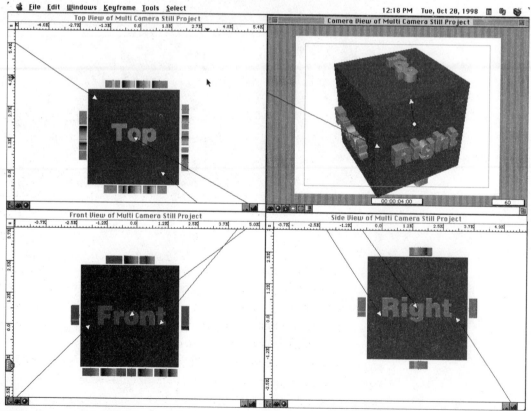

FIGURE *With a typical scene, this is all you get as far as viewports are concerned.*

8.1

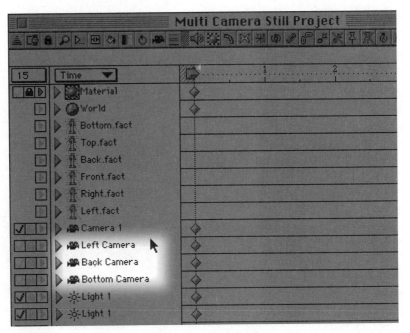

FIGURE *Here I've added three additional cameras.*
8.2

Adding cameras couldn't get much easier. Just go to **File>Add>Type>Camera** and then click roughly where you want the camera to be positioned. You can fine-tune the placement later.

Once you have your new cameras in the scene you can jump back and forth between them by holding down the **Option** key and clicking in the **Camera View Window's** title bar. When you do this, you'll get a pull-down menu similar to the one in Figure 8.3. Simply select the camera you wish to view from and let go.

With all of these cameras in your scene, you may have difficulty managing them. Several things can help here. For starters, name your cameras. If you have one camera that is to be your rendering camera, name it *Rendering Camera, Rendering Cam,* or some such thing. The same thing applies for these other view cameras. If it's a right view camera, name it as such.

With a world full of cameras, you'll quickly find it difficult to select things close to cameras because the tools tend to favor cameras, or so it seems. It's rather frustrating trying to select an object close to a camera because the camera always seems to be the one to get picked. To avoid this, you can either lock the cameras or turn them off altogether. Turning off cameras only removes

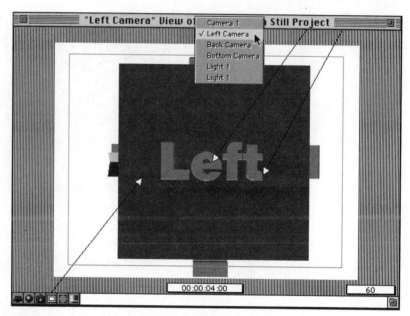

FIGURE *You can switch cameras by option-clicking on the Camera View Window's title*
8.3 *bar.*

them from the World View Windows. You can still view the scene through them and also move them around by using the navigational controls in the Camera View Window.

Using Rotoscoping for Bleeds

Being an illustrator, I'm often being asked to provide a specific amount of bleed around my images, or I'm being asked to create an illustration that fits a certain design format such as a magazine or book cover. Animation work often has the same problems due to title safe and action safe zones and post-production composites. EI comes with some great title safe and action safe guidelines as well as a grid for placement purposes, but, if precision is what you want, these tools don't really cut it.

For example, say you get a job to do a magazine cover. The layout of the cover of the magazine isn't going to move much to fit your illustration, your illustration must accommodate the layout of the cover. Let's take the cover mockup in Figure 8.4 as an example.

If you're really lucky, the client will give you something like this. If you can't get one for the current issue, you can at least get a past issue. The first thing you want to do is get it into some form of bitmap image that you can open in Pho-

FIGURE *This is a sketch of a fictional magazine cover.*
8.4

toshop, so scan it, rasterize it, or grab a screencap. You don't need a whole lot of resolution here because we're just going to use it as a template. Pull the image into Photoshop and consult your other specs.

The specs say that, not only does the image need to fit the provided design template, but you also have to provide about 2 inches of bleed so that they can have a decent trim area and also because they want to use the same illustration on the inside of the magazine but want plenty of room to move things around. OK. Fair enough, but your title safe areas aren't going to cut it here and eyeballing the render in the Camera View Window would require a lot of trial and error renderings. So what do you do? You make your own *Bleed Safe* area.

FIGURE *Add the bleed area by increasing the size of your canvas.*
8.5

With your template open in Photoshop, make sure your background color is something that stands out from the main color of the magazine and choose **Canvas Size** from the **Image Menu**. Add 4 inches to both measurements and leave the image centered. In this case, the image size was originally 8.5 by 10.013 so I made the new dimensions 12.5 by 14.013 as shown in Figure 8.5. Figure 8.6 is what you should get. Save that out as an Image file.

Now, in EI, double-click on the camera you plan on using for your render. You'll get the **Camera Info Window**. Click on the **Roto/Comp** tab and add the template in the background section as shown in Figure 8.7. Make sure the map is on by checking to see if that little blue ball is showing next to the map's name. If it's not, click in the little blank area next to the map and the ball should appear.

Now go to your Camera View Window and **Option-click** on the **Paint Image Icon** at the bottom of the window as shown in Figure 8.8. You'll get a pull-down menu where you can select the background image you just imported. Select it and Presto! you have your background template with a clearly delineated bleed area. Use this while building and test rendering your scene and composition will be a breeze (see Figure 8.9).

When you're ready to do your final render, double-click again on your rendering camera and go to the Roto/Comp tab again. Uncheck the **Render Rotoscope/Composition** box, as shown in Figure 8.10. You'll still be able to see the background image to guide you through those last-minute tweaks, but it won't show up or interfere with your alpha channel during the render.

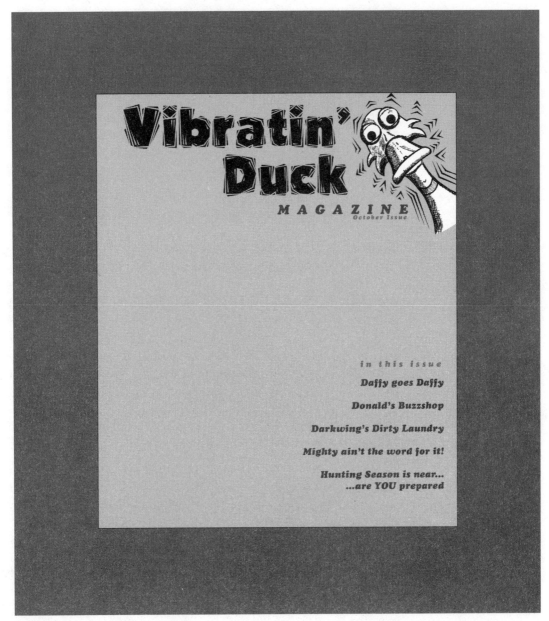

FIGURE   *This is the resulting image.*
8.6

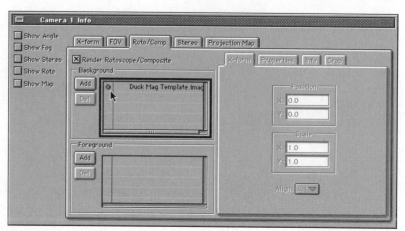

FIGURE *Import the template into the Background section of the Camera's Roto/Comp*
8.7 *Tab.*

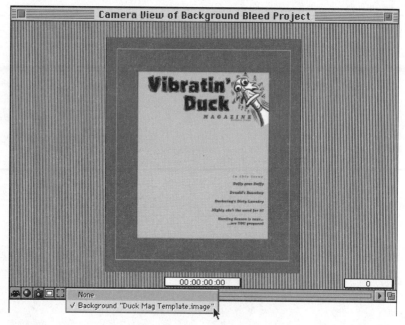

FIGURE *Option-click on the Paint Image Icon.*
8.8

Use Look At Object

Want to keep your camera pointed in the right direction all of the time? Or maybe you want it to track one object for a while and then switch to another object. You could animate this by hand by dragging the reference point around

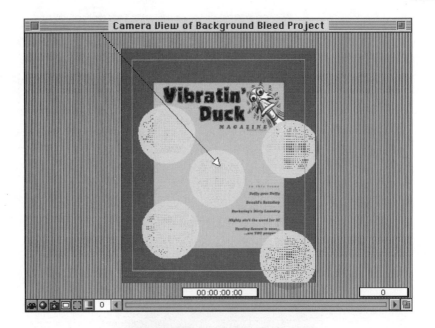

FIGURE *It's easy to set up your scene using your image as a template for placement.*
8.9

or you could just use the **Look At Object Tool**. We played with the Look At Object Tool a bit in the Lighting Techniques chapter, but it works great for cameras, too.

Figure 8.11 shows a simple scene set up with one camera and two standard shapes, a cube on the left and a sphere on the right. If I select the camera and then the **Look At Object Tool** shown in Figure 8.12, I can click on either one

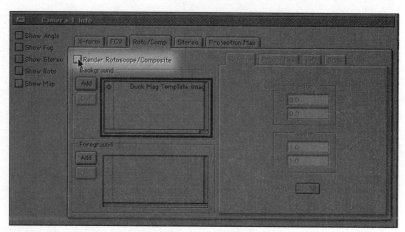

FIGURE **8.10** *Uncheck the Render Rotoscope/Composition box to keep your template out of the final rendering.*

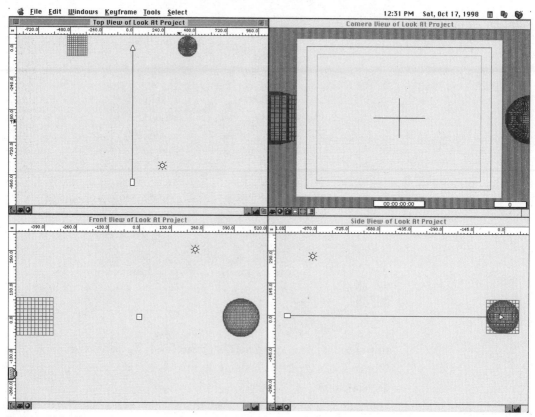

FIGURE **8.11** *A simple scene with a couple of primitives.*

FIGURE   *The Look At Object Tool.*
8.12

of the objects to have the camera immediately center its view on that object. Figure 8.13 shows what happens when I select the cube as my object to be looked at. Notice that the cube is centered in the Camera View Window. Now anywhere we move this cube, the camera will keep it in view. This is a very handy tool for keeping up with high-action shots.

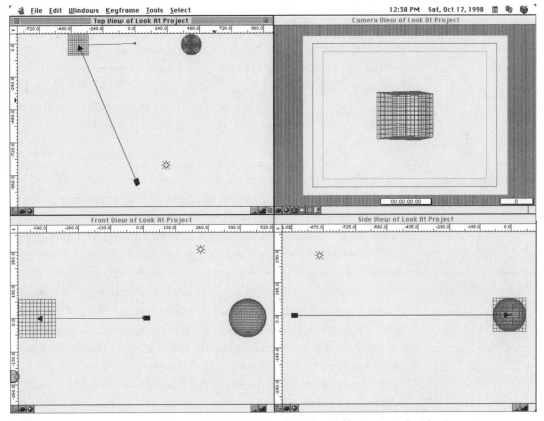

FIGURE   *Selecting the Cube as the object to be "looked at" results in the cube being centered in the Camera View*
8.13   *Window.*

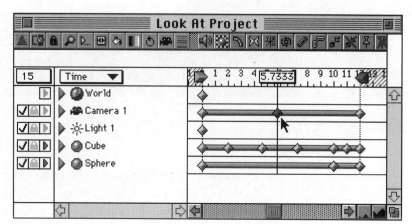

FIGURE 8.14 *During the animation, I changed the camera's target from the cube to the sphere so the camera follows the cube through the first half of the animation and then changes its focus to the sphere.*

You can change the target object mid-animation as well. In Figure 8.14, you can see they keyframe where I've changed the looked-at object from the cube to the sphere. The animation now follows the cube until it and the sphere cross paths and then it follows the sphere off into the distance with the cube in hot pursuit.

Fisheye Lens

ElectricImage offers a fantastic amount of control over its camera settings, but one thing it doesn't offer is a spherically distorted fisheye lens type of camera. The good news is that many of the optical properties that can be exploited in a real-world 35mm camera can be applied to the virtual camera in EI. Figure 8.15 shows one of the many effects that can be accomplished with a little ingenuity.

Picture this. You're holding a camera to your eye, poised to take a photograph. You lift a round, reflective ball into place directly in front of the camera lens. Looking through the viewfinder of the camera, the ball fills the frame.

On the surface of the ball, you see yourself reflected in the middle of an almost 180° view of all that lies behind you. This is the poor man's fisheye lens, and it works just as well in the EI world as it does in the real world. Actually, it works much better.

The camera "sees" the reflection of whatever is in the scene—except itself, of course (ah, one of the beauties of the virtual camera)—and renders the scene as

FIGURE *The fisheye technique employed.*
8.15

a reflection based on the optical distortions created by the shape of the object. Take into account that you can use objects other than a sphere and also tweak the other material attributes for varying effects, and you're well on your way to some very creative and unique possibilities for how your virtual camera might see your scene.

So let's get started on this, shall we?

STEP ONE

You can create your own scene or you can use the scene on the CD-ROM called FISHEYESTART.PROJECT. If you render the scene as is, you'll get something like Figure 8.16.

Remember that your fisheye view will bring a great deal more of your scene into view than the normal camera settings; take that in account as you work on your own projects. You may need to add additional background objects or zoom in closer to your scene to fill out the frame. You can work with a normal camera with a wider angle if you want a semi-accurate preview while setting up your scene, or you can just bracket your positioning and settings with various test renders.

FIGURE *This is your scene rendered without the fisheye effect.*
8.16

STEP TWO

Now add another camera to your scene (**File>Add>Type>Camera**). This will be your rendering camera so name it *Fisheye Camera* and position it as shown in Figure 8.17. Figure 8.18 shows the actual settings I used in case you need them, but the specifics aren't horribly important here. Also, make sure you have this Fisheye Camera selected as your rendering camera by option-clicking on the Camera View Window's title bar and selecting *Fisheye Camera*.

STEP THREE

Using the **Standard Shape** socket, create a sphere using the default settings. This should position the sphere directly in front of the Fisheye Camera you just created. Name the sphere *Fisheye*.

Open Fisheye's Material editor to set the properties that will turn it into a fully reflective object. Leave the Geometry settings alone and, in the **Diffuse** tab, uncheck the **Use Polygon Color** box and enter a Value of **0** for the **Amount**. In the **Specular** tab, change the **Amount** to **0**.

Leave the **Ambient** settings alone and click on the **Reflectivity** tab. Change the **Amount** to **1.0** and uncheck the **Reflection Bias** checkbox. Click on the color swatch next to the Amount field and make it 100% white. Now, in the

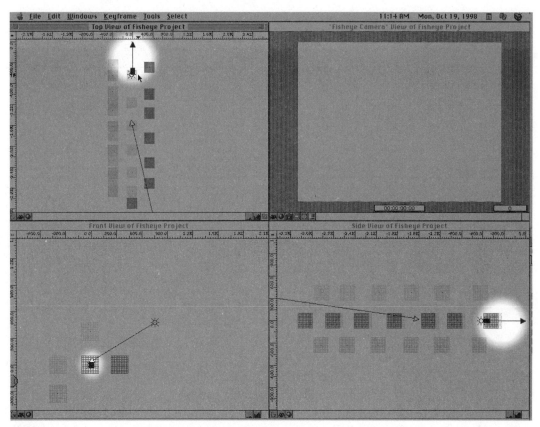

FIGURE *Position your Fisheye Camera as shown here.*
8.17

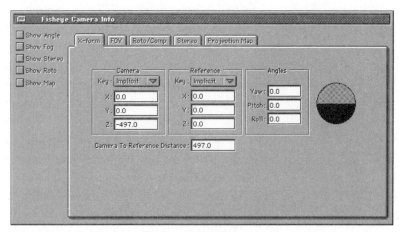

FIGURE *These are the actual settings I used for the project.*
8.18

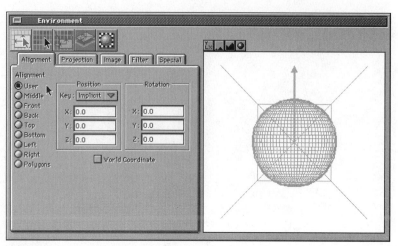

FIGURE *Configuring your environment map.*
8.19

Environment Reflection section, click on the **Environment** radio button. This should automatically put a check next to the **Use Environment Reflection** box in the **Reflection Map Configuration** options.

Click on the **Configure** button and you'll get the window shown in Figure 8.19. Leave the **Alignment** settings alone and move on to the **Projection** tab. If you are rendering a large image, you'll want to increase this buffer size a tad. For this 320×240 image, I left it at 320.

You can skip the **Image** tab because you can't change anything in there for an environment reflection, so move on to the **Filter** tab. Uncheck **Interpolate** and **Anti-Alias** because these will blur the quality of your final image. Feel free to play with these, but leaving them off got the better image for me in this case. In the **Blur** field, enter a value of **0**. The whole point with this technique is to keep it from looking like a reflected image, so you have to turn off everything that will blur it needlessly. I left the samples on 5 for this image, but, as with the buffer setting, if you're working on a larger image, you may need to increase this.

So, with all of that done, close out this texture info box and your material is finished. You don't need to alter any more material settings, so let's just do a quick check on the setup of your scene. It should look similar to Figure 8.20.

If everything is set up right, you can render and get an image similar to the one back in Figure 8.15.

So this works great for stills, but what if you want to animate? Well, that's pretty simple, too. Just select the *Fisheye Camera* and link it to *Fisheye* using the

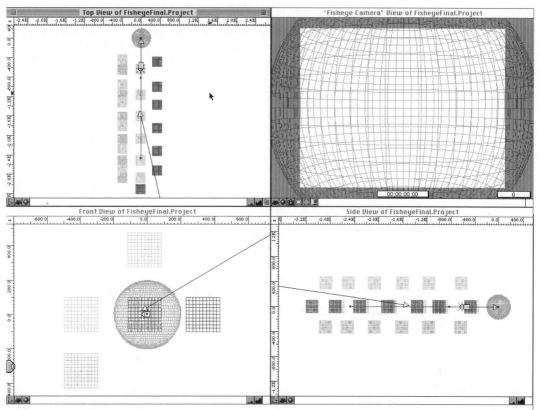

FIGURE *This is what your scene should look like at this point.*
8.20

Link to Parent Tool. In this particular file, you might want to link Light 2 to the fisheye, too, so you have illumination all the way through your tunnel. Figure 8.21 shows the final setup in the Project Window. Alternately, you could also link the fisheye sphere and light 2 to the Fisheye Camera. Both produce pretty much the same results. I chose to link the camera to the sphere and then animate the sphere traveling through the tunnel. You can view the finished animation on the CD-ROM. Look for FISHEYE MOVIE FAST.

You can adjust the level of visual distortion of this effect by changing the camera's FOV settings and also by moving the camera closer to or further away from the sphere.

Be warned that this environmental reflection stuff can cause a big hit in rendering time but it's there if you need it.

—*Rick Greco*

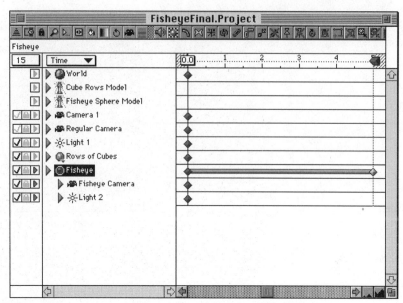

FIGURE *The hierarchy setup of my final scene.*
8.21

Creating Depth of Field Using Fog

You might be wondering why there's a tip in here about using Fog for a depth-of-field effect. It is true that EI 2.9 shipped with a new Depth-Of-Field feature that is great for many things, but I prefer to use this other technique for three reasons. The first reason is because, if you're using the DOF feature in EI and you change your mind about your settings, you have to rerender the entire animation. With this technique, you simple have to reapply the blur in Photoshop or After Effects. The second reason is because EI's automatic DOF feature eats rendering time like crazy because it relies on multi-frame motion blur for its effect. The effect looks good, but it comes at a price. The final reason I prefer this technique is because I own EI 2.9 Broadcast, not the film resolution version, so when I want to do high-resolution illustrations, I can't use the multi-frame motion blur because you can't use motion blur with the high-resolution **Still Camera**. So now that I've listed all of my reasons, I'll show you how it's done.

STEP ONE

Open the file on the CD-ROM called DEPTH OF FIELD PROJECT. Go ahead and render this project as is, and you should get what you see in Figure 8.22. Save the render as *Depth of Field 1 Image*. We'll use it later.

FIGURE   *The initial render for our Depth of Field project.*
8.22

These four primitives are spaced out relatively evenly starting close to your camera and then progressing deeper into the scene. What we want to do here is focus on the foreground element while blurring out the background elements in a progressive fashion. That is, the last object in the line should be blurred more than the second object in line. Follow me? Good. Let's move on.

STEP TWO

What we're going to do here is use a feature of 2.9's **Fog** to create an alpha channel that we can use to control the blurring of our objects. Double-click on the **World Object** in the Project Window. Enable the **Fog** checkbox and change the **Fog to** option to **Alpha** as shown in Figure 8.23. Now make the **Radius** of the fog **700 to 1600** but leave the Amount the way it is. If you click on your camera at this point, you should see two circles surrounding it, as shown in Figure 8.24. This represents your Fog's Radius (you know, the two numbers you just poked into those holes). If you don't see these circles, open the Camera Info Window and make sure the **Show Fog** option is checked (see Figure 8.25).

Now, to explain what these circles mean to you, basically the objects that fall between the camera and the first circle will render as pure white in the alpha

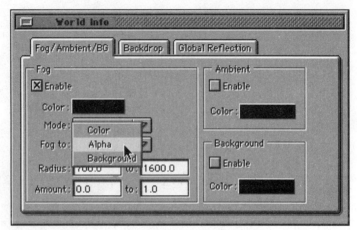

FIGURE *Change the Fog to option to Alpha.*
8.23

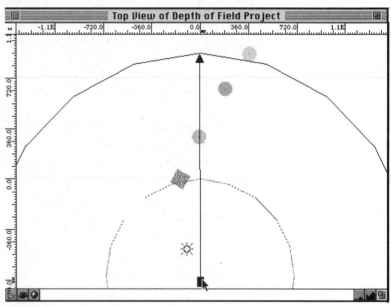

FIGURE *The camera with the fog preview circles.*
8.24

channel and the objects behind the outer circle will render as solid black with objects between the two rendering at a corresponding level of gray.

But before you render anything, go back into the **World Info Window** and click on the **Background** tab. Uncheck the **Enable** boxes for the **Sky** and the **Ground** because rendering these will overwrite your alpha channel.

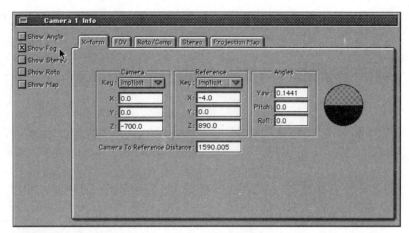

FIGURE *If you don't get the circles, enable the Show Fog option in the Camera Info*
8.25 *Window.*

STEP THREE

We're not going to render just yet. First, I want to show you how to save a lot of
time rendering this second pass. Open your **Render Info Window (command-r)** and make sure you're in the **Render** tab. You'll see a section here called
Flags. Uncheck all of these flags. We won't need them for this particular project. Unchecking these flags reduces the amount of work EI needs to do to render an image. Since all we want from this image is an alpha channel, we can
disable all of these flags. When it comes time to use this technique on your own
project, you might want to be more selective. For example, if you were using
clipping maps or displacement maps, you'd want to keep those flags enabled so
that the appropriate information would be written to the alpha channel. Same
goes for the other channels such as transparency, glow, and so on.

For this image, though, we don't need any of them, so uncheck everything
and render the image. Name this render *DOF for Mask Image* and save it to
your hard drive.

What you will get here will just look like a totally black image but that's OK.
We only want the information in the alpha channel, and it should be intact.

STEP FOUR

Now open both of your renders in Photoshop or other image editing application. Go to the **Channel** tab of the *DOF for Mask Image* and click on Channel
4. Do a select all and copy. Now bring the *Depth of Field 1* image to the foreground, select its Channel 4, which should be completely white due to the ren-

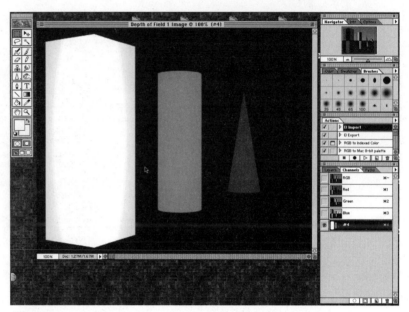

FIGURE *Pasting channel 4 from our Alpha channel render to channel 4 of our initial*
8.26 *render.*

dering of the background. Select all and then paste. You should have something similar to Figure 8.26.

If you wanted to blur the foreground element the most and leave the background elements in focus, you'd want to keep the alpha channel as it is. For this tutorial, however, we're going to blur the background elements so you'll want to invert the alpha channel by typing **command-i**. You should wind up with an alpha channel that looks just like Figure 8.27. So you can see from here that by using this alpha channel as our mask for our blur, the areas that are 100% white (the background) will receive the most blurring while the areas in black (the foreground) will receive 0% of the effect and the varying levels of gray in the middle will receive varying levels of the effect.

STEP FIVE

Now go back to the RGB composite channel of your image and load Channel 4. Hide your selection (**command-h**) so you can see the full effect of the blur. Now choose **Blur** or **Blur More** from Photoshop's **Filter>Blur** menu. You may have to apply the filter you choose several times to get the effect you're going for, but you should wind up with something like Figure 8.28.

As with everything else in EI, all of the parameters are animatable so you can animate these effects.

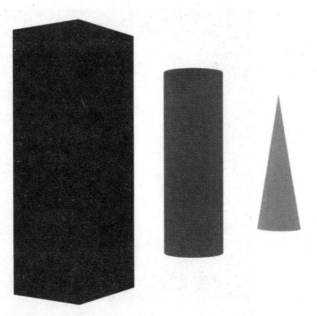

FIGURE   *Inverting the mask should leave you with a channel that looks like this.*
8.27

FIGURE   *The final image with blur applied.*
8.28

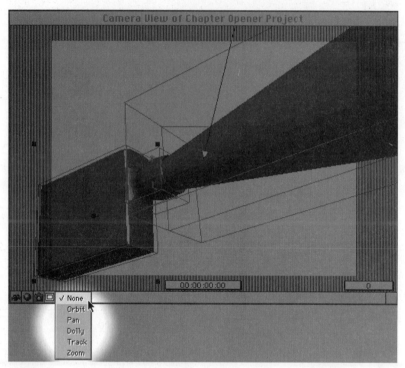

FIGURE *All of these control options can be accessed via keyboard combinations.*
8.29

Learn the Camera Control Keyboard Controls

There is one last quickie tip I want to cover before wrapping up this chapter: Learn the camera control keyboard controls. I run into far too many people who don't even know these exist. Well, I'm here to tell you that they do exist— along with many other keyboard shortcuts for many other aspects of EI. I'm not going to cover them all here but you can find them all in the back of your EI 2.7.5 Reference Supplement book.

If you take a look at Figure 8.29, you'll see the familiar camera control options found in the **Camera View Window**. You can access all of these controls on-the-fly simply by holding down various key combinations and dragging the mouse. These key combinations are:

Spacebar:	Track
Command-Spacebar:	Orbit
Option-Spacebar:	Pan
Control-Spacebar:	Dolly
Shift-Spacebar:	Zoom

Learning these will save you tons of time and oodles of mouseclicks.

9 Animation Tips

H ere are a few quick animation tips that will help you streamline your workflow and add a little punch to projects with minimal effort.

Using Movies as Projections to Create Realistic Shadows

The introduction of projection mapping has made it very easy to create realistic shadows without the use of gobos. Just take movies of things like blowing leaves or passing trees, posterize and blur them in your favorite video app, and then load the resulting movie as a **Projection Map** for a light. The results can be very realistic.

Using Standard Shape 2 for Animated Primitives

Use the **Standard Shape 2** socket from Northern Lights Productions instead of the **Standard Shape** socket that ships with EI. There are several reasons for this, the first reason being that Standard Shape 2 provides several shape options, such as toruses, tubes, and hemispheres that the regular Standard Shape socket doesn't offer.

The second reason, and probably the most important (especially considering that this is the Animation Tips chapter), is that all of the parameters for Standard Shape 2 are all animatable. Take a look at Figure 9.1 to see what I mean. This screencap shows a Standard Shape 2 Torus object and a regular Standard Shape Sphere object with their animation channels expanded to show you the differences between the two. Notice the **Socket** animation channels for the Standard Shape 2 group.

The third reason is that the Standard Shape 2 socket gives you the option of using separate polygon resolutions for EI and for Camera (see Figure 9.2). What this means is that you can work with a low-poly version during setup that will speed redraw, but then replace it with the high-poly count version upon rendering.

The fourth reason, and the last big reason that I can think of, is because of a neat auto-naming feature. When you have this option enabled, the objects you create are named according to what they are. So if you create a cube, a sphere, and a cone, your objects come into EI named **Cube**, **Sphere**, and **Cone**. If you were using the generic Standard Shape socket, you'd get **Standard Shape**, **Standard Shape**, and **Standard Shape**.

Be careful with this one, though. If you have this **Auto-name** option checked and you rename your object in the Project Window then jump into the socket to make some changes, when you exit the socket, your custom name will be gone and replaced with the default object name.

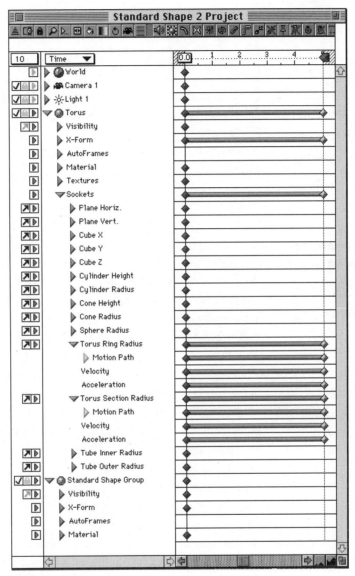

FIGURE   *All of the parameters for a Standard Shape 2 object are animatable.*
9.1

You can find the Standard Shape 2 socket in the 3rd Party Stuff folder on the CD-ROM that came with this book. You can also find it on Northern Light's Production's web site (www.northernlightsprod.com).

FIGURE *Separate resolutions for EI and Camera mean that you can work with low*
9.2 *resolution models but render them at higher resolutions.*

Don't Use "Add Keyframe"

When you want to freeze a certain object parameter (for example, Y Rotation), for a period of time, so that it doesn't start to rotate until you want it to, don't use the **Add Keyframe** command. You shouldn't use this command is because it creates keyframes for every single animation channel of the group. This can make editing of the other channels more difficult. Figure 9.3 shows what you get with the Add Keyframe command.

Instead, go to the point in time where you would add your keyframe, click in the **Y Rotation** box and enter a value. It doesn't matter what the value is. It can be 1 degree more than the current value, if you like, just so that it adds a keyframe. Once you've entered that value, reenter the previous value. This locks the one animation channel for the specified amount of time, leaving your Project Window uncluttered, as shown in Figure 9.4.

Now there are times when you may want to use the Add Keyframe command but for general use, you'll probably find that this method works better.

Use the Timeline as an Infinite Undo

ElectricImage has a great command in under the **Keyframe** menu called **Clear All Keyframes**. This basically turns your timeline into an infinite undo device. If you're experimenting with settings of some form or another, all you have to do is set up a range of keyframes, each with its own variation of your experimentation. Render these keyframes and decide which one you like the most. Then move the time thumb to the keyframe that contains the preferred settings and choose the Clear All Keyframes command. This deletes all of the existing keyframes but leaves the object at frame 0 with the last settings intact. So you can experiment to your heart's content without worrying about losing anything.

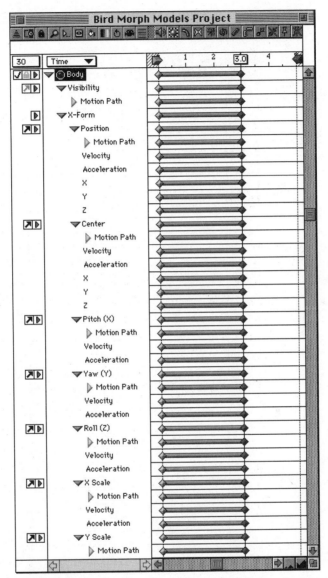

FIGURE   *Adding a keyframe using the Add Keyframe command creates a mess of*
9.3   *additional keyframes.*

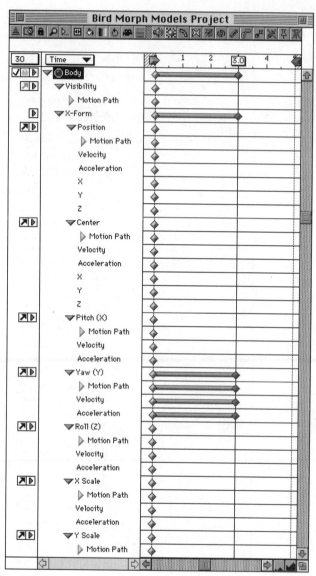

FIGURE *Adding the keyframe with this method leaves your Project Window uncluttered.*

9.4

Morphing's Not Just for Facial Animation Any More

When most people think of morphing, they think of a great way to do facial expressions, but it's also good for many other forms of animation. I recently had a project where I had to animate a cartoon-style flying bird. Since this bird is a bit stylized, the first thing I tried was using segmented wings. The client didn't like the "stuck on" look of the wings and asked that I smooth the seams out.

I thought about this for a while and decided that a single mesh bird body was the way to go. I remodeled the bird but still needed a decent way to animate the flapping motion. I tried a few options from bones to deformers but nothing worked very well at all. Finally I decided to give the **Morph Window** a shot. I jumped back into my modeler and created two morph targets for my bird. Figure 9.5 shows the bird anchor object (in the middle) and the two morph targets.

I opened the morph window, loaded the two morph targets, laid down a few keyframes and presto! . . . a wonderfully smooth flying bird—not to mention a happy client.

FIGURE *The anchor bird (middle) with the two morph targets at the top and bottom.*
9.5

10 Animation Techniques

The following is a collection of general all-around good animation stuff. Take a few hours and go through the following and I guarantee you'll run into applications for this stuff later on down the road.

Controlling Your Cameras with Effectors: Upside Down Project

This tutorial will illustrate how an effector can be used to control the camera's Y orientation. The concepts that will be covered are adding effectors to scenes, parenting effectors to objects, and aligning effectors with objects. With that cleared up, let's get started.

STEP ONE

Start ElectricImage and open the UPSIDE DOWN PROJECT located on the CD-ROM. Choose the **X Rotate** tool and then, in the **Side View Window**, click and drag on the camera's reference point to rotate the camera above the words *Upside Down*. You *can* just drag the body of the camera up, but by rotating the reference point, you'll get a better understanding of why this technique works in the end.

While rotating the camera, pay careful attention to what happens in the **Camera View Window**. As you rotate the camera, the text comes into view as in Figure 10.1, but as the camera passes over the top of the words, it

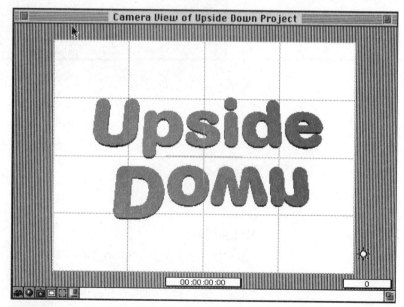

FIGURE 10.1   *As you begin to rotate the camera, everything looks fine . . .*

FIGURE . . . *but when you get to the top of the rotation, the camera suddenly flips*
10.2   *over.*

abruptly flips over once the yaw angle exceeds -90 degrees, as shown in Figure 10.2.

You can confirm this by double-clicking on the camera to open its info window. Select the **Transform** tab and rotate the camera again, paying attention to the **Angles** data fields. You will notice that the Pitch angle abruptly snaps to -180 degrees once the **Yaw** angle passes the -90 degrees mark. The camera does this because it is programmed to always maintain the same Y-axis orientation to the world space. In cases where you need to rotate the camera fully around the world's x-axis, this can be a problem. Linking the camera to an effector can be the solution.

Now before moving on, either undo your rotation, or close the file without saving and reopen it.

STEP TWO

With the camera at its original starting point, choose **File > Add > Type > Effector** to add an effector to your scene. Then align the effector exactly to the camera's reference point. To do this, double-click on the camera and the effector to open their info windows. Transfer the values from the **Reference** boxes of the **Camera Info Window** into the **Position** boxes of the **Effector Info Win-**

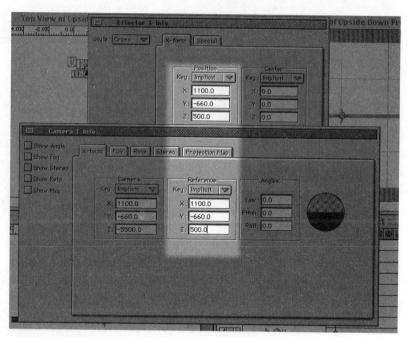

FIGURE **10.3**   *By using the camera's reference position values for the effector's position values, you place the effector directly over the camera's reference point.*

dow, as shown in Figure 10.3. This will position the effector directly on top of the camera's reference.

STEP THREE

Change the display style in the Effector Info Window to **Box** and then select the **Special** tab and change the **Size** to **1000** on X, Y, and Z. For the **Origin**, enter **-500** in the X, Y, and Z fields to keep the box perfectly centered with the camera's reference (see Figure 10.4). Changing the display method to *Box* will make the it easier to see how the rotation of the effector relates to the camera.

STEP FOUR

Select the camera and click on the **Link to Parent** tool. Choose the effector as the item to link to. The camera is now linked to the box effector, as shown in Figure 10.5.

STEP FIVE

Turn on the **Enable Animation** box for the effector, and move the time thumb to 3 seconds. Choose the **X Rotate** tool and, in the **Side View Window**, rotate

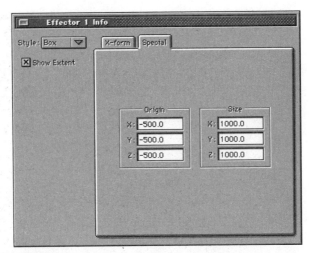

FIGURE *Give the effector a physical box shape.*
10.4

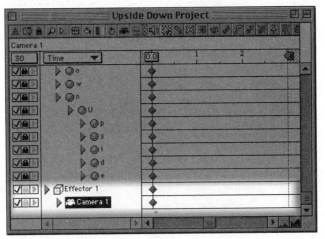

FIGURE *Link the Camera to the Effector.*
10.5

the effector all the way around until the camera is pointing at the underside of the *Upside Down* model, as shown in Figure 10.6.

Preview your animation. The camera will rotate around the words without flipping the Y-axis. Why does this work? Because technically the camera's rotation values aren't changing. Only the effector's values are changing. The camera doesn't know to flip the Y-axis! You can see this by opening the **Group Info Window** for the camera and for the effector. Position both windows so you can

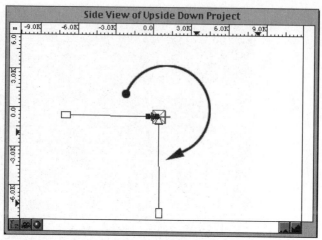

FIGURE *Rotate the effector all the way around until it faces the bottom of the text.*
10.6

see them. Move the time thumb to different locations in the Project Window and look at the Group Info Windows. The angles for the camera stay at 0, but the X-rotation for the effector is changing.

You may have also noticed that the camera is making a perfect circle around the model. The is a great technique to use anytime you need the camera to make a perfect orbit on any axis.

—Chris Weyers

Creating Layered Animation: Photon Torpedo

In this exercise we'll learn how to create a photon torpedo and animate it using linked effectors to control the streak rotation and position of the torpedo. The concepts we will cover are creating a hierarchy of effectors and objects and Creating an animation by layering different attributes to effector groups.

STEP ONE

Open ElectricImage and create a new project called PHOTON TORPEDO PROJECT. When prompted to add a model, choose **Done**. Set the duration in the Project Window to 5 seconds.

Select the default light, *Light 1,* and double-click on it to open its info window. Click on the **Show Glow Radius** and **Show Size** boxes to enable them, as shown in Figure 10.7. In the **X-Form** tab, set the values in the **Light** and **Angles** boxes to **0**. This will locate the light in the center of the world, and take any rotation out of it (see Figure 10.8). In the **Properties** tab, leave the color set

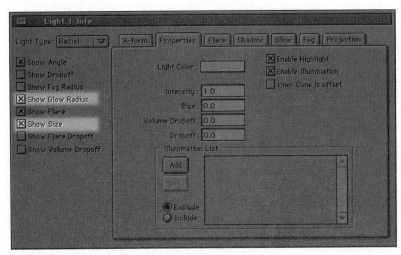

FIGURE *Click on the Show Glow Radius and Show Size Boxes.*
10.7

to white. This will create a hot center for the torpedo. Change the **Intensity** to **.25**, and set the **Size** to **50** units. You should see a black circular line surrounding the light in the world view windows. This is the indicator you turned on by enabling **Show Size** (see Figure 10.9).

In the **Flare** tab, choose *LightFlare* from the pull-down menu. Uncheck **Use Red Outer Glow** and **Use Central Ring**. Set the **Star Filter** to **4+4 Point** as

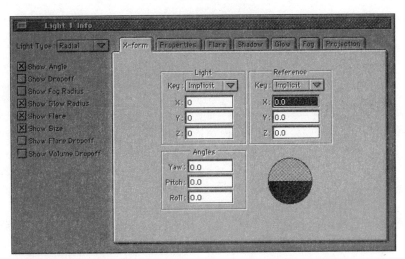

FIGURE *Positioning the light.*
10.8

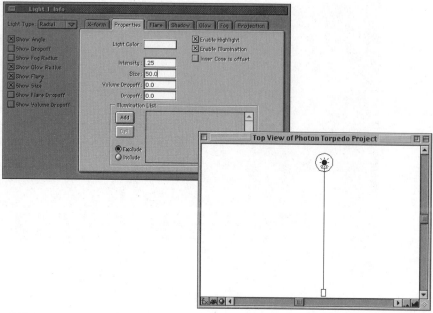

FIGURE
10.9 *Creating the center of the torpedo.*

shown in Figure 10.10. Several concentric circles will show up in the world view windows. These represent the radius of the LightFlare (see Figure 10.11). To turn the flare radius indictors off, uncheck the **Show Flare** box in the **Light Info Window**.

In the **Glow** tab, check the **Enable Glow** box. Click on the **Outside Color** box and choose a very dark green. Click on the **Inside Color** box and choose a

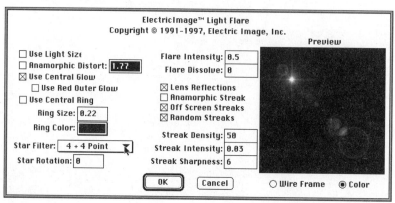

FIGURE *Setting up the LightFlare.*
10.10

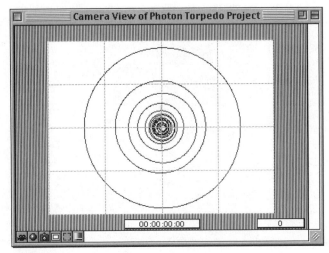

FIGURE *Circles show the radius of the LightFlare.*
10.11

bright green. This will create a glow that is bright green, falling off to near black. In the **Inner Radius** box enter **5.0** units. Again, you will see a black circular line surrounding the light. This indicates the inner glow area, which will be bright green. Set the **Outer Radius** box to **100** units. You will see a second black circular line that indicates the outer radius of the glow, as shown in Figure 10.12. The area between the inner and outer radius lines will be filled

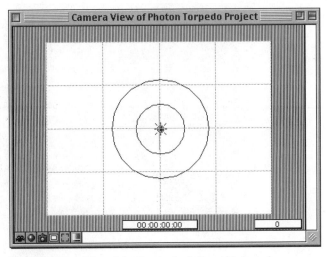

FIGURE *The radius of the glow is also indicated by a circle.*
10.12

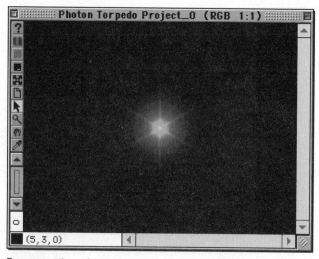

FIGURE   *Increase the Factor to 2.0.*
10.13

with a gradient of color that mixes between the inside and outside colors. Set
the **Factor** to **2.0**, as shown in Figure 10.13.

Do some quick test renders of the project to see your glow/flare. Move the
camera to different positions and do a few more. You get a nice green lightflare
with streaks, but it looks a little flat, as you can see in Figure 10.14. We need to
add some dimension to it. Before proceeding, rename Light 1 *Flare Center* and
lock it so you can't accidentally move it.

FIGURE   *The preliminary rendering of our torpedo.*
10.14

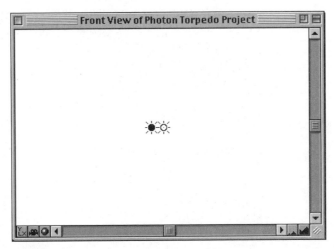

FIGURE   *Add a new light to your scene.*
10.15

STEP TWO

Choose **File > Add > Type > Light**. Click in the front view window to add the new light near the *Flare Center* Light, as shown in Figure 10.15, and double-click on the new *Light 2* to open its info window.

Change the **Light Type** from **Radial** to **Spot**, as shown in Figure 10.16. You now have a spotlight pointing inward toward *Flare Center* Light (see Figure 10.17). Constrain the **Move** tool horizontally by tapping the tab key,

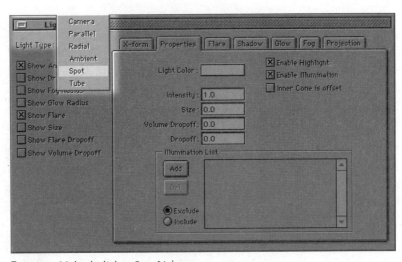

FIGURE   *Make the light a Spot Light.*
10.16

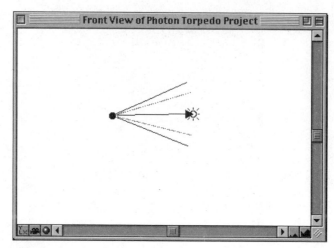

FIGURE **10.17** *This shows roughly how your Spot Light should currently be positioned and aimed.*

and drag the triangular light's reference point away from the *Flare Center* Light until it points in the positive X direction, as shown in Figure 10.18. Now, enable the **Show Glow Radius** box. We're going to use the spot light to add a directional streak that will rotate and give the effect dimension.

In the **Properties** tab, change the light's color to bright green. Set the **Outer Cone** to **8.0** units and the **Inner Cone** to **3.0** units. This will create a very narrow cone "streak" effect. Uncheck the **Enable Illumination** and **Enable Highlight** boxes, and set the **Intensity** to **0** as shown in Figure 10.19. Doing this

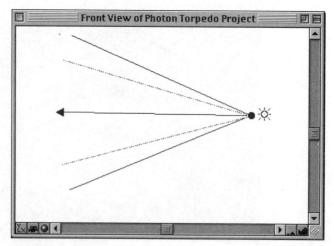

FIGURE **10.18** *Drag the new light's reference point so that it faces away from the first light.*

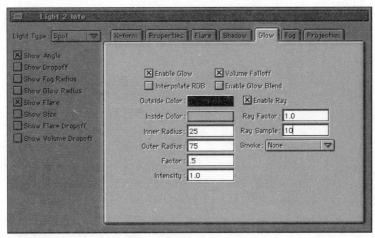

FIGURE   *Uncheck the Enable Illumination and Enable Highlight boxes.*
10.19

ensures that the light will not add an extra illumination or intensity to the scene, but will still display its inner and outer cone.

In the **Glow** tab, set the **Outside Color** to black and the **Inside Color** to bright green. Doing this will make the spotlight cone green at the light's origin and black at the outer edge of the spotlight cone. Set the **Inner Radius** to **25** units and the **Outer Radius** to **75** units. Change the **Intensity** to **.5**. Also check the **Enable Ray** box and change the **Ray Sample** to **10**, as shown in Figure 10.20.

FIGURE   *Setting up the Glow Parameters.*
10.20

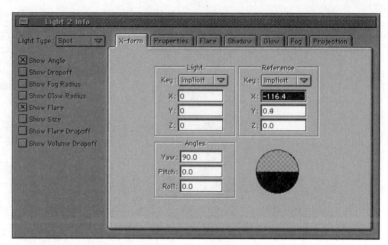

FIGURE *AUTHOR: Please supply caption for this figure ********
10.21

In the **X-Form** tab, enter **0** for the X, Y, and Z position of the light. Also enter **0** for the X and Y position of the reference, as shown in Figure 10.21. This will center Light 2 on top of *Flare Center* Light and make the spotlight cone look like it's coming out of the flare center. Now, rename your Light 2 to *Streak Light*.

Duplicate the *Streak Light* and double-click on the duplicate. Change its **Yaw** angle to **-90**. This will rotate it around the world Z-axis. You should now have two identical lights that are opposite each other in the front view window, as in Figure 10.22.

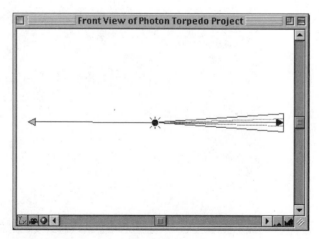

FIGURE *Changing the Yaw of the duplicate creates an identical light facing the*
10.22 *opposite direction.*

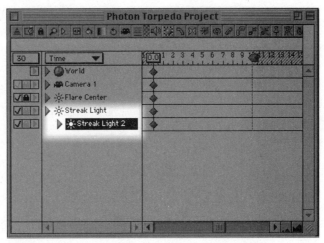

FIGURE   *Link* Streak Light 2 *to the original* Streak Light.
10.23

Now, rename the duplicate streak light *Streak Light 2,* click on **Link to Parent** tool and select *Streak Light* as the parent (see Figure 10.23).

Select *Streak Light* and duplicate it again. You will get a copy of the *Streak Light* and *Streak Light 2* hierarchy. Select the duplicate *Streak Light* and double-click on it. Change the **Pitch** angle to **90** degrees. You should now have a "cross" of lights in your front view window, as shown in Figure 10.24. Rename the duplicate Streak Light *Streak Light 3,* as shown in Figure 10.25.

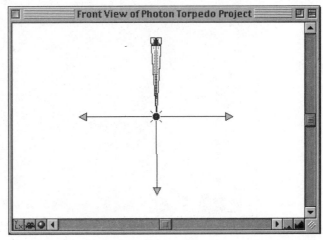

FIGURE   *Rotate the duplicated* Streak Light *combo to get a cross of lights.*
10.24

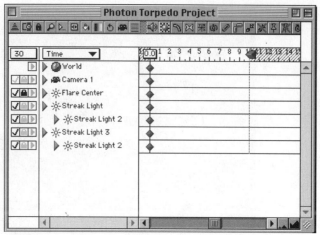

FIGURE *Rename the new duplicate* Streak Light 3.
10.25

Now do a quick test render of the project window and you should get something similar to Figure 10.26.

The cross of Streak Lights add some dimension to the Flare Light. They will add even more dimension once we animate them. We want to find a way to rotate the Streak Light chains around the Flare Light while moving the entire hierarchy forward. To do this we will use effectors to layer position animation for the entire hierarchy on top of rotational animation for the streak lights.

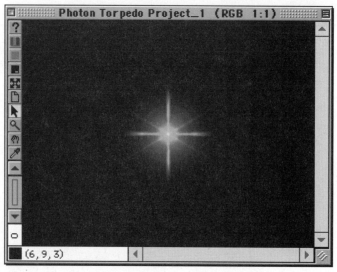

FIGURE *Your test render should look something like this.*
10.26

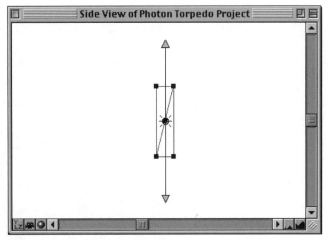

FIGURE   *Creating the first effector.*
10.27

STEP THREE

Choose **File > Add > Type > Effector** and click in the front view window near the center of the *Flare Center Light*. Double-click on the effector to open its info window. In the **X-Form** tab, set its position to **0** for X, Y, and Z. This will center it over our lights. Change the display type to **Box**. In the **Special** tab, change the X and Y size to **100**, and the Z size to **25**. In the **Origin** box change the X and Y size to **-50** and the Z size to **-12.5**. You should get something similar to Figure 10.27. We want to create "skinny boxes" that will align with the two streak light chains. This will make it easier to identify which effector is controlling which chain. Rename this Effector **Rotate Z**.

Select the *Rotate Z* effector, duplicate it, and rename the duplicate *Rotate Z2*. Double-click on the *Rotate Z2* effector to open its info window. In the **X-form** tab, enter **90** degrees in the Y rotation field, as shown in Figure 10.28. You should now have two intersecting "skinny box" effectors, as shown in Figure 10.29.

Now select *Streak Light* and parent it to *Rotate Z*. Select *Streak Light 3* and parent it to *Rotate Z2*. Your Project Window should look like Figure 10.30. These two effectors will control the rotation of our streak lights separately in the final animation.

Now what you want to do is add a third effector to the scene. Again, set its position to **0** on X, Y, and Z. Change the display type to **Box**. In the **Special** tab, set the size to **200** on X, Y, and Z. Set the origin size to **-100** on X, Y, and

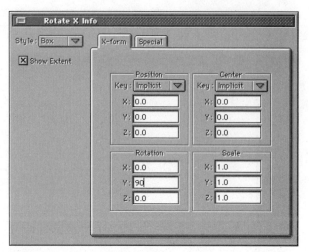

FIGURE *Change the Y rotation.*
10.28

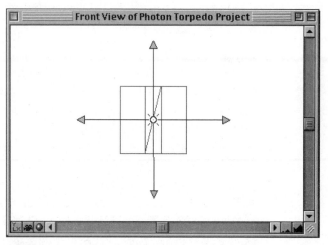

FIGURE *Similar to the two-light cross, you should have two intersecting effectors.*
10.29

Z. The new box effector should be completely surrounding your lights and rotation effectors as shown in Figure 10.31. Rename the new effector *Mover*.

Finally, hold down the **Shift** key and click on *Rotate Z, Rotate Z2,* and *Flare Center* in the Project Window. Select the **Link to Parent** tool and choose *Mover* as the parent. You now have a completed hierarchy that's ready to animate in layers (see Figure 10.32).

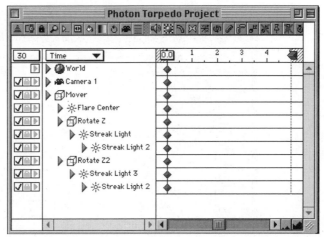

FIGURE *Parent the* Streak Light *hierarchies to the corresponding effectors.*
10.30

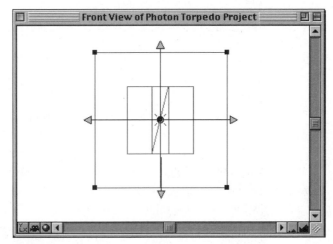

FIGURE *Creating the third effector.*
10.31

STEP FOUR: ANIMATING LAYER ONE

The first thing we're going to do is create the photon torpedo's camera flyby. To do this, hold down the **Option** key and click the lock icon next to *Flare Center*. This will lock all of the lights and effectors below the *Mover* so they can't accidentally be moved.

We're going to set up our animation backwards, setting the last keyframe in the animation first and the first keyframe in the animation last. Since we're fly-

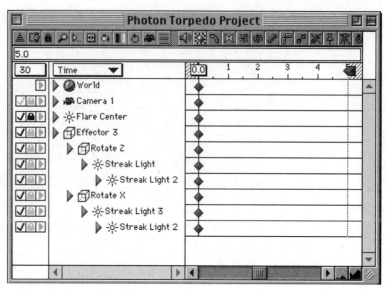

FIGURE *Link everything to this new effector.*
10.32

ing by the camera, it makes more sense to set the keyframe that's nearest the camera and pull the photon torpedo away, rather than trying to pull it closer from a distance.

Before you start animating anything, be sure turn on the **Enable Animation** arrow for *Mover* and then drag the time thumb to 5 seconds.

Working back and forth between the top view, side view, and front view windows, position the photon torpedo so it's below and to the left of the camera, just outside its field of view. Make sure you get the photon torpedo as close as you can to the camera, as in Figure 10.33. Do test renders to be sure the lights are all out of the camera view for the final frame.

Once you have that set up, drag the time thumb back to 0. Select the *Mover* and translate it back on -Z and up so that it's in the upper right-hand corner of the camera's view as shown in Figure 10.34.

Hold down the **Option** key, click on the shaded display ball in the **Camera** window and select **Display Paths**. You should see an animation path for the *Mover* running diagonally through your **Camera View Window** (see Figure 10.35).

If you preview your animation in the Camera View Window, you will see that the photon torpedo floats at the upper right-hand corner a little too long. To correct this we need to adjust the animation path so it curves away from the camera in the top and side views (see Figure 10.36).

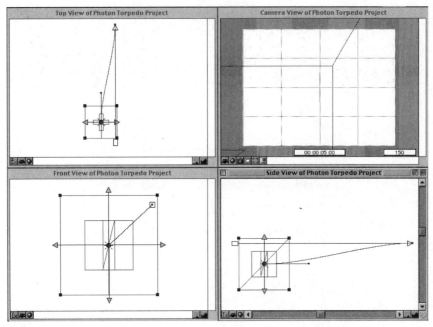

FIGURE
10.33
Setting up the last keyframe of the animation.

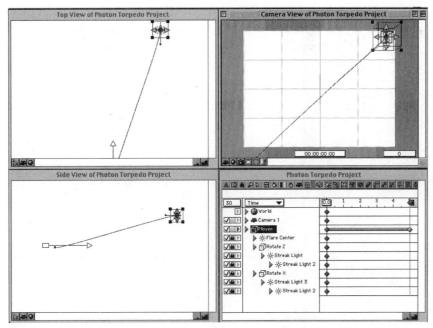

FIGURE
10.34
Setting up the first keyframe.

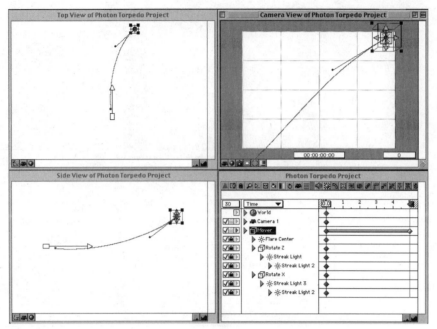

FIGURE
10.35
Showing the animation paths in your Camera View Window will give you a good idea of the direction the animation will follow.

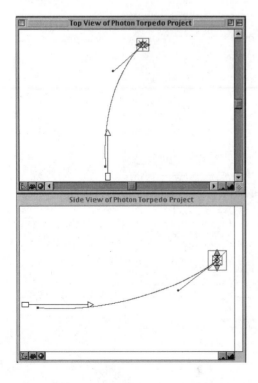

FIGURE
10.36
You need to adjust the animation paths a little to keep the action going.

STEP FIVE: ANIMATING THE SECOND LAYER

Once you've got the basic motion of the photon torpedo down, it's time to give it a little more life by spinning the Streak Lights around the center of the flare.

Preview the animation in the Camera View Window a few times to determine how you want to rotate the streak lights. Plan to make at least one of the Streak Lights rotate toward the camera. Once again, we're going to set the end keyframes first.

Set the time thumb to 5 seconds and lock the *Mover* effector. Unlock the *Rotate Z* effector and enable it for animation by clicking on the green arrow to the left of its name in the Project Window. Since we called this effector *Rotate Z,* we're going to rotate it around its Z axis.

Double-click on *Rotate Z* to open its info window. In the **Rotation** area of the **X-form** palette enter **1800** in the Z rotation field. This will make the lights rotate once per second of animation.

Preview the animation in the Camera View Window. The *Rotate Z* effector and the lights that are attached to it should be spinning around counter-clockwise as the animation plays.

Now set the time thumb back to 5 seconds if it isn't still there. Lock the *Rotate Z* effector and unlock the *Rotate Z2* effector. Guess which axis we're going to rotate it on? Double-click on the *Rotate Z2* effector and enter **-1800** in its Z rotation data field. By rotating this effector 90 degrees on the Y axis earlier, we aligned the object's Z axis with the worlds X axis. This is why we use a Z rotation, even though the effector's direction is aligned with the world X axis.

Finally, render your scene. You should have a photon torpedo with spinning, dimensional flare streaks. To add to the effect, you could go back and animate the *Mover* again to add a gentle tumbling action.

By layering your animation into separate effectors, it's very simple to achieve complex effects.

—Chris Weyers

Creating Perfect Arcs: Rotating Planets

We want to create an animation with a moon orbiting a planet, which is orbiting the sun, while at the same time rotating around their local Y axis. Sounds complex, but thanks to effectors, once again the problem is easily solved.

What we'll be doing here is adding Skeleton Effectors to a scene, using Skeleton Effectors to create multiple rotations on the same axis, and finally, creating perfect arcing motions.

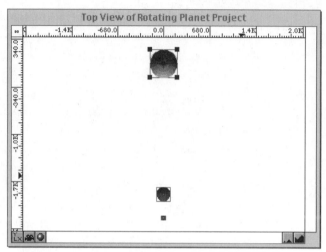

FIGURE *The planets, ready for orbit.*
10.37

STEP ONE

Open the ROTATING PLANETS PROJECT. You will see a yellow sun, a blue planet, and a gray moon, as shown in Figure 10.37.

STEP TWO

Choose **File > Add > Type > Skeleton**. In the top view, click once in the middle of the Sun, a second time in the middle of the Earth, and a third time in the middle of the Moon. **Hit Command+.** to stop the drawing. Don't worry if your skeleton arm joints don't line up perfectly. You should have something similar to Figure 10.38.

Now, parent the Earth to Skeleton Arm, and parent the moon to Joint 2, as shown in Figure 10.39. When the skeleton arm is rotated the earth will rotate, when Joint 2 is rotated the moon will rotate.

STEP THREE: ANIMATE PLANET ROTATIONS

We want the planets to be rotating around their local Y axis, so we'll set that up first.

Select the Earth and open its **Group Link Window**. Change the joint type to **Custom**, and click all limits except for Y-rotation, as shown in Figure 10.40. This will prevent all movement, except for rotation around the Y axis. Select the moon and do the same thing.

Now, enable animation for the Earth by clicking on the little green arrow in the Project Window and move the time thumb to 5 seconds. Double-click on

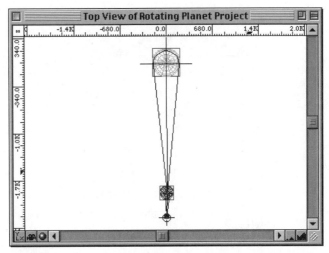

FIGURE   *Your skeleton effectors should look something like this.*
10.38

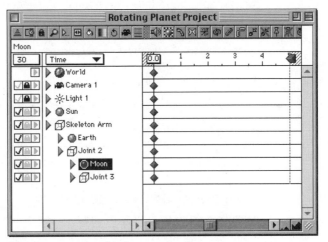

FIGURE   *Parenting the planets to the effectors.*
10.39

the Earth to open its Group Info Window, and set the Y rotation field to
357.6. This will allow a perfect looping rotation.

To create an animation that will loop perfectly from the last frame to the
first frame, you need to figure out how many degrees your object is rotating per
frame and subtract that amount from the end of the animation. If we had entered 360 degrees in the Y-rotation field, our animation would stutter when it

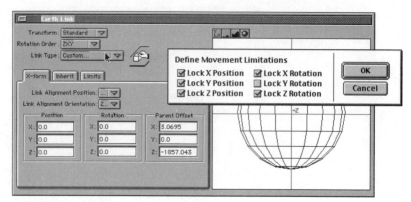

jumped between frame 150 and frame 0. To find the degrees of rotation per frame simply divide 360 by the number of frames you have in your animation.

Here's the example from this project:

360 degrees / 150 frames = 2.4 frames per second

360 degrees − 2.4 degrees = 357.6 degrees

Now you'll want to select the moon and open its Group Info Window. The time thumb should still be at 5 seconds. Set the Y-rotation value to **-357.6**. If you preview the animation now, you will see that the moon and earth are both rotating around their center points on the Y axis.

STEP FOUR: SET UP THE ORBITS

Now we need to set up the rotations of the skeleton arms that will orbit the moon and the earth.

We want the moon to orbit the earth at an angle, so we'll adjust Joint 2's X-rotation to slant it. Select the **X Rotate** tool and click on *Joint 2* in the side view window. Rotate it until the moon is slightly above the earth, as shown in Figure 10.41.

Open the Group Link Window for Joint 2 and change its joint type to **Custom**. Disable all position and rotation parameters, except for the Y axis. (Since we rotated Joint 2 on the X-axis *before* we locked X-rotation, the joint will be locked in its slanted position.)

Open the Group Info Window for Joint 2. Notice that there are values for rotation in the Y and X rotation fields. In order to create a perfectly looping

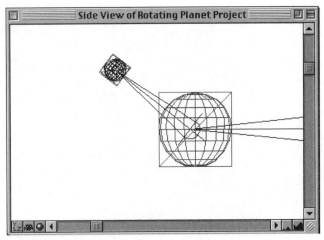

FIGURE *Setting the angle of the Moon's axis of rotation.*
10.41

orbit, we'll have to add these values into the equation. Or we can take the easy way out by parking the skeleton arm.

With the Group Info Window for Joint 2 open, click on the **Park** icon in the **Tool** palette (see Figure 10.42). Notice that the rotation and position values in the Group Info Window have reset themselves to zero as shown in Figure 10.43. Now we can use our standard 357.6 degree rotation to create a perfect orbit.

With Joint 2 selected and its animation enabled, move the time thumb to 5 seconds. Enter **-357.6** in the Y rotation field. Preview the animation in the side view window. The moon should now be making a perfect orbit of the earth. It should also be dropping below the earth's equator in the middle of the animation and moving above it at the beginning and end.

To set up the orbit for the Earth, select *Skeleton Arm* and open its Group Link Window. Change the joint type to **Custom** and disable all position and rotation boxes except for Y-rotation.

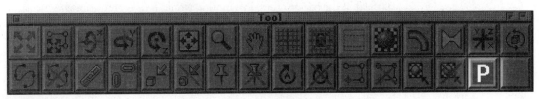

FIGURE *The Park tool.*
10.42

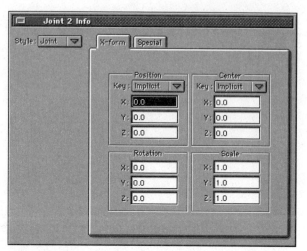

FIGURE   *Using the Park tool zeros out all of the X-Form parameters of an object.*
10.43

Double-click on *Skeleton Arm* to open its Group Info Window. Notice that there is a small value in the Y-rotation field. Enter a zero for Y-axis rotation. In this case, since we're not changing more than one axis, it's easier to set the joints rotation back to zero rather than parking the joint.

Move the time thumb to 5 seconds and enter **-357.6** in the Y-rotation field in Skeleton Arm's Group Info Window.

Preview your animation. The Earth should be rotating on its own axis, while orbiting the sun. The moon should be rotating on its axis, while orbiting the earth.

Chances are that the Earth and Moon are leaving the frame at certain points in the animation. To stop this, and add some excitement to our animation, select the camera and parent it to *Skeleton Arm*. Preview your animation in the project window again. The Earth, Moon, and Sun should all remain perfectly centered within the frame. At first glance it looks like the camera isn't moving at all. But upon closer inspection you will see that the Sun appears to be rotating, even though we haven't set any rotation animation for it. If you added a starfield in the background, this motion would be even more apparent.

If you preview your animation in the side view window, you will see that the camera is indeed moving around in perfect synch with the Skeleton Arm.

Note that just because the camera is parented to the skeleton arm doesn't mean you can't move it. Because the camera's link type is set to free, it can also be animated. Experiment with it.

—Chris Weyers

Chain Link Project Part 1: Setting up Skeleton Effectors

The goal of this project isn't to create an animation, but to learn how to set up a hierarchy of **Skeleton Effectors**. We touched on this a little bit in the previous tutorial but will go into more depth here.

The concepts we'll be covering here are setting joint position and rotation limits, creating an extendable hierarchy, and aligning Skeleton Effectors to each other. So let's get started.

STEP ONE

Open the CHAIN LINK PROJECT on the CD. You should have one object called *Chain link* in your Project Window. Duplicate the chain link once. Constrain the **Move** tool vertically (tab) and, in the front view, move the duplicate down on the Y axis until the inner curves of the chain links barely touch one another, as shown in Figure 10.44.

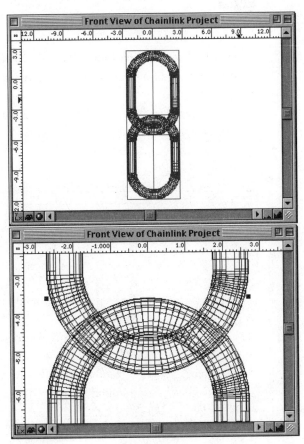

FIGURE   *Setting up your first links.*
10.44

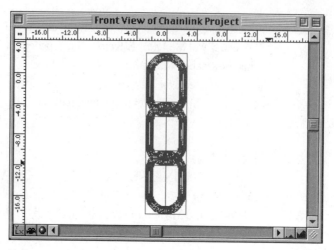

FIGURE
10.45
Making the last link.

Duplicate the chain link again and move it down vertically to the bottom of the middle chain link so its curves are barely touching, as shown in Figure 10.45.

With our links ready, we'll add the skeleton effector joints that will control these links.

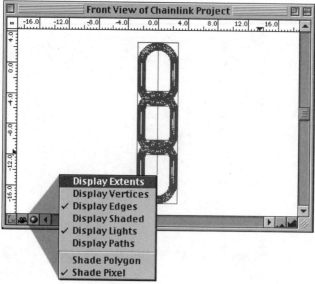

FIGURE
10.46
Turn on Display Extents.

STEP TWO

Expand the front view window to full screen and frame the chain links to fill the entire screen. This will make it easier to see what you're doing. It will also help to have **Display Extents** turned on so you can use the center lines as a guide for placing the effectors. You can do this by holding down the **Option** key and clicking on the shading button in the lower left hand corner of the window (see Figure 10.46).

Before we start creating the effector chain, turn on the snapping grid, as shown in Figure 10.47, to help keep your chain in s straight line.

Now that we have that taken care of, choose **File > Add > Type > Skeleton** and start the chain by clicking in the center of the top chain link's upper curve. Click a second time in the center of the middle chain link's upper curve, and finally, click a third time in center of the bottom chain link's upper curve. You should have something similar to Figure 10.48. Check the top and side views to make sure your skeleton joint chain is centered within the chain links.

FIGURE   *The Grid Snap Tool.*
10.47

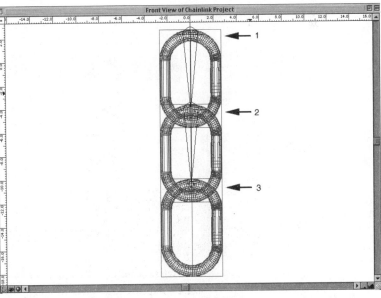

FIGURE   *Creating the initial skeleton.*
10.48

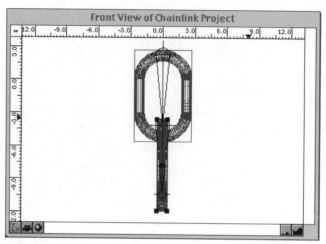

FIGURE
10.49 *Rotate the bottom link 90 degrees.*

Once you're all set up, turn off the visibility for the bottom chain link model by clicking on the little checkbox next to its name in the Project Window. This chain link was only used as a place-marker so we could position the second skeleton arm. We'll use it again when we set joint rotation limits.

Select the new bottom chain link and rotate it 90 degrees on the Y axis, as shown in Figure 10.49, then select the top chain link and parent it to *Skeleton Arm*. Select the bottom chain link and parent it to *Joint 2* as shown in Figure 10.50.

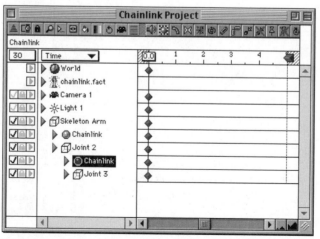

FIGURE
10.50 *Parent the bottom chain link to Joint 2.*

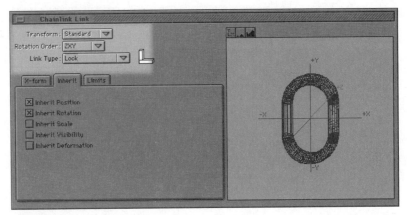

FIGURE   *Change the Link Type to Lock.*
10.51

Now select the top chain link and open its Group Link Window. Change the link type to **Lock**, as shown in Figure 10.51, and then do the same for the bottom chain link. This will ensure that the chain links go everywhere the skeleton effectors go.

If you switch to the side view of the chain link hierarchy, you will see that we've created a chain link with an "open" joint that duplicate links can be attached to.

Now that we've set our links up, we'll need to set joint limits for the skeleton arms to make sure our chain link geometry doesn't intersect when we animate. Let's move on, shall we?

STEP THREE: SETTING JOINT ROTATION LIMITS

Select *Joint 2* and open its Group Link Window. Change the joint type from **Socket** to **Custom** and uncheck the Z-position lock as shown in Figure 10.52.

Now select the **Limits** tab in the Group Link Window for *Joint 2* and select **Rotation**. Entering values in these fields will allow us to control how far our link can rotate.

FIGURE   *Change the Joint Type from Socket to Custom.*
10.52

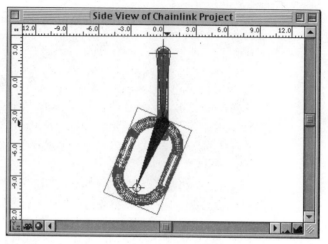

FIGURE   *Rotate Joint 2 until the outsides of the link almost touch.*
10.53

Double-click the **X Rotate Tool** in the **Tool** palette. (Double-clicking any of the rotation tools will lock them as current, until you pick another tool from the tool palette. Alternately you can also choose the tool from the **Tool** menu. This will also lock the current tool until you choose another.) Rotate *Joint 2* on the X axis until the chain link's curves appear to be touching, as shown in Figure 10.53.

In the Group Link Window click on the small arrow next to the **X Minimum** data field and choose **Use current value**, as shown in Figure 10.54. This will insert the current rotation of the joint into this field. Or will it? Notice that the value was actually entered into the **X Maximum** field.

When working with joint rotation and position limits, ElectricImage will automatically insert larger values in the maximum boxes and smaller values in

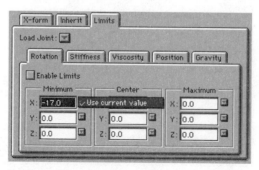

FIGURE   *Select Use Current Value.*
10.54

the minimum boxes. You don't have to try and figure this out yourself. Using just the move and rotate tools, you can easily position joints and insert the proper position and rotation limits in the proper fields.

Now rotate Joint 2 in the opposite direction with the **X Rotate** tool until the middle chain link appears to be touching the upper chain link. Just like last time but in the opposite direction. Click on the small arrow next to the **X Minimum** field in the Group Link Window to insert *Joint 2*'s current rotation value into the field. Don't worry if these values aren't the same, as long as everything looks good.

Double-click on *Joint 2* to open its info window and set its X-rotation back to 0. Switch to front view and open *Joint 2*'s Group Link Window again. Double-click on the **Y Rotate** tool. (Remember, a skeleton effector's Z axis always runs along the *length* of the joint's vector. This means that Y and Z axes are reversed from the world views, in this case.) Rotate *Joint 2* on its Y axis until the bottom curve is somewhat above the midpoint of the top joint, as shown in Figure 10.55, and choose **Use Current Value** in the **Y Minimum** box. Again, the value may be transferred into the **Y Maximum** field. Rotate *Joint 2* to the opposite side and repeat the process (see Figure 10.56).

Double-click on *Joint 2* to open its Group Info Window. Change the Y-rotation value back to 0 and then switch to a top view.

Double-click on the **Z Rotate** tool and rotate *Joint 2* until it nearly touches the edges of the top chain link, as shown in Figure 10.57. You may need to lock *Skeleton Arm* to keep from accidentally moving it. Click on the **Use Current Value** arrow next to **Z Minimum** in *Joint 2*'s Group Link Window. Now rotate

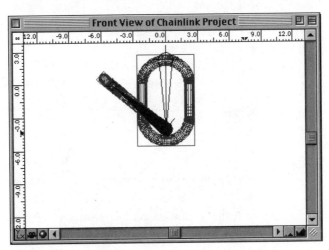

FIGURE   *Rotate the link again until the curves almost touch.*
10.55

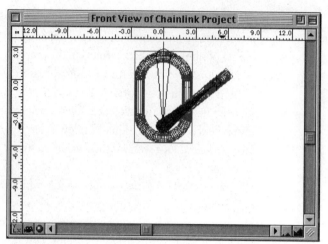

FIGURE *Same as before but backward.*
10.56

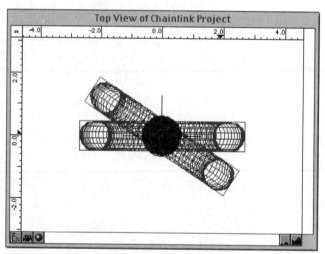

FIGURE *Setting the limits for the Z rotation.*
10.57

Joint 2 in the opposite direction and set the **Z Maximum** rotation limit. You should have this part down to a science by now.

At this point, you should have rotation limits set for *Joint 2* on all axes. To make these limits active, check the **Enable Limits** checkbox shown in Figure 10.58.

Take a moment to experiment on *Joint 2* with the various rotation tools. Notice that you can't rotate the joint past a certain point. Setting these limits

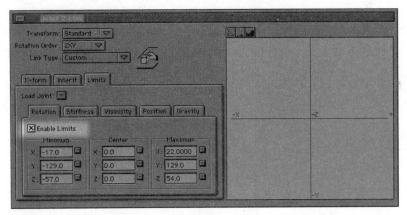

FIGURE   *Check Enable Limits.*
10.58

will ensure that our chain links won't pass through each other when they're animated.

STEP FOUR: SETTING JOINT POSITION LIMITS

Because a chain link needs to be free to move within the interior of the chain it's contained by, we'll need to set a Z-position limit. Remember that the X and Y position channels have been turned off, so they can't receive any motion.

Open the Group Info Window for *Joint 2* and reset all the rotation fields to **0**. Open the Group Link Window for *Joint 2* and switch to the **Position** tab (under the **Limits** tab) as shown in Figure 10.59. Select the **Move** tool and

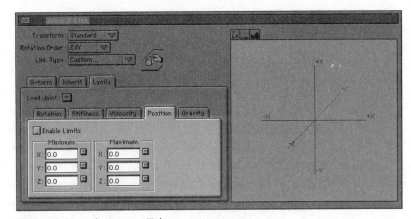

FIGURE   *Go to the Position Tab.*
10.59

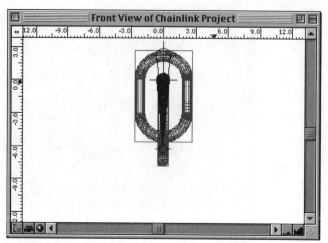

FIGURE   *Reposition Joint 2.*
10.60

constrain it vertically. Select *Joint 2* and move it up about three-quarters of the way into the interior of the top chain link, as shown in Figure 10.60. Insert the current position of the joint to into the **Z Maximum** field in the **Position** box. Leave the **Z Minimum** set to **0**. Click on the **Enable Limits** box and close *Joint 2*'s Group Link Window. Open *Joint 2*'s Group Info Window, and reset its Z-position to **0**.

STEP FIVE: SET UP JOINT ROTATION AND POSITION LIMITS FOR SKELETON ARM

By now you should have the hang of setting up joint rotation and position limits. Now we'll let you set up the limits for the top *Skeleton Arm* joint. Before you can do this, however, you'll need another chain link to reference to.

Turn on the visibility for the original bottom chain link. Constrain the **Move** tool vertically and move this chain link up so that the lower curve just barely touches the upper curve of the top chain link, as shown in Figure 10.61. Open the Group Info Window and rotate the reference link 90 degrees on the Y axis. In the Project Window, lock the reference chain link and *Joint 2,* so they don't accidentally get moved.

Open the Group Link Window for *Skeleton Arm* and change its joint type to **Custom**. Uncheck X and Y position to disable those parameters.

Now go through the same procedure for *Skeleton Arm* that you did for *Joint 2* to set the rotation and position limits. Compare your results to the ones in Figure 10.62.

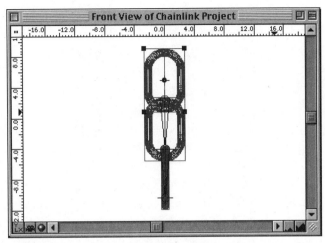

FIGURE
10.61
Like before, we want to set the links up so that they almost or just barely touch to simulate their actual physical mass.

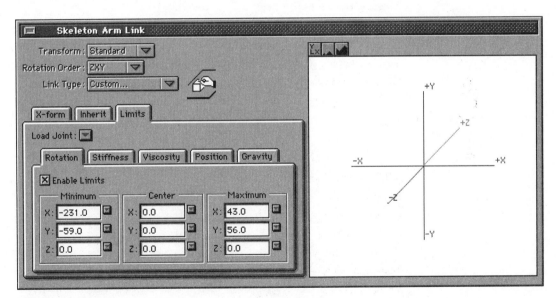

FIGURE
10.62
The Skeleton Arm's limits.

STEP SIX: JOINING LINKS

At this point you've got a chain link that can be repeatedly duplicated and linked to create a chain of any length.

Select *Joint 3,* open its Group Link Window and change its joint type to **Lock**. Because our duplicate links will join each other at Joint 3, we want to make sure there is no extra rotation at this point. Select *Skeleton Arm* and duplicate it (**Command + D**). You will get a duplicate of the entire *Chainlink* hierarchy. Rename the duplicate *Skeleton Arm 2*. Constrain the **Move** tool vertically and drag the duplicate down so that the center of *Skeleton Arm 2* lines up with the center of *Joint 3*.

You're probably having problems doing this. That's because we've already set a position limit for this joint. Since we're moving it down, we'll need to open the Group Link Window and turn off position limits by clicking on the **Limits** tab, then the **Position** tab, and then by unchecking **Enable Limits**. Because position limits are calculated in world units, you will have to reset the position limits for the chain links each time you duplicate and move them.

With position limits turned off, you can now position the duplicate Skeleton Arm over *Joint 3*, as shown in Figure 10.63. We want to have an exact match here, but there's another problem. When the *Skeleton Arm 2* is selected, it turns black, obscuring *Joint 3*. To line these joints up, we need to change *Skeleton Arm 2*'s display style.

Double-click on *Skeleton Arm 2* to open its Group Info Window. Change the display style from **Joint** to **Cross**. Now you will be able to exactly position *Skeleton Arm 2* over *Joint 3*, as shown in Figure 10.64. Once you have *Skeleton Arm 2* positioned, change its display style back to **Joint**.

With *Skeleton Arm 2* selected, click on the **Link to Parent** tool, and choose *Joint 3* as the parent, as shown in Figure 10.65.

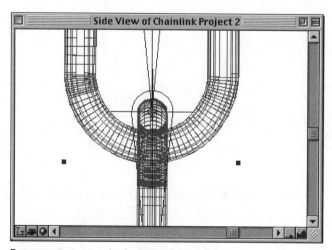

FIGURE　*Reposition the duplicate Skeleton Arm.*
10.63

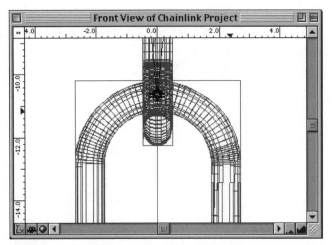

FIGURE   *Exact positioning.*
10.64

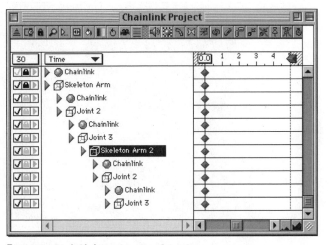

FIGURE   *Link Skeleton Arm 2 to Joint 3.*
10.65

STEP SEVEN: MANIPULATE THE CHAIN WITH IK

You can now manipulate your chain with the **Inverse Kinematics** tool. To do this, select the **IK** tool from the toolbar. Going down the new hierarchy, shift-select *Joint 2, Joint 3, Skeleton Arm 2, Joint 2,* and finally, *Joint 3,* as shown in Figure 10.66.

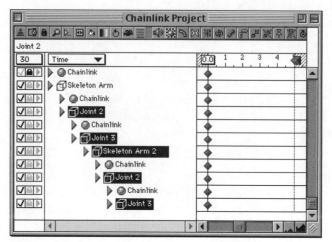

FIGURE *Adding IK.*
10.66

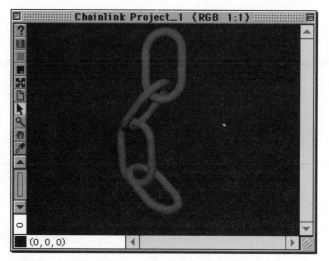

FIGURE *All of our work, in action.*
10.67

Now click on *Joint 3* of the *Skeleton Arm 2* chain and drag the chain into a new position. By moving *Joint 3,* you are forcing all the other joint rotations to be calculated by the IK tool. Notice how the links are both rotating, and moving up and down in the interior of each other. See Figure 10.67 for an example. This concludes the first part of our Chain Link project tutorial. Grab yourself a well-deserved snack.

—*Chris Weyers*

Chain Link Project Part 2: Forward Kinematics, Inverse Kinematics, and Auto-IK

Now that we've got a nicely built hierarchy, we should utilize it to learn about forward kinematics, inverse kinematics, and Auto-IK constraints. Our chain links provide us with a perfect opportunity.

The concepts we'll cover here are animating a hierarchy with forward kinematics, animating a hierarchy with inverse kinematics, animating a hierarchy with an Auto-IK constraint, and setting an Auto-IK termination point.

STEP ONE: SETUP

Open the CHAIN LINK PROJECT you created in the previous part of this tutorial. You can load the CHAIN LINK PROJECT 2 file from your ElectricImage Handbook CD-ROM if you need the project prebuilt and ready to go.

Before we can start animating, we need to give the root of the chain a little more freedom to move. Select *Skeleton Arm* (the topmost Skeleton Joint on the chain) shown in Figure 10.68 and open its Group Link Window. Change the **Link Type** to **Free**. Select the **Limits** tab and then the **Position** sub-tab. Uncheck **Enable Limits**, as shown in Figure 10.69. Even though we set the joint type to free, the position limits would have still been honored if the Enable Limits box had been left checked.

To prevent confusion, rename *Joint 2* (the child of *Skeleton Arm 2*) as *Joint 2B,* and rename the *Joint 3* Effector, at the bottom of the hierarchy, *End Effector,* as shown in Figure 10.70.

Do a **Save As...** on you project and call it *CHAIN LINK PROJECT 2*. We'll

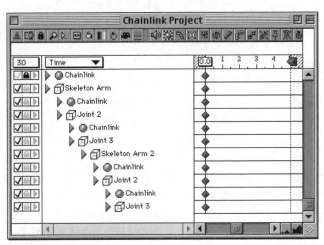

FIGURE *Selecting Skeleton Arm.*
10.68

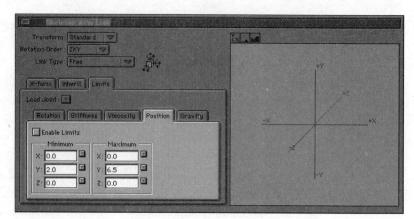

FIGURE   *Uncheck the Enable Limits checkbox.*
10.69

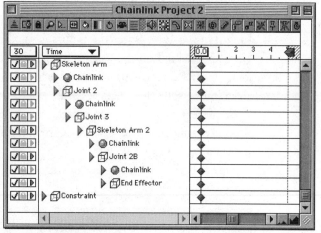

FIGURE   *Do some renaming.*
10.70

be doing a short forward kinematics exercise, a short inverse kinematics exercise, and a short Auto-IK constraint exercise. Make sure to do a different **Save As...** if you decide to save your work during any of these steps. We'll be using the CHAIN LINK PROJECT 2 as the master project we revert to after trying each type of animation.

STEP TWO: FORWARD KINEMATICS

First, we're going to try to animate the chain swinging with forward kinematics tools. In the Project Window, enable animation for *Skeleton Arm, Joint 2,*

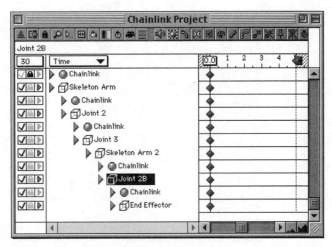

FIGURE *Enable the Animation Arrows.*
10.71

Skeleton Arm 2, Joint 2B, and the *End Effector* at the bottom of the hierarchy, as shown in Figure 10.71. Move the time thumb to 1 second.

Frame the entire chain link hierarchy in the side view window and double-click on the **X Rotate** tool. This will make it the active tool until another is chosen. Rotate *Joint 2* to the left and it will stop when it hits its rotation limits (see Figure 10.72).

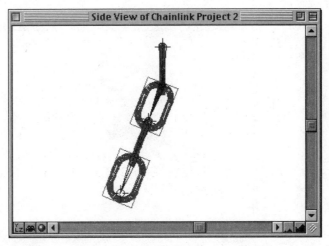

FIGURE *Rotate Joint 2 with the X-Rotate tool until it hits its rotation limits.*
10.72

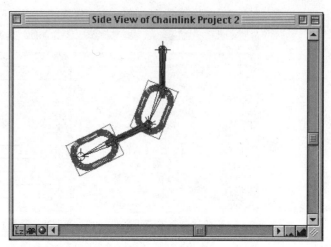

FIGURE
10.73
Rotate Skeleton Arm 2 and observe what happens.

Move down the chain one level to *Skeleton Arm 2* and use the **X Rotate** tool to rotate it to its limits, as shown in Figure 10.73. Notice that rotating this joint only affects the children below it. The chain links above it don't react to the change at all.

Now move down the chain one more time to *Joint 2B* and use the **X rotate** tool to rotate it to its limits, as shown in Figure 10.74. Take a look at your Project Window. You've got three keyframed joints. If you change the position of any of these joints, it will affect all of those below it.

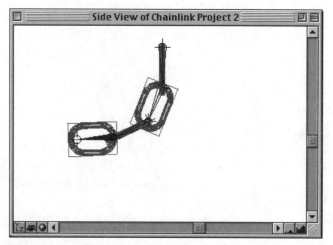

FIGURE
10.74
Rotate Joint 2B.

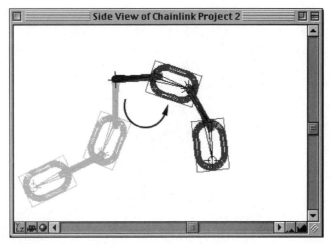

FIGURE *All the other objects will follow Skeleton Arm as it is rotated.*
10.75

Now select *Skeleton Arm* with the **X Rotate** tool and rotate it around. None of the other objects lose their individual orientation, but they all follow along the arc the root creates when it rotates (see Figure 10.75).

This is how animating with forward kinematics works. You animate the hierarchy from the top down, one joint at a time, until you reach your goal. Play back the animation you've created so far in the side view window. Hardly convincing, is it. To make this chain swing more authentic we would have to work out the exact timing for when each joint should rotate—a time-consuming process. Imagine if this chain were 1000 links long!

STEP THREE: INVERSE KINEMATICS

There is a better, more intuitive way to create the swinging motion of the chain. We can use the **Inverse Kinematics** tool to move the entire hierarchy at once. By applying Inverse Kinematics to the chain, we can work up the hierarchy from the bottom, passing the movements of the lowest child on the chain to the root of the chain.

Return the time thumb to 0. Hold down the **Shift** key and select all of the skeleton joints in the Project Window (even the ones you haven't set keyframes for). Choose **Keyframe > Clear All Keyframes**. This will clear out all of the keyframes you set in the previous exercise.

Now move the time thumb to 1 second. Hold down the **Shift** key and select all of the skeleton joints in the Project Window (see Figure 10.76). Select the **IK** tool from the **Tool** palette, as shown in Figure 10.77, and, in the side view

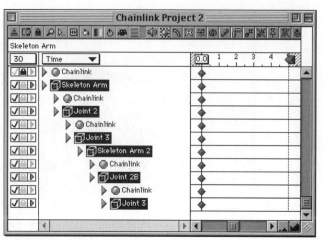

FIGURE   *Shift-select all of the skeleton joints.*
10.76

FIGURE   *Select the IK tool.*
10.77

window, click on the *End Effector* that sits at the bottom of the chain. Drag it around in any direction you like and release.

Your entire joint hierarchy will move as a whole in reaction to the *End Effector*. You will notice that the chain links have been both translated and rotated, as shown in Figure 10.78. The **IK** tool will move and rotate any joint within the limits that have been set for it.

You should also notice that keyframes have been created for all of the selected joints in the Project Window (see Figure 10.79). In one simple move, you set a keyframe for all the links in the chain. Think how long this would have taken with forward kinematics.

Now select *Skeleton Arm 2, Joint 2B,* and *End Effector* in the Project Window. Use the **IK** tool again to rotate them into a new position. Notice that only the bottom two chain links react. This is the way Inverse Kinematics works in ElectricImage. You select all of the joints you want to move and use the IK tool to move them.

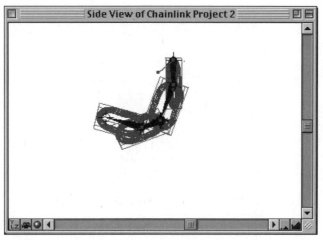

FIGURE *Everything gets translated and rotated.*
10.78

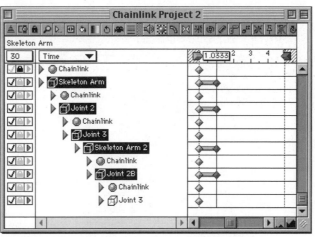

FIGURE *Keyframes will be created for all selected objects.*
10.79

Click on the **Move** tool in the tool palette. Select *Skeleton Arm* in the side view window and drag it left. Notice that the rest of the joints follow along as expected without reorienting themselves (see Figure 10.80).

What if we wanted to have the top chain link move left in the side view window, but we also wanted the bottom chain link to stay right where it is, as if it were fastened down to something? Let's try to do this with IK.

Select *Joint 2, Skeleton Arm2, Joint 2B,* and *End Effector* in the Project Window, as shown in Figure 10.81. Select the **IK** tool, then click and drag right on

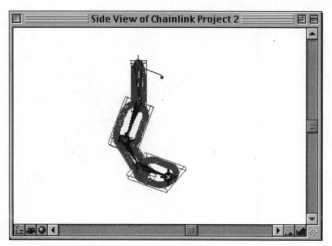

FIGURE   *With the Move tool, everything just follows along.*
10.80

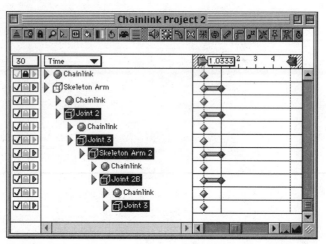

FIGURE   *Shift-select* Joint 2, Skeleton Arm2, Joint 2B, *and* End Effector.
10.81

the *End Effector* in the side view window. The chain will reorient itself as if it has been pulled tight (see Figure 10.82). There's only one problem. Play back your animation in the side view window.

The chain is moving from right to left as it pulls itself tight. The lowest chain link is moving right as the top chain link is moving left. Why is this happening? It's happening because the keyframe that moves the *Skeleton Arm* (root) to the left is pulling all of the children (and their motion paths) with it.

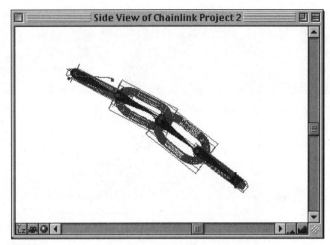

FIGURE   *The chain will reorient itself.*
10.82

This is a fine example of a forward kinematics solution conflicting with an In-verse Kinematics solution. We got the positioning of all the joints with the IK tool, but when we want to move the parent, we translate a new set of com-mands down to the children. They have to follow their parent. So, the question is, *Is there an easy way we can make our chain pull tight?*

STEP FOUR: USING AN AUTO-IK CONSTRAINT

In order to have a child on a chain stay in position as one of its parents moves, we need to constrain it. The only way to create a constraint on the child is to force it to follow an object that lies outside of its immediate hierarchy. This is what the **Constrain to Object** tool, shown in Figure 10.83, and **Auto-IK** are for.

Return the time thumb to 0 and clear all keyframes once more. Select the *End Effector* at the bottom of the Project Window and duplicate it (**Com-mand+D**). With the duplicate selected, click on the **Unlink From Parent** but-ton shown in Figure 10.84. Rename the duplicate *Constraint*. This constraint

FIGURE   *The Constrain to Object Tool.*
10.83

FIGURE   *The Unlink From Parent button/tool.*
10.84

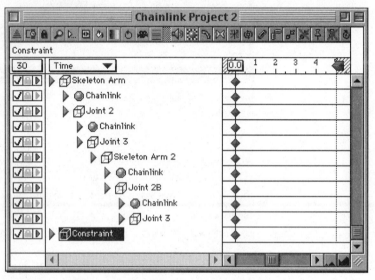

FIGURE   *The* Constraint *object is not part of our chain hierarchy.*
10.85

object now lies outside of the chain link hierarchy, as shown in Figure 10.85. This is the object we will Auto-IK constrain the end of our chain to.

Double-click on the *Constraint* effector to open its Group Info Window. Change the display style from **Cross** to **Box**. In the **X-form** tab, change all rotation values to **0**. (Zeroing out the rotation for the effector will ensure it doesn't pass any skewed rotation information on to our chain link hierarchy.) In the **Special** tab, change all of the **Size** values to **6**, and the **Origin** values to **-3**. This will put a box effector on the end of your chain link hierarchy as shown in Figure 10.86.

Select the *End Effector* in the Project Window and click on the **Constrain to Object** tool. Pick *Constraint* as the object to follow. Notice that two keyframes were automatically set for *End Effector* (see Figure 10.87). These represent custom keyframes that will be recalculated every time the *Constraint* moves.

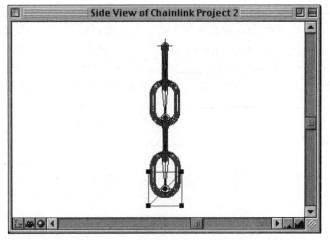

FIGURE   *Placing a new box effector.*
10.86

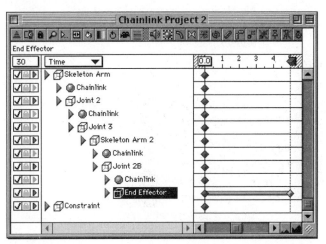

FIGURE   *Two keyframes are set for* End Effector.
10.87

You can disable the automatic calculation of Auto-IK keyframes by choosing **Edit > Keyframe...** *and unchecking the* **Calculate Attach/Look At/AutoFrames** *box shown in Figure 10.88. With this option disabled, AutoFrames will only be calculated when you do a preview or a render. If you want to force an AutoFrames calculation during your work, choose the* **Keyframe>Calculate AutoFrames** *command.*

FIGURE **10.88** *Disabling the automatic calculation of your Auto-IK keyframes.*

Select *Constraint* with the **Move** tool and drag it to the right. The chain links shouldn't follow. Hit **Command+Z** to undo the move. Select *Skeleton Arm* with the **Move** tool and try to move it. It's not going anywhere, even though its joint type is set to free.

What's happening here? Right now the entire chain is constrained, but it hasn't been told what to be constrained to. Or where the constraint should stop. To fix this problem we need to set the **Auto-IK** termination point for the constrained part of the chain.

Select *End Effector* in the Project Window. Change the display method from **Time** to **Keyframe**. Twirl down the arrow next to *End Effector*. Find the arrow for **Auto Frames** and twirl it down as well. At the very bottom, you will see an **Auto IK** field (see Figure 10.89). This is where we set the Auto IK termination point.

Click the **Auto IK** popup menu at frame 0. Select *Joint* 2, as shown in Figure 10.90. By doing this, we are telling ElectricImage stop passing IK information up the chain at *Joint 2*. (The joint you select as the termination point is included in the IK calculations.) Now each time we move the *Constraint* object, all the joints in the chain will be oriented to it with an IK solution, *except* for *Skeleton Arm*.

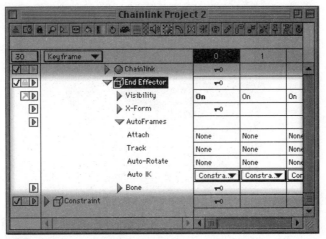

FIGURE   *Look for the Auto IK field.*
10.89

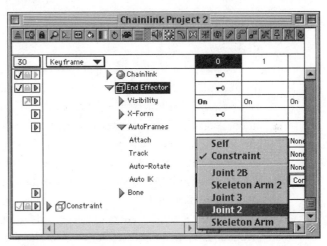

FIGURE   *Select* Joint 2.
10.90

Twirl the arrows for *End Effector* back down and switch the Project Window display back to **Time**. Set the time thumb to 1 second.

In the side view window, select the constraint with the **Move** tool. Drag it to the left and upward. Be patient here, it could take a few seconds for the calculation to occur. All the links in the chain should reorient themselves to the position of the constraint object.

Notice that the entire chain hierarchy reorients itself to follow the constraint object. Unless you've changed your joint types, your chain is also breaking apart

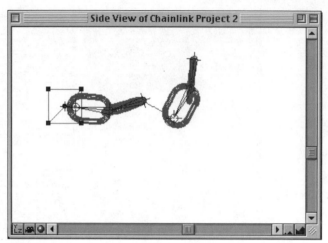

FIGURE *The chain breaks apart.*
10.91

in the middle, as shown in Figure 10.91, so undo the move you just made for *Constraint.*

The reason the chain broke apart is because *Skeleton Arm 2* has some positional freedom on the Y axis, and *Joint 2* above it has freedom on the Z axis. Normally, this wouldn't be a problem, but because we're both constraining the end of the chain *and* animating the chain root, we're able to orient the *Joint 2* and *Skeleton Arm 2* to their maximum positional freedom. By pulling on both ends of the chain, we've forced it to break in the middle. The lesson here is that you need to be thinking about how you're going to animate your hierarchy while you're creating it. When using Auto-IK to animate a chain, you need to make sure the entire portion of the chain you want to animate is part of the IK solution. This often means adding an extra effector to the beginning or end of a chain. In our case we want to add an extra effector to the top of the chain and make it the new root. We also need to change the joint type for *Skeleton Arm 2.* We'll do that first.

STEP FIVE

Select *Skeleton Arm 2* and open its Group Link Window. Change the joint type from **Custom** to **Socket**. This will remove the positional freedom. Select the *Constraint* effector and duplicate it. Rename the duplicate *Root,* constrain the **Move** tool vertically, and align the root object with *Skeleton Arm,* as shown in Figure 10.92. You will need to lock the *Constraint* effector so you don't accidentally move it, too.

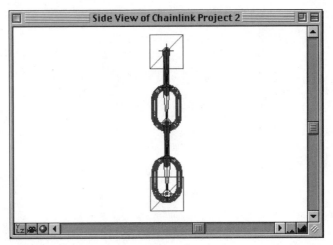

FIGURE   *Aligning the* Root *object.*
10.92

Select *Skeleton Arm* and click on the **Link to Parent** tool. Select *Root* as the parent. Open up *Skeleton Arm*'s Group Link Window and change the link type to **Socket**. This will prevent *Skeleton Arm* from breaking apart from the root object as we move it.

We also need to reset the termination point for the *End Effector* to include *Skeleton Arm* in the Auto-IK solution. To do this switch the Project Window to **Keyframe** mode and twirl down *End Effector*'s arrow. Twirl down the **AutoFrames** arrow and set the Auto-IK termination point to *Skeleton Arm,* as shown in Figure 10.93.

Switch the Project Window back to **Time** display and move the time thumb to 1 second. Now try to animate the chain again. In the side view window select the *Constraint* effector and drag it to the left and upward (see Figure 10.94).

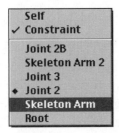

FIGURE   *Set the Auto IK termination point to* Skeleton Arm.
10.93

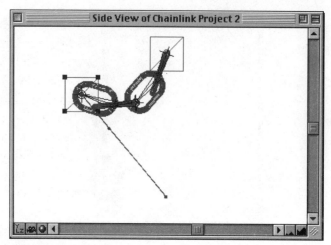

FIGURE *Drag the* Constraint *effector again.*
10.94

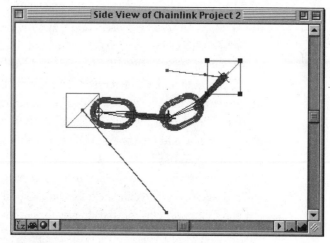

FIGURE *Drag* Root *to the right.*
10.95

Move the time thumb to 2 seconds and select the *Root* in the side view window. Drag it to the right, as shown in Figure 10.95. Notice that if you drag the root far enough, the *End Effector* will pull away from the *Constraint*. This is because the constraint is doing just what its name suggests—constraining the chain. It's not linked to it hierarchically. If the root pulls the chain away from the constraint object, the chain will follow but stay oriented to the constraint.

—Chris Weyers

Creating Bulging Muscles with Bones

Bones are wonderful tools that allow you to create believable motion in body parts like arms and legs, but let's take a look at how to overcome a basic shortcoming of realistic motion using bones: muscle bulge. If you look at your arm, for example, you'll see that your bicep muscle bulges up and in, as you raise your forearm. However, the basic bones setup (a bone in the upper arm, a bone in the forearm) will not automatically create this muscle bulge for you—you'll notice, in fact, that a "wave" using only the standard bones setup looks rather weak if you focus on the completely unchanging profile of the upper arm (see the NoMuscleWave.mov file on the CD). Therefore, in order to gain that extra degree of realism, we have to add a little something to the project.

STEP ONE

Begin by opening the MUSCLEWAVE.PROJECT on the CD. There you'll find a nice blue hand (generously donated for this project by Keith Lango—thanks, Keith!) and a basic bones setup (see Figure 10.96).

If you would like practice setting up bones, delete the ones in the project, and recreate them from scratch (good practice); if not, just use the already linked and ready to go project as is.

Next, we need to add another bone to the project to create the muscle movement. After some experimentation, I found that laying the bone along the same axis as the upper arm bone and near (but above) the upper arm bone gave the best approximation of a biceps muscle (see Figure 10.97).

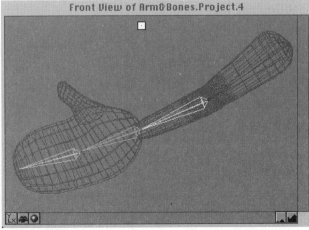

FIGURE **10.96** *The basic setup, including linked bones for upper arm, forearm, wrist, and hand.*

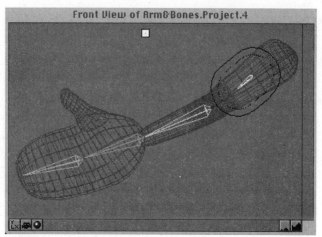

FIGURE **10.97** *The muscle bone highlighted, along with its regions of influence (black ovals).*

The reason for this is that the "region of influence" of bones is cylindrical about the length of the bone (the ovals around the selected muscle bone in the above image). As the muscle runs in the long direction of the arm, it makes sense to place the bone along the same axis as the upper arm bone. Vertically (from the top), this bone is lined up directly on top of the upper arm bone. Once this bone is added, the hierarchy should look like Figure 10.98.

Note that the muscle bone has been childed (linked) to the *Upper Arm Bone,* so that it will follow position and rotation of the upper arm.

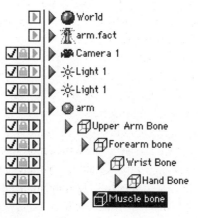

FIGURE **10.98** *Bones hierarchy, with the muscle bone highlighted.*

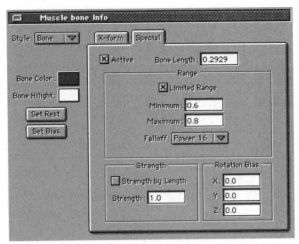

STEP TWO

After bone placement, the next step is to set the bone up to have the proper region of influence and fall off. After experimentation, I was fairly happy with the settings in Figure 10.99.

Please note in this dialogue that I have set the **Limited Range** checkbox to active, set the **Minimum** and **Maximum** ranges, and set the **Fall off** to **Power of 16** rather than the default **Ease**. This makes the bulge of the muscle more well-defined. Essentially, the higher-order falloff rate simulates a bodybuilder's muscle more closely. Having a lower-order exponent, or **Ease**, creates a less-defined muscle. Also, setting the **Minimum** to **0.6** and the **Maximum** to **0.8** creates a region of influence for the bone that encompasses the biceps area without straying into the forearm area or the shoulder area. But don't just copy my settings, play with them to get the look *you* like!

So now we have a muscle bone attached to our upper arm bone. How do we animate the muscle bulge? Simple: We animate the Y scale of the bone (we can animate the X scale as well if we want a more circular muscle). Note in Figure 10.100 how changing the Y scale to 1.5 creates a nicely defined muscle bulge.

This looks just wonderful! The only problem is, how do we get the muscle to bulge just when the forearm rotates up and down? There are actually two different methods to do this, one using **Copy** and **Paste** of data cells and a little spreadsheet work; the other using EI 2.9's great new F-Curve feature.

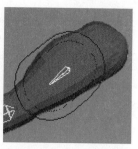

FIGURE *With a Y scale of 1.5, the arm bone "bulges" the upper arm, simulating a*
10.100 *muscle.*

STEP THREE: METHOD 1 (SPREADSHEET METHOD)

In the MUSCLEPLAIN.PROJECT included, I've already created a waving
motion for the arm, including the rotation of the forearm (rotation about the
forearm bone's X axis). Obviously, when the forearm is rotated up (a negative
X-rotation in this case), it is closer to the upper arm, and the muscle should be
contracted (or bulged). When the forearm is rotated down (close to 0 rotation),
the muscle should be more at rest and not as bulged. The question now is how
to translate the X-rotation of the forearm into the Y scale of the muscle bone.
This is where the spreadsheet comes in. After some experimenting, I decided
that I thought a Y scale of 1.5 looked good for the "maximum bulge" for the
muscle. The maximum rotation (which happens in my project at time 1.125)
is about -60 degrees. What I need to do, then, is scale the results of the X-rotation of the forearm so that the largest rotation (–60 degrees) changes to the
largest value we want for the Y scale (1.5). Before we sit down and do the math,
there is one other important point: the *rest* value of the Y scale is 1.0, *not* 0.
Therefore, when the forearm's X rotation is 0, the muscle's Y scale should return
to 1.0. How to we do this? We scale our X-rotation to be a maximum of 0.5,
and then add 1.0 to it. When all is said and done, the formula for doing this
conversion is:

$$- (X \text{ rotation})/120 + 1 = (Y \text{ scale})$$

Minus the X-rotation gives us a positive value (at least when the forearm is
rotating closer to the upper arm); dividing by 120 ensures that when the X-rotation value is 60 (its maximum value), we will generate 0.5; adding 1 scales
this number back up to 1.5, which is the maximum Y scale we want. Also consider: If our X-rotation is 0 (rest position), the Y scale is 1.0, *and* if our X-rotation is 10 (i.e., its less than rest position), our Y scale value will be 0.9167, a

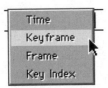

FIGURE *Changing the Project Window mode.*
10.101

scale less than one (in other words, the Y scale will make the muscle "squash" the arm a little, flattening out the muscle).

We thus have a good formula; now how do we get it into the Y scale values for the whole animation? We use EI's copy and paste features. First, change the dropdown menu in the Project Window to **Keyframe** or **Frame** mode, as shown in Figure 10.101.

Next, still in the Project Window, twirl down the arrows under the *Forearm bone,* then twirl down the **X-Form** channels, revealing the **Pitch (X)** frames. There, you'll see the actual values for the rotation for each frame. Select these frames from first to last by selecting the first frame, scrolling to the end of the animation, and selecting the last one while holding down the shift key. You should have something similar to Figure 10.102.

Once this is done, simply select **Copy** from the **Edit** menu (or press **Command-c**). You now have all the frames for X-rotation stored in the clipboard.

Now open your spreadsheet program of choice, and select **Paste** (or **Command-V**). One *important* note here: ClarisWorks™ (and likely other spreadsheets as well) does not include enough data cells in the horizontal direction to allow all your data to be pasted directly in. What you must do first is add columns to the spreadsheet manually. In ClarisWorks, this involves selecting several columns and selecting **Calculate>Insert Cells...** (or **Command-Shift-I**). You may need to do this several times before you get enough data cells to successfully paste in the values.

Forearm bone	⊷0		
Visibility	**On**	On	On
X-Form	⊷0		
Position	⊷0		
Center	⊷0		
Pitch (X)	**0.0**	0.0	0.0
Yaw (Y)	**0.0**	0.0	0.0

FIGURE *The Forearm bone's frames in spreadsheet mode, showing the first several*
10.102 *frames for X-rotation selected.*

	A	B	C	D	E	F
1	0	0	0	0	0.6195	0.7194
2						
3	1	1	1	1	0.9948375	0.994005

FIGURE
10.103 *Some data cells in ClarisWorks, showing how the scale (in row 3) relates to the rotation (in row 1).*

Once the data is pasted into the spreadsheet, simply use the formula we came up with, above. For data cell A1, the formula would look like this:

$$= (-A1/120) + 1$$

(You can move to data cell A3 and simply type this formula into the edit box.) Then, select the entire row (A3 in this instance), and select **Calculate>Fill Right...** (or **Command-R**). This will fill all data cells in row A3 with the proper formula and present the results in the cells. If you look at the numbers, you'll see that they move around 1.0, down a little, and then up to about 1.5, which is just what we wanted. Figure 10.103 is what you should have.

One other little note here: I was not totally satisfied by simply pasting these numbers back into EI starting at cell 0. As a muscle generally begins bulging just before the arm starts to move, I pasted the values back into EI starting at spreadsheet cell E3, rather than A3. This made the muscle bulge "anticipate" the movement of the arm by 4 frames (or, at 24 fps, about 0.16 seconds). This simple frame offset was a subtle but effective change to the basic plan outlined above. The one problem with this is that you have 4 frames at the end of the animation that don't have corresponding movement. Solution? I just cut the last 4 frames out of the animation!

Once this is done, select row A3 (if it isn't already selected) and copy (**Command-c**) the values back into the clipboard. Then return to EI, twirl down the arrows under the *Muscle bone* and **X-Form** and find the Y scale row. Select the first cell and paste (**Command-V**) the values into these cells as shown in Figure 10.104.

That's about it! Simply preview the animation, and you should see the muscle bulge with the movement of the arm! If you don't want to take the time to run out this preview, simply check the MUSCLESPREAD-SHEET.MOV on the CD for a fully rendered movie. If things didn't work out exactly right, you can look at MUSCLESPREADSHEET.PROJECT on the CD to see how I did it.

Was method 1 too mathematical? You don't want to go outside EI? Do you just love F-Curves? Well then, Method 2 is for you.

▶ Y Scale	1.0	1.0	1.0	1.0	0.9948

FIGURE 10.104 *The "Muscle bone's" Y scale values, pasted in from the spreadsheet.*

STEP FOUR

In method 2, we will assign the X-rotation of the forearm and the Y scale of the muscle bone to F-Curves and change the data curve to fit right within the **F-Curve Window.**

First, let's add the forearm X-rotation and muscle bone Y scale to the F-Curve Window. Once again, twirl down the arrows next to the *Forearm bone,* then twirl down the **X-form** channels, revealing the **Pitch (X)** row. If you're using my project, there will already be keyframes for this property, and you'll see that the little black arrow (far left) is grayed out, as shown in Figure 10.105.

If the arrow is not grayed out, simply double-click on **Pitch (X)**, answer yes to any dialogue box that might appear, and the arrow will go gray. Now do the same thing for the Y scale property of the *Muscle bone* effector. Once both channels have been added to the F-Curve Window, select **Windows>Function Curve Editor** (**command `**) and the F-Curve Window will appear as shown in Figures 10.106 and 10.107, with at least 2 items in it (if it's my project, more will be there).

FIGURE 10.105 *The Pitch (X) property, its black arrow (far left) grayed out.*

● ▢ Forearm bone_X-Form_Pitch (X) (1C
○ ▢ Wrist Bone_X-Form_Pitch (X) (100.'
○ ▢ Wrist Bone_X-Form_Yaw (Y) (100.%
○ ▢ Wrist Bone_X-Form_Roll (Z) (100.%
○ ▢ Hand Bone_X-Form_Pitch (X) (100.%
○ ▢ Hand Bone_X-Form_Yaw (Y) (100.%
● ▢ Muscle bone_X-Form_Y Scale (100.C

FIGURE 10.106 *The F-curve selection area, with* Forearm bone *and* Muscle bone *checked (the black dots are filled in).*

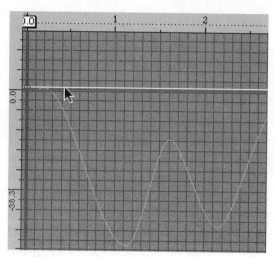

FIGURE **10.107** *The F-curve main window, with Pitch in green and Scale in white (straight line with the mouse pointing at it).*

Before doing anything else, make the Y scale an F-Curve by double-clicking the Y scale text and selecting F-Curve from the **Motion type** pop-up, as shown in Figure 10.108.

Now that the Y scale is an F-Curve, we'll copy and paste the X-rotation curve into the Y scale curve (replacing the straight line). Unfortunately, at this revision (2.9Q), EI will not allow direct copy and paste. To get around this, highlight the **Pitch (X)** text, selecting the entire F-Curve for the **Pitch (X)** channel, then click the small piece of paper icon, and select **Save all...** (see Figure 10.109).

In the dialogue box that comes up, save the envelope wherever you wish. Next, select the Y scale F-Curve, click the paper icon and select **Load To Replace All...**, find the envelope you just saved, and double-click it. This will replace the straight line in the Y scale with an exact copy of the X rotation's curve (in other words, both curves will look the same). To reformat this curve to fit

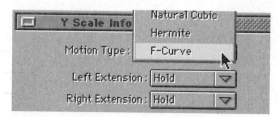

FIGURE **10.108** *Forcing the Y Scale to become an F-Curve.*

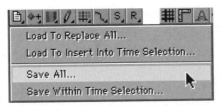

FIGURE **10.109** *Selecting Save all to save an envelope of the X-rotation data curve.*

what we want (a curve that gets bigger when the X-rotation gets smaller, and that is scaled from 1.0 to 1.5 (see method 1 for a detailed discussion of these numbers), we must first invert the curve so that when the X-rotation curve goes down, the Y scale curve will rise. First, drag a box around all the keyframes for the Y scale in the F-curve window (use the mountain icons to shrink the F-Curve window until you can see the whole curve), then select, under the **R** icon, **Reverse Data**, as shown in Figure 10.110.

Now that the data is reversed, we need to reduce its scale to less than 0.5 (we will move it so that it is centered around 1.0 in just a moment, so hold on). To do this, we must first set our ranges. From the **R** icon, select **Set Ranges…** and set the ranges as shown in Figure 10.111.

Note that the maximum Data value is now 0.5, so that the largest keyframe will only have a value of 0.5. Now simply select **Fit To Data Range** from the **R** icon menu. This will squash all keyframes to 0.5 or less. However, you will see that the actual curves are now all over the place. Don't worry about them, for the moment. First, with all the keyframes still selected (solid red squares), drag the first keyframe up until it is at 1.0 on the Y axis. To keep from moving the keyframes forward and backward, press the tab key twice to select **vertical**

FIGURE **10.110** *Reversing the Y scale data.*

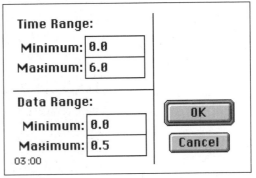

FIGURE **10.111** *Setting the Time and Data Ranges for the Y scale conversion.*

movement only (pressing the tab key twice more takes you back to a regular mouse pointer). Now comes the fun part. First, drag the mouse anywhere there are no keyframes in the F-Curve Window to deselect all keyframes. Then it's time to tilt the little blue handles for each of the keyframes to get the curve nice and small again. If you find that selecting one handle doesn't move the other handle for the keyframe (in other words, the curve gets a spike where you're moving the handle), click **Undo** to undo the change, then **Command-click** the blue handle. This will force the curve to be continuous at this point, which will make things look much better in the final animation. In Figure 10.112, I merely flattened out the handles:

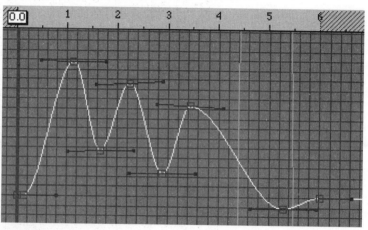

FIGURE *Flattening out the handles causes the curve to appear thus.*
10.112

Now we've got a basic muscle movement that matches the rotation of the forearm. But don't think you're done—this is just the beginning! Since the values here are F-Curves, you can change them (maybe you want one of the muscle bulges to be larger), move them around in time (perhaps you would prefer, as I do, that the muscles move just a few frames before the arm), and even alter the shape of the curve. All of these actions can create subtleties of motion that will make the muscle bulge look just that little bit more natural than the spreadsheet method You are now ready to really have fun!

As always, consider this tutorial not as a recipe but as an inspiration. Play with values during all the steps of the tutorial, and even try some crazy variations you might come up with. Make your work your own, not simply a copy of mine—and always have *fun* doing it!

—John L. Kundert-Gibbs

11 Rendering Tips

The Different Renderers and When to Use Each

Wireframe, Flat, Gouraud, and Phong are the different renderers available to you in EI's Camera Shading popup window shown in Figure 11.1. This setting basically sets a limit on the highest level of rendering a scene can have. The reason I say that it's the highest level of rendering you can have is that each renderer selected here will allow all other modes under it to be rendered in the same scene. Now when I say "all other modes under it," I mean all other modes under it in the hierarchy of renderers. If you look at the arrangement of options in the popup menu, Wireframe is first, followed by Flat, then Gouraud, and finally Phong. This is actually backwards, or rather upside down. In the hierarchy of renderers, Phong is at the top of the food chain and Wireframe is on the bottom.

To illustrate how this works, take a look at Figure 11.2. This image shows four teapots. Each has a different rendering level assigned via its shading popup menu found in the **Shading** tab of the Group Info Window (see Figure 11.3). The global rendering setting in the Camera Shading popup window was set to **Phong** so all four teapots render with their individual shading mode intact. That is because the Phong renderer, being the highest in the hierarchy, allows all other shading modes to be rendered. If we were to set the global rendering mode to **Flat** and rerender this scene, we'd get Figure 11.4. Notice that teapots 2, 3, and 4 all have the same surface qualities, yet teapot 1 is still wireframe. This it because, by setting the global rendering limit to Flat, the Gouraud and Phong render, which are higher up on the hierarchy of renderers, are forced to render flat. Teapot 1, however, is set to Wireframe, and since wireframe falls under Flat in the grand scheme of rendering importance, it still renders. So, if we were to set the Camera Shading popup to wireframe, all of the teapots would render in wireframe. If we were to set it on Gouraud, teapots 1, 2, and 3 would render exactly how they are supposed to but teapot 4, even though it's

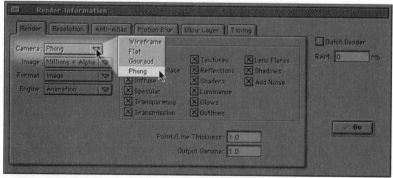

FIGURE
11.1 *The Shading popup window determines the maximum rendering level for your scene.*

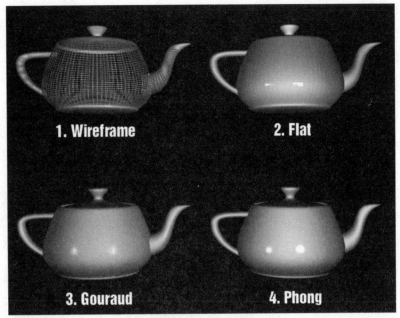

FIGURE   *Four teapots with four different renderers.*
11.2

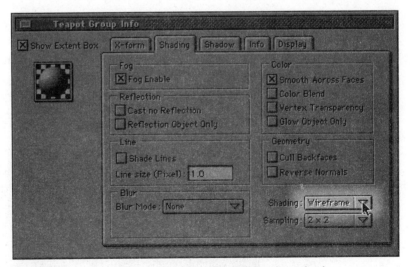

FIGURE   *This is actually where you set how an object is to be rendered.*
11.3

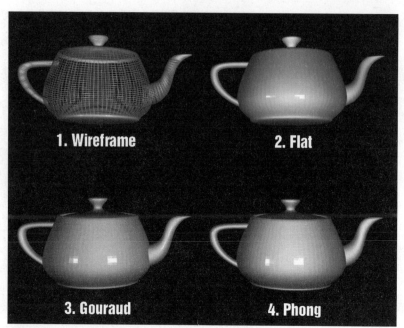

FIGURE
11.4
The same scene with the global rendering mode set to Flat.

set to render in Phong, would render Gouraud. So, just so we make this as clear as possible, setting the render mode in the Camera Shading popup doesn't really determine how the various objects in a scene are rendered. It merely determines the highest rendering quality for the scene as a whole. As I mentioned above, the Shading popup menu in the Group Info Window's **Shading** tab determines how an object is supposed to be rendered;t.;t.;t. and these always default to Phong, so don't worry about winding up with wireframes by mistake even though you have the global renderer set to Phong. You would have had to tell an object to render in wireframe mode by selecting Wireframe from that **Shading** tab in order for that to happen.

So now why would you want to limit the rendering for a scene? Well, when I actually started writing this, I was writing that it was to save a great deal of time while rendering motion-tests. Then I had a conversation with one of the brilliant EI people, in which they said something to the effect of, "Things have gotten so fast, I don't know why anyone would use anything but Phong." This statement started me thinking, so I decided to do some actual calculations, and what I found out was that they were right. Take a look at Figure 11.5. These three cars were rendered, from top to bottom, using Flat, Gouraud, and Phong.

FIGURE   *Three cars. Three renderers.*
11.5

In this picture, the Flat version rendered in 50 seconds on my 233Mhz 604e. The Gouraud version rendered in 51 seconds, and the Phong version rendered in 79 seconds. Now there is a big difference between 51 seconds and 79 seconds, but that extra time on the Phong version was due to the shadow, which was not calculated in Flat for Gouraud versions. When I turned off the shadow, the Phong version rendered in 52 seconds. Now, I don't know about you, but saving 2 seconds per frame is not enough to make me want anything but the best. Of course, with a more complicated scene, the savings *might* be more justifiable, but with differences like these, there's only so much justification available.

So I thought, "Well, that's fine. This pro-Phong idea can't include wireframe though. Wireframe is still the fastest of them all and is way out ahead of the solid renderers in the speed race. Right?"

So I did another test render. This same scene, rendered in Wireframe, popped out in 16 seconds. A big difference from the lowest solid renderer score of 50 seconds. But then it occurred to me that I had all of the Render Flags enabled and decided to disable everything except for Diffuse and Specular and rerender the scene. Figure 11.6 is what I got and the times for Flat, Gouraud, and Phong were, 13 seconds, 14 seconds, and 18 seconds (without the shadow) respectively. Just to make sure I was being thorough, I rerendered the Wireframe version and it came in at 12 seconds. So OK, you'll basically buy yourself one minute for every 15 frames you render by rendering in Flat over Phong (providing every frame renders at the same speed, which it won't) and that means that you'll save yourself an extra hour every 900 frames, which makes it look a little more attractive, but at 4 seconds per frame, Phong is a great deal.

With all of that said, I do want to point out that sometimes a job might call for a particular look that can easily be achieved by using one of the lower-end algorithms. The Science Fiction, Science Fact, and Industrial scenes out there all love Wireframe and Flat shaded images for certain effects, or to illustrate certain points. So using them might not buy you that much time, but it can give you some interesting looks.

Disable Rendering Flags

Since I just spent a good deal of words talking about speeding up test renders, and, in doing so, made it pretty obvious that disabling some Render Flags decreased rendering times much more than using the different renderers, I thought I should throw this in here just to cover more of the bases.

If you're rendering for motion or lighting tests, you can disable all of the flags that are unnecessary for checking motion. This includes just about all of them. In Figure 11.7, I've unchecked everything but Diffuse and Specular. The

FIGURE
11.6 *Disabling several Rendering Flags speeds things up quite a bit and also shows the difference between the shading algorithms better.*

FIGURE *Disabling the Render Flags.*
11.7

reason I've left these two flags enabled is because unchecking Diffuse gives you flat black holes where your objects would be. If you're rendering against a black background, you wouldn't be able to see anything to motion-test. I've also left Specular checked because I wanted to make sure my highlights traveled across my objects the way I wanted them to. The rest were pretty much superfluous for the task at hand.

These Flag options are not only for test renders but can also aid you when doing separate pass renders for post-production. For example, you can choose to render out a scene with no shadows and then rerender it again with only the shadows. Then you can composite the two in a separate application. This allows for more precise control of the shadows and shorter rendering times, should the client change his or her mind about something. It's much quicker to rerender parts of a scene than to rerender the entire scene.

Turn off Unseen Items to Reduce Rendering Times

Another trick for speeding up renders is to turn off the visibility of items that aren't being seen by camera. So if an object is off-camera or totally obscured by another object, make it invisible so camera doesn't have to think about it. Be careful though. You'll want to make sure that shadows or reflections from these objects don't appear in the rendered portion of the scene.

To hide an object, go to the Project Window and change it to **Keyframe** or **Frame** view. Then expand the gray arrow next to the object you wish to make invisible. You should see an option for **Visibility** directly under the group name. Click in the frame where you want the object to become invisible and type *Off* (see Figure 11.8). You'll still be able to see the object in the **World View** and Camera View Windows but it will not be rendered.

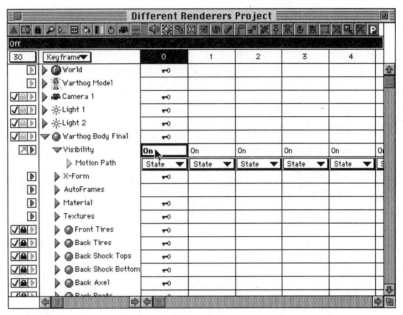

FIGURE   *Setting the Visibility for an object.*
11.8

If you want a group and all of its children to be invisible as well, you don't have to go through this procedure for every single child group if you've got the **Inherit Visibility** checkbox enabled for them in the Group Link Window's **Inherit** tab.

Render Extra Footage for Editing Purposes

This may be obvious to some, or even most, but it wasn't obvious to me when I first started animating. Say you're putting together a 30-second piece comprised of three 10-second clips. You set up your scenes and render your three clips at exactly 10 seconds each. You might have even put a great deal of thought into where the scenes were going to cut and set the animation up just perfectly. But along comes the client and says, "I really don't like those abrupt cuts between clips. Can you change them so there is a fade between clips 1 and 2 and a nice special effect transition between clips 2 and 3?"

If you only rendered 10-second segments, the answer would be *no* because you wouldn't have any footage to fill in those transitions. They would have to overlap some and if you overlap each of your 10-second clips by 1 second, you'll wind up with a final piece that is 28 seconds long instead of 30.

The answer to this problem is to pad your clips a little bit on both sides of the area of clip you know (or at least think) you're going to need. If you're coming to animation from the print field, think of this extra footage as the animation equivalent of *bleed*. Having this extra footage will give you room to transition your clips any way you see fit and even allow for a little bit of linear offset if necessary.

At What Resolution Do I Render This for Print Work?

EI offers resolution and aspect ratio presets for most, if not all, of the commonly used animation and multimedia formats. What it doesn't offer, however, are presets for print work.

If you're an animator who has to render a still for print work or an illustrator who purchased EI specifically for print work, you might find its resolution settings a little confusing when the printed page is the destination for your piece.

In the world of print, measurements are not usually referred to as straight pixel dimensions but usually as real-world measurements, such as inches, with a dots-per-inch (DPI) or pixels-per-inch (PPI) figure for resolution. (Those of you on the metric system can replace the inches with centimeters. The concept is the same.) The reason for this is that in the physical world, you typically have a precise amount of space that you're trying to fill with your image, but the resolution within this space can vary. For example, you might be creating an image for the cover of a book that measures 7.38 inches by 9.25 inches. Well, that's great but you also need to know what resolution, or pixels-per-inch, the image needs to be for the printer or printing method being used. The reason for this is that you can take any number of pixels and stretch them out to fit these real-world measurements, but a 7.38×9.25 image at 72 pixels-per-inch is not going to give you a very good print piece. Basically speaking, the higher the resolution, or dpi, the higher the quality of the printed piece. There is a ceiling, however, for this quality and not all printing devices (printers, presses, imagesetters) can handle the same resolutions. The situation gets even further complicated because of another measurement known as lines-per-inch (LPI). Just because your laser printer is a 600 dpi printer doesn't mean the images you print to it need to be 600 dots-per-inch. And if your piece is being printed on an offset press, this doesn't even work by the dots-per-inch metaphor. These areas are where the lines-per-inch measurement comes into play. A laser printer might be 600 dpi printer but it might only be able to print an 80-line screen (or 80 lines-per-inch). Anything over that will just be a dark mess or wasted information. Offset and web presses typically print anywhere from 120 to 175 lines-per-inch, but if you don't know how that relates to dots-per-inch, or worse yet, to the overall pixel dimensions, you're hosed. Just how do all of these strange measurements fit together? Well, stay tuned, I'm about to tell you.

Let's start with figuring out how to determine the pixel dimensions for a printed piece with a specified dpi and entering that information into EI. Let's say you need to create an illustration that is 8 inches by 10 inches at 300 dpi. The first thing you should do is figure out your pixel dimensions.

There are several ways you can do this. The first way is to figure out the measurement for both the height and width. This is easy enough. You take your real-world measurement unit and multiply it by your dots-per-inch figure. So you'd get 2400 pixels wide and 3000 pixels tall.

The next thing you want to do is open your **Render Info Window** in EI and click on the **Resolution** tab. It probably looks something like Figure 11.9. I won't say it looks exactly like this because the size of your monitor can affect the actual numbers in the box, but you get the general idea. Simply type 2400 into the X field and 3000 into the Y field, and you're done. Your Camera View Window will update to your new measurements and you're ready to go.

The second way to do this is to change your **Aspect Ratio** first. There are advantages to this method, and I'll get to them in a moment. First, let's just set it up. Click on the **Aspect Ratio** pulldown menu and choose **Custom**. When the dialogue box comes up, click on the pulldown menu next to the **Horizontal** and **Vertical Size** fields and change them to **inch**. Then type **8.0** into the **Horizontal Size** field and **10.0** into the **Vertical Size** field (see Figure 11.10). You don't need to worry about the **Frame Aspect**, because that automatically updates from the numbers you just entered. This sets the aspect ratio of your render. The advantages to this method, as I mentioned before, come in two flavors. The first advantage is that you really only need to know one of the pixel dimensions of your image. Take a look at the little lock boxes next to the Horizontal and Vertical Size fields. These are constraint boxes. So if you leave the

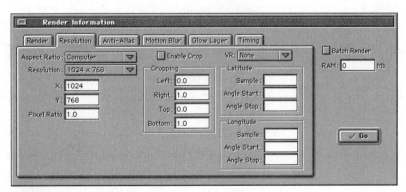

FIGURE   *Meet the Resolution Tab.*
11.9

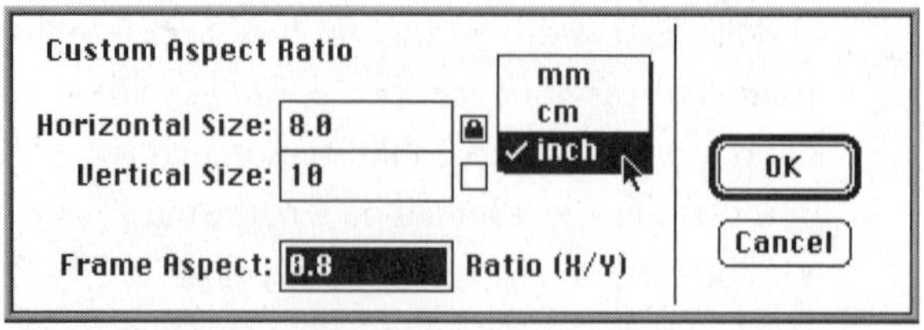

FIGURE **11.10**   *The Custom Aspect Ratio Dialogue.*

Horizontal field locked, the only dimension you need to know is the horizontal one. If you typed 2400 into your X field in the **Resolution** tab, your Y field would update to 3000 automatically. If you only knew your vertical pixel dimensions, you could click on the lock next to the **Vertical Size** in the **Aspect Ratio** dialogue box and then enter the pixel dimensions in the Y field of the **Resolution** tab and the X field would update automatically.

The next advantage to this method is that you can set up test renders more quickly. It would be silly to do test renders at the full resolution because they would take so much time. If you have your Aspect Ratio set up correctly, you can simply type a lower resolution into one of the fields and the other will update automatically. So, say we have our Horizontal Size constrained in the Aspect Ratio dialogue box. We could then change our X field to 600 pixels and our Y field would automatically update to 750 pixels (see Figure 11.11). It's still the proper aspect ratio as our full 2400 × 3000 pixel image, but a 600 × 750 image will render much faster. Want a little higher of a resolution? Simply type it in. A figure of 1200 in the X field automatically updates the Y field to 1500

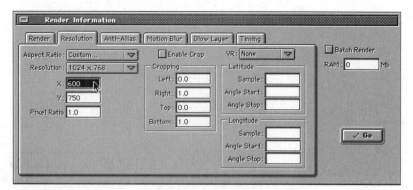

FIGURE **11.11**   *Changing the locked dimension automatically updates the other to match.*

to give us a bigger preview but still renders much faster than the 2400 × 3000 image. We can reserve that size for when we render the final image.

OK. Now that we know how to control our overall pixel to dpi ratio thing, we have to figure out this whole lines-per-inch thing. Sometimes you won't be given a dpi to go by. Your client or printer may say, "I need an 8 × 10 inch image with a 150 line screen."

What on earth does that mean? Well, basically the lines-per-inch figure is directly related to the dpi figure. The dpi you would need would be anywhere from 1.5 to 2 times your lpi. So a safe dpi for a 150 lpi image would be 300 dpi, but you could get away with as low as 225 dpi. 225 dpi would be pushing it as far as quality goes, but anything in the middle should be fine. I personally always go to the high end whenever possible. That way, if the client needs to size the image up a little, he or she can do so without fear of the image deteriorating, but if the deadline requires a faster turnaround, I'll cut some corners on the dpi.

For a quick lpi to dpi conversion, you can use Photoshop's **Image Size** dialogue box. Figure 11.12 shows the **Image Size** dialogue box. Notice the measurements and the dpi. If you click on the **Auto** button, you'll get the dialogue shown in Figure 11.13. This is basically just a calculator. You type in your requested lpi, click on a **Quality** button and then click **OK**. Then you'll get Figure 11.14. Notice that it automatically tells you what dpi you need. Not only that, but it also does your dpi to pixel dimensions calculation as well.

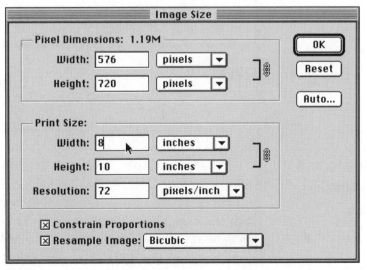

FIGURE   *Photoshop's Image Size dialogue box makes a great dpi to pixel dimensions*
11.12   *calculator.*

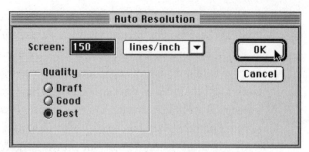

FIGURE　*The Auto button takes care of the lpi to dpi conversions.*
11.13

FIGURE　*You wind up with all the numbers you need.*
11.14

Sampling and Anti-Aliasing Basics

In the most basic of terms, Sampling makes things sharp and Anti-Aliasing makes things blurry.

Sampling is how EI gets its information to create the pixels that you see in your final image. The renderer must decide what color to make a pixel in your render based on the information from all of the colors in the area of the scene that is being represented by that one pixel. The sampling level tells EI how closely to look at this area of your scene before deciding what color the pixel that represents it should be.

If your sampling level is set on 1 × 1, it looks at that area once and quickly averages the colors together to get the color of the pixel. If you bump up your sampling level up to 2 × 2, the renderer is breaking that 1-pixel area up into four separate sections, two horizontal and two vertical, taking the color information of each section and then averaging those areas together at the end. So the color information you get is more accurate, which makes your final image sharper, but it costs you in rendering time. You may have upped your level from 1 × 1 to 2 × 2, but this doesn't mean you've doubled your rendering time—it means you've quadrupled it. If you bump the sampling up to 4 × 4, you've increased your rendering time 16 times what it was when you were using 1 × 1 sampling. Take a look at Figure 11.15 for a visual breakdown of what's going

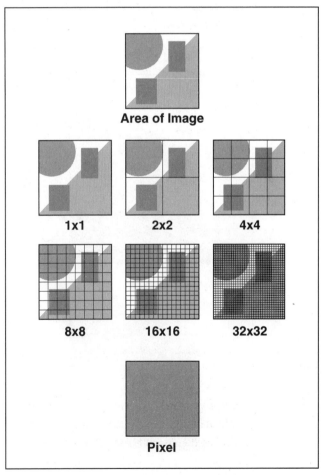

FIGURE *Here is a basic breakdown of what's happening when you increase your*
11.15 *sampling levels.*

on with this sampling thing. Your image gets crisper with the higher levels but at a definite cost. Believe it or not, this can also cost you in image quality. If you're doing print work, it most likely won't be a problem, but for doing animation for TV or video, there is such a thing as *too* sharp. If there is too much contrast between any two given pixels and these pixels do not stay in exactly the same place, they will appear to jump around on your TV screen. I'm sure you've all seen this "sizzling" effect. High sampling rates are a great way to ensure that your high-detail scenes sizzle like crazy.

This is where *anti-aliasing* comes into play. What anti-aliasing does is soften the areas between pixels so you don't get these high-contrast areas that tend to sizzle. Basically, it takes two areas of pixels that are different colors and blends the area in between them to form a smooth transition between the colors. Take a look at Figure 11.16. The top image shows a non-anti-aliased set of pixels or and the bottom image shows what anti-aliasing does to smooth these areas out.

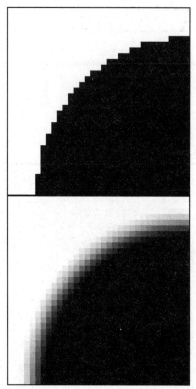

FIGURE   *The top image is not anti-aliased and shows a high contrast between pixels.*
11.16   *The bottom image shows how anti-aliasing smooths everything out and creates a much more pleasing line.*

Unlike sampling (and unlike the anti-aliasing in most 3D applications, specifically raytracers), anti-aliasing in EI doesn't cause much of a rendering hit.

Now you may be wondering how to balance your sampling and anti-aliasing levels. Basically, you just do what you need to. There is no magical solution because all scenes are different. You just want to try to get your images as sharp as possible, while avoiding sizzling, and not cost yourself an arm and a leg in rendering time. So increase the sampling to sharpen to taste and then watch for sizzles or moirés. If they pop up, try raising the anti-aliasing or lowering the sampling. Sometimes you just have to compromise.

Here are several tips for sharpening images while keeping the render speeds as fast as possible.

SELECTIVE SAMPLING

Since you can select your sampling level on an object-by-object basis, only increase the sampling levels on the objects that really need it. If you have an object that is simply too blurry, try increasing the sampling levels of the object itself. The sampling level of an object can be found in Group Info Window's **Shading** tab as shown in Figure 11.17. Like the global shading level set in the Render Info Window **Render** tab, the sampling level in the Render Info Window **Anti-Alias** tab sets the highest level of sampling available. So if you set your sampling level to 2 × 2, objects set to 1 × 1 will still render at 1 × 1 sam-

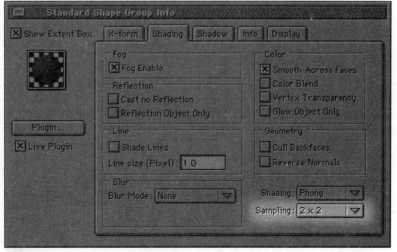

FIGURE *Setting the sampling level for an object.*
11.17

pling and objects set to 2×2 sampling will still render at 2×2, but objects set to 4×4 sampling will only render with 2×2 sampling. Also, like the global shading settings, this is a great way to do quick test-renders.

RENDER LARGE AND THEN DOWNSIZE

Although it may seem strange, a quick way to sharpen your images is to simply render them larger, like one and a half times larger, and then resize them in Photoshop or After Effects. Although it does take longer to render, it doesn't take as long as increasing the sampling and the results may be just as pleasing. Depending on what you're looking for, they may be even better.

ADAPTIVE ANTI-ALIASING

Another way to sharpen your images a bit is to use Adaptive Anti-Aliasing. Adaptive Anti-Aliasing can be chosen by pulling down the **Anti-Alias** popup in the Render Info Window's **Anti-Alias** tab, as shown in Figure 11.18. Now, don't really think of this as so much a different type of anti-aliasing but as **Oversample**. Think of it as more of a means of telling EI where to do the oversampling. When you choose **Adaptive**, you'll get several settings to change for the **Threshold** of the Anti-Aliasing effect. Basically, this threshold gives EI a determiner for what to anti-alias a little and what to anti-alias a lot, based on the contrast between the pixels. The larger the spread between the minimum and maximum, the blurrier the image. So to sharpen your image, try increasing the minimum value to 245 or 250 or even up to 254, but keep an eye on this because you really don't want jaggies.

One thing about this form of anti-aliasing is that it should not be used when working on broadcast or video jobs, which are the most susceptible to sizzling.

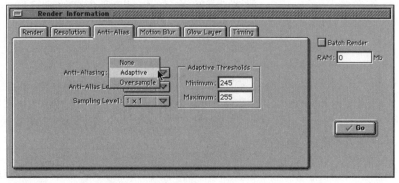

FIGURE   *Choosing Adaptive anti-aliasing.*
11.18

The Oversample method is the safest way to ensure you won't have a problem in this area. TV images like a good bit of blur.

TEXTURE MAP SAMPLING AND ANTI-ALIASING

Another thing you can do is play with your texture map settings. Typically, they are fine at their default settings, but there are some things you can do. Take a look at the **Texture Info Window Filter** tab in Figure 11.19. There are several ways to sharpen (and blur) your maps by adjusting some of these options. The first are the **Map Filter** check boxes. **Interpolate** helps prevent your map from aliasing, but, as a result, can also soften it. You can uncheck it for a sharper image but, as the manual states, this is not recommended. You could also uncheck the Anti-Aliasing box. This is another map filtering option that is basically a pre-anti-aliasing before the final anti-aliasing that happens during the render. Unchecking this will sharpen your images, but if you have a high Anti-Aliasing value for the final render, you may not notice it. This is helpful if most of the objects in your scene look fine but this one texture map is just a little fuzzy. As with many of the options, just use it when you need it, otherwise, leave it alone.

Your other options are in the **Map Quality** edit boxes. You'll notice right off that there is a Blur field with a setting of 1.0. If you want to sharpen a map, lower that puppy or zero it out completely. It should be noted here that you don't always want a map to be sharp, that's why this setting is here.

The **Samples** box is similar to the sampling level for objects but only con-

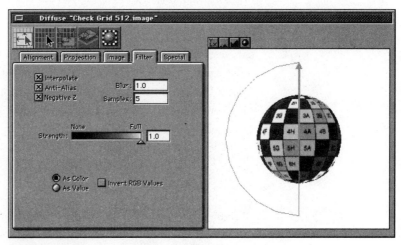

FIGURE   *The Texture Info Window's Filter Tab.*
11.19

cerns itself with texture maps. I typically leave this alone, but occasionally, if I don't want to increase my overall sampling or an object, I'll just increase this setting to see what happens. Like the normal sampling, this will increase rendering time, but basic math will tell you that it'll take less time to have a higher sampling rate on one map than an entire scene.

Control-Go (and Aliases)

If you're one of those lucky people who either have a whole lot of RAM, or an additional super-fast computer lying around not doing much, you should be taking advantage of the **Control-Go** rendering option.

If you're not familiar with Control-Go, basically it's a way to send a full render to Camera while still keeping EI open—like a preview render, but it's the full-blown thing. It's often used to send a render to an additional computer on your network, but it works just as well on the same computer where you're running EI.

To use Control-Go, you simply hold down the **Control** key and click on **Go** in the Render Info Window. EI will prompt you to find the copy of Camera you wish to use. Navigate to that copy of Camera and click **Find**. EI will then prompt you for a destination for the final render.

This is a great way to ease tension if you're tired of waiting for EI to open back up after each and every render, but it does have a downside. EI doesn't even venture a guess as to where your Camera is or where you want to save your render. So, when you do a Control-Go, the first place you're put is wherever you were the last time you opened or found a file. So you have to navigate out of there and into your EI folder so you can choose camera. Then you have to navigate out of your EI folder and then back to the folder where you want to save your movie. If your projects are in deeply nested folders and/or on different drives/computers, this can add up to a whole lot of clicking.

One of my recent projects had ridiculously long filepaths to get to and from camera. Yes, this is partially my fault, but what can I say, I like my hierarchies. I had several nested folders so a typical file path to get from the job folder to Camera looked like this:

```
Mongoose>Sprites>Sledd Art>Slithereens>A Work
Drive>Desktop>Lazarus>Applications>EIAS Broadcast
2.8>Camera
```

And that was just to get to Camera. Then when I was prompted to save my movie, I had to retrace all of those steps in reverse. Now granted, I'm making it look a little worse that it really is here because you can cut out several of those steps by clicking on the **Desktop** button in the navigation dialogues, but that only helps so much. Needless to say, I got very tired of this so I decided to make good use of system aliases and streamline the entire procedure.

I first created an alias for my EIAS folder, named it *A_Camera* and placed it in my Mongoose folder. Then I created an alias of the Mongoose folder, renamed it *A_Mongoose,* and placed it in my EIAS folder. Adding that *A_* to the beginning of the names was simply to place them at the top of the list so I didn't have to go scrolling to find them in the navigation dialogues.

From then on, when I did a Control-Go, all I had to do was open the *A-Camera* alias, select Camera, then when prompted for a destination for my render, I just opened the *A_Mongoose* alias (which was right above Camera) and clicked **Save**. Figure 11.20 shows the new filepath. Four steps replacing twenty is always a good deal.

For future projects, you can just drag your *A_Camera* folder to a new location and replace your equivalent of the *A_Mongoose* folder with an alias from your new project. It takes a teeny bit of preparation in the beginning, but you'll be glad you took the time.

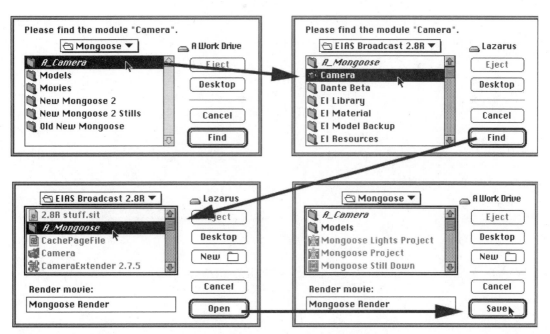

FIGURE   *Using Aliases makes for much shorter filepaths.*
11.20

12 Postproduction Tips and Techniques

The world of postproduction in 3D is huge. There are so many things that can be covered under this title that it could warrant a complete book. Since I don't have enough pages to insert a whole new book, I'm going to try to get you pointed in the right direction with a few handy tips and a killer technique.

Dodging and Burning to Grunge Things Up

This tip is typically more useful for illustration, but the concepts can apply to animation as well. You've probably read by now that grunge is good. Mixing surfaces up is a great way to make a rendering more interesting. You don't always have to work this into your texture maps, though (although this technique works just as well on maps *before* you render them). Some of it can be done as an afterthought and can actually save you time.

Take a look at Figure 12.1. The texture maps are pretty good as it is, but it still needs a little tweaking to mix up the surfaces. Dodge a little highlight here, burn a little shadow or oil-splash there. I do this for practically every illustration I do because I like the control you have over doing it in the texture maps. I dirty my maps up, too, but almost always work in a few extra touches to give the piece a little extra oomph. In Figure 12.2, you can see where I've gone over seams, through shadows, and around highlights to give the car more of a grungy look.

FIGURE *The textures look pretty good, but it could use some more "oomph."*
12.1

FIGURE   *Dodge a little highlight here and burn a little shadow there to give the*
12.2   *textures more depth.*

Add Motion Blur to Still Images

Even though still images don't move, that doesn't mean they don't need to look like they are moving. The quickest way to do this is to add some motion blur to them. Take a look at Figure 12.3. I've really gone overboard to illustrate a point here, but the same car with some motion trails can take it out of the showroom and put it in the action.

FIGURE   *Adding some motion blur to still images can spice up an otherwise static*
12.3   *image.*

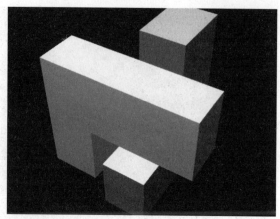

FIGURE *Two overlapping objects.*
12.4

Instant Masking (Using the Opacity Slider in the Diffuse Channel)

Say you've rendered out a project using the two objects in Figure 12.4. The client comes along and says, "I don't like the back block. Could you change its color to better match the block in front of it?" Begrudgingly you say "Um. OK." You know it took you three days to render the completed animation and you're really not looking forward to that big render again. He then says, "Good. I need the corrections in two days."

So what do you do? You change the color and render out the scene again but with only the second block, as shown in Figure 12.5. The problem is, there are areas of the animation, just like the one in this picture, where the front block

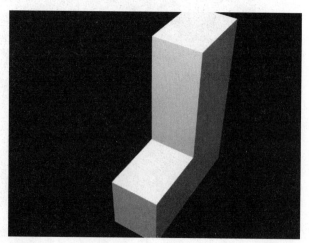

FIGURE *Render with only the second object.*
12.5

FIGURE   *The alpha of this image wouldn't aid you in compositing at all.*
12.6

overlaps the back. If you just turned off the front block and rerendered, you'd still have those areas that you needed to mask out and the alpha channel you'd get out of this image wouldn't even really help here (see Figure 12.6).

Well, luckily, you don't really need to do it that way. EI provides a great way to chop an object out of your render while leaving space where it used to be. Allow me to introduce you to a nifty little slider in the Material Info Window's **Diffuse** tab. Take a look at the **Mask** slider in Figure 12.7. This is like Trans-

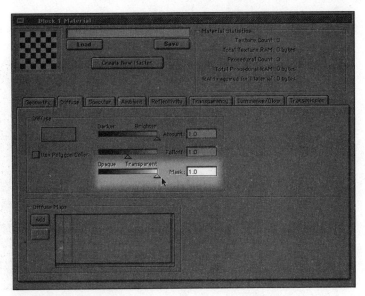

FIGURE   *The Mask slider.*
12.7

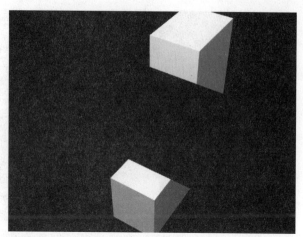

FIGURE **12.8** *Rendering using this Mask option makes the first object invisible but also cuts out the area where it was.*

parency on steroids. Not only does it make the object invisible, but it subtracts its area from the alpha channel as well. Figure 12.8 shows what happens when you render this scene, and Figure 12.9 shows the resulting alpha channel. So now you can either just composite your new render with your existing scene or you can use the mask generated by the new render to simply alter the color of the first render.

FIGURE **12.9** *The object is also cut out of the alpha channel, making compositing much easier.*

Creating a Comet

In this tutorial you'll learn how to use EI's built-in particle engine to create a comet. Then you'll render several passes of the comet for more precise control over the final composite in After Effects, which we'll use to create a more believable comet effect. Oh yeah, and we'll talk just a little bit about orbital dynamics and solar winds too (oh, no, not astronomy!).

Between all the recent science fiction movies, television shows, and 1997's Hale-Bopp comet sighting, everyone today seems interested in creating a believable-looking comet in a 3D animation program. How does one create such an ephemeral object as a comet, however? The secret to creating a believable comet is twofold: First, we must understand what a comet is and how it moves; and second, we must know how to transfer this knowledge about what comets are into the 3D animation world. Along the way, we'll also learn how to create multi-pass renderings in EI and how to put them together in interesting ways in After Effects (AE).

First, the theory: Comets are tiny (or not so tiny) balls of frozen liquids and gasses (like water vapor, carbon dioxide, ammonia, and so forth). The comet consists of a nucleus (the frozen gasses and water), a coma, which is a kind of halo of gasses around the comet, and, most importantly for us, a tail of gasses, which only appears when the comet is close to the sun.

The coma and tail are generally only visible when the comet is near the sun because of a phenomenon known as solar winds. Solar winds are streams of high-energy particles that effectively shoot out from the sun into space. We are (very fortunately) protected from these dangerous particles by the earth's magnetic field, and by our ever-shrinking ozone layer. If you have ever seen the aura borealis (northern lights), it is caused by the high-speed particles from the sun being trapped and moved around by the earth's magnetic field. For a lone comet traveling about our solar system, the solar winds are a kind of baking wind: They melt off the outer layer of the nucleus of the comet (creating the halo), and when the comet is close enough to the sun, the solar wind blows the melting gasses and water off of the halo and away from the sun. At this point, you get the famous comet tail. Because the solar wind creates the comet tail, it *always* travels directly away from the sun—even if the comet is moving away from the sun. Thus, sometimes, the comet's tail actually *leads* the comet as it circles the sun. The comet's tail is less like a jet's exhaust trail (which always follows the jet) than it is like a strong wind that always blows a flag in one direction, no matter which way the flag holder marches.

In addition to the fact that the comet's tail always blows directly away from the sun, a comet's path is highly elliptical (remember your high school geome-

try class!), with one end very near the sun, the other end very far out (most of
the time past the orbit of Pluto). When the comet is far away from the sun, it
travels very slowly. When it nears the sun, it gets pulled in by the sun's enor-
mous gravity and moves more quickly. For our purposes, we'll only be animating the portion of the comet's path when it is very near the sun, so the motion
path will look nearly parabolic (a wide U shape).

STEP ONE

All right, enough theory! How do we actually build this beast? The comet is
comprised of three parts, so we need to build the three parts of the comet. The
nucleus is simply a sphere. You can create a new project, or open my Comet-
New.Project file from the CD. If you open my project, you'll see a star field
(Stars), a Standard Shape 2 sphere already added to the file (see Figure 12.10),
and its motion path defined (note how the motion path looks like a parabola).

If you create the project from scratch, first add the Stars.fact group from the
files on the CD, and then add either a Standard Shape, or a Standard Shape 2
sphere—or import one from your favorite modeler. The settings I used to create the "nucleus" sphere are shown in Figure 12.11.

Now we need to build the glowing coma around the nucleus. There are several ways to create a glowing object, including doing it in AE (we'll do some-

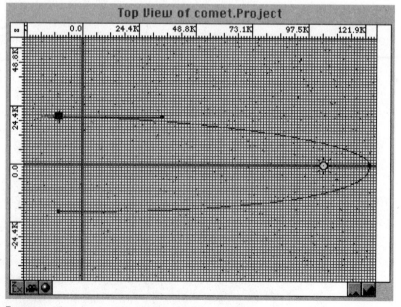

FIGURE   *The sphere's path, which is nearly a parabola.*
12.10

Standard Shape 2

Shape: Sphere

Shape color:

☒ Auto-name   ☒ Smooth

Orientation

Radius: 250.0

○ +X   ○ −X
◉ +Y   ○ −Y   ☐ End cap
○ +Z   ○ −Z

☐ Hemisphere

	EI	Camera
Latitude:	9	30
Longitude:	9	30

Number of polygons (EI): 81
Number of polygons (Cam): 900

v 1.0.0b6 March 2, 1998
© Northern Lights Productions
www.northernlightsprod.com

[Cancel]   [OK]

FIGURE **12.11** *The Standard Shape 2 dialogue box, with the settings I used to create the comet's nucleus.*

thing like this for the tail). In this case, let's use one of the new features added in EI 2.9 and create a glow right in EI using glow layers. First, we have to create a set. From the menu, choose **Select>By Set>Edit Set**.

Under Selection Sets, click **Add**, choose the existing Glow.set (or create your own), and click **OK**. Next, in the Project Window, highlight the **Sphere** group. Then, back in the **Selection Sets** box, select the Glow.set. Move over to the **Members** area, and click **Add**. You will then see Sphere added to the Glow.set set as in Figure 12.12. You have now created a set of objects (OK, so it's only one object!) that will receive a glow pass when camera renders the images.

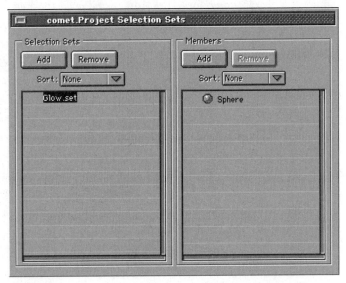

FIGURE **12.12** *The Edit Sets dialogue box, with elements already added.*

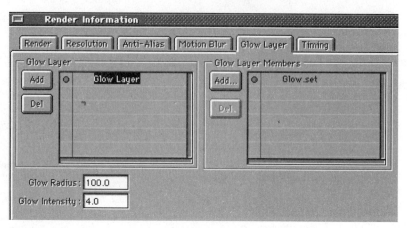

FIGURE *The Glow tab in the Render dialogue box, showing the Glow Layer and*
12.13 *Glow.set already added.*

But wait, you're not yet done. If you don't believe me, try rendering out a test image—see, no glow. What's missing is that you have to go to the render dialogue box (**File>Render;** or **command-r**) and essentially repeat what you just did.

In the **Glow Layer** area, click **Add** and accept the default name, *Glow Layer*. Then, with the *Glow Layer* highlighted, move over to the **Glow Layer Members** area, click **Add...**, and make the only choice you can: Glow.set (see Figure 12.13). What you've just done is tell camera that there will be a glow layer (appropriately enough named *Glow Layer*); then, you have defined what lies within that glow layer (its Members): the Glow.set you had just created. One other note here: When the *Glow Layer* is highlighted, you will see two other boxes at the bottom (**Glow Radius** and **Glow Intensity**). These two boxes tell the camera how big the glow is (radius) and how bright it will be (intensity). After some experimentation, I arrived at the two numbers shown in Figure 12.13—however, as always, feel free to play with these numbers to create a look you like.

If you think you're done, guess again: There is one final step that you must make to get the sphere to glow (sheesh!). Open the sphere's information box, then click the materials ball, and then select the **Luminance/Glow** tab.

I set the luminance to about 0.25, and the glow amount to 1.0 with a light blue color, as shown in Figure 12.14. In addition, I made the **Diffuse** tab settings the same light blue color, reduced the specular reflection to 0, and made the sphere 0.25 percent opaque (in other words, mostly transparent). If you

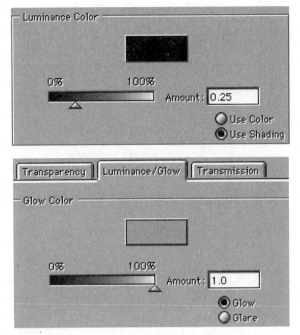

FIGURE *The Luminance and Glow Color areas of the Luminance/Glow tab.*

12.14

have trouble understanding these settings, try opening the Comet.Project file on the CD, because it is the finished project containing all the materials.

Now that we've added the glow color and amount, you will (finally!) see the sphere glow when you test render a scene. Try it and notice the difference between no glow and a glow—very nice!

We've created a semi-transparent nucleus and a glowing coma; now, how do we produce the famous comet tail? Easy, we use EI's built in particle generator (or a third-party particle generator like Northern Lights' Dante, or CEI Software's Power Particles). From the file menu select **File>Add>Socket>Particle....** For the standard particle generator, I found the settings in Figure 12.15 worked pretty well.

Let's work through the (many) numbers here, starting at the top. **Maximum Particles** sets the maximum number of particles EI will allow. If the particle generator makes the maximum number on some frame, it will thereafter only replace the particles that have "died" in subsequent frames (see **Particle Life Time**, below). The **New Particles Per Second** boxes tell EI how many new particles to create each second. The ± box gives a variance to this first number—in other words, in this case, EI will generate 2500 new particles per sec-

Maximum Particles:	20000		
New Particles Per Second:	2500	±	1000
Particle Life Time:	1.5	±	0.25
Create Particles From Time:	-0.7	To:	100

X Position:	-5	±	5	Direction:	-1
Y Position:	0	±	100	Direction:	0
Z Position:	0	±	100	Direction:	0

Deviation Angle:	-0.01	±	0.15
Velocity:	11000	±	1500

Gravity X:	0	Y:	0	Z:	0

Y Ground Level:	-1000	Air Resistance:	0
Bounce Factor:	0	Bounce Friction:	0

Energy 1.0: [   ] 0.5: [   ] 0.0: [   ]

[OK]   [Cancel]

02:57

FIGURE *The Particle... dialogue box, showing the settings I used in my project.*
12.15

ond *plus or minus* 1000 (so anywhere from 1500 to 3500 new particles will be created each second). As the ± boxes all function in the same way, I won't draw attention to most of them. The **Particle Life Time** boxes show how long each particle lives (with a variance range). If particles live for 1 second, they will appear, and then disappear about 1 second later in the animation. **Create Particles From Time...To** tells EI when to begin making these particles, as well as when to stop making them. Notice that you can begin creating particles *before* the animation starts (in this case, at -0.7 seconds). This allows you to get the particles "up and running" before your animation starts.

The **X**, **Y**, and **Z Positions** tell EI where to place the particles—0, 0, 0 will make the particles generate at the exact center of the coordinate system. The **Direction** boxes tell EI in which direction to emit the particles. A positive Y value will make the particles shoot straight up. A negative X value (as here) will make the particles shoot backward across the X axis. It is worth noting the ± boxes for X, Y, and Z positions: They allow you to make the particles shoot from a circle (or sphere) instead of a point. If we defined our particle fountain to emit from 0,0,0 with all the ± boxes at 0,0,0 (and an X direction of -1), we would get a point emitter that shoots the particles straight sideways (try it!). If, however, we change the Y Position and Z Position ± boxes to 100 and 100 each, the particles will emit from a circular surface (do this and check the side view of the particles). Thus, we can make the particle tail appear to have a volume at the start, rather than coming from a tiny point source.

The **Deviation Angle** is also a crucial setting: A large deviation angle (such as 360) will emit the particles in all directions. A small deviation angle (as in our case) will make a very thin cone instead. The **Gravity**, **Air Resistance**, **Bounce**, and **Bounce Friction** boxes are all useful in some animations, but not ours (as we're in outer space), so they are all set to 0. The **Y Ground Level** has been set to about -10,000 units, making the ground effectively so far down that the particles will never hit is (hitting the "ground" would look awfully weird in space!).

Finally, the three **Energy** boxes tell EI what color to make each particle as it ages. At the beginning of its life, particles will be colored like the far left box; at middle age, they will appear as in the second box; and when they are old (about the fade from the animation), they will look like the third box. Notice that in my case, I made all the colors the same in hue (approximately 230 degrees), and only changed their brightness values over their lifetimes. This tends to work best, as changing from red to blue to green over a particle's lifetime is not only ugly but can create some very strange colors in the particle stream. Once you have good settings, select **OK** and the particle group will be created (in our case at 0,0,0). Remember that you can, at any time, change the particle's settings by double-clicking the particle group, then selecting the **Plugin...** button. At this point, you should have a sphere and a particle group, both located at the 0,0,0 center of the coordinate system. Be sure you are at time 0 in the Project Window and link the particle group to the sphere group, as shown in Figure 12.16.

FIGURE *The Particle Group linked to the Sphere Group (the Big Dipper Group is*
12.16 *independent).*

Now that the Particle Group is linked to the Sphere, wherever I move the sphere (and whichever direction I rotate it), the particles will move and rotate with it.

Great, we have a completed comet!

STEP TWO

Now let's animate the sphere/particles combination around a sun (light) over the course of about 10 seconds (that's one *fast* trip around the sun!). At time 0, enter the following values for the sphere: X=-10,000; Y=0; Z=20,000 (you can, of course, change these numbers to suit your needs). Move to time 5.0 seconds, and enter the following: X=124,000; Y=0; Z=0. Move to the end (time 10), and enter the following: X=-10,000; Y=0; Z=-20,000. Now pull on the beziér (blue) handles for each keyframe until you get something like Figure 12.17.

As the comet changes speed during the approach to the sun, we need to use velocity curve to make a hump shaped velocity curve like the one shown in Figure 12.18.

Now that we have the motion path, we need to animate the comet tail's direction change so that it always points away from the sun. First, let's put the sun (the light that came with the project) at X=104,000, Y=100, Z=0, placing the sun/light near the far end of the comet's path. What we need to do now is to

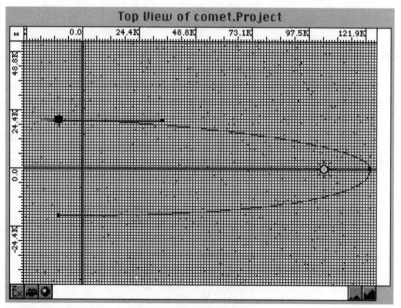

FIGURE *The elliptical orbit of the comet (sphere).*
12.17

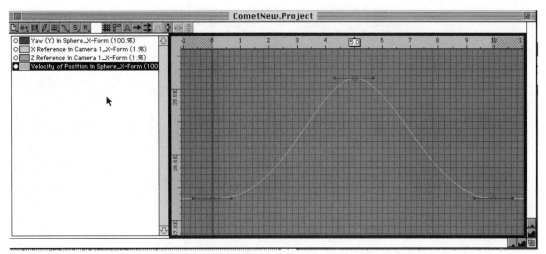

FIGURE 12.18 *The reshaped velocity curve, showing highest velocity near the middle of the animation.*

make the comet tail always point directly away from the sun. At the beginning, the Y rotation value of the *sphere* (as the sphere rotates, so does the particles group) will be about 11 degrees. At the 5-second mark (center keyframe), the rotation will be 180 degrees. At the end of the animation, the rotation will be about 350 degrees. Basically, it almost makes one complete circle. If you now make a Quicktime preview of the top view of the action, you'll see that the tail rotates out of synch with the animation, so it doesn't always point directly away from the sun (note that you can turn off **Live Plugin** in the particle groups info window, which makes creating a Quicktime preview *much* faster).

To overcome this problem, the easiest method is to add the Y rotation to the F-Curve editor and adjust its path to match the motion of the comet's travels. (I don't have space to venture into working in the F-Curve window here; if you need help working in this window, see the Muscle tutorial in Chapter 10. After some playing, you should get a curve shaped something like the one in Figure 12.19.

We're getting very close to completing the basic motion of our animation. The final step is to get the camera to follow the comet. The simplest way to do this is to use the **Look At** function to force the camera to always look at the comet head. This, however, is uninteresting, and I chose to keyframe the camera by hand (and using F-Curves). The camera's position is always at X=0, Y=0, Z=-30,000. The reference point of the camera is moved in the X and Z directions, creating the curves in the F-Curve window shown in Figure 12.20.

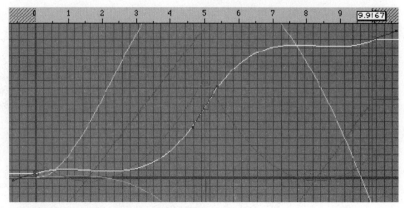

FIGURE **12.19** *The white path represents the Y rotation of the sphere/particles during the animation.*

If you don't feel like messing around with all these F-Curves, simply open the Comet.Project file on the CD, which contains the completed project.

The last step is to make the sun/light visible. I added a light flare with the settings shown in Figure 12.21. These settings give a nice "distant sun" feel to the light.

STEP THREE

Render out a Quicktime preview to see if everything looks all right. If you like it, you can render out a completed animation with everything on to see what the comet looks like at this point. Not bad, but could still use some improvement, right?

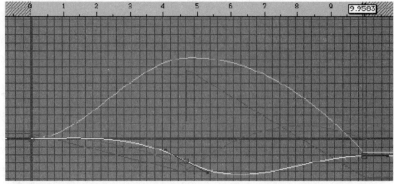

FIGURE **12.20** *The X and Z elements of the camera's reference point position, adjusted to follow the comet.*

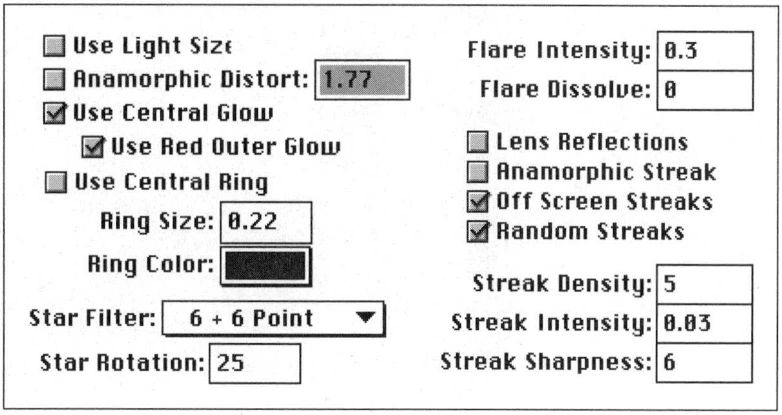
Use Light Size
Anamorphic Distort: 1.77
Use Central Glow
Use Red Outer Glow
Use Central Ring
Ring Size: 0.22
Ring Color:
Star Filter: 6 + 6 Point
Star Rotation: 25
Flare Intensity: 0.3
Flare Dissolve: 0
Lens Reflections
Anamorphic Streak
Off Screen Streaks
Random Streaks
Streak Density: 5
Streak Intensity: 0.03
Streak Sharpness: 6

FIGURE 12.21 *Light Flare settings for the "sun."*

To make these improvements, we'll use a technique called *multi-pass rendering* to generate several different movies we'll then composite in AE. The first question we need to answer when using this technique is: What layers do we need to render separately? Given what we're going to do in AE, just about everything. First of all, we need to render out the background stars. Then we need to render out the comet head (twice) and tail separately. Finally, we need to render the sun twice to get the proper look we're after in AE. Fortunately, as all the objects in this scene are self-lighted (luminous), we don't need the sun light on in all the scenes. Thus, when we don't need it, we can simply turn off the sun (alternatively, we can simply reduce the intensity of the light flare to 0, effectively making the sun invisible).

Let's do the easy passes first. The stars will provide the backdrop for the scene, so turn off all other items by unclicking the checkboxes next to them as shown in Figure 12.22, and turn on point/line motion blur for them to get a convincing effect. Then render out the stars to a movie at whatever resolution

Light 1
Sphere
Particle Group
Big Dipper™ #2 Group

FIGURE 12.22 *All visibility checkboxes off except for the Big Dipper Group.*

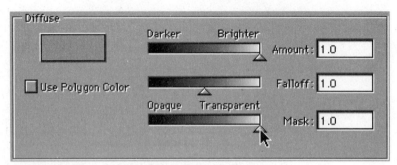

FIGURE *Moving the Opaque/Transparent slider to the right.*
12.23

and frame rate you wish (Be careful: All the renders have to be at the same frame rate and resolution!).

Next, turn off everything except for the particle group and render that to another movie file. Next, turn off everything except for the sphere group and disable the **Glow** flag in the Render Info Window—we will use this pass for some special tricks in AE—and render the non-glowing comet head. Then, render the sun alone. Be sure to name all these movies with meaningful names (like "comet.sun.movie").

The last two render passes are a bit more tricky: Since the comet moves both behind and in front of the sun, we need to "cut out" the sun where the comet comes in front of it. Fortunately, EI can do this very easily. First, be sure glow is disabled in the render dialogue box (unless you want the render to take twice as long for no gain!). Second, turn on sun, sphere, and particles (but not stars). Third, for *both* the sphere and particles, go into the Material Info Window, find the **Diffuse** tab, and move the **Opaque/Transparent** slider all the way to the right (setting the mask to 1.0) as shown in Figure 12.23.

Be sure the **Use Polygon Color** checkbox is off as well (by default, this will be checked On for the particle group). Now render out this pass, calling it something like *Comet.SunBlocked.movie*. When the comet moves in front of the sun (toward the end of the animation), notice how the parts of the sun that are covered disappear behind some invisible object. This will allow us to use AE to effectively composite the comet on top of the sun even while the comet resides in a layer *behind* the sun.

Next, go back into the **Diffuse** tab in the Material Info Window for the sphere group and slide the **Opaque/Transparent** slider all the way back left (setting the mask to 0). In the Render Info Window, turn the **Glow** flag back on and render this pass. This will produce the glowing comet head, while at the same time cutting out areas blocked by the particle trail. This pass will take longest to render, which is why I saved it for last. When you finish this pass, you will have six individual passes that you will composite in AE. I named them:

comet.stars.Movie
comet.sun.Movie
comet.tail.Movie
comet.head.Movie
comet.sunBlocked.Movie
comet.headBlocked.Movie

Congratulations! You are finished with the EI portion of this tutorial. Now, let's close EI and open AE.

STEP FOUR

In a new project, first import all six of your movie files (stars, sun, blocked sun, comet head, blocked comet head, and comet tail). Next, add a new composition to the project, set its time to 10 seconds, and its frame rate and size to whatever frame rate and size you used when you created your EI movies. Next, add all your movies as layers to the composition time line (be sure the time line is at time 0 first!). Now arrange the movies as follows (from top to bottom—the order is critical): sun blocked, comet head blocked, comet tail, comet tail (again), comet head (unblocked), Sun (unblocked), and finally stars (see Figure 12.24).

If you now scrub through the time line, you will see how the movie now looks like "the real thing" (all the layers combine to make a fully rendered image). However, merely layering these movies is no better than rendering one movie with everything on in EI. Where we can start to have fun now is in our ability to make changes to each layer *independently* of all the others. For this

▷ 🎞 1 : comet.SunBlocked.Movie
▷ 🎞 2 : comet.headBlocked.Movie
▷ 🎞 3: comet.tail.Movie
▷ 🎞 4 : comet.tail.Movie
▷ 🎞 5 : comet.head.Movie
▷ 🎞 6 : comet.Sun.Movie
▷ 🎞 7 : comet.stars.Movie

FIGURE   *The layers in an AE composition time line. Note the order of the layers, which*
12.24 *is crucial.*

project, we'll leave the sun and stars layers alone (though their brightness, contrast, and other characteristics could be altered to suit your taste). We will deal with the comet head layers, adjusting its opacity and brightness, and, most importantly, with the two comet's tail layers, which looks all right in its present form, but can be far more convincing with just a little bit of work.

First, highlight the comet head movie (the one without the glow) and press the letter "t" on the keyboard. This will bring up the **Opacity** channel, which we can click on and select some number less than 100% opacity. A value of about 70 makes the comet head very ephemeral, which is nice (and also allows the backgrounded sun to shine through the comet head late in the animation—which is why that layer is there). If you wish, feel free to add effects like **Brightness/Contrast** to the comet head as well, creating a brightly glowing, but insubstantial object.

Now let's move on to the first comet's tail layer, where we'll have most of our fun. The first thing we'll do is add a time echo to the comet tail. Highlight the first comet tail layer, then select **Effect>Time>Echo** from the menu. Make the settings as shown in Figure 12.25 (or change them as you like).

What the time echo does is to use the **Echo Time** setting to offset several copies of the image of the tail, effectively stretching it out behind the comet when the echo time is negative, and moving it in front of the comet when the value is positive. Other settings affect how the echo behaves. Once you have these settings in, move the time bar to about 5.01 seconds, and create a

FIGURE *The time echo settings for the comet tail layer.*
12.25

keyframe for the **Echo Time** channel of the Echo effect (do this by twirling down the arrows, finding the Echo Time channel, and clicking the little stop-watch next to it). Now move the time marker back to about 5.0 seconds, and create a new keyframe for Echo Time by clicking the number (0.01) next to the Echo Time title, and changing this number to -0.01. These two keyframes will cause the comet's tail to stretch out behind the comet for the first half of the an-imation, and then "precede" the comet during the second half of the animation (when it is moving away from the sun).

Using Echo has stretched our comet a bit, but it still looks a lot like regular old EI particles. The next step will help solve this problem. From the effects menu (with the comet tail layer selected), choose **Effects>Blur&Sharpen>Ra-dial Blur** and create the settings shown in Figure 12.26.

Creating a radial blur will cause the comet's tail to spread and thin out as it moves away from the comet head—if, of course, we can keyframe the center of the radial blur to always lie where the comet head is. Here is where the pro-duction bundle of AE is useful. If you don't have the production bundle of AE, move the time marker (about 1 second at a time) through the animation and set the Blur Center on top of the comet's head for each frame (do this by click-ing the little cross-hairs, and then clicking in the comp window where the comet's head is). This will get you close to accurate, but not nearly as close as AE production bundle's Motion Tracker feature will.

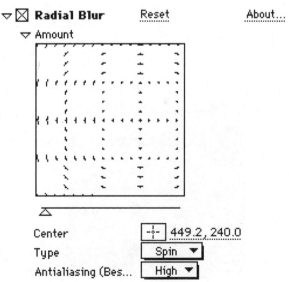

FIGURE   *Settings for the radial blur for the comet's tail and the unglowing comet head.*
12.26   *The Amount setting, numerically, is 3.0.*

If you have AE production bundle, here's a neat trick to learn. First, add a radial blur layer to the non-glowing comet head (not the tail this time). Make the blur amount 0; the settings are unimportant, as we only care about the fact that this effect is now part of the comet head layer. Be sure the time line marker is reset to 0, then choose **Layer>Keyframe Assistant>Motion Tracker....** In the layer window that appears, select the default option of **Track Position**, and then move the two concentric boxes on top of the comet head and adjust their size to approximate Figure 12.27.

The inner box tells AE what feature it is looking for (the comet's head, obviously). The outer, larger box tells AE how far to look around to find this feature. As the comet head gets much larger at the end of the animation, I've made the outer box relatively large.

Next, go into the Options dialogue box and set it as shown in Figure 12.28.

Note that the Apply Motion To radio button is set to Effect point control, allowing the motion tracker information to flow to the Radial Blur/Center channel (for the comet head), setting its keyframes. Now the reason to add the Radial blur to the comet head becomes clear: we can directly create the 'follow' keyframes to center the radial blur around the comet head *only* within the comet head layer itself. Click Track, allow the keyframes to render, and then click Apply. Now, twirl down the arrows in the comet head layer, uncovering the Radial Blur>Center channel. You will notice the entire time line is full of keyframes, created by the motion tracker. Drag a marquee box around these keyframes using the mouse, highlighting them all, and then select copy (command-c) from the menu. This copies all keyframes from this channel onto the clipboard. Next, highlight the comet *tail* layer, and paste (command-v) the information into the (already created) radial blur channel. Check to see the information has been transferred by twirling down the arrows until you see the

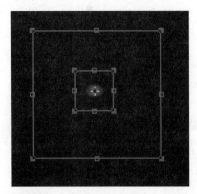

FIGURE   *Positioning and sizing the Track Position boxes.*
12.27

```
┌─ Apply Motion To ──────────────────────────────────────────────┐
│  ○ Layer:          comet.SunBlocked.Movie              ▼       │
│  ● Effect point control:    Radial Blur/Center         ▼       │
│  ┌─ Frame Rate ──────────────────────────────────────────────┐ │
│  │    24      Frames per second                              │ │
│  │  ☐ Track Fields (doubles frame rate)                      │ │
│  └───────────────────────────────────────────────────────────┘ │
│                                                                 │
│  ☒ Subpixel Matching:   1/4     ▼   pixel                      │
│  ☐ Blur Before Match:          pixels                          │
│  ☐ Track Obscured Objects with Tolerance of        %           │
└─────────────────────────────────────────────────────────────────┘
```

FIGURE *The Motion Tracker Options dialogue box.*
12.28

keyframes in the comet tail's Blur>Center layer, then go back to the comet head layer and delete the effect from there (by selecting the name of the effect in the effects control box, and pressing the delete key). Now that we have moved the radial blur into the comet tail layer, we no longer need the effect for the comet's head. Still with me?

Why do use such a strange method to create our motion tracker keyframes? Because if we had simply tried to apply the motion tracker to the tail layer, the motion tracker would have quickly become very confused given the long and changing shape of the comet (go ahead and try it!). Using the well-defined comet head as a substitute for the tail was a great way to 'cheat' the information into the comet tail layer.

Finally for a little more flair, I added a fast blur (Effects>Blur&Sharpen>Fast Blur) to the first comet tail layer and reduced its opacity to about 60% as shown in Figure 12.29.

The fast blur layer smudges out the particles, making them less solid looking and less banded from the radial blur effect. The order of the effects for the

```
▽ ☒ Fast Blur        Reset            About...
   ▽ Blurriness        3.0
       0.0                              127.0
        △
```

FIGURE *Fast blur settings for the first comet tail layer. The 'name,' which can be used*
12.29 *to drag the effect around the effects window, is highlighted here.*

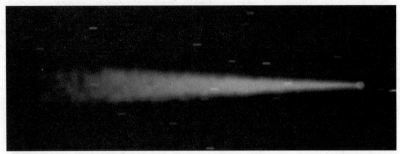

FIGURE *A detail of one frame of the final comet animation.*
12.30

comet tail layer is very important for achieving the appropriate effect. They should be (from top to bottom in the effects window): Echo, Radial Blur, and Fast Blur. If they are in another order, simply grab the 'name' of the effect and drag it up or down to properly position it. Try moving the order of the effects around and observe how the image changes. Reducing the particles' opacity to 60% makes them a little less substantial still.

The final steps will add just that little *je ne sais quoi* to the animation, making it just a bit better. First, with the first comet tail layer (still) selected, choose **Layer>Mode>Luminance** from the menu. This will change the way in which the top, blurred, and stretched comet tail layer interacts with the underlying one. Notice that it is now easy to see the particles from the second comet tail layer showing through a kind of "haze" from the first layer. To correct the rather harsh edges of the underlying layer, I added a fast blur with a Blurriness of 3.0 to this layer as well and then reduced this layer's opacity setting to about 60% also. When all the layers and effects are added up, we get quite a striking effect (see Figure 12.30).

Should you wish to see it, the full Quicktime animation of this file is CometFinal.mov on the accompanying CD-ROM.

If you have successfully negotiated this tutorial, then congratulate yourself! The techniques described here are advanced tricks used by professionals who use EI for such impressive work as the rereleased "Star Wars" trilogy. With a little work and experimentation, you may be on the team for the next movie!

As always, consider this tutorial not as a recipe but as an inspiration. Play with values during all the steps of the tutorial and even try some crazy variations you might come up with. Make your work your own, not simply a copy of mine—and always have *fun* doing it!

—*John L. Kundert-Gibbs*

W ith all of the talk up to this point about how to do this and how to do that, it's time to go inside the head of one of the most talented and demanding users of ElectricImage. Keith Lango has produced some amazing character animation with EI, and here's a little bit of info on how he produced a recent work called *Daycare for Junior*.

Daycare for Junior

THE GERM OF AN IDEA

Daycare for Junior is my latest independent animated short film detailing the trials and travails of Junior, a young preschool space alien who's facing his first day outside the loving care of his parents (see Figure 13.1). In the nearly 3 minutes of animation, Junior runs the gamut of emotions from innocent sleepiness, to anger, sadness, despondency, hesitant apprehension, curious exploration, resignation, inquisitiveness, relief, and then finally, at last, the joy of a newfound friend.

Over the course of bringing this story to life, I came across many hurdles using ElectricImage, as I would have using any application. Character animation is a tricky business to begin with, but there are a few things that can help

FIGURE   *Meet the star of* Daycare for Junior, *Junior.*
13.1

convey the emotion of a piece and to help it transcend a technological curiosity to a story that engages the viewer. It was with this goal in mind that I entered into the six-month odyssey of making my short film, *Daycare for Junior*, using ElectricImage to help realize this goal.

MODELING: SPLINES TO THE RESCUE

First thing I needed to do was model Junior. Since the ElectricImage Modeler was still under development, I turned to Martin Hash's 3D Animation for my modeling needs. Using its intuitive and flexible spline patch modeling techniques, I was able to construct Junior in a few days. His prominent feature, his head and eyes, were going to be the main vehicle for expressing his thoughts, so I made them extra large. I did this to also help convey a sense of his cuteness. Kids have large heads relative to their body size. So I went with this.

I modeled his hands and arms as one section, then duplicated it for the feet with some scale and pitch modification. Junior's five body parts were then exported as subdivided DXFs from MH3DA. Before wrapping up the modeling stage, I made some emotion targets for the weighted morphing feature in EIAS 2.8. Selecting spline control points for different areas of Junior's head, I created morph targets for the right and left brows. A total of six targets were created, R&LBrowUp, R&LBrowDown, R&LBrowMad. These six targets were exported as subdivided DXFs for use in EIAS morpher. To bring these targets into the morpher, I made a blank project, imported each DXF, and saved it as a FACT file. Then I threw out that blank project and brought the Default base body model into my animation project. I then opened the Keymorph Dialog for it. Within the morph dialog I added the six targets I had created. I was then able to animate his eyebrows by adjusting the sliders to set keyframes. Using this feature, I was able to enhance the emotion Junior was showing at any given moment. Used in concert with the eyes, this was the magic that made it possible to allow the viewer to know what Junior was thinking (see Figure 13.2).

The last thing to model was Junior's eyes. Using a technique I had developed for my first short story character animation, Yum-Yum, I made spherical eyes and matching eyelids in another polygonal modeler. The eye was a sphere and the lids were lathed caps that covered the top and bottom hemispheres of the sphere accordingly. I named the sphere Eyeball and the lids Upper and Lower lid (see Figure 13.3). I then imported this model into EIAS where I used the Scale and Bezier deformations to shape the eye. To set the blinking I opened the eyelid's Link Info Window and set the lids to inherit deformation, as shown in Figure 13.4. This way, any deforming I did to the eyeball, the lids would follow suit. I then adjusted their center of rotation to be the center of the

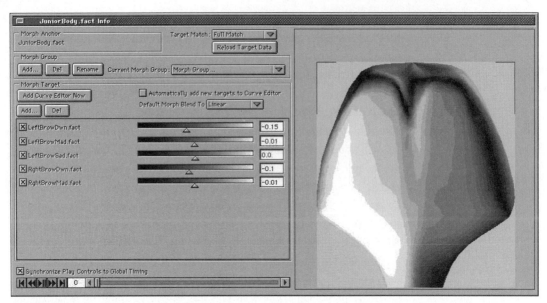

FIGURE **13.2**   *Once modeled, the individual targets were imported into EI's new keymorph editor where the shape of the head could be animated. By blending different percentages of these targets, Junior was able to produce an infinite amount of expression.*

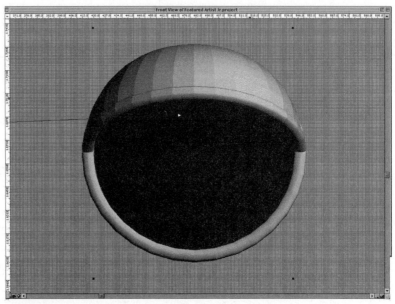

FIGURE **13.3**   *Junior's eye before adding the bezier deformation.*

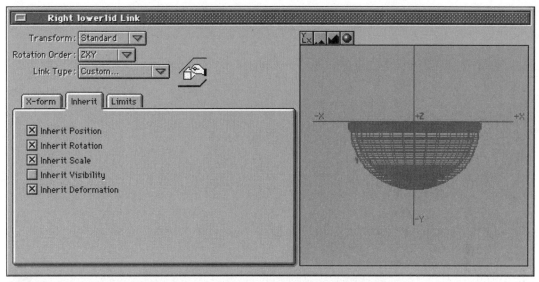

FIGURE
13.4 *By checking the Inherit Deformation feature, the lids follow along with the eyeball as it is deformed.*

eyeball sphere. I could then just rotate the lids on their X axis to make them "blink." Next, I gave the eyeball a scale deformation of -50% for the Z axis to thin out the eyeball and have it lie against Junior's flat-fronted head. Then I added a bezier deformation to the eye along its Y axis. By grabbing the top and bottom control points of the bezier deformation, I could shape the eye into what I wanted. The eyelids inherited this and followed along for the ride, still blinking perfectly when rotated on their X axis. I later animated the shape of the bezier deformation for the eyeball to form the eyes into different shapes to show different emotions (see Figure 13.5). Using just the eyes, body language, and the morph targets, I was able to convey the wide range of emotions Junior exhibits over the course of the story.

Bones and Linking: Digital Rheumatism

When EIAS 2.9 came out, with it came the long-awaited bones feature. What bones allowed me to do with Junior was take this simple five-mesh character and make him move all over the place. I could make the fingers bend, his back arch, his head turn, and his legs walk; all without having to break Junior into dozens of little pieces. What bones also did was add tons of complexity to a relatively simple character.

The first obstacle to overcome was making the mesh behave with bones applied. Because there is no vertice tagging in EIAS bones, it's all proximity

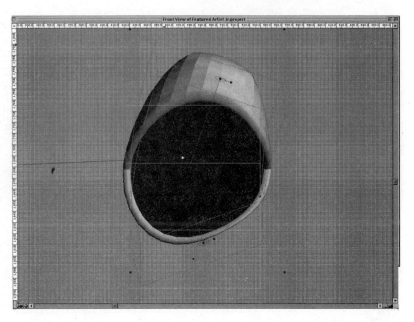

FIGURE **13.5**   *As we see here with the bezier deformation applied, the eyelids glide along smoothly. Using the bezier deform Junior's eyes could be made any number of shapes.*

based. What's bad about that is that when a hand reaches across to scratch a belly, as Junior does upon waking, the mesh in the hand and the belly get all twisted around because the bones in the hand and torso are fighting with each other. After weeks of experimenting with different hierarchy settings and linkings, I settled upon a workable hierarchy that let me animate Junior in a somewhat predictable and worthwhile manner (see Figure 13.6).

I wanted the arms and legs separate from the torso for a number of reasons. One of them was simplicity of modeling; the second was in an attempt to bypass the problems introduced when trying to use bones on a single mesh character. Well, the modeling was simpler. But I still had unique challenges in the setup.

At the base of it all was a box effector to which I parented the body and subsequently all the bones as well. Anytime I needed Junior to bend forward, turn, lean sideways, or shift his weight I animated this main root effector. I did this to reduce the tearing of the mesh when I animated the torso bone. The torso bone was the internal base structure to which I linked the arms. What I ended up doing with the arms and legs in order to get them to play nice with the torso was to bone each arm and leg separately with its own bone chain structure.

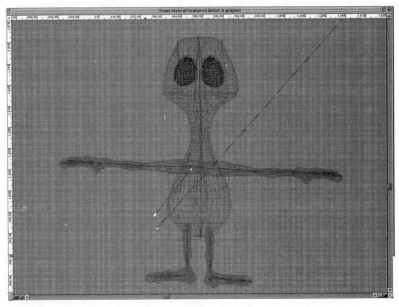

FIGURE 13.6 *The final bone structure for Junior.*

This allowed me to not have to fight with custom bone regions for influence. This chain was then activated and added to the relating arm or leg. I then took the arm model (the mesh, not the bone) and linked that to the torso bone running down the spine of Junior and told it to inherit deformation. This way when the torso bent, the arms would follow suit. But parenting the arm mesh to the torso bone also acted as a sort of insulation from keeping the arms from getting all messed up by the body's bones. When I linked the arms to the body mesh (as you would logically assume you should do) I got all kinds of nasty results, as you can see in Figure 13.7. But linking to the bone in the body solved most of those problems (see Figure 13.8).

Another problem was that the arms were interfering with the body when moved, so to minimize that I added placeholder bones to the body to keep the mesh more in shape when the arms and legs moved. I also did this for Junior's large head. His head was so large that just adding one bone up there to move around that mesh would result in his head distorting all over the place when he looked up or down turned his head, as you can see in Figure 13.9. So I added a series of six placeholder bones to his head to keep its shape. The placeholder bones are parented to whatever the controlling bone is (in this case it was the headbone, the one I set keyframes to animate his head) and are not in a chain.

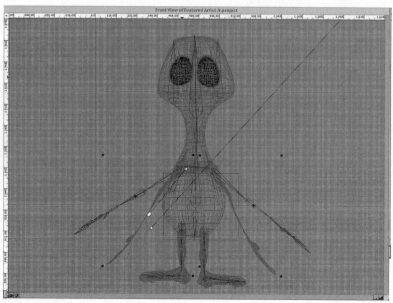

FIGURE **13.7** *When parenting the arm to the body mesh, the deformations got extremely ugly and unmanageable.*

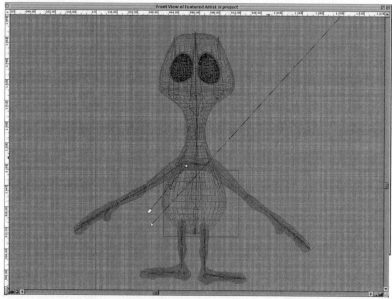

FIGURE **13.8** *But by parenting the arms to the torso bone, we were able to get desirable and predictable deformation results.*

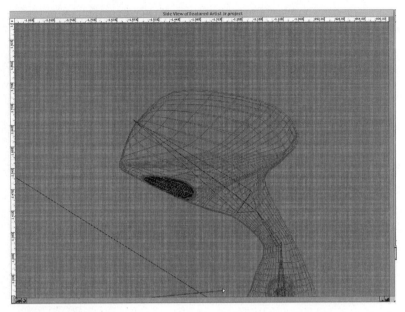

FIGURE   *Without placeholder bones, Junior's head got very messy and squashed when he*
13.9   *moved.*

They are all usually lock-linked so as to not move and mess up the mesh shape. And then, for good measure, I turned off their visibility and then locked and hid them in the project window to keep myself from accidentally messing with them (see Figure 13.10). Occasionally I needed to get at them, but not often, and they saved the day in allowing me to move Junior's body parts around in the odd and weird ways I did.

All told, Junior ended up with 54 bones to make him move around. When he was in the same scene as his newfound friend Sloopy, I had no less than 108 bones to keep track of. All of them had anywhere from 3 to 12 data channels for motion to keep track of and edit. Without some way to keep track of this immensely complex amount of data, I was looking at a white-walled rubber room in my not-so-distant future.

ANIMATING: HOW F-CURVES SAVED MY SANITY

Once I was happy with the way Junior was all set up and was moving him in a safe and predictable manner (for the most part), I decided to get right down to it and start making him do his thing. The story evolved a bit as I made it. The nice thing about being the producer, director, and animator is I can change things as I go without any arguments from the staff. My storyboards were ex-

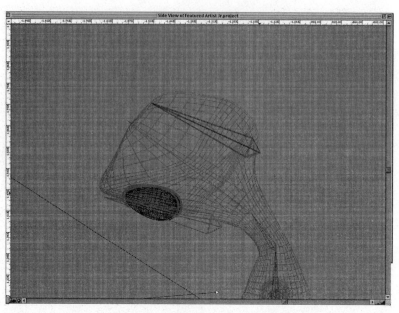

FIGURE 13.10 *By adding several bones to the head and lock-linking them to the main headbone we were able to allow Junior's head to maintain its shape integrity. This was key since so much of the emotion of the character would be expressed in his head and eyes.*

tremely simple concept sketches. Just stick-drawings really. Since the only person I needed to communicate with was myself, I could cut this corner. If I had other animators working on this project, detailed storyboards would have been essential to getting things the way I needed them to be.

I had originally planned on a different ending than the one I ended up using, But over time, three more possible endings popped up in my head. So I developed a story path that would lead me to a cross roads where I could choose either one of those three endings. I ended up going with the one used for a number of reasons. But the main reason was because I had run the emotional gamut on the darker side of Junior and had not shown him happy at all. A friend and fellow animator commented that he didn't think Junior could ever be made to look happy because he was modeled sad. So I chose to end the story happy in an attempt to see if I could make this sad-looking character look happy. In the end I felt I was able to do that successfully (see Figure 13.11.)

But before I could get to the end, I had to tell the story along the way. There are principles to cartoon character animation that have been developed since the early days of Disney, Schlesinger Productions, Warner Bros. MGM, and

Junior and Sloopy in the end. Both look happy enough.

others. Building on the pioneering work of such animation greats as Jones, Avery, Clampett, Freling, Thomas, and Johnston, I went to work.

One of the main keys to good animation is snappy motion. Snap can mean to hit a pose and hold it to allow the viewer to read the action/idea/emotion. It can also mean to anticipate a motion to help the audience read what's happening. Snap is like the black lines of a drawing. It helps set the boundaries of individual motions, just as lines help to set the limits of individual elements in a drawing or picture. A picture with no discernible lines looks like a painter's dropcloth. While some folks like that style, nobody is certain what the picture is of. Similarly, animation without snap is also difficult to read and understand exactly what is going on in the scene. Mushy motion is generally bad motion. It's like watching someone get seasick. After awhile you end up feeling queasy as well. With EIAS 2.9 came the single greatest advancement in the program since the days of version 2.0—Function Curves. F-Curves allowed me to edit the data channels of motion directly and graphically. By allowing me to go in and edit the motion curves, I was able to add snap, moving holds, overshoot, extremes; avoid motion symmetry; and generally add the organic subtlety that

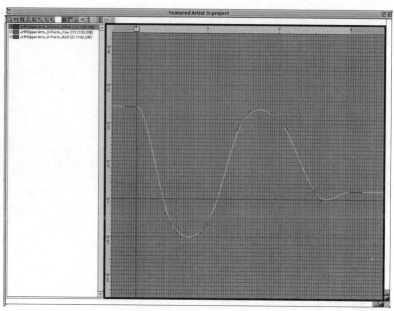

FIGURE **13.12**   *Left to its own devices, the motion of an object would tend to be very smooth and mushy. This F-Curve shows how the motion would blend from one into the other, with little or no discernible definition to separate the motion and make it easier to read when viewed at full speed.*

makes Junior a living, breathing character instead of a mechanical study in moving around (see Figure 13.12).

When Junior needed to hold a pose to add drama to a moment, F-Curves allowed me to flatten out the curve data, as shown in Figure 13.13. Flatter curve data equals less movement, since the F-Curve is a graphical representation of data changing over time. Less data change means less motion. And less motion is a stronger pose hold; a stronger pose hold adds zip and life to a character animation. While I was looking for flatter motion data for hold, sometimes I wanted to overshoot a keyframe to really emphasize that motion. So by adding a little hiccup to the F-Curves I can get some exaggerated motion. If I wanted Junior to be still, but not perfectly still, I could use the F-curve editor to slightly offset a keyframe in value. When a computer-generated character comes to a perfect, complete standstill and is frozen, it loses life. Drawn animation has some variance from frame to frame to keep the character alive while it is still, but the computer is too good at understanding a drop-dead stop. So to add moving holds and keep the illusion of Junior as a living creature, I just twiddled a bit with the F-Curves. Without F-Curves, animating Junior with the degree of subtlety and control I had would have been downright impossi-

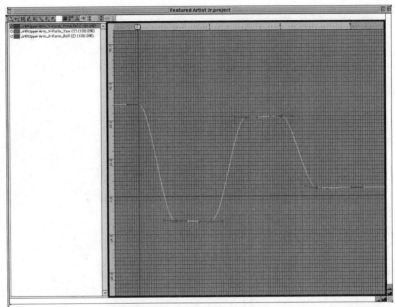

FIGURE   *By flattening the curves where Junior is supposed to hold a pose, we add snap*
13.13   *to the animation, making it much easier to understand what is going on. The
flatter areas of the curve are where he's holding the pose. The slope is where
he's moving. Note the flat areas aren't perfectly flat. This is called a moving
hold and helps to keep the character "alive" while holding a pose.*

ble. When dropping tens of thousands of keyframes for three minutes of complex character animation, you need that kind of control or you'll go crazy (see Figure 13.14.). F-Curves saved my life.

TEXTURES, SURFACES, AND LIGHTING: WHY IS EVERYTHING SO PURPLE?

With Junior, I wanted to experiment with a very stylized color palette and lighting scheme. Much of my professional 3D work involves creating realism. Much of this realism is achieved with lighting and textures. Conversely, if I wanted to break out of that mold and create an oddly colored universe where all the colors are thrown together to create a patchwork of brightly arranged contrasts and open up a world unknown, then textures and lighting would be how I would do it.

Junior's body color is the result of another EIAS 2.9 feature—procedural shaders. Using a customized Fractal shader, I was able to give Junior his subtle and organic look. The same Fractal shader was used for the ground on the pur-

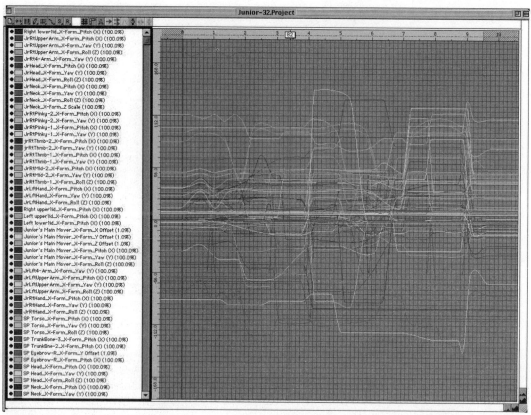

FIGURE *A snapshot of the F-Curve editor for the scene Junior35. And you think your desk is cluttered!*

13.14

ple planet. Using the Wisp shader, I was able to create many different textures to the inside walls of the ship and the daycare. I used the Veins shader for the floor of the daycare, as well as the seats in the flying saucer. Using the Crust shader, I could make his bed. All these shaders, with their organic and procedural nature, allowed me to create surrealistic surfaces that were free from pattern repeating and the tiling common to texture mapping. With their editable parameters I was able to create dozens of customized surfaces from just a few shader bases.

When I did need a texture map, EIAS 2.9's new Materials editor, with its unlimited texture mapping, came in very useful. For the text on the side of the daycare, in the daycare on the walls and floors, as well as on the doorbell, I used custom black and white texture maps to create bump, diffuse, luminance and glow patterns. I used the new Glow feature in 2.8 extensively on the bottom of the space ship, on the daycare sign as well as the text in the daycare walls. The ability to render those glows directly in 3D freed me from having to create all of those effects in post production, which would have made the job of post a lot more difficult. Plus I really liked the look of the glows. I wanted to use them to enhance the overall nuttiness of the universe Junior lives in. I did this to accentuate just how strange the world can look through the eyes of a child. To them everything is odd-looking, strange, new, fascinating, and colorful. They're not old enough to be jaded about how light falls on a pattern. So to thrust the viewer into a world as strange to them as it would be to a child, I broke down the walls of realism with textures (see Figure 13.15).

Lighting also played a huge role in creating this tapestry of weirdness and unsettling oddness. Using an odd combination of purple, yellow, blue, green, orange, and white lights, I was able to create the style I wanted. Allowing those odd lights to be shown in even more vivid array was the surface of Junior's eyes. Everywhere the story goes, the eyes lead it. To create that highly glossy, but not purely reflective surface, I dropped the diffuse values all the way down. I then set the specular value to 100% white and decreased the specular size to 50 to make the hot spot on his eyes very large. Then the final touch was to set the

FIGURE
13.15   *Some frame grabs detailing the use of several procedural shaders and textures, layered glow and luminance maps, and object glows. Also some hints at the lighting used to set the mood in Junior.*

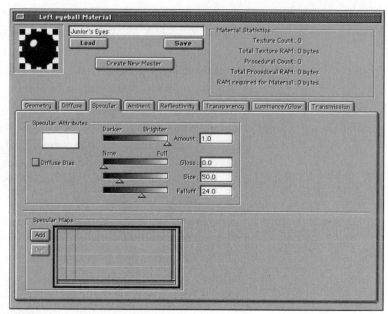

FIGURE **13.16** *A snapshot of the Materials editor detailing the specular settings for Junior's ultra glossy eyes.*

specular dropoff to an extraordinarily high number of 24 (see Figure 13.16). In my realism work, I usually lower this setting to 0.2 or 0.4 to soften the specular highlights. CGI images often suffer from telltale specular highlights that aren't natural and tend to make 3D renderings look plastic and fake. But rather than fight this, I took it to the absurd and created a style of surface for Junior's eyes that was exactly what I was looking for.

I chose not to use pupils to indicate direction of view or emotions, but threw the weight of that responsibility upon the bezier deformations and the body language. Everywhere I turned, I tried to boil the essence of the emotion down to the eyes and the pose. By skipping pupils (and a mouth) I was able to focus my energies on conveying feeling in a universal language.

POST: PUTTING IT ALL TOGETHER

The job of taking the end result of 41 different EIAS projects, 46 rendered movies, numerous special effects shots, adding dialog and subtitles as well as credits, music, and sound effects all fell to Adobe's After Effects. This powerhouse application made bringing all this stuff together possible. The main After Effects project had 4 sub comps consisting of 124 total layers, 50 sound effects files and brought over 2 gigs of data into a cohesive film.

FIGURE   *Two frame grabs detailing the use of faked depth of field achieved in After*
13.17   *Effects using track mattes.*

Many of the effects were done directly in ElectricImage, but some things were faster and easier to handle in After Effects. The simulated depth-of-field, as shown in Figure 13.17, was faster to fake in After Effects than ElectricImage. EIAS 2.9 added depth-of-field as a rendering effect, but it made the render take five times as long as it normally would have due to its multiframe sampling for the effect. While the effect is beautiful, it was too costly for me to use in this film. Since realism wasn't something I was necessarily aiming for, I simulated depth-of-field switching and effects using gray scale images made in Photoshop and blended with a track matte in After Effects.

For sound, I sampled in a collection of sounds I have, as well as recording new ones and customizing them to fit the situation. The dialog tracks of the parents, which are a garbled alien language, are actually a recording of myself speaking the lines with odd inflections and emphasis. These then were then reversed and warbled, and tone pitch was changed and reverbed. Junior's snoring and yawning were also recordings of my own voice, with tone pitch changes to give the impression of a small child making the noises. As for the music, that was superbly written and performed by Michael Bastedo of Atlanta, GA and then dropped into the After Effects project.

THE RESULT: MY DAUGHTERS LIKED IT

While making this short-form animation was a labor of love, done for the sheer joy of creating something worthwhile and of quality, *Daycare for Junior* has served me well professionally. By sharpening my skills as a character animator and finding work-arounds to problems, I've managed to grow as an artist. *Daycare for Junior* will be making the rounds at film and animation festivals the world over, hopefully allowing for 3 minutes of some joy for those who see it.

APPENDIX

A

Contributor Profiles

This book is an expression of the cumulative experience of several ElectricImage artists, each of whom has been gracious enough to share this experience with you. In the next few pages, you'll have an opportunity to learn more about each artist and his background. If you'd like to comment on their contributions to the book, there's contact info here, too. You can even find out more about their work or trade additional tips and techniques. (This book is by no means exhaustive!)

JOHNATHAN BANTA

Johnathan Banta is a lead Animator at Sassoon Film Design, the Director of Agrapha Productions, and the programmer of AG_shaders. He has worked on films such as "Air Force One", "Desperate Measures", "Starship Troopers", "Meet the Deedles", and numerous IMAX and special venue features.

JOHN CRANE

John B. Crane is the principal of Sandhill Studios, a 3D illustration and animation studio based in Santa Fe, New Mexico. His work has been published in a variety of national and international computer graphics/art magazines has and won numerous awards, including recognition from the New York Society of Illustrators. His clients include some of the largest national labs in the country. John is also a contributing editor to *3D Artist* magazine and a 3D columnist for a popular web e-zine. He can be reached by email at jbcrane@sandstudios.com. More samples of his work may be seen at http://www.sandstudios.com.

SHARKAWI CHE DIN

Sharkawi Che Din is from Malaysia and is currently a lecturer for computer animation at the faculty of applied and creative arts. After graduating from New

Zealand as a Computer Graphics major, he taught Graphic Design at the Universiti Malaysia Sarawak for about a year before earning his master's degree in the USA as the Savannah College of Art and Design. About two years ago, he began to work in 3D on both Macintosh and Silicon Graphics workstations and has recently had his 3D work published in *DV magazine*, *Computer Artist*, *Computer Graphics World*, *Electronic Publishing*, and *In-FormZ magazines*, 1998 Form•Z Calendar, and *Mac International Art and Design Magazine*, Sweden . His animation called "The Time Passage" won second prize in the Animation category for MetaCreation's 1997 "Beyond The Canvas" International Art and Design Contest. Sharkawi can be reached at: **sharkawi@earthlink.net** or by snail mail at **Faculty of Applied and Creative Art, Universiti Malaysia Sarawak, 94300 Kota Samarahan, Sarawak, Malaysia**.

DON FOLEY

Don is a freelance illustrator/animator/author who, when not chained to his computers, can be found out sailing somewhere on the Chesapeake Bay. With over 15 years of experience in both traditional and digital media, Don has won over two dozen international, national, and regional awards for his work. He has written two books on computer animation and to escape his home studio, he teaches a college course on animation. You can reach Don at don@foley-media.com or http://www.foleymedia.com.

RICK GRECO

Rick Greco is currently the Photo/Image Editor for Casino Journal Publishing Group, the largest and most highly respected publisher of gambling trade and consumer magazines in the casino industry. Rick specializes in custom editorial feature and cover art, applying photography, 2D, and 3D digital techniques to achieve his powerful and unique imagery. Greco's strengths stem from his 12 years' experience as an artist and editor in the publishing industry, developing and creating quality visual solutions in a fast-paced deadline-oriented environment. Check out his webfolio at http:/members.aol.com/ripix, and e-mail him at ripix@aol.com to inquire about his freelance availability.

ALBERT KIEFER

Albert Kiefer formed his company, Sector A (www.sectora@euronet.nl, sectora@euronet.nl), in 1989 and has since been developing his 3D and imaging skills using various packages and hardware platforms. Working for clients in both the corporate sector and broadcast media, his most recent broadcast project was Zeeuws Meisje. As a series intended for children, Sector A provided

3D modeling and animation sequences, and, in cooperation with Illustrator Frans Mensink, produced very convincing matte and texturing work for all of the series' digital backdrops. His passion clearly reaches out to film and broadcast effects work.

JOHN L. KUNDERT-GIBBS

John Kundert-Gibbs is assistant professor and director of the Multimedia Program at California Lutheran University. His BA is in physics, from Princeton University, and his Ph.D. is in dramatic literature from The Ohio State University. He teaches computer animation and post-processing using ElectricImage and Adobe's AfterEffects. the especially enjoys working out animations that mimic physical actions or phenomena. Additionally, he has lectured extensively on the effects of new computer technology on society and the arts.

GORD LACEY

Gord Lacey is working at his former college, where he creates websites. He also maintains the ElectricImage Resources Page and is the creator of the website that accompanies this book. His company, BlueFrog Studios, has developed many successful websites for Edmonton area businesses, yet he'd rather be animating. Gord can be reached at bluefrog@shaw.wave.ca or bluefrog@home.com. The ElectricImage Resources Page can be found at http://www.eiresources.com.

KEITH LANGO

Keith Lango has been creating digital art and 3D animation professionally since 1993. He has created digital environments and complex creative character animation for the game, CBT, broadcast video, and film markets. Keith lives with his lovely wife Kim and their two daughters Candice and Laura in upstate New York, only a stone's throw from the Erie Canal. If you would like to contract Keith to develop character animation for your next project, contact him via e-mail at keith.lango@velocityfx.com or visit his website.

"Daycare for Junior" was Keith's third independent short animated story. Junior and his previous efforts, "Yum-Yum" and "10-Pin" can be viewed on his website at http://www.velocityfx.com/KeithLango.

MATT SILVERMAN

After studying traditional and CG animation at San Francisco State University's Cinema department, Matt Silverman moved on to Silicon Valley where he specialized in 3D animation and motion graphics for the high-tech industry. Matt's freelance work and fulltime employment at CKS/Pictures led him to projects for clients including Apple Computer, Compaq, Visa, Timberland, Psygnosis, and Northwest Airlines. In addition, Matt worked as a contracted demo artist for ElectricImage Inc., Adobe Systems, TGS Software, and Puffin Designs. Matt is currently working for Puffin Designs, as the Product Manager for the Knoll Software product line. When he isn't traveling the globe demoing Puffin Designs' software, he continues to work on personal animation projects and independent films. You can reach Matt at matt@puffindesigns.com.

CHRIS WEYERS

Chris Weyers is an award-winning animator and digital designer. He won first place in the scholastic division of the inaugural ElectricImage animation contest in 1996. He can be contacted through his web site at http://www.over-thruster.com.

Resources

The following is a list of web sites for tons of stuff related to ElectricImage and 3D in general. If you don't feel like typing it all in, Gord Lacey created a great support site for the book which is included on the CD-ROM. Enjoy.

ELECTRICIMAGE RESOURCES:

3Dimentia
http://www.3dimentia.com/
> An electronic newsletter for Form*Z and ElectricImage users. 6 issues a year, once every 2 months.

Listserve Searchable Archive
http://lists.anapraxis.com/forms/email/ei-search.html
> Weston Houghton has created a searchable archive of the ElectricImage Listserve.

PostForum—Electric Image Forum
http://www.postforum.pair.com/ElectricImage/
> An online forum for discussion on ElectricImage.

ToolFarm Electric Image Listserve
http://www.toolfarm.com/resources/lists.htm
> This listserve has over 1000 subscribers around the world. There are two versions of the list; regular and digest. Toolfarm has also added a "How-To" list for help with specific EI questions.

The Electric Image Resources Page
http://www.eiresources.com

> A collection of resources for anyone interested in ElectricImage. The information includes tutorials, links to models and textures, the latest plugins and links to other net resources. A must see for any EI user.

MAGAZINES:

3D Artist
http://www.3dartist.com

> The web version of this magazine includes many links to 3D resources on the 'net and some articles from the newsstand copy.

3D Design
http://www.3d-design.com

> Online articles, tips, links and a user forum can be found here.

Computer Graphics World
http://www.cgw.com

> Although it's main focus is on PC's, there is some excellent information related to 3D on the Macintosh.

Digital Video
http://dvlive.com

> Online articles from the current issue and back issues of this digital video magazine.

New Media
http://www.newmedia.com

> A magazine that covers 3D, digital video and multimedia.

Serious 3D
http://www.serious3d.com

> A new magazine that focuses on tutorials. There is a broad range of programs covered on both Mac and PC systems. ElectricImage tutorials will be included in the Magazine starting with it's September issue. The magazine is released every 2 months.

MODELS:

3D Cafe

http://www.3dcafe.com/meshes.htm

> Lots of different models that are free to download. Nicely organized so it's easy to find what you're looking for.

3Name3d

http://www.3name3d.com/

> 3Name3d sells the "Cyberprops" Volumes 1-15. Each CD contains a wide variety of objects.

Acuris

http://www.acuris.com/

> Various models in the following categories: animals, architecture, geography, medical, sports, vehicles and miscellaneous.

Avalon

http://avalon.viewpoint.com/cgi-bin/nav.pl?key=o&site=vp

> A huge collection of models that are free to download. Nicely organized so it's easy to find what you're looking for.

Electric Image Model Repository

http://www.mediav.com/ei_model/

> A great resource for animators who need a model for ElectricImage. People are constantly submitting models so there's always something new to look at.

Geo-Metricks

http://www.geo-metricks.com/

> Geo-Metricks sells highly detailed models of characters and objects. There are a few models that're free to download.

Mesh Mart

http://www.meshmart.org/

> Lots of different models that are free to download. Nicely organized so it's easy to find what you're looking for.

Model Masters

http://www.modelmasters.com/

Model Masters allows you to order your models online, and they offer models in many popular categories; Automobiles, Characters, Sports, and many others.

Plastic Thought

http://www.plasticthought.com/

"Active Art" and "3D Active" are collections of 3DMF objects (also includes animated gifs and VRML).

Star Wars Modelling Alliance

http://www.surfthe.net/swma

The archive contains some of the most amazing 3rd party Star Wars models ever made.

Viewpoint Datalabs

http://www.viewpoint.com/

One of the largest collections of high quality models on the net. This is a must see for 3D animators.

TEXTURES:

Arcitex

http://www.arcitex.com/

Seamless stone, wood and flooring textures that were scanned using a drum scanner. Available on 2 CDs or separately.

Artbeats

http://www.artbeats.com/frames/prodmain.html

Artbeats sells collections of textures as well as video clips of fire and explosions.

Avalon

http://avalon1.viewpoint.com/cgi-bin/nav.pl?key=t&site=vp

Links to some free textures on the Avalon site. Various themes in a few different formats (gif, jpeg, tiff).

Axem

http://axem2.simplenet.com

Free textures ranging from stones and marbles to wood and tiles.

Electric Image Texture Repository

http://www.mediav.com/ei_model/texture

Free textures provided in .image of Photoshop file formats.

Maps of the Solar System

http://maps.jpl.nasa.gov/

Very detailed maps of planets in our solar system taken from satellites.

Mesh Mart

http://www.meshmart.org/textcat.htm

Textures and links provided by Mesh Mart.

Pixar

http://www.pixar.com/products/renderman/toolkit/textures/

These seamless textures work well with any 3D program. There are two volumes; Classic Textures 1 and 2.

Ransom Interactive Texture Collections

http://www.forgotten.com/textures/

18 collections of seamless textures (and bump maps) in 12 different categories. Nice, affordable textures.

Skintures

http://www.lh.net/client/magus/skintures/main.html

A set of shareware textures used for skin. There are different textures for various ethnic skin colors; nicely done and very inexpensive.

Surface of Reality

http://www.wellsite.com/surface/index.html

A collection of grunge textures created by Alex Lindsay of ILM.

COMPANIES:

Adobe Systems Inc.

http://www.adobe.com

Adobe has developed some of the "must have" programs associated with 3D. After Effects for video compositing and special effects, and Photoshop for texturemaps and;t.;t.;t.;tpretty much everything else.

auto_des_sys

http://www.formz.com

form-Z is the flagship product from auto•des•sys. Many people use this to model and ElectricImage to render.

Electric Image Inc.

http://www.electricimage.com

The company that brings you the leading animation program on the Macintosh.

Endless Corporation

http://www.endless-corp.com/

Endless and Endless 2000 are the plugins created by Endless Corp.

Motional Realms

http://www.reelmotion.com

Reel Motion is a physics based app/plugin for Electric Image. It allows you to drive a car (or fly a plane/helicopter) and use the motion data in Electric Image.

Northern Lights Productions

http://www.northernlightsprod.com

Big Dipper, Cable Craft, Dante, DaVinci's Chisel, Flock This, Liquefy, Pathfinder, Placer Deposit, and Zeus are part of the Artifex Series 1, 2 and 3. Auto-Bank, Flag for 2.8, and Standard Shape 2 are free plugins from Northern Lights Productions.

OLBI Card Co., Inc.

http://users.aol.com/olbicard/index.html

Image2Mesh is a widely known plugin from this company. They've also brought us Image2Relief, KeyMorph, NthPoly and Texturer.

Onyx Computing

http://www.onyxtree.com/

TreePro has spawned two plugins for Electric Image; Tree EIAS and Tree Storm.

Puffin Designs

http://www.puffindesigns.com/

Puffin Designs was co-founded by ILM Visual Effects Supervisor Scott Squires. Puffin Designs has released Commotion and markets Knoll Lens Flare Pro developed by another wizard at ILM, John Knoll.

TripleDTools Inc.

http://www.powerparticles.com/

The company that developed the plugin PowerParticles and the AG_Shaders for EI.

Valis Group

http://www.valisgroup.com

Although Kitchen Appliances is still in beta, you can get a sneak at the plugins that many are eagerly awaiting.

Zaxwerks

http://www.zaxwerks.com

Zaxwerks products include EPS Invigorator, The Vector Lathe, Surface Materials Training CD and the Fundamentals of Electric Image video series.

PLUGINS

Auto-bank—Northern Lights Productions

http://www.northernlightsprod.com/auto.html\

Auto-bank samples camera data and creates realistic roll information for creating better fly-through type animations.

Big Dipper—Northern Lights Productions

http://www.northernlightsprod.com/dipper.html

Creating 3D star fields for your space ships to blast through has never been easier. Big Dipper can place geometry in place of stars. Part of Artifex volumes 1 &2.

Cablecraft—Northern Lights Productions

http://www.northernlightsprod.com/cable.html

Allows you to create animateable extruded B-Splines. Part of Artifex Volume 3.

Dante—Northern Lights Productions

http://www.northernlightsprod.com/dante.html

A full featured particle generator. Dante lets you create fire, water, explosions, fireworks and a few other effects. Part of Artifex volumes 1 &2.

Da Vinci's Chisel—Northern Lights Productions

http://www.northernlightsprod.com/chisel.html

Da Vinci's Chisel is a 3-dimensional wipe tool for revealing on consuming your models. Part of Artifex volumes 1 &2.

Endless 1.5—Endless Corp

http://www.endless-corp.com/products/plugin/eias_1_5.ht

This plugin expands the texture mapping features found in ElectricImage. Endless allows you to have precision mapping allowing you to work with groups at the vertices and facets level. Endless works well with Metacreations Detailer.

Endless 2000—Endless Corp

http://www.endless-corp.com/products/plugin/eias_2000.htm

Endless 2000 includes all the features of Endless 1.5 as well as Trooper. Trooper lets you create hair, fur, and many other effects.

EPS Invigorator—Zaxwerks

http://www.zaxwerks.com/EI_InvigMain.html

It's been described as a "must-have plugin for any EI user". EPS Invigorator imports EPS and Adobe Illustrator files and creates geometry inside ElectricImage. There are over 100 ways a file can be extruded, giving you almost endless possibilities.

Flag 2.8—Northern Lights Productions

http://www.northernlightsprod.com/updates/Flag28.hqx

A recompiled version of this unfinished plugin that simulates a flag blowing in the wind.

Flock This—Northern Lights Productions
http://www.northernlightsprod.com/flock.html

> Gives you the ability to simulate flocks, herds, and schools. Part of Artifex Volume 3.

Image2Mesh—OLBI Card Co., Inc.
http://users.aol.com/olbicard/index.html

> Using a grey scale image or QuickTime movie you can create a mesh. Great for creating water or other natural effects.

Image2Relief—OLBI Card Co., Inc.
http://users.aol.com/olbicard/index.html

> Similar to Image2Mesh, Image2Relief can only use still images to make meshes.

Knoll Lens Flare Pro
http://www.webcom.com/puffin/products/klf/intro_knoll.html

> Create professional lens flares with this plugin developed by John Knoll at ILM. The Pro package includes plugins for EI, Adobe After Effects and Adobe Photoshop.

Liquefy—Northern Lights Productions
http://www.northernlightsprod.com/liquefy.html

> Liquefy melts your models into a puddle, or reverse the effects to have objects appear from ooze. Part of Artifex volumes 1 &2.

Pathfinder—Northern Lights Productions
http://www.northernlightsprod.com/path.html

> Lets you use a model as a motion path. Part of Artifex volumes 1 &2.

PowerParticles—TripleDTools Inc.
http://www.powerparticles.com

> A powerful particle plugin that no user should be without. Excellent collision detection, emission of models as particles, and the ability to set 100 colors to be displayed during the lifetime of the particle are just some of the features offered by PowerParticles.

Placer Deposit—Northern Lights Productions
http://www.northernlightsprod.com/placer.html

> Allows you to quickly and easily place copies of models on the surfaces of other models. Part of Artifex Volume 3.

ReelMotion—Motion Realms

http://www.reelmotion.com

> A Physics based simulation program that produces unbelievable results. Want a car to drive on a country dirt road? Use ReelMotion with a terrain file of the road to have your car bumping along. Imagine key framing that! Although it was designed for simulating cars and planes, there are endless uses for this plugin.

Standard Shape 2—Northern Lights Productions

http://www.northernlightsprod.com/shape.html

> A free replacement to the Standard Shape plugin, Standard Shape 2 includes all the shapes found in Standard Shape as well as circular disks, hemispheres, and toroids.

Tree EIAS—Onyx Computing

http://www.onyxtree.com/treeeias.html

> Tree EIAS lets you import trees made in Tree Pro (or Tree Painter) for use in ElectricImage.

Tree EIAS Storm—Onyx Computing

http://www.onyxtree.com/storm.html

> Tree EIAS Storm has the same features as Tree EIAS, but it allows you to apply a wind force to animate the trees.

Texturer—OLBI Card Co., Inc.

http://users.aol.com/olbicard/index.html

> Texturer allows you to texture child objects of a model.

Vector Lathe—Zaxwerks

http://www.zaxwerks.com/EI_VectorLathe_Main.html

> Vector Lathe is a great way to lathe (or revolve) EPS files to create geometry inside ElectricImage.

Zeus—Northern Lights Productions

http://www.northernlightsprod.com/zeus.html

> So you want lightning? Better pick up Zeus then. Zeus allows you to easily create complex, 3D electricity and lightning. Part of Artifex volumes 1 &2.

About the CD

The Enclosed CD contains many of the ElectricImage project files (and their supporting textures, models and rendered movies) used within this book, as well as a few nifty little things here and there to make your life easier, including several models from the ElectricImage Model Repository.

It also includes software from the following companies:

Credo Interactive
LifeForms 3.0 (demo)

Northern Lights Productions
Standard Shape 2 (free)

Puffin Designs
Commotion Player, Commotion, CyberMesh, and Knoll Lens Flare Pro (demos)

Zaxwerks
EPS Invigorator, Vector Lathe (demos)

And if that isn't enough, it also includes a wonderful supporting web site created by Mr. Gord Lacey, which will point you in just about any direction related to ElectricImage and 3D creation, in general. You'll find links to Magazines, Plugin developers, Model and Texture Libraries, Mailing Lists and more, and it looks mighty spiffy to boot.

There are some other nifty little things in there that you'll just have to find for yourself. Feel free to explore.

System Requirements:

Power Macintosh 6100 or better
System 7.5 (or later)
40 MB RAM (minimum)
CD-ROM Drive
Large capacity hard drive
Full color monitor
ElectricImage 2.9 (to open project files)
Bitmap graphics viewing application such as Adobe Photoshop to view and/or edit texturemaps and other images

Using the CD:

All of the project and texture files on the CD can be used directly from the CD. Just insert the CD into your CD-ROM drive and start browsing folders. Demo software should be dragged to your Harddrive and used from there. Some demo software may have installers. In this case, double-click on the installer and follow the installation directions. Demo or freeware sockets should be placed in the EI Sockets folder found within your ElectricImage application folder.

Index

The EPS Invigorator™

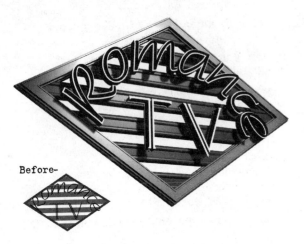

Before—

• Zaxwerks EPS Invigorator Highlights •

Extremely Fast:
- Speeds up the production process a thousand percent!

Very Easy to Use:
- The 3D modeling is done for you. You don't have to be a professional modeler.
- The interface encourages playing "what if" scenarios.

Power and Flexibility:
- All parameters remain "live". Changes can be made at ANY point. Nothing is locked.
- Independent control over Horizontal and Vertical Mesh density.
- 100+ preset profiles included.

Advanced Technology
- The most advanced model creation engine ever developed for this type of work. Cleans up garbage in poorly constructed files. Creates perfect miters where other modelers fail.
- Imports any Adobe Illustrator™ format file from 88 to 8.

The Vector Lathe™

• Zaxwerks Vector Lathe Highlights •

- Animatable lathing of objects for growing longitude/latitude lines.
- Superb curve sub-division.
- "Live" modeling enables changes at any time.
- Unique "one-way" faceting (See space gun in picture.)

This is it! If you want to eliminate the frustration of 3D production graphics...

if you want to make money doing Opens, Titles, Promos, Spots, Logos, Announcements or Intros...

Then you need the Invigorator and the Vector Lathe.

These tools give you the power to make client revisions on the spot and make your deadlines.

It's an amazing system for creating models, and it's fully integrated into ElectricImage!

"Where the Invigorator really saved us was in changes. The client made literally hundreds of changes."
- r.v.

"I want to write you every time the Invigorator saves me time... but then I'd have to write you every day!"
- a.p.

"This plug-in paid for itself MANY times over in the first couple of months. You will never know how you did without it."
- j.l.

"Invigorator ROCKs!"
- j. h.

The proven master of heart pounding, nerve shattering, deadline crunching, production graphics.

**Find out more on the Web at www.Zaxwerks.com
or call 1-800-549-0250 to order today!**

Learn ElectricImage™ from a Master

Now that you have taken your first steps on the road to mastering ElectricImage, expand your training with the Zaxwerks Reference Series CDs.

The Reference Series is full of techniques and tricks that will save you hundreds of hours of production time, and give you the road map to solve the most puzzling 3D riddles.

Written and hosted by one of the masters of ElectricImage, these lessons lead you directly to the core of how and why ElectricImage works the way it does.

You'll not only learn how to make ElectricImage sing, you'll also learn why it's singing. This powerful knowledge then helps you figure out future projects and encourages independent problem solving.

- Learn by watching.
- CD movies are crisp. They duplicate every pixel of the interface.
- Lessons are divided into fast, understandable sections.
- Every lesson comes with exercises and projects for you to work through.
- Contains complete project files, maps & models.
- Each Reference Series CD covers a different topic such as Lighting, Texture Mapping, Animation, and Inverse Kinematics/ Bones.
- Learn secrets that only the Pros know!

Lots of great artistic insights. Great examples and marvelously clear teaching.
- m.r.

All I can say is WOW! ElectricImage needs to ship this with every license.
-m.a.

I have Zax's brain! Ha Ha Ha! After using Zax's Brain I found that I was able to navigate my way through the EIAS environment with the speed of an electron! My kinky deformations gained new life and zest. My keyframes now shine like brand new!
-c.m.

— Zax Dow —

" Training is the great Enabler... With good training you can do anything! "

Zax Dow is a professional animator for film and broadcast graphics, and the former Product Evangelist for Electric Image Inc.

He teaches ElectricImage at the American Film Institute and conducts animation workshops throughout the country.

Find out more on the Web at www.Zaxwerks.com or call 1-800-549-0250 to order today!

PUFFIN DESIGNS

commotion™

Pro Tested. Pro Developed.

Commotion was developed by Puffin Designs founder Scott Squires, an award-winning Visual Effects Supervisor at Industrial Light and Magic, whose credits include Starship Troopers, The Mask and Dragonheart. Used in production since 1991, Commotion has benefitted from years of professional users' experience and feedback. Built to offer workstation functionality on the desktop, Commotion offers realtime paint, rotoscoping, motion tracking and software-based playback for work with film and video files.

Paint and Roto

Commotion is an excellent complement to ElectricImage™. With it's realtime paint and cloning tools, 3D shots which normally require a long re-rendering can now easily be fixed in minutes. Commotion can read ElectricImage IMAGE files natively, and play them back in realtime speeds of 24, 25, or 30 fps. The sophisticated rotoscoping tools can provide detailed animated mattes, complete with accurate motion blur, for compositing live footage with your 3D animation.

Motion Tracking

Commotion's fast and accurate motion tracker allows artists to easily track position, scale, rotation, and anchor point data, which can easily be exported into other applications, including ElectricImage. By tracking a point in your live action shot, Commotion can export the data with a specified field of view as an .obm file. This file can be imported into ElectricImage, and the exact live action camera move will be applied to your 3D camera. Match moving has never been easier!

For more information,
and to download the latest demo,
visit www.puffindesigns.com

80 Liberty Ship Way, Suite 7
Sausalito, CA 94965
415-331-4560 voice
415-331-5230 fax

Ask a Tough Question. Expect Solid Direction.

Help on the Horizon. Arnold Information Technology points corporations and organizations to information that get results. Access our experienced professionals who can help senior managers identify options and chart a course.

Since 1991, we've proven we can help in a range of capacities:

BUSINESS DEVELOPMENT
- Knowledge Management
- Competitive Intelligence
- Marketing & Sales
- Acquisitions & Mergers
- Patent Evaluations
- Technology Startups

INFORMATION TECHNOLOGY SERVICES
- Intranets, and Extranets
- Web-based Technologies
- Database Management
- Digital Work Flow Planning
- Information Engineering

ACTION FROM IDEAS. We helped build the service known as the Top 5% of the Internet, found at www.lycos.com. Our latest competitive intelligence tool can be explored at abcompass.com. It builds a personal daily news feed that only you receive.

A TEAM WITH STRATEGIC VISION. Our seasoned consultants can build, research, prototype, budget, plan, assess, and tackle some of the toughest jobs in information technology. Our managers have taken a leadership role in U.S. corporations and elsewhere in the world.

GET WHERE YOU WANT TO GO. TODAY.
We move corporations and organizations into the future. Our work spans a variety of industries, including publishing, telecommunications, government agencies, investment banks, and startups. We welcome confidential, informal discussions of your challenges and opportunities.

CONTACT:

Stephen E. Arnold, President
Arnold Information Technology
P.O. Box 320
Harrods Creek, Kentucky 40027
Voice: 502 228-1966
E-Mail: ait@arnoldit.com
Facsimile: 502 228-0548